Food Around the World

A Cultural Perspective

Margaret McWilliams, PhD.

Professor Emerita
California State University, Los Angeles

Holly Heller, M.A.

Prentice
Hall

Upper Saddle River, New Jersey 07458

Library of Congress Cataloging-in-Publication Data

McWilliams, Margaret.
  Food around the world : a cultural perspective / Margaret McWilliams,
Holly Heller.
    p. cm.
  Includes bibliographical references.
  ISBN 0-13-094456-4
  1. Food. I. Heller, Holly. II. Title.
  TX353 .M396 2003
  641.3—dc21

                                    2002004325

Editor-in-Chief: Stephen Helba
Executive Editor: Vernon R. Anthony
Executive Assistant: Nancy Kesterson
Editorial Assistant: Ann Brunner
Director of Manufacturing and Production: Bruce Johnson
Managing Editor: Mary Carnis
Production Liaison: Adele M. Kupchik
Marketing Manager: Ryan DeGrote
Production Management: Pine Tree Composition, Inc.
Production Editor: Russell Jones
Manufacturing Manager: Ilene Sanford
Manufacturing Buyer: Cathleen Petersen
Creative Director: Cheryl Asherman
Cover Design Coordinator: Christopher Weigand
Interior Design: Pine Tree Composition, Inc.
Printer/Binder: Courier Westford
Cover Designer: Kevin Kall

Pearson Education LTD.
Pearson Education Australia PTY, Limited
Pearson Education Singapore, Pte. Ltd
Pearson Education North Asia Ltd
Pearson Education Canada, Ltd.
Pearson Educación de Mexico, S.A. de C.V.
Pearson Education – Japan
Pearson Education Malaysia, Pte. Ltd

PHOTO CREDITS

Dorling Kindersley Medialibrary: Figures 3.6, 4.4, 9.1, 13.1, 13.2, 13.3, 13.4, and 16.8. Color plates C24, the Treasury; C7, Sphinx; and C28, statue head.
Ruth MacFarlane: Figure 12.1. Color plates C26, Bedouins; and C27, goat herd.
Paul F. Peterson: Color plate C63, Chichen Itza.
Eileen Welsh: Figure 15.3. Color plates C40, Tibetan Monks; and C41, yaks.
Shaun Egan, Getty Images Inc.: Figures 3.4, and 8.2.
Dave G. Houser: Color plate C12, "Onion" domes.
Wolfgang Kaehler: Figure 4.5, 5.1 and Color plate C24, Island fortress.
Ted Streshinsky: Figure 5.4.
Chris Hellier: Color plate C19, The Lion's Gate guards.
Michael Nicholson: Color plate C23, Krak de Chevalliers in Syria.
Owen Franklin: Color plate C44, Loatian women.
All other photos were supplied by the author, Margaret McWilliams.

10 9 8 7 6 5 4 3 2

ISBN 0-13-094456-4

Contents

Preface

No matter where we grow up and live, eating is one of the most personal experiences of life. We all find pleasure and comfort in eating foods associated with our childhood and heritage, but personal perspectives on eating and what is good to eat are only part of the global picture. With the remarkable increase in diversity within the American population, we all need to learn more about the cultural backgrounds, geographic parameters, and social and economic factors that have shaped other nations and the people who have emigrated from them to become residents and citizens of the United States. Better relationships between individuals, within schools, and throughout communities and the nation begin with people learning about each other, what they value, and what they seek. Food preferences and eating habits provide a fascinating and very approachable avenue for promoting understanding between all of us.

Each of us is a member of (or soon will become a part of) a minority in the United States, but most of us have much to learn about the foods preferred by people in different subgroups within our increasingly polycultural nation. This book will help you gain a broader knowledge of what people eat around the world; it is based on the assumption that what people eat is shaped over the centuries by geographic, historical, cultural, and economic factors. Rather than focusing only on food, the reader will develop a broader understanding and appreciation of the cultural uniqueness of the food patterns in nations around the world. Numerous photographs, maps, and recipes will help you visualize and sample the actual heritage of new immigrants and other people whose ancestors came from abroad.

In recognition of the several religions discussed in this book and the influences they have imparted to food patterns, the dating system used is BCE (before the common era) and CE (common era) rather than the traditional BC and AD. Also, some of the recipes have been slightly modified to simplify the problems of finding particularly exotic ingredients without sacrificing the character of the dishes. Changes have not been made to accommodate the palate of the unadventurous diner.

As you explore the world and its foods in these chapters, new images and a spirit of adventure about the world of food will develop. Knowledge of cultural food preferences is particularly important for dietitians, nutritionists, and food technologists so they will succeed in meeting the challenges of helping people from cultures other than their own achieve healthy and satisfying food patterns in this country. Regardless of your professional goals, you will perhaps find that you are willing to experience a broader range of foods by the time you finish this book. You may find that you are picturing the romantic days of the Mughals the next time you dine at an Indian restaurant, or perhaps images of the Ming Dynasty are flashing through your mind as you feast on Chinese food. The possibilities could go on and on. When you finish this book, you will be acquainted with the many cultures and their foods around the world.

So, now it is time to grab your imaginary passport and journey around the world with us through the pages of this book.

Bon voyage!

Acknowledgments

In addition to thanking the above photographers, the authors wish to express their appreciation to Toni Empringham for her invaluable comments in the preparation of this manuscript.

Margaret McWilliams
Redondo Beach, California
Holly Heller
Irvine, California

Food Around the World

A Cultural Perspective

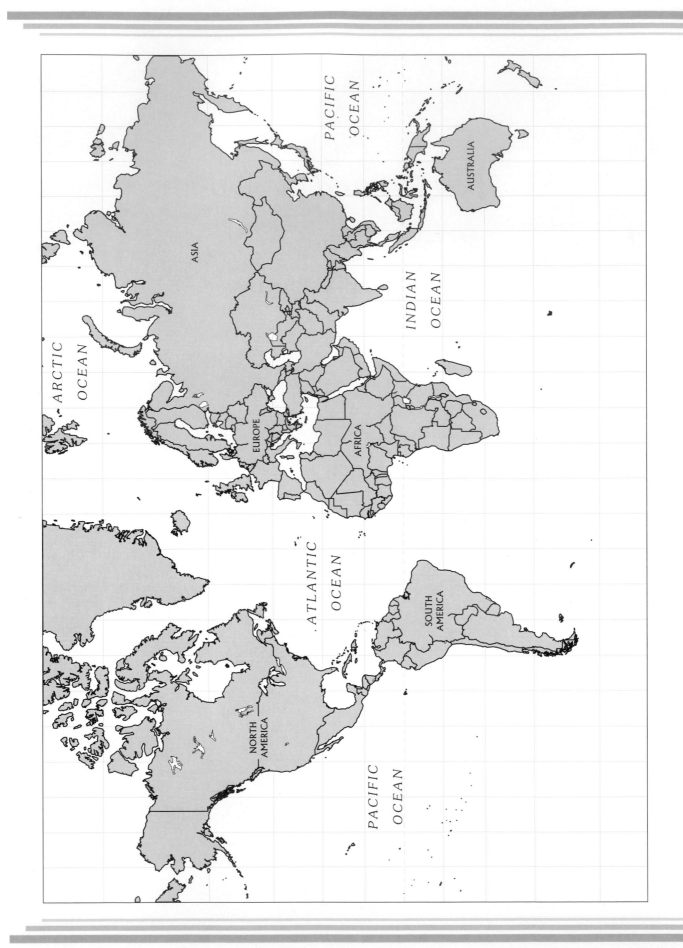

Part I

Influences on Food Around the World

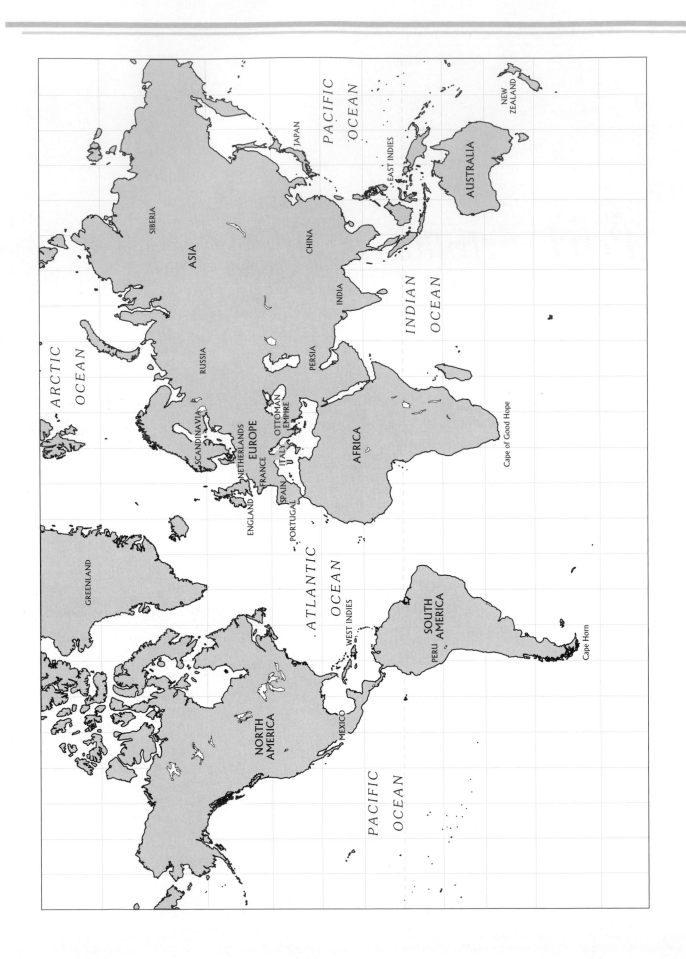

1

Food Origins and History

The story behind the food that you and people all around the world choose to eat today is one with many twists and turns. Development of today's food supply goes far back in history and is still evolving. Geography plays a key role in defining the types of foods and the quantities of crops that can be produced around the globe. Knowledge of the wide variety of foods grown in distant regions was acquired as adventurers began to contact (and often conquer) other people and learn of their cultures. Trade evolved to bring exotic foods from distant locales. These are key aspects of the evolving tale of the foods that are on your table now.

Food Origins

Early man's food habits derived strictly from what was available in the near environment (Figure 1.1). Hunter-gatherers were restricted to the particular plants and prey indigenous to where they lived. Survival was the driving force that determined what was eaten. Archaeologists have been able to identify some of the foods eaten by the people who lived at the sites being studied, although many food samples have been destroyed by time.

Geographic features of their immediate environment determined significantly what foods were available to early people. If they were living in an area next to an ocean, the possibility of food from the sea was a nourishing, if challenging, prospect. Similarly, some people were fortunate enough to live near a lake or a stream where they could catch fish to eat. Civilizations with access to either fresh or salt water fishing developed dietary patterns in which fish played a very prominent role. Evidence of shellfish being used as human food as far back as 127,000 years ago has been found in southern Africa.

Figure 1.1 The immediate environment was early man's only source of food.

Civilizations that flourished in temperate river valleys were able to grow wheat or other cereal and vegetable crops. They also were able to domesticate animals, which were allowed to graze or were fed portions of the crops reserved for that purpose. Central Europeans developed this type of agriculture, and their dietary patterns took on quite a different character from the Japanese and others around the world who lived near the sea.

Around 12,000 BCE, people in Upper Egypt and Nubia were using grindstones to make flour from wild grasses. In Palestine, wild emmer (wheat) was being harvested by 10,000 BCE, and einkhorn (a type of wheat) was eaten in Syria by 9000 BCE. Wheat, barley, and pulses (legumes) were cultivated around Jericho and also in the favorable locales from Syria to Mesopotamia and Egypt by 8000 BCE. Sheep were domesticated to add to the diet in this region. Taro was a cultivated crop in New Guinea by 7000 BCE, approximately the same time manioc was being grown in the upper region of the Amazon in South America.

Mountainous regions were inhospitable settings for early people. The rugged terrain made agriculture virtually impossible, and the extreme cold due to the high elevations added to the hazards of attempting to live in the upper elevations of the Alps, the Hindu Kush, and the Himalayas. Lower valleys in the mountains could be used for grazing animals in the summer, but the mountains were not the regions where early civilizations developed.

Civilizations based on farming in early times were established where the land was fertile enough for good crops to be raised. The region in Mesopotamia where early civilization and agriculture flourished in the valleys of the Tigris and Euphrates rivers was dubbed the "Fertile Crescent" by historians, a name clearly reflecting the importance of rich farmland.

The land available for habitation by people on the earth was limited. About 80 percent of the world was covered by oceans. Mountain ranges restricted use of large parts of Asia and South America plus many regions in Europe and North America. The climate of approximately the northern half of Asia was not only dry and arid, but also severely cold in winter due to its northern latitude and some high elevations. Northern China was dry, but southern China had a wet, tropical climate. Northern Africa had a very hot, dry climate, with the Sahara Desert occupying a huge area. Western Asia was rather desert-like, especially the Arabian

Peninsula and portions of the western interior. Europe and the eastern half of North America had moderate climates more amenable to a wide variety of agricultural products than can be produced in desert lands.

Several environmental factors determined the feasibility of early farmers growing a crop in a particular location. Adequate moisture, but not too much, was vital to a crop. In some parts of the world, rainfall was adequate most seasons for early people to raise a crop, while in other, more arid regions irrigation was required for crops to flourish. This necessitated building a functional irrigation system with an adequate supply of water each year if farmers were to be successful. In other regions of the world, early farmers faced failure of crops when they were inundated with rainfall to the point where fields were flooded and crops were washed away. The need to control water for crops has been addressed for centuries, as can be seen in the terracing of rice paddies in Bali and other Asian regions, the irrigation systems developed in Mesopotamia around 5000 BCE, and in the Roman aqueducts.

Natural rainfall has served for growing many crops around the world, and this reliance on nature influenced the early crops that were raised in various regions. For instance, rice was the staple grain for centuries in the monsoonal areas of the world, from India to Japan, while wheat was the favored grain crop in farm areas that received moderate amounts of rain. The ease of raising rice in the Far East made this grain of key importance in diets there; wheat was not available to the early people in the rice-growing areas because it did not grow well in such wet soils. It did thrive in Europe, Asia, and the northern part of China, where it was the staple cereal in the diet. These contrasts illustrate how rainfall influenced the diets of people in different regions, particularly when trade between regions was limited.

Temperature was a key determinant of crop successes. An early illustration of this geographic factor is that oranges were a successful crop, and so were dates, in the warm climates at the eastern end of the Mediterranean Sea, but they were unknown to the Norsemen, whose climate was far too severe for citrus and dates to survive. The length of the growing season (the number of days at temperatures warm enough for active growth) also determined whether or not a crop could be grown in a particular location. For example, corn requires a growing season of at least 140 days to mature. Countries at very high or very low latitudes did not have enough warm days for corn to mature. Vegetables requiring a comparatively short growing season to reach maturity could be grown in such northern latitudes as Alaska with surprising results because of the almost continuous daylight available in the height of summer.

Topography was yet another geographic dimension that influenced agricultural land use. Extremely steep slopes were appropriate only for raising goats, or perhaps sheep. On the other hand, gently rolling or flat lands were well suited to growing a variety of crops. Some regions required labor-intensive terracing for crops or animal husbandry efforts to produce food.

Before 7000 BCE, goats and pigs were domesticated as sources of meat from Anatolia (now southern Turkey) as far east as Pakistan. Barley became a food crop in India, and farming was developing in the region between the Indus River and the Baluchistan Hills around 7000 BCE. Domestication of goats and sheep and the raising of cereal crops had spread into the Balkans from Anatolia by approximately 6500 BCE.

By 6000 BCE, farming was established in central Mesopotamia and China, and Peruvians were raising potatoes. Around 6200 BCE, farming was extending into western Europe and along the Mediterranean Sea, but use of cattle for plowing did not begin until around 4500 BCE near the lower Danube. Use of animals for milk and wool did not occur in Europe until about 3500 BCE, at which time the plow was introduced in western and northern areas of Europe.

Around 5000 BCE wet rice farming was being carried on in eastern China, maize was being cultivated in Mexico, and irrigation was being developed as an aid to farming in Mesopotamia. Millet began to be cultivated in Korea about 3000 BCE. Wet rice farming was not begun in Japan until 500 BCE. Water buffalos began to be used as draft animals in Southeast Asia in approximately 200 BCE.

Lives of these early people were gradually evolving beyond the basic pursuit of food for mere survival. At several points around the world, pockets of rather sophisticated cultures developed. These civilizations began to create riches that were coveted by adventurers who happened to stumble upon them. Such discoveries sometimes led to efforts to conquer such territories to build empires at the expense of those who had created the wealth. Some selected illustrations of these developments that ultimately led to today's expanded food experiences are presented in the next section.

A Capsule of Cultures and Conquests

Early Cultural Sites

Egypt is likely to be the first early culture that comes to mind, for the dramatic temples and pyramids built by early Egyptians more than 4,000 years ago remain as testimonials to these people. They controlled land along the eastern end of the Mediterranean Sea and the northeastern corner of Africa as far south as the Sudan before they began to be conquered by various invaders.

The lands to the north of the Persian Gulf also fostered the development of cultures. Sumerians came south from Persia around 2000 BCE. Their contemporaries, the Hittites, who were flourishing in the region that is now Asian Turkey, conquered Sumeria's Babylon and ruled Syria as well for four centuries, until 1200 BCE. Assyrians, the next group to conquer the region, ruled until the Persians took Nineveh in 612 BCE.

Meanwhile, Chinese culture was developing and flourishing on the eastern edge of Asia, beginning to be of significance about 1800 BCE under the Shang dynasty. In contrast to the history of many other parts of the world, China has been essentially a political unit with the exception of the Mongol incursion from 1280 CE to about 1350 CE. The dynastic sequence after the Shang period included Chou, Ch'in, Han, Sung, Ming, and Ch'ing.

In the western hemisphere, enduring evidence of the early culture of the Olmecs, who lived along the Gulf of Mexico in what is now Mexico and also in Central America, dates from 1200 BCE for almost 1,000 years. They peacefully coexisted with the Zapotecs near Oaxaca, who also left enduring ruins as evidence of their culture around 500 BCE.

Some Significant Empires

Cultural centers developed at various points around the world during the two millennia prior to the birth of Christ, but these tended to be quite isolated from each other. However, geographical barriers eventually began to be breeched, and knowledge of other groups led to the desire for conquest and possible riches. When conquerors established themselves by settling among the conquered for extended periods, considerable sharing of such aspects of both cultures as their foods and their arts resulted in lasting changes, many of which are still evident today.

The Persians conquered a vast empire by the 6th century BCE. This empire (the Achaemenid Empire) included present-day Turkey, the eastern end of the Mediterranean Sea, Armenia, eastward in Asia beyond the Caspian Sea and Samarkand, southward over the Hindu Kush mountains of Afghanistan to the Indus River in India, then westward to the Persian Gulf and Mesopotamia.

Particularly prominent among the various rulers of the Achaemenid Empire (also called the Persian Empire) were Cyrus, Darius, and Xerxes. The ruins of the great palace at Persepolis in Iran still reveal some of the artistic glory of the Persian Empire, which finally was ended by Alexander the Great in 331 BCE (Figure 1.2).

Crete's Minoan civilization was snuffed out dramatically following the gigantic volcanic eruption on Thera (today's Greek island of Santorini) in 1625 BCE. However, the Myceneans on the Greek Peloponnesus then established control over Crete, Sicily, Sardinia, and Troy at the eastern end of the Mediterranean and even as far as the Baltic Sea and Britain. This situation lasted about 400 years (from about 1500 BCE to 1100 BCE). Agamemnon was the most prominent ruler of this vast trading empire. The demands of fighting the Trojan War in Turkey led to the downfall of the Myceneans.

However, classical Greece began to emerge about 400 years later. The artistic achievements of the Greeks are among the leading cultural gifts. These include the Acropolis in Athens (with its dramatic Parthenon, Erechtheum, and the Theatre of Dionysus) and Ephesus and Priene in Turkey (Figure 1.3), as well as numerous beautiful marble sculptures. Greeks extended their influence over the entire northern shores of the Mediterranean Sea to the eastern part of Spain and eastward along the Turkish shores of the Black Sea. The Macedonian military leader Alexander the Great was able to extend the conquests to central Asia by such feats as defeating the Persians at Persepolis and then marching to Afghanistan and on southward to northern India before his death in 323 BCE at the age of 33.

The Roman Empire began in Italy, but gained immense dimensions as its armies sent its legions to various points, starting with lands bordering the Mediterranean Sea. Romans fought three Punic Wars against Carthage in Tunisia from 264 BCE to 146 BCE to gain control not only of Carthage itself, but also of its territories (Sicily, Corsica, Sardinia, the Balearics, and Spain). Later conquests included the Dalmatian coast of the Adriatic Sea, the western part of Anatolia (part of Turkey in Asia Minor), land along the Black Sea, the Levant (from Syria almost to the Red Sea), and finally France and England. Among the significant contributions of the Romans were the legacy of law and government, roads, aqueducts, and baths.

The enormity of the Roman Empire made it difficult to defend from the warlike tribes challenging the borders. Emperor Diocletian split the territories in 284 CE to establish the Eastern Roman Empire with its headquarters in Byzantium (subsequently renamed Constantinople by Constantine, its emperor). This part of the Roman Empire lasted until 1453 CE when the Ottoman Turks conquered it. The Western Roman Empire was overrun by northern barbarians, thus ending

Figure 1.2 Bas relief from the ruins of the Persian palace at Persepolis in Iran.

Figure 1.3 Dramatic columns provide the centerpiece of the ruins at the Greek settlement of Priene in Turkey.

that part of the Roman Empire in 493 CE. Over the course of the centuries that Rome dominated its vast empire, it was ruled by many different emperors; Julius Caesar is perhaps the best known.

The Mongol Empire presents a sharp contrast to the ways of the Roman Empire. It lasted for only 200 years (1206 to 1405 CE), beginning under Genghis Khan. He united very fierce warriors from the various tribes of Mongolia and central Asia, who breeched the Great Wall and invaded China in 1211 CE. He also sent troops westward toward northern Tibet and on to encircle the Caspian Sea and penetrate Kashmir and northern India. One of the consequences of the westward push beyond the Caspian Sea was the acquisition of many Turkish-speaking people, which ultimately led to the demise of the Seljuk sultanate in Turkey and the establishment of the Ottoman Empire there. One of the surprising consequences of the Mongol Empire was a weakening of Christianity (which had been fairly strong in Constantinople) and tremendous gain in support of Islam, as well as some strengthening of Buddhism (in the Far East only). Even after Genghis Khan died in 1227 CE, Mongol hordes attacked Russia in 1237 CE and then went on to conquer Poland and Hungary in 1241 CE. Fortunately for Europe, the Mongol leader, the Great Khan Ogedei, died, and so did the Mongol threat to Europe. However, Mongols held control in Russia until the last ruler, Tamerlane, died in 1405 CE.

An interesting footnote to the Mongol Empire is provided by Babur (a descendant of Tamerlane), who invaded India in 1526 CE to begin the Mughal Empire, which extended eastward from the Arabian Sea well into Afghanistan and included all of Kashmir, southward along the Indian side of the Himalayas, and a long coastline of the Bay of Bengal before turning westward to the Arabian Sea just north of Bombay. Akbar, the grandson of Babur, fostered the unique artistic style that blended Persian and Indian influences. The Taj Mahal, built by Shah Jahan, is the architectural masterpiece of the Mughal Empire, which ended in 1707 CE.

Three empires (Mayan, Incan, and Aztec) were dominant in different areas of the Americas, the earliest of these being the Mayan Empire (350 BCE to about 1200 CE). Remains of this culture still stand on the Yucatan Peninsula of Mexico and in the jungle lowlands of Guatemala. The Incan Empire was the leading civilization in the mountains of Peru and beyond in South America from about 1300 CE until Pizarro arrived from Spain, conquering the Incas and seizing Cuzco in 1533. The Aztecs gained control of land near today's Mexico City when they arrived in 1345 CE and built their capital, Teochitlan. By the time Spain's Cortez arrived in 1519, they ruled the land from the Gulf of Mexico to the Pacific from central Mexico to Guatemala, land which immediately became Spain's.

Emerging Trade Routes

The growth of trade was a natural result of the conquests mentioned above, as well as many others around the world. Wheat was one of the early items traded from the Fertile Crescent of Mesopotamia, for this was a crop that could be transported long distances to such places as Europe, Scandinavia, and the British Isles without spoiling. By the end of the 15th and beginning of the 16th century, wheat had even been carried to the Caribbean and Argentina. Spanish conquerors and friars aided in the introduction of wheat to North America.

Maize was developed in Central and South America, and then it was introduced to Europe when the Spanish expedition returned to Spain, carrying some maize from Mexico, in 1493. A century later maize from South America was introduced to West Africa. European voyagers in the 16th century not only transported maize to Europe, but also carried Mexican maize to eastern South America and on to part of India and northeastern China. Rice originated in China, spread to India, and then was carried by traders to the Fertile Crescent and throughout the Mediterranean and North Africa by about 300 BCE.

Central America was the origin of the tomato and sweet potato. From there, they were introduced to Europe in the very late 15th and early 16th centuries. Europe provided not only onions and cabbage, but also tomatoes to North America in the 19th century (long after tomatoes had ventured to Europe from Central America). Potatoes went from western South America throughout Europe and also to eastern Africa and India by the 17th century.

Coffee appears to have originated in eastern Africa. Its acceptance spread rapidly to Amsterdam and all along the routes of the Dutch traders around Africa and to Southeast Asia. Tea originated in northern China and then spread rapidly all along the trade routes back to Europe. Cocoa is the only popular beverage that originated in the New World. The wonderful discovery of chocolate was carried in about 1520 CE to a very appreciative audience in Europe.

Another gift of the New World to Europe was the sunflower, with its excellent oil. Palm oil had its origins in the western part of Africa around the Niger River. From there, its use spread to both Americas and Southeast Asia in the 19th century. Much of the production of palm oil for the world is centered now in Malaysia, where it is an agricultural commodity of considerable importance.

Spices offered very early traders two particularly outstanding characteristics that spurred the spice trade: long shelf life and high market value per volume. Various spices were known and highly prized from China all the way to Rome and beyond long before the time of Christ. Traders carried their valuable cargoes thousands of miles, often under extremely difficult conditions. Despite these long ocean voyages, the spices from Southeast Asia brought such high prices when they finally reached their markets that many traders became very wealthy. It is said that the spices carried back in the hold of Magellan's only ship that returned from his 3-year voyage of 1519 to 1522 returned sufficient money to pay for the entire expedition! Traders from various European nations plied the seas between Indonesia and Europe, bringing home fortunes in spices. The exciting flavors were appreciated not only for their uniquely pleasing variety, but also for their ability to help disguise off flavors in food in the era when refrigeration was not available to extend the useful life of foods.

𝒦ey Terms

Aztec Empire—Empire extending to both coasts of central Mexico south to Guatemala that was controlled by Aztecs from 1345 to 1519 CE.

Carthage—Important trading city on the Mediterranean shore of Tunisia.

Einkhorn—Wheat species native to the Balkans, Anatolia, and adjacent areas of western Asia.

Emmer—Early form of wheat native to Palestine and Syria; main form of wheat in prehistory and later grown in parts of Europe into the Christian period.

Incan Empire—Region of Andes in Peru controlled by Incas from about 1300 CE until Pizarro conquered it after his arrival in 1533 CE.

Manioc (cassava)—Tropical plant from the lowlands of South America used as a source of root starch.

Mayan Empire—Region including the Yucatan Peninsula and Guatemala controlled by Mayans from 3000 BCE to about 1200 CE.

Minoan civilization—Well-developed, artistic culture centered on Crete in the second millennium BCE until the volcanic eruption of Thera in 1625 BCE.

Mycenea—Site of Agamemnon's palace and the governmental center of the Greek Peloponnesus and the eastern Mediterranean from the late 1500s BCE to about 1100 BCE.

Olmecs—Dominant cultural group in Central America from 1200 to 150 BCE; settled predominantly on the coast of the Gulf of Mexico along the Bay of Campeche west of the Yucatan Peninsula.

Punic Wars—Three wars fought between Carthage and Rome between 264 and 146 BCE.

Taro—Tropical plant from Southeast Asia noted for its edible, starch-rich root.

Summary

The food supply available to people not only in the United States, but around the world, is the result of geographical parameters and historical developments over the ages. Early people were able to obtain food only in their immediate environments. However, they eventually acquired agricultural skills that enabled them to grow crops and domesticate some animals for their use. Emmer and einkhorn were early crops, followed by barley and legumes in the Middle East, taro in New Guinea, and manioc in South America.

Early agricultural sites were near sources of water in relatively flat lands with comfortable climates suited to success in raising crops. Subsequently, animals were domesticated as sources of food and labor, with sheep and goats being particularly suited to rather rough terrain.

Mountains, very cold regions, and deserts were hostile to agriculture. However, terracing and irrigation eventually were developed, adding significantly to the use of land for agriculture, as can be seen in the terraces of Southeast Asia and Japan.

Adequate food supplies paved the way for the development of civilizations such as existed in Egypt, the Middle East, China, and coastal Mexico for centuries prior to the Common Era (CE). However, conquests began to take place around the world as some groups sought to take over the food and riches of other settlements and populations. Among the empires that existed at various times over the ages were the Persian or Achaemenid (6th century BCE to 331 BCE), Mycenean (1500 to 1100 BCE), Greek (about 700 BCE to 323 BCE), Roman and subsequently the Western and Eastern Roman (about 3rd century BCE to 493 CE for the Western and 1453 CE for the Eastern), Mongol (1206 to 1405 CE), Mughul (1526 to 1707 CE), Mayan (350 BCE to 1200 CE), Incan (1300 to 1533 CE), and Aztec (1345 to 1559 CE).

Concomitant with the increasing interaction between groups of people was the growth of trade, including the shipping of various foods to other places. Wheat was well suited to trade because of its ability to withstand the rigors of long trade routes and to arrive in marketable condition. Maize was taken from the Americas to Europe and then brought back to Mexico, as well as being shipped as far as India and China. Rice came from China via traders to Europe and Africa. Tomatoes and sweet potatoes were shipped from Central America to Europe, which then introduced onions and cabbage to the New World. Potatoes were shipped to Europe, India, and Africa from the western side of South America. Africa contributed coffee and palm oil to the trading scene, Central America gave chocolate and sunflowers, and spices came from various points in Southeast Asia.

Study Questions

1. What geographic characteristics were found in the Fertile Crescent that were favorable to the development of an agrarian society?
2. Why is development of a culture dependent on the food supply?
3. Identify 10 of your favorite foods and the part of the world where they probably originated.
4. Where did the food that you ate yesterday come from? As much as possible, indicate where each ingredient probably was produced.
5. Why was rice the staple cereal in Japan? Why was wheat the traditional grain in Central Europe?
6. Briefly describe each of the following empires: Western Roman, Mughal, Persian, Mycenean.
7. Why are food patterns influenced by empire builders?

Bibliography

Barraclough, G., ed. 1998. *Harper Collins Atlas of World History.* 2nd rev. ed. Border Press. Ann Arbor, MI.

Brander, B. 1966. *River Nile.* National Geographic Society. Washington, D.C.

Grun, B. 1991. *Timetables of History.* 3rd ed. Simon and Schuster/Touchstone Books. New York.

Harper Collins. 1997. *Past Worlds: Atlas of Archaeology.* Border Press. Ann Arbor, MI.

Huot, J. L. 1965. *Archaeology Mundi: Persia I.* World Publishing. Cleveland, OH.

Pan American. 1978. *World Guide.* McGraw-Hill. New York.

Pearcy, G. E. 1980. *World Food Scene.* Plycon Press. Redondo Beach, CA.

Shahbazi, A. S. 1976. *Persepolis Illustrated.* Institute of Achaemenid Research. Persepolis, Iran.

Ward, S., C. Clifton, and J. Stacey. 1997. *Gourmet Atlas.* Macmillan. New York.

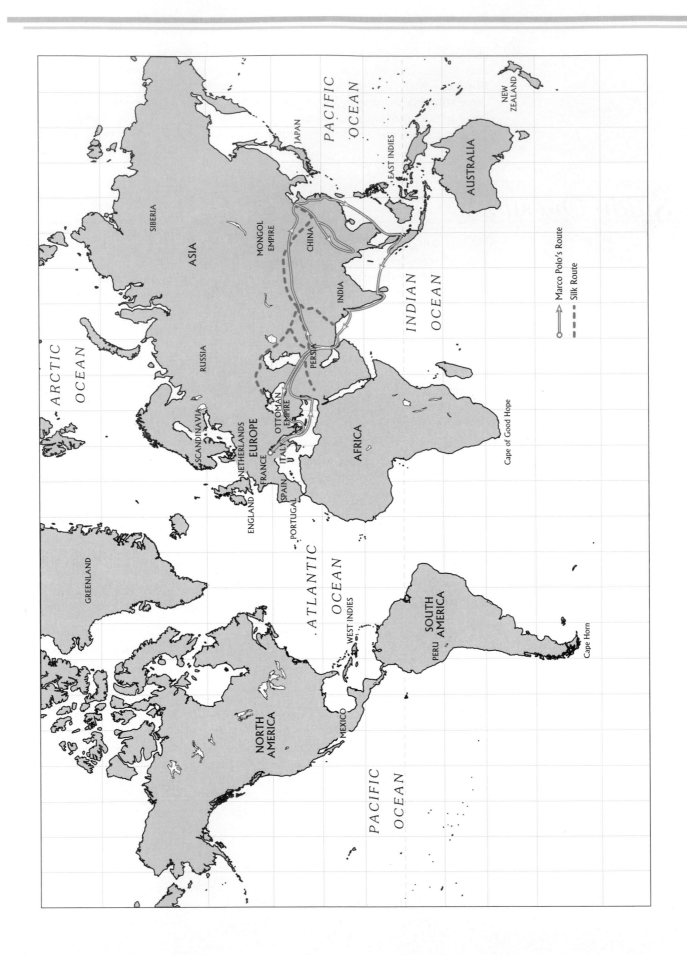

2   Cultural Landscapes

If food is thought of as only the means of getting the nutrients needed for life, the important subtleties that influence what people actually eat will be missed. What a convenience it would be if achieving adequate nutrition for people simply meant defining the requirements for each person according to age and sex and then providing the nutrients in the correct amounts via supplements. Unfortunately, this simplistic approach not only is unable to provide all of the requirements, but it also would rob people of the pleasures that food adds in their lives. Favorite flavors, textures, and aromas (especially when provided in familiar and preferred recipes) give immediate pleasure and also evoke happy memories of people and places associated with these foods.

Components of Culture

Culture may be defined in somewhat different ways, one of which is the customary beliefs, social forms, and material traits of a racial, religious, or social group. Ethnicity is the affiliation with a race, people, or cultural group. Culture and ethnicity are essential foundations of the study of food and people. Knowledge of the major cultures around the world and appreciation of the cultural richness that is a part of the food patterns not only adds pleasure to our lives, but also strengthens the ability of food professionals to work effectively with people from cultures other than their own.

      To an extent, the country where a person is born and resides shapes the food patterns of the individual and families. The geographic realities of climate and terrain suitable for productive agriculture define the local foods that may be available. Other resources of the country will influence whether or not manufacturing and business and other commercial endeavors generate a vigorous economy. In countries where all is favorable, an abundant and varied food supply can

Culture refers to the way of life of a people: what they make, do, and think. Customs, habits, language, knowledge, housing, tools, and the arts all contribute to the uniqueness of a culture.

be obtained by virtually all people in that country. In less favored locales, food may be in very short supply and unavailable in adequate amounts. In other words, the economy and the agricultural conditions combine within a country to define one of the parameters of the nation's food culture.

Housing is another dimension of a person's culture. People in some cultural groups live in elegant, single-family dwellings; some live in cottages; while others live in apartments or condominiums. The roof may be anything from a leaky thatch to an orderly, fireproof tile. Some people have a bedroom for each person, while others live in a one-room house in which the entire family must eat and sleep. The kitchens range from spotless and completely equipped with every appliance to those in which refrigeration is unavailable or extremely limited in space, a situation which imposes serious problems of food safety or necessitates daily shopping. A family of a cultural group often lives in housing that is similar to the others in the group.

Lifestyles add to a cultural identification. For example, where are young children cared for, and by whom? Are parents with their children most of the day, or are they away from home for long hours while working many miles away? What mode of transportation is common—trishaws, buses, bicycles, cars, trains, or foot? Do families eat all meals together at home, or do they eat in some other setting for one or more meals daily? Who prepares these meals? These are some of the practical questions that help to develop some understanding of a specific cultural group.

One of the important threads that tends to identify a culture and to continue to hold its members together as a group is that of art. Styles of art vary over the ages and around the world, yet most cultural groups have an artistic heritage that they feel to be their own (Figure 2.1). In fact, paintings and other forms of art provide a somewhat historic documentation of the earlier people who helped to define the group's artistic culture. These visual works often serve as a strong tie to a person's cultural roots.

Music and dance are other art forms that communicate directly to individuals and draw them toward the local culture. Moscow's Bolshoi Ballet, performing such works as Tschaikovsky's *Swan Lake* and Ireland's *River Dance,* are evidence of the cultural heritage from Russia and Ireland respectively. Musical examples also abound. Sibelius's *Finlandia* is an orchestral work that causes Finnish people to swell with pride in their heritage, while also providing an appreciation of Finnish people to all who hear this rich and very strong composition.

Public architecture affords additional insights into a culture. The survival of the Summer Palace and the Hermitage, as well as other grand buildings from the Tsarist era, provides mute testimony to the appreciation that the citizens of Leningrad (now St. Petersburg, once again) held for their cultural heritage even through the Revolution and eventual break up of the Soviet Union. In the United Kingdom, the stern and imposing palaces and castles are proudly viewed as the cultural heritage of the country. The Welsh (and tourists in Wales) see the strength and independent nature of earlier citizenry clearly expressed in the castles that were built and defended so heroically to keep invaders from their stark and windswept coastland (Figure 2.2). The Parthenon on the Acropolis in Athens, with its open and inviting style, is a reflection of the early Greeks and today's citizenry as well. Karnak Temple in Luxor, Egypt, affords a glimpse of yet a different ancient culture that is an important part of a nation's culture even more than three millennia later. The famed Taj Mahal in Agra, India, is a dazzlingly lovely and graceful tribute to Shah Jahan's dead wife, its intricate inlaid designs of semiprecious stones attesting to the highly developed skills of the craftsmen and artists in India. Deeply carved bas-relief adorning the long walls of the huge Angkor Wat complex in Cambodia add a different artistic dimension to the cultural context of architecture. The Forbidden City, with its temples and mazes of buildings and rooms within its encompassing walls, affords a remarkable look at the cultural heritage of both Beijing residents and all people of China.

Figure 2.1   Imaginative and intricate art decorates the walls at Angkor Wat in Cambodia.

Figure 2.2   Conway castle in Wales clearly was built for defense in a style typical of architecture in the United Kingdom.

These glimpses of the importance of all of the arts in creating emotions and feelings that cause individuals to embrace parts of their specific heritage are presented to help you begin to think about similar artistic works that contribute to your definition of your cultural inheritance.

Additional Dimensions of Culture

Other defining aspects of cultural groups are national histories and religions. When people live within a region that constitutes a nation or possibly just a portion of a nation, common experiences related to government of the land and beliefs and values can either unite people or create civil unrest and even wars. From such influences, cultural identity and groupings often result, and these groups continue for many centuries when governments are stable, as is true in Great Britain. Examples of the strength of such ties can be seen today when you consider the many political refugees who have sought asylum and new beginnings in countries quite distant from their country of origin. Frequently, these new immigrants will gravitate in the new country to regions where others from their own culture have already begun to gather.

Religion is a particularly strong factor in cultural identity. Sharing common beliefs and practices that are central to a particular religion creates common threads that bind people together into a culture. By the same token, the fact that people practicing a different religion do not have the same beliefs and customs serves to separate the followers of each major religion into isolated groups or into groups who respect each other, but who are not as close between as within religious groups. Even though groups are defined, knowledge and appreciation of various religions can do much to reduce possible tensions and enrich the fabric of our American culture.

Special Messages of Food

Food sometimes carries special meanings beyond simply providing nutrients. The subtle messages conveyed by a particular food may be a nonverbal exchange between people at a meal or a social occasion. Certain foods may be absolutely essential on a particular occasion. For example, matzo (unleavened bread) must

Figure 2.3 Chunks of salt being marketed on a street in Nepal.

be served for Jewish Passover. Special green tea prepared in the Japanese tea ceremony conveys total welcome and hospitality to guests. The specific foods and traditions vary greatly around the world. Some of these will be discussed in later chapters in this book. However, the importance of salt is sufficiently universal to all people that it warrants some attention here.

Salt, a simple yet essential part of the diet for both man and animals, has been valued throughout the world for many centuries. The Romans were well aware of the importance of salt for their troops in their military conquests as they carved out their vast empire. Caesar's armies had persons responsible for making salt (by boiling down brine) for the troops. In remote Tibet, during the time of Marco Polo (around 1300 CE), salt cakes served as the currency (Figure 2.3).

Emperor Yu, in 2200 BCE, attempted to control and tax salt in his domain. Throughout the centuries taxes on salt have punctuated numerous political upheavals, including the French Revolution. Even in the 20th century, England's tax on salt in India and its ban on personal harvesting of salt from the sea triggered Mahatma Ghandi's famous 200-mile protest march to the sea in 1930.

The universality of the importance attached to salt can be seen in various religious and cultural traditions of the past. Catholic priests used to place a little salt on the baby's tongue during baptismal rites so the baby would "receive the salt of wisdom." Early Jewish rites required that salt be a part of their offerings. Both Jews and Christians had a tradition of rubbing salt on infants to ensure a long life. Friendship between Arabs was sealed with the expression "There is salt between us." This meant that they would not do harm to each other when they had shared salt. The negative predictions of bad luck from spilled salt are immortalized in Leonardo's "The Last Supper" in which the salt is spilled by Judas.

Key Terms

Angkor Wat—Very large temple complex built by the Khmers in northwest Cambodia.

Bolshoi Ballet—World renowned Russian ballet ensemble.

Culture—Customary beliefs, social forms, and material traits of a racial, religious, or social group.

Ethnicity—Affiliation with a race, people, or social group.

Forbidden City—Walled area in Beijing built by Chinese emperors as the seat of government and power.

Ghandi, Mahatma—Famous pacifist in India who led a 200-mile march to the sea in 1930 to protest the salt tax.

Parthenon—Classical Greek structure dominating the Acropolis in Athens.

Sibelius—Composer from Finland who lived from 1865 to 1957; his most famous orchestral work is *Finlandia*.

Taj Mahal—Graceful marble monument inlaid with semiprecious stones in graceful designs, which was built in Agra, India, by Shah Jahan in memory of his favorite wife, Mumtaz.

Summary

This chapter discusses components of culture. These include beliefs, social forms, and material traits of a racial, religious, or social group. Geography of the region where a person is born and lives is of great importance, and so is the economic strength of that nation and of the individual families. Housing has a tangible influence on lifestyles, as do the choices about working. Both of these factors certainly influence food patterns. Art, music, dance, and architecture make significant contributions to cultural identity. World history and religions are other key components defining cultural groups.

America today is made up of a kaleidoscope of immigrants from virtually all parts of the world. Regardless of how long ago immigrants first came to America, they or their descendants have stories of remembrances or at least some knowledge of their country of origin. Appreciation of this heritage helps bind people of similar backgrounds into cultural groups that reinforce the customs and traditions to maintain a richness of memories and experiences in the next generation. Often, these traditions are shared with others in the community. Such sharing increases understanding and appreciation of the wonderful diversity that is becoming America.

Study Questions

1. What are the characteristics that describe the cultural group with which you identify most closely?
2. What are some of your food preferences and patterns? Do any of these gain this status with you because of your cultural group (or groups)? If so, explain the foods you have identified in terms of your cultural identity.
3. Using a recent newspaper, describe a current example of how some aspect of culture (as described in this chapter) is influencing the food intake of the people involved.

Bibliography

Barer-Stein, T. 1979. *You Eat What You Are*. McClelland and Stewart. Toronto, Canada.

Brown, L. K. and K. Mussell. 1984. *Ethnic and Regional Foodways in the United States*. University of Tennessee Press. Knoxville, TN.

Kurlansky, M. 2002. *Salt*. Walker and Co. New York.

McIntosh, E. N. 1995. *American Food Habits in Historical Perspective*. Praeger. Westport, CT.

Norris, R. E. and L. L. Haring. 1980. *Political Geography*. Charles E. Merrill Publishing Co. Columbus, OH.

Stoddard, R. H., B. W. Blouet, and D. J. Wishart. 1986. *Human Geography: People, Places, and Cultures*. Prentice Hall. Englewood Cliffs, NJ.

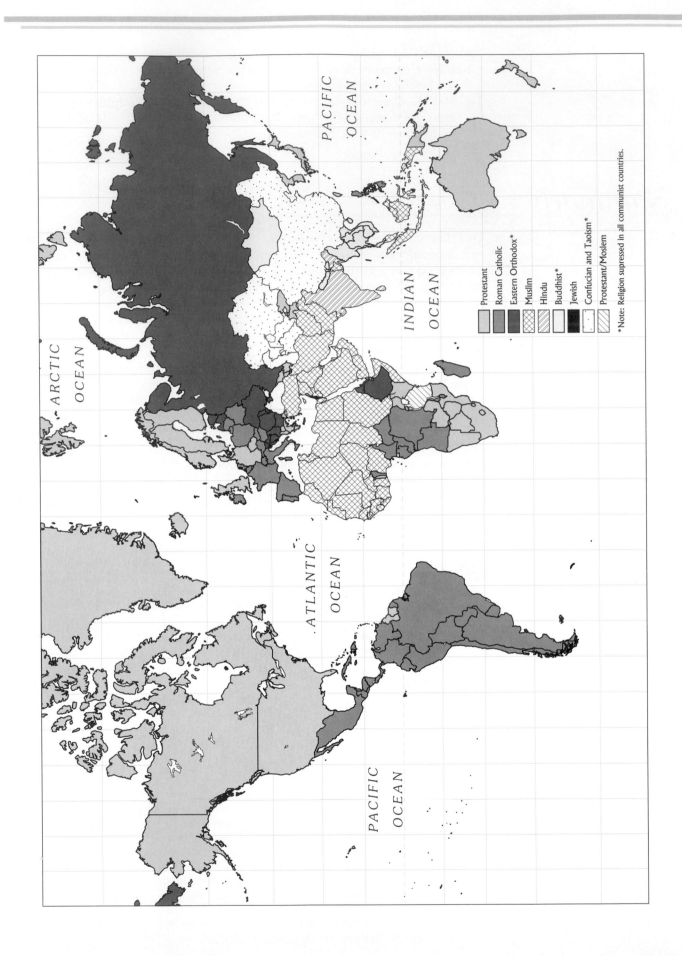

ARCTIC OCEAN

PACIFIC OCEAN

PACIFIC OCEAN

ATLANTIC OCEAN

INDIAN OCEAN

Protestant
Roman Catholic
Eastern Orthodox*
Muslim
Hindu
Buddhist*
Jewish
Confucian and Taoism*
Protestant/Moslem

*Note: Religion supressed in all communist countries.

3 Religions

Beliefs in a god (or gods) have shaped behaviors and cultural patterns of people around the world since very early times. The beliefs and the deities differed quite considerably. Sumerians worshiped Mother Goddess Innin and her son Tammuz around 3000 BCE. Isis and Osiris were important as an Egyptian goddess and god respectively around 2500 BCE, approximately the time when Minoans were viewing the snake and bull as religious symbols. Early Greeks had a pantheon of gods and goddesses, including Zeus, Poseidon, Athena, Aphrodite, and many more during the millennium preceding the birth of Christ.

During the intervening centuries, different religions have emerged as dominant in today's world. Christianity includes Protestant, Roman Catholic, and Eastern Orthodox, which together comprise the most followers of a religion. Islam is the second most numerous when both the Sunni and Shiah branches are counted. Hindu believers are the third in terms of numbers, although they are clustered primarily in India and Nepal. Buddhism also has many followers (somewhat more than half as many as Hinduism). Confucianism has many followers in the Far East; in the same region Shintoism and Taoism are found, but with a smaller group of followers. Judaism is a religion with far fewer followers than the other major religions, but with a very significant influence in today's world.

In the United States, significant changes in religious preferences have been taking place even since 1970, due in part to the large numbers of immigrants from many parts of the world who brought their religious heritages with them. The practice of these religions attracted attention and heightened interest in learning about these different approaches to spirituality. Conversions to these different religions and immigrants who already practiced the predominant religion of their cultures account for an increasing religious diversity, which adds to the breadth of cultures in America (Table 3.1).

Table 3.1   Estimates of Religious Affiliations in the United States in 1970 and 2000

Religion	1970 (millions)	2000 (millions)
Protestants	70.7	88.8
Roman Catholics	48.4	61.8
Jews	6.7	5.5
Muslims	0.8	4.0
Buddhists	0.2	2.0
Hindus	0.1	0.95
Sikhs	0.001	0.22

Adapted from *Encyclopedia Britannica Book of the Year.* 1998. Association of Statisticians of American Religious Bodies.

All of these religions are of considerable importance in influencing not only spiritual beliefs of people, but also their value systems and their cultural behaviors, which may include dietary practices. This chapter provides a review of the major religions of the world. It offers some knowledge about each of these religions, but not an in-depth philosophical examination. These glimpses will add insight into the dietary patterns found in the countries and regions where each of these religions holds considerable influence.

Hinduism

Hinduism probably is the oldest religion in the world, with its roots going back to about 2000 BCE. India and Nepal are the primary countries where Hinduism is found. A distinctive aspect of this religion is that it is not based on the life or teachings of a single person or on the worship of a single god. Hindus believe in reincarnation and that the spirit is reborn in another form in a seemingly eternal cycle in pursuit of spiritual perfection. Manu was the name for the progenitor of the human race and the source of the Vedas. The Vedas are four volumes, which are the collective statements on how Hindus must live.

Although there are many gods and goddesses in Hinduism, three are dominant: Vishnu and Shiva, the two of prominence today, and Brahma. The belief is that Brahma was responsible for creating the present world and that Shiva will destroy it after about 425,000 years so that Brahma can make the world once again. In short, Brahma is the creator god of the triad of Hindu gods. In contrast, Vishnu is the preserver god and Shiva (or Siva) is the destructive god of Hinduism.

Hinduism is a religion with definite emphasis on mysticism and on becoming free of desires—in short, living an ascetic existence and rising above desires of the flesh. Hindus believe that some people, designated as *avatars,* are incarnations of deities here on earth. Ramakrishna, a prominent Hindu saint, is viewed as an avatar of Shiva. Hindu worship includes chanting of incantations, or mantras. The sound involved is *om* (pronounced with a long *o* and extended *m* sound). With extended chanting, a religious energy presumably is generated. Another prayer form is the chanting of "The Thousand Names of Sivasahastranaman (Shiva)."

Inherent in Hinduism is the caste system, which socially divides people into classes that are required to maintain distinct divisions and privileges (or lack of privileges) associated with each specific caste level. Brahmans are the highest of the castes, and the untouchables the lowest. The Brahmans were the priests and teachers, and were viewed as being derived from the mouth of Brahma, the universal spirit. Next is the caste called Kshatriyas, thought to be from the arms of Brahma and designated as the warriors and rulers. Vaisyas, the farmers and business people, were from the thighs. Brahma's feet were the caste of menial workers, the Sudras. Believers in Hinduism were born into the caste of their ancestors. Anybody who was not born as a Brahman, a Kshatriyas, a Vaisyas, or a Sudras was deemed unworthy and was designated as an untouchable. Fundamental to Hinduism is the lack of upward mobility through the good deeds one might do during life. However, such deeds are believed to be able to exert influence on the soul in which a person is reborn in the next life. The way a person lives is the responsibility of the individual. The fact that status in rebirth is the direct result of the acts in the previous life is a powerful motivation to live according to Hindu beliefs. The new form of the soul in the next life can be far lower than in the present life, or it can be better. The whole purpose is to constantly strive to reach the universal spirit during some future rebirth. The deeds performed in all previous lives determine the nature of a person's next existence; this force is called karma.

All life, whether human or animal, is highly respected by Hindus and is believed to be sacred, because part of the spirit of Brahma is thought to be a part of any living thing. An extension of this belief is that one's ancestor might actually be the spirit of the life that is taken if something is killed. Cows occupy a particularly revered niche because they are thought by Hindus to have been created by Brahma at the same time that people were created. This reverence for cows is still seen in India, where they are allowed to wander freely on any street, road, or land they wish.

The high respect for life means that many Hindus are vegetarians. Not surprisingly, Brahmans are the caste most likely to forgo eating meats and also eggs, which potentially represent life. Castes below that of Brahman may avoid beef but eat other meats. However, chickens and pigs, viewed as unclean because they may scavenge for food, also may be avoided. Fish seem to be more acceptable than other flesh foods. Animals that are to be killed for food can be killed by people who are in the Kshatriyas caste, for they are designated as the leaders and soldiers. Good sanitation underlies activities in a Brahman kitchen, for this is considered a holy place. The cook must have a ritual bath before cooking. Lower castes should not prepare the food, but they can give uncooked foods or those cooked in ghee to Brahmans. All Brahmans eating the food also need to bathe the entire body and dress in clean clothes. The foods they eat are designated as *pakka* foods, which are foods offered to the gods and then to guests of high rank. All pakka foods contain ghee. The next level of food is designated as *kacca* and does not contain ghee, which makes the products, such as bread, drier. If any kacca is left over, it is designated as *jutha* (garbage). Jutha is suitable for animals, lower castes, or untouchables. Only wives or others of lower status are allowed to scrape kacca from plates.

Brahmans tend to avoid garlic and onions to avoid association with lesser classes. Avoidance of alcohol by Brahmans is required to avoid any possible loss of self-control. Lower Hindu castes, however, are allowed to drink alcohol.

Hindus have numerous gods and goddesses, some of which are prominent in their holidays at various times throughout the year. Krishna, worshiped as the eighth incarnation of the god Vishnu, is a figure celebrated as Janmashtami or Gokul Ashtami on the occasion marking his birthday. This unusual celebration features pots of milk curds hung very high so that they can only be reached by boys or men forming a human pyramid topped by someone swinging a stick to break the pots.

Kama, the Hindu god of love, and Krishna are honored at Holi, a lighthearted celebration in which brightly colored powdered dyes are thrown at others as men play pranks and dance around.

On a more somber note, the festival called Dussara is a time of pageantry to honor Devi, the goddess who is Shiva's wife. This celebration continues for 10 days.

One of the more unusual gods is Ganesha, who is easily recognized because of the happy elephant head and the rotund human belly of his figure. His birthday is celebrated with the holiday Ganesha Chaturthi. Not surprisingly, quantities of food offerings (milk, fruit, and puddings) are featured at this 3-day holiday.

Brahmans get new clothing and give away their old sacred clothing as a part of their celebration of Rakhi Purnima to honor Shiva (who has three eyes). The coconut, with its three eyes, is traditional for this celebration, and it is broken at a shrine as part of the festivities.

Rama Navami is another holiday featuring coconuts. In this celebration, a coconut is placed in a cradle to represent the birth of Rama, the seventh incarnation of Vishnu. Dancing and entertainment are featured at this particularly important festival.

Divali is the joyous celebration of the new year. Even fireworks are included. The greeting for the occasion is "A happy Divali and a prosperous new year!"

Hinduism has had many rituals in years past, although today, some have been eliminated either by law or by practice. An example is *sati*, which occurred occasionally in centuries past when a widow would throw herself on her dead husband's funeral pyre and die in self-immolation. Sati was outlawed over 100 years ago. Furthermore, Hindu widows now are allowed to marry again. The class of untouchables also has been eliminated.

Underlying some rituals is the notion of purity and pollution. The ritual of bathing is dictated by the need for purity and the elimination of pollution. Since human wastes are all considered pollution, there are various rituals that are to be followed when coping with these sources of pollution. *Dharma* is a term that encompasses the rituals of daily life. These include rituals for praying, which Brahmans are to do three times daily. When a child is born, the house must be purified, and the newborn's horoscope must be determined. On the sixth or twelfth day, the baby is named, and the occasion is marked by feeding the baby its first solid food. Ear-piercing may also be done then or at some later time. The child's head may be shaved at the age of one to thank the *deva* for safeguarding the child through infancy.

Weddings are of greatest ritual importance, and every Hindu is expected to marry, because it is a religious duty. The religious debt to the couple's ancestors is paid by having children. The rituals associated with the marriage may take more than a week and involve such acts as the couple walking seven times around the sacred fire.

Funerals are needed to empower the departing spirit to leave the present world and also to take care of the pollution that is associated with death. The funeral pyre is lighted by the oldest son of the departed. The mourning period, which lasts 10 or 11 days after the cremation, is marked by various rituals that restrict what the relatives can do during that time. The ending ritual involves offerings of balls of rice or barley and some milk. These offerings are also presented annually from then on. This ritual is intended to help the departed get a new spiritual body.

Worship can be done as temple worship, home worship, or in congregational worship. Priests are responsible for conducting the rituals associated with the god and goddesses of the particular temple. The ceremonies are marked by a variety of practices, including food and flower offerings, ringing of bells, prayers, music, and possibly other practices. Each household also maintains an area for worship, which may include images, yantras (geometric designs), and offerings, all of which are kept in a state of purity. Pilgrimages are undertaken to such holy sites as Banaras in the hope of achieving a spiritual experience. These efforts often are well arranged and may include religious fairs.

Buddhism

Buddhism is the religion of vast numbers throughout Southeast Asia, including Taiwan, Vietnam, Cambodia, Laos, Bhutan, Nepal, Tibet, China, Japan, Myanmar (Burma), Thailand, and Sri Lanka. This far-reaching religion began in northeastern India in about 530 BCE and was based on the teachings of Siddhartha Gautama, who became known as Buddha.

During his lifetime, he renounced his worldly position and spent 6 years searching for the truth. His "enlightenment" occurred while he was sitting under the bodhi tree, where he reached Nirvana and all worldly desires disappeared. The religion that flowed from his teachings represented a departure or reformation movement from the Hindu roots of India. It was a religion that spread successfully over vast regions, but did not replace Hinduism among most Indians. Asoka, the strong Mauryan ruler of India, was converted to Buddhism and did much to spread Buddhism to China, Japan, Korea, and beyond.

Although Buddha is central to the Buddhist religion and is important for his teachings, he is not worshipped as a god (Figure 3.1). Buddhism has no gods, and thus is quite different from Hinduism. Also, there is no caste system. The ultimate goal of Buddhism is to reach Nirvana, a process that could involve countless rebirths. The basic teachings, called the Four Noble Truths, are

1. Existence is suffering.
2. The origin of human suffering is craving pleasure, possessions, or cessation of pain.
3. Craving is cured by detachment from oneself and from all things.
4. Detachment is achieved by following the Eight-Fold Path:
   a. Right conduct
   b. Right effort
   c. Right intentions
   d. Right livelihood
   e. Right meditation
   f. Right mindfulness
   g. Right speech
   h. Right viewpoint

Figure 3.1 Large statue of Buddha presides over temple ruins at Sukhothai, the first capital of Thailand.

The code of conduct, called the *dasa-sila* or Ten Precepts, includes

1. Thou shalt not take another's life.
2. Thou shalt not take that which is not given.
3. Thou shalt not engage in sexual misconduct. (Monks are to be celibate, and others are not to be adulterous.)
4. Thou shalt not engage in false speech.
5. Thou shalt not use intoxicants.
6. Thou shalt not eat after midday.
7. Thou shalt shun worldly amusements.
8. Thou shalt not adorn with ornaments or perfume.
9. Thou shalt not sleep on high or luxurious beds.
10. Thou shalt not accept gold or silver.

The mantra (chant) is repeated three times: "I take refuge in the Buddha. I take refuge in the teachings. I take refuge in the community."

Buddhism is broadly divided into three sects: eastern (Japan, Korea, and China), northern or Mahayana (Tibet, Mongolia, and the Himalayas), and southern or Theravada (Thailand, Myanmar, Sri Lanka, Cambodia, and Laos). The Theravada in Southeast Asia developed as a monastic sect (Figure 3.2). The Mahayana in the north developed a somewhat more mystical approach and included *bodhisattvas* (supernatural, semidivine beings who helped people achieve Nirvana). The Dalai Lama is considered to be the reincarnation of Bodhisattva of Mercy, Avalokitesvara.

In Thailand and the other countries where Theravada Buddhists worship, it is a common sight to see monks strolling about during the mornings with a beggar's bowl (usually brass) (Figure 3.3). This enables the woman of a house to fill or add to his bowl with food she has prepared. Her generous act allows her to gain merit *(kutho)* and of course enables the monk to eat during the day until midday, after which he is not to eat. All Buddhist males following the practices of the Theravada sect are expected to become monks, although their "careers" as monks may be as short as only a few days. The monasteries provide education for

Figure 3.2 This Theravada Buddhist monk in Cambodia has dedicated his life to his religion.

Figure 3.3 Three young monks in Myanmar (Burma) are seeking food for their begging bowls before the end of the morning.

boys who remain in their group, and the boys provide help to the older monks and to the monastery.

Not surprisingly, Buddhists do not believe in killing animals to obtain food, and so generally abstain from eating meat. However, it is possible for a non-Buddhist to kill an animal and for the Buddhist to eat some of the meat if that animal was not killed to feed him. Interestingly, fish can play a role in Buddhist diets because they are considered to have died as a consequence of coming out of the water and therefore were not killed by the person who caught them.

Buddhism has resulted in the creation of innumerable statues of Buddha in different positions—sitting, standing, and reclining. Another feature of Buddhism is the construction of *stupas,* which are hemispherical mounds with a central mast or decorative feature. Pagodas of various designs and with several stories also serve as shrines for Buddhists. Relics of religious significance may be found in these stupas and pagodas: a tooth from Buddha, an alms bowl he used, or an object that symbolizes Buddha, for example.

Buddhist festivals are calculated according to lunar months, with the full moon being especially important. Festivals of agricultural significance are found in many places where Buddhism is practiced. Festivals of lights typically celebrate the full moon and Buddha's first sermon, and also celebrate the sending out of the first Buddhist missionaries. Local pilgrimages are done by individual Buddhists, such as can be seen in Lhasa, Tibet, as pilgrims prostrate themselves repeatedly on the road surrounding the Jogkhang Temple as they painfully circumambulate this most honored temple. In Tibet a special type of stupa called a *chorten* is built to house religious relics or to honor a special figure, such as a deceased Dalai Lama. Prayer wheels and prayer flags are other familiar aspects of Buddhist worship in Tibet, Nepal, and Bhutan. By whirling the prayer wheels, Buddhists send their prayers. Prayer flags strung along ropes and tied against the strong breezes of the Himalayas are an efficient way for Buddhists to pray.

In Tibet, China, and Japan as well as in much of Southeast Asia, Buddhism has been influenced by wars and politics. However, Buddhism is practiced in all of these places today in whatever form it has evolved to in the various cultures. One of the enduring attributes of Buddhism over the centuries has been its flexibility to adapt to change and to the needs of its followers, regardless of the sect.

Confucianism and Taoism

Religion in China for the majority of the people is a blend of Confucianism, Taoism, and Buddhism. Confucianism underlies the morality and behavior of people, including rites of passage. Taoism provides for the needs and healing of the sick and is a basis for regulating festivals. Buddhism is the source of compassion in life and salvation after life. The three together provide for all aspects of life, both during and after.

Confucianism and Taoism can be traced back to at least six centuries BCE. Confucianism evolved into a school collected into the *Four Books and Five Classics* (Hong Kong University Press, 1960). The founder of Confucianism was considered to be a 6th century BCE man named Confucius, or K'ung Fu-tzu (Master Kung). He taught that the way to live was by correct ethical conduct, which would allow one to achieve ideal harmony with the "way of Heaven" and make one become more than human.

Taoism was founded slightly later, based on teachings from the Chuang-Tzu and Lao-Tzu in the 6th century BCE. The goal of Taoism was to achieve a passionless oneness with the divine Absolute, a process that encouraged a passive approach to living one's life and a peaceful acceptance while awaiting death. Retreat into meditation and nature or into a life as a monk or isolated person allowed for connecting with the ways of nature. Thrift, humility, simplicity, patience, contentment, and harmony are the basic principles of Taoism.

Contributions from Taoism in current Chinese religions stem from the cosmic concept that Tao gave birth to the primordial breath (the One), which birthed yin and yang (the Two), which gave birth to water, earth, and heaven (the Three), which birthed the myriad creatures. This becomes a never-ending cycle in Taoism as the myriad creatures return to Tao. From Confucianism come the norms for behaviors, which embrace (1) respect, (2) family love, (3) benevolence toward strangers, and (4) loyalty to the state. The concept of cosmos can be summarized in terms of yin and yang: pure yang is heaven, the visible world of life is both yang and yin, and the underworld (in nine stages) is pure yin. The soul is believed to sink into the domain of pure yin for a period following death, where it can ultimately be freed to ascend to heaven.

Rituals are important in the Chinese religious culture. For example, pregnant women are excused from a variety of chores that might impose undue physical or psychological pressures. They also are expected to be fed a diet rich in protein and vitamins by other family members for one month following delivery. Gifts that might include eggs and rice or other special healthy foods to symbolize good health and prosperity are given in the first, fourth, and twelfth month after birth. The new mother's family is expected to give all of the clothing and diapers at these times too.

Traditional marriage rituals begin with a 3-day period when the characters representing the year, month, day, and hour of birth of both the prospective bride and groom are placed on the family altar in the bride's family home. If all goes well in that household during those three days, invitations are sent for the wedding. A special procession is the means for transporting the bride's vanity box and dowry to the groom and his family, where he opens the vanity box (symbolizing sincere love) and the dowry is counted. The groom matches the value of the dowry in such items as jewelry or clothing for the bride. The groom then must go to his bride's home and take her back to his home, which she enters by stepping over a cooking pot, a saddle, and an apple. At the reception following the marriage ceremony, a small rice wine toast is done by the bride and groom before proceeding with toasts (tea) at each of the tables of guests at their wedding dinner. The next morning the bride serves breakfast to her new in-laws, including dried dates and seeds to signify many children as a gift from the bride; then they serve her breakfast. Finally, she is a guest in her own parents' home on the third day.

A death in the family also invokes religious rituals, beginning with wailing at the moment of death, followed by removal of jewelry and fine clothes as mourning begins. White paper-wrapped money or other talismans are placed as a cover over the body as symbols of protection from harm and of purification for the deceased. Money gifts and condolences are given to help the family with the funeral. The burning of a paper house with its furnishings, symbolic clothes, and paper money combines appreciation of the merits of living and prayers for eternal salvation for the dead. A willow branch to represent the deceased is a part of the family's procession with the coffin to the grave, and it then is carried to the family altar at home to put the soul into the memorial tablet. Special liturgies are to be performed by the deceased's minister 7, 9, and 49 days after the burial as well as on the first and third anniversaries of the death.

Some festivals have food traditions as a part of the celebration. The lunar New Year (festival of spring) is celebrated by a big gathering of family from all over to share a banquet. To celebrate the family's ancestors, five or seven sets of chopsticks, bowls of cooked rice, wine, and tea are placed at the family altar. The family members then share a huge banquet (16 or 24 courses): three or five kinds of cooked meat, noodles, bean curd, vegetable dishes, cake, sweets, dried fruit, and fish. The celebration includes gifts and cash in a red envelope for children. Women don flowers in their hair, and fireworks add to the festivities, which include visits to friends, to shrines, and to churches.

The third day of the third lunar month is a festival day for cleaning graves and a family picnic. Rice cakes are eaten for the festival on the fifth day of the fifth lunar month (the first day of summer), and dragon boat races are held where possible. The 15th day of the seventh month is the all souls' day festival, which is the occasion for another large family banquet. Fresh fruits and round mooncakes are the traditional fare for the harvest festival on the 15th day of the eighth lunar month.

Shintoism

Shinto was the religion of early Japan and still is in practice today, as also is Buddhism and sometimes blends of religions. Ancestors are revered in Shinto; each ancestor is assumed to become a *kami*, or supernatural being, following death, and as such remains as a life within the family. Kami can be either good or evil, depending upon the life the person led on earth. Among the patron saints in Shinto is a dwarf named Okuninushi, or Master of the Great Land, who is the saint of rice wine brewing. The Emperor of Japan is the person who symbolically shares new rice and rice wine with Shinto deities, according to a very careful ritual, and by doing so assumes his own divinity. Some Japanese homes still maintain two altars—a kami altar for life and its activities, and a Buddha altar for death and ancestral veneration. Both altars are maintained with fresh food and drink at the start of each day.

Festivals highlight the religious calendar in Japan at various times of year. The 3-day New Year celebration is marked by thoroughly cleaning house and yard and paying all debts, as well as by visits to elderly relatives, teachers, and others. If a family member has died during the year, the family does not celebrate, but it does send cards to friends, asking them not to send New Year's greetings this time. The Bon festival is held in the summer, at which time many return to the family home to honor their ancestors who are on their ancestral tablet. Family graves are cleaned and freshened on the occasion of the spring and autumnal equinoxes, and a family picnic is held at the graves. Children are taken to their Shinto shrine to be presented to the kami at the end of the first month of life and again at ages 3 and 7 if a girl and at age 5 if a boy to place them under the divine care of the kami. Religious rites associated with death tend to follow Buddhist traditions.

Judaism

The history of Judaism traces back to ancient Hebrews who developed their religion based on their belief in one God, who was revealed to them, the Chosen People. The Torah (Pentateuch, or first five books of the Old Testament of the Bible) provided the foundation to which were added the Neviim (the Prophets) and Ketuvim (writings) to ultimately comprise a 24-book Hebrew Bible. The Talmud contains extensive oral teachings and many other important interpretations of the Jewish faith. Maimonides, a Spanish Jew who lived from 1135 to 1204, authored the Mishneh Torah, which provided the great law code of Judaism.

The stories of early Judaism are those of the books of Genesis, Exodus, Leviticus, Numbers, and Deuteronomy, and of such powerful figures as Abraham (patriarch and founder of the Hebrews) and Moses (Hebrew prophet who led the Israelites out of Egypt). Although Judaism was centered in Judea, history has chronicled the Jewish diaspora to far-flung regions over a period of centuries. The conquest of Babylonia and the destruction of the First Temple in Jerusalem resulted in Jews being exiled to Babylon. Invasion of Judea by the Romans in 63 BCE started another dark period for the Jews, a time in which the Temple was again destroyed (70 CE), and the brave rebels who had fled to Masada (overlooking the Dead Sea) all died dramatically in 73 CE (Figure 3.4). Jews gained some prominence in Rome because of their cultural and economic abilities, talents that they revealed wherever they settled. Eventually, Jews were living in much of Europe. In Spain they played very significant roles in commerce and the economy. However, the adoption of Christianity in the Roman Empire in the 4th century CE caused increasing isolation for Jews throughout the Empire. The conquest of Spain by Muslims in 711 CE gave considerable acceptance and recognition to the Jews there, but they were expelled when the Moors were driven out of Spain and Christianity ruled in 1492.

The Jews who lived in Spain and Portugal were identified as Sephardic Jews, and those who were situated in northern Europe and on over toward Russia were called Ashkenazi Jews. Sephardic Jews were treated with some degree of

Figure 3.4 View of the site of the Roman encampment from Masada, the high plateau where Jewish rebels held off their enemy until all the Jews perished in 73 CE.

tolerance by people in the Muslim world, but the Ashkenazi Jews suffered extreme persecution in many cases. These two divisions have some differences, but they both believe in the foundations of Judaism.

The Jewish ritual calendar has 12 lunar months, which requires leap months to accommodate the 11 days that would be missing to keep in step with the agricultural seasons. On this calendar Rosh Hashanah (the New Year) occurs in late September or early October (2001 was 5771 on the Jewish calendar). Ten days later is Yom Kippur (the Day of Atonement). Five days after Yom Kippur is Sukkot (the Festival of Tabernacles), which is a 9-day event. About 2 months later, Chanukah (Festival of Lights) is celebrated for 8 days. Asarah Be-Tevet (the 10th of the month of Tevet) is a fast day. The 14th day of the Jewish month of Adar is Purim, a festival based on the book of Esther (from the Bible). Pesach (Passover) is an 8-day celebration that is held in the spring. Shavuot (Festival of Pentecost) is held 7 weeks after the second day of Passover. A 3-week period of mourning begins 5 weeks after Shavuot with a daytime fast (Shivah Asar Be-Tammuz) and ends with a 25-hour fast (Tisha Be-Av). There also are minor festivals at the beginning of each lunar month (Rosh Codesh), and Shabbat is celebrated each week, beginning at sunset on Friday and ending when it is dark on Saturday. These holidays are summarized in Table 3.2.

Traditions are very important in Judaism on special occasions and in daily living. Children born of a Jewish mother are considered to be Jews; the father does not have to be Jewish, although a Jewish father is preferred. If the baby is male, circumcision is done on the eighth day to symbolize the baby's entry into the covenant God made with Abraham and his descendants; a feast celebrates this event. Careful and thorough instruction in Hebrew and in the translations of parts of the Torah and prayers continues for both boys and girls until they reach maturity (12 for girls and 13 for boys), at which time their maturity is celebrated by the Bar Mitzvah for boys and Bat Mitzvah for girls. At a boy's Bar Mitzvah, he will read from the Torah in the synagogue, and a very elaborate family party, which also includes friends, will be held. Bat Mitzvah celebrations usually are somewhat less elaborate (and may not occur in Orthodox families).

Special foods are important in Jewish traditions. Although each family has special favorites, certain dishes are familiar in most homes, especially for holidays and feasts. Some of these are listed in Table 3.3.

Marriage in Judaism is extremely important, for the family occupies a central position in the religion. The ceremony is held under a canopy, sometimes in the synagogue (unless the marriage is with a non-Jewish person) and occasionally outdoors (the preference of some Ashkenazi Jews). A ritualistic service often is presented by the rabbi and the synagogue cantor and includes the traditional breaking of a glass, symbolizing the poignancy of the great joy of the wedding with the tragedy of the destruction of Jerusalem.

Funerals for Jewish people also have many traditions. The burial needs to be done immediately or just as soon as possible after death, and a little dirt from Israel is thrown on the coffin before it is lowered into consecrated ground in a Jewish cemetery. Official mourning is done by the next of kin for a week and includes sitting on low stools, not wearing leather shoes, and praying with people who come to comfort them.

Worship in the synagogue is shorter during the week than on Saturdays, but there are prayers for morning, afternoon, and evening in which worshipers face Jerusalem and the Ark of the synagogue where the Torah is placed. Saturday morning services may last as long as 3 hours and include more reading from the Torah, prayers, and chanting. Orthodox services are conducted by men, with the women attendees seated in a special gallery, whereas Reform and Conservative services, if held in a temple rather than a synagogue, have combined seating and participation in the service. Orthodox and Conservative Jewish men wear the

Table 3.2 Jewish Holidays: Their Timing, Significance, and Mode of Celebration

Holiday	Timing	Significance	Mode of Celebration
Rosh Hashanah (New Year)	2 days; late September or October	New Year; divine judgment (fate of world for next year determined).	Shofar blown 100 times to symbolize awareness of shortcomings and repentance. Sweet foods on first day symbolize good year to come; fast on second day remembering tragic event in past.
Yom Kippur (Day of Atonement)	10 days after Rosh Hashanah	Seek atonement from God for past sins.	Fast day (25 hours beginning at dusk). Mostly spent in the synagogue in worship. No leather shoes are worn.
Sukkot (Tabernacles)	9 days; begins 5 days after Yom Kippur	Commemorates flight from Egypt.	Ritual of Tabernacles: taking of palm branch, willows, myrtle, and a citrus shaken together during prayers. No work is done on first 2 days or on last day. End yearly cycle of Torah readings and begin reading Genesis again. Singing, dancing, and alcohol.
Chanukah (Hanukkah, Feast of Lights)	8 days; 2 months after Sukkot	Commemorates victory of Hasmonean priests over non-Jewish and rededication of second Temple in 165 BCE; Feast of Lights recalls Talmudic tale of 1 day's oil burning in Temple for 8 days.	One candle is lighted each day on the menorah (total of eight); fruits, nuts, and sweet treats are served; children receive small gifts of wrapped money. Star of David and gifts wrapped in blue and white paper are prominent during the celebration.
Asarah Be-Tevet	10th day of Tevet	Remembers tragic event.	Fast day.
Purim	14th day of Adar	Commemorates rescue of Jews from Persia and its leader Haman (as told in book of Esther).	Elaborate, dressy day with gifts, a big feast in afternoon, and much alcohol.
Pesach (Passover)	8 days; 1 month after Purim	Commemorates the Passover and Exodus of Israelites from Egypt. Very important family holiday.	Complete cleaning of house, removal of all leaven. Seder (ritual meal) and the story of the Exodus the first night; 4 cups of wine are drunk; bitter herbs and unleavened bread are ritual foods.
Shavuot (Pentecost)	7 weeks following Passover	Festival of Pentecost; celebrates time when Moses received the Ten Commandments on Mt. Sinai.	Study the Torah all night.
Shabbat (Sabbath)	Begins every Friday at sunset; ends Saturday at dark	Sabbath, or seventh day; day of rest and worship.	Mother lights candles before Shabbat begins, father blesses children for reciting kiddush and says blessing over two loaves of challah (special bread); hymns sung at the three Shabbat meals; Shabbat ends with prayer over wine, incense, and lighted candle.

yarmulke (type of skullcap) in the synagogue, and Orthodox men wear it at all times to show respect and reverence to God. Orthodox married women also cover their hair, at least in the synagogue.

In Orthodox homes, strict practices are followed. The men may choose to wear the black hats and long black coats that have so long been a traditional garment. Another traditional male garment is a four-cornered vest with strings fastened to each corner, which is a version of the prayer shawl used for morning prayers. In the Orthodox kitchen, separate utensils and dishes must be used for meat and for dairy foods, and strict dietary laws (*kashruth*) are practiced.

Kashruth spells out kosher requirements for Orthodox Jews and others wishing to have the purity connoted by selecting foods designated officially as kosher. Meats that can be eaten include only those from animals that chew their

Table 3.3   Selected Traditional Jewish Favorite Dishes

Dish	Description	Holiday
Latke	Fried potato pancake.	Chanukah
Gefilte fish	Baked or stewed fish balls containing egg, bread, and seasonings.	Sabbath eve dinner
Matzo[a]	Unleavened flat bread made of flour and water and baked in a very hot oven.	Passover
Matzo meal	Coarsely ground matzo used in place of flour or bread crumbs during all of Passover.	Passover
Matzo farfel	Coarse pieces of matzo similar to flaked cereals; replaces noodles and pasta during Passover.	Passover
Matzo cereal	Used in place of cream of wheat and as a thickener in place of flour.	Passover
Hamantashen	Prune and poppy-seed-filled three-cornered cookies (eat Haman's hat).	Purim
Challah	Two circles or loaves baked for Sabbath, symbolizing double portion of manna provided by God on Fridays for Sabbath during 40 years in the wilderness.	Sabbath eve
Challah	Bread with birds or ladders to carry Rosh Hashanah prayers to heaven. With slice of apple and honey, gives wish for sweet new year.	Rosh Hashanah
Kreplach	Pasta-wrapped meat morsels (Jewish tortellini).	Meal before Yom Kippur fast
Honey cake	Spicy, sweet cake made with honey and perhaps dried fruit.	Rosh Hashanah or to break fast of Yom Kippur

[a] Matzo in various forms is used in preparing foods during Passover. Flour is not to be used (actually, no flour is in the house nor are any products made with regular flour in the house at that holiday).

cud and have a cloven (split) hoof, and these must be slaughtered and bled according to kosher requirements, which includes slaughter by a butcher *(shochet)* who uses a very sharp knife *(challef)* following the prescribed kosher method. The meat is soaked in cold water, then salted with kosher (coarse) salt for an hour and allowed to drain on a slanted board to remove the blood. Finally, the meat is washed before it is considered fit for consumption. The types of meat that can be eaten when following kashruth include beef, sheep, goat, and deer. Fish with scales and fins are also approved, but mollusks and crustaceans are prohibited. Chickens and turkeys are approved, but ostrich is not. These and other dietary laws are contained in Leviticus and Deuteronomy. The quote in Deuteronomy and also in Exodus suggests that a kid should not be cooked in its mother's milk, which is the basis for waiting between 1 and 6 hours between eating meat and dairy products, the timing being quite variable between rabbis. Hasidic Jews who trace their sect to 18th century Poland follow particularly strict kashruth rules, even requiring that such egg-containing products as egg noodles be prepared by a Hasidic because there is a very remote possibility that the egg might have a blood spot. Kosher products in the market are designated with such markings as K.U. or COR, signs that indicate rabbinical approval.

Among Jewish people in the United States today, there are differences in traditions and approaches to Judaism, which are creating potentially sharp divisions within the faith. A 1997 survey among Jewish households throughout metropolitan Los Angeles found that 4.3 percent of those surveyed were Orthodox, 28.2 percent were Conservative, 39.9 percent were Reform, and 2 percent were Reconstructionist. The trend since 1979 has been a reduction in the numbers of both Orthodox and Conservative, and an increase in Reform and Reconstructionists.

*C*hristianity

Christianity as a religion separate from Judaism developed in the early centuries following Jesus' death. The Old Testament was accepted as a record of early important events, which is not surprising, since Jesus and his disciples were born as

Jews and lived in that context during at least a part of their lives. However, the interpretation of Jesus on earth and thereafter provides the schism between Judaism and Christianity (Figure 3.5). The name *Christian,* derived from the Greek *Cristos* (translation from the Hebrew word *Messiah*), was coined in about 35 CE in Syria to describe a group worshiping there. The New Testament, with its first four chapters attributed to the apostles Matthew, Mark, Luke, and John, and other books added later, provided the written foundation for the period that included Christ, and the combination of the Old and New Testaments became the Bible for Christians.

Although early believers in Christianity had been born as Jews, the religion fanned out from Jerusalem and attracted many converts who had never been Jews. Eventually, Christianity became widespread among Gentiles, and new traditions gradually evolved. Hellenistic influences contributed to the developing religion, with a large role being played by the apostle Paul. The Roman Emperor Constantine became a Christian, which led to a strong Christian influence in the Roman Empire for centuries, especially in the Eastern Roman Empire.

The Roman Catholic church was split permanently when the branch in Constantinople officially broke away in 1054 CE. The Eastern Orthodox Church, which also is referred to as the Greek Orthodox and the Russian Orthodox Church, is a version of Christianity in which icons are the tradition, and Jesus, the Divine Son, is the icon or image of what man can aspire to be. The four patriarchates (Jerusalem, Antioch, Alexandria, and Constantinople) of Eastern Orthodoxy exist even today, although they are diminished in numbers of followers. Eastern Christianity also had an ancient group of churches that were termed *Oriental* and that remain today as the Coptic Orthodox Church (Egypt) and as the Church of Ethiopia and the Church of Armenia.

The Roman Catholic Church was the branch of Christianity that developed in Roman times and remains today, with its headquarters at the Vatican and the Pope as its head (Figure 3.6). The sacraments of the Roman Catholic Church included the rites of baptism, confirmation, marriage, Eucharist, penance, anointing of the sick before death, and ordination. Latin became the language of the Roman Catholic Church and was spread throughout the western part of Europe from Scandinavia to the Danube region despite the confusion of the Middle Ages.

Figure 3.5 The large Catholic cathedral in Strasbourg, France, is representative of the large cathedrals built by Christians in Europe.

Figure 3.6 St. Peter's cathedral in the Vatican is the Pope's primary place to celebrate mass.

However, discontent was festering in the northern region of the European continent.

October 31, 1517, was a historic day in Wittenberg, Germany, for it was there that Martin Luther (an ordained Roman Catholic priest) nailed to the cathedral doors his 95 theses enumerating objections to practices within the Roman Catholic Church. This posting sparked the break with Rome that resulted in the Protestant branch of Christianity and its several independent groups around the western world, including Methodists, Presbyterians, Congregationalists, and many others.

Protestant churches used the language of the regions where they were practiced rather than the Latin of the Roman Catholic Church. The freedom of religious thought generated by the Protest movement engendered the start of the rather wide range of church groups that are considered Christian now, but are clearly not Roman Catholic or Orthodox. Despite the many differences among Christian groups, there is agreement that God is the Holy Father, the Spirit, and the Holy Ghost; that He made Heaven and Earth; that Jesus was God's only son and that Jesus rose from the dead. Baptism and communion (the ingestion of wine and bread, symbolizing the blood and body of Christ) are unifying rituals in Christianity.

Religious holidays for Christians are focused particularly around Christ's death and also his birth. Christians dwelt more on the event of death and the hereafter than did Jews, so it is not surprising that the events around Christ's death were honored before traditions arose around his birth. Easter was established as the Sunday following the first full moon after the vernal equinox, falling between March 22 and April 25. The Eastern Orthodox Church observes its Easter only after the Jewish Passover, which can represent a delay of a month from the Easter celebration of other Christian churches. Sunday was the holy day in the Christian calendar because it was the first day of the week, a description in Mark 16:2 stating that the resurrection occurred early in the morning of the first day of the week. This designation had the advantage of distinguishing the Christian holy day from the Jewish Sabbath, which was on Saturday. Coincidental with the selection of the date for Easter was the pagan celebration of Eastre, the fertility goddess of Spring. The tradition of the Easter bunny for Christian children may have sprung from the acknowledged fertility of hares. Another Easter pagan ritual was the sacrificing of a horned bull, which led to the practice of tracing the pattern of the crossed horns into the top of bread, probably the forerunner of Easter's traditional fare of hot cross buns.

The observance of Lent for 40 days prior to Easter evolved as a time to contemplate and consider one's life and behaviors. The precedent for the 40-day period may have been Jesus' fast for 40 days after he was baptized, or it may refer to the time Moses and Elias spent wandering in the wilderness, or it may even symbolize the 40 years the Jews wandered in search of the Promised Land. The first day of Lent is Ash Wednesday, a time when a smudge of ash in the shape of a cross is marked on the forehead, the ash preferably being from the palm leaves kept from the previous Easter's Palm Sunday celebration.

The actual week of Easter is a 7-day event, beginning with Palm Sunday, commemorating Christ's triumphant entry into Jerusalem. Holy Monday of that week is in recognition of Jesus chasing the money lenders from the Temple. Holy Tuesday honors Christ's speaking to his disciples on the Mount of Olives outside Jerusalem, and it also recognizes the plotting of the Pharisees to trap Jesus. Holy Wednesday is in recognition of Judas agreeing to betray Christ for 30 pieces of silver. Maundy Thursday is marked as the Last Supper, at which Christ washed his disciples' feet, emphasized brotherly love, and initiated the sacrament of the Eucharist (communion). On Good Friday the march to the cross and the Crucifixion are remembered. The especially sober period is the 3 hours from noon until 3:00 when Christ was on the cross. Holy Saturday is the eve of Christ's Ascension into Heaven, which is celebrated with Easter sunrise services by many Christian churches today.

December 25 is celebrated as the birth of Christ by all Christians, despite the fact that his real birth date is far from certain. In the 4th century this date was picked because it coincided with a pagan celebration, which allowed Christians to celebrate without too much attention. Christmas became a firm tradition on December 25 in 337, when Emperor Constantine was baptized, an act that symbolized that Christianity was the state religion. The period from November 30 until Christmas Eve has been designated as Advent, a time for spiritually preparing for the wondrous gift of Christ to all Christians. January 6 is celebrated as the Epiphany because three major events in Christ's life occurred on that date: the visit of the Magi at his manger in Bethlehem following his birth, his baptism at the River Jordan, and the miracle at Cana when Christ, at a marriage feast, changed water to wine.

The apostle Paul is credited with freeing Christians from the dietary laws practiced by the Jews, which thus served as a means of distancing the new Christian religion from its Jewish origins. In fact, the symbolic drinking of wine as a representation of the blood of Christ clearly was a great departure from the strong avoidance of blood proscribed in the Jewish dietary laws. The prohibition of meat on Fridays apparently was an economic measure that derived from shortages in England during the reign of Edward VI. The practice not only relieved shortages of meat a bit, but also bolstered the sale of fish, an industry that needed a boost. Meat has been returned to the tables of Roman Catholics since the 1960s by the decree of then Pope John XXIII.

*I*slam (*M*uslim)

The youngest of the major religions of the world is Islam, the religion spawned on the Arabian Peninsula by the Prophet Muhammad in about 622 CE. Muhammad apparently led a somewhat unremarkable life from his birth in around 570 CE until he was 40, the time when he began seeing visions and revelations and started preaching about them in Mecca, the town where he lived. His protests against the worshiping of various gods at the stone shrine (Ka'ba) in the center of Mecca resulted in his being banished from Mecca, and he lost the protection of his clan, the Hashim. He and his followers were allowed to settle a little less than 300 miles north of Mecca in a town now called Medina, meaning the city of the Prophet. Muhammad and his group gained such strength and support between 622 and 630 that Mecca surrendered to them in 630 without a fight, and he continued to lead his movement until his death in 632 CE. The Koran is the book containing the writings that Muhammad is believed to have received from Allah through the Angel Gabriel. Muslims are guided by the Koran with its 114 writings (some brief, some long) that are called *suras*. Considerable study and debate have been carried on over the centuries involving the interpretation and the contradictions that occur between the Koran and the hadith, which discusses the Prophet and daily life (in many volumes). The combination not only defines the spiritual life, but also the practical daily life for all practicing Muslims.

Islam spread very rapidly into many parts of the known world. The Arabs conquered the Fertile Crescent, Iran, and Egypt by the end of the 7th century, and built the Dome of the Rock in Jerusalem starting in 691 on the site where Muhammad is said to have ascended to heaven. In 711 they invaded Spain and went to the Indus River in India. People quickly converted to Islam, and large portions of this vast region remain in the Muslim realm to this day. Among the remarkable buildings constructed by the Muslims are the great Mosque of Damascus (705), the Great Mosque at Cordova in Spain (785–987), the Alhambra in Granada, Spain (1333–1391), the Mosque of Suleyman the Magnificent in Istanbul (1550–1560), and the Taj Mahal in Agra, India (built by the Mughal Emperor Shah Jahan from 1632 to 1652). The Crusaders mounted vigorous attacks on the Muslims in the Levant and captured Jerusalem from them in 1099 CE, only to lose the city to Saladin (who had been ruling from Cairo while Jerusalem was in Christian hands) in 1187. The Mamluks, who had been ruling in Egypt from 1254 to 1517, captured Tripoli from the Crusaders in 1289. The Moors (and Muslims from North Africa) were forced out of Spain in 1492. Istanbul was controlled by the Ottomans from 1453 until Ataturk's successful overthrow in 1922. Pakistan was formed as a Muslim country in 1947 at the time of the British partition. Muslim is the principal religion in many nations, according to surveys in 1990 (Table 3.4).

Table 3.4 Estimate of the Percentage of Muslims in Selected Countries in 1990

Country	% Muslim
Iran	98
Iraq	95
Afghanistan	99
Turkey	99
Syria	87
Saudi Arabia	95
Yemen Arab Republic	99
Jordan	93
Democratic Yemen	90
Lebanon	70
West Bank, Gaza	92
Israel	14
Pakistan	97
Bangladesh	86
India	12
Indonesia	87
Malaysia	58
Central Asian Republics	19
Thailand	4
Myanmar (Burma)	4
Singapore	15
Albania	70
United States	2

Source: Kurian, G. T. *Encyclopedia of the First World* (2 vols.), *Second World* (2 vols.), *Third World* (4th ed., 3 vols.) Oxford; Facts on File 1990, 1991, and 1992. *Europa World Year Book*, 1992. London.

Muslim calligraphy is done using a pen made from a reed that has been buried in manure for 4 years to achieve the desired red color, ink made from ground soot, and paper dyed with tea and coated with egg white to make it easier to correct mistakes. These practices stem from the 7th century.

The Muslim calendar not only is a lunar calendar, but it also starts at a different year in history than is used by most countries. Year 1 was 622 CE. The Muslim year 1420 began April 18, 1999, and 1421 corresponds with April 6, 2000. Since the Islamic calendar has 12 lunar months and no extra days added in, the seasonal timing for various Muslim holidays shifts over time.

The basis of Islam is the Five Pillars, consisting of the Shahada (creed), Salat (prayers), Saum (fasting), Zukat (purifying tax), and Hajj (pilgrimage to Mecca). The Shahada or confession consists of two statements from different places in the Koran: "There is no god but God (Allah)"; and "Muhammad is the Messenger of God." Performance of the Salat has evolved over the centuries from the two times indicated in the Koran to the present practice of five times daily: at sunrise, midday, midafternoon, sunset, and evening, the times when the *muezzin* (usually now a recording of the crier) chants out the call to prayer from the minaret of the mosque. Before going into the mosque, Muslims are required to achieve purity by washing according to a defined ritual in the place provided for this in the courtyard of the mosque. Inside the mosque, worshipers pray facing Mecca with all of the other worshipers, and are led by the *imam* in a carefully structured communal prayer service that involves changes in position, including prostration, semi-kneeling, prostration again, standing, kneeling, and sitting at various points in the prayer.

Fridays are the holy day in Islam, and the noon Salat on Friday is extended into a special worship service. The original selection of Friday as the holy day apparently was made because that was the day for the weekly market in Muhammad's town of Medina, which made it possible for many people to attend. It also had the advantage of distinguishing the Muslim holy day from the Jewish choice of Saturday and the Christian selection of Sunday. The service, like the Salat during the week, is held in a mosque. Mosques have a niche *(mihrab)* in the interior wall, indicating the direction of Mecca. The *minbar,* an ornate pulpit atop a straight staircase, is the place where the Friday sermon is read by the *khatib* and daily prayers are led by the imam in the mosque. The floor of the large interior room of a mosque is carpeted, and no seats are placed anywhere, which leaves all of the floor available for the many men praying together. Women are allowed in galleries around the side of the main room. Distinctive features of the exterior of a mosque include one or more minarets, or towers, for the muezzin to call people to prayer and the fountain or pool for ablutions.

Saum is the Pillar that is observed during the ninth month of the Muslim lunar calendar, when the 30-day fast of Ramadan takes place. At this time, adult Muslims are expected to fast from just before sunrise until sunset. The fast requires abstaining from all food and drink during that period, as well as from smoking, intentional vomiting, and sex. Travelers, sick people, and women who are menstruating are excused from fasting, but are required to make up the day(s) immediately following the celebration that ends Ramadan. Children are not expected to participate in fasting. Since the lunar calendar causes Ramadan to occur at different times of year, the temperatures in the very hot climates may make the fast of Ramadan extremely difficult when it falls in summer. Even when the weather cooperates, this long period of fasting places considerable physical strain on many people, although a few seem to welcome the opportunity to lose a few pounds while pondering religious truths. The end of Ramadan brings the very joyous celebration of Id al-Fitr (Feast of the Breaking of the Fast), a 3-day holiday highlighting wonderful food, new clothes, and family visits.

The giving of alms, the Zukat, was originally a means of sharing one's blessings with the less fortunate. It evolved into taxes collected by the nations in which the Muslims lived, and eliminated the voluntary aspect of giving. Now, Zukat is sometimes done as an optional giving in addition to the required governmental taxes.

The Hajj is the last of the Five Pillars and often is the event of a lifetime for a Muslim if the trip is financially and physically possible. The final parts of the Hajj can be done only on certain days in the 12th lunar month. The two parts of the pilgrimage can be completed in two segments or in a continuous effort. A white garment is to be worn, and the mosque is to be visited in Mecca as soon as ablutions are finished. Pilgrims must circumambulate around the Ka'ba, and hair is either shaved off or trimmed. Official ceremonies are held on the seventh and eighth days, and a sermon is given on the ninth day while the pilgrims stand on the hillside in the hot sun, listening for many hours. The tenth day there is a ritual throwing of stones at a pillar representing Satan, followed by ritual slaughtering of many animals in preparation for the Feast of the Sacrifice, which remembers Abraham's willingness to sacrifice for God. Three more days of celebration are held in Mecca before pilgrims begin to disperse for a visit to Medina and the long journey home. In recent years there have been such crowds making the Hajj that people have been killed when stampede-like situations erupted. The small area around the sacred Ka'ba and the mosque in Mecca creates what sometimes can become fatal congestion.

In the Islamic world, men are to provide for their wives and children and to protect them, a traditional situation that has tended to curtail opportunities for women that are assumed to be their rights in other countries. Theoretically, Muslim men are able to have four wives, as long as they treat them all equally. However, this is not the general practice today. Women have traditionally been veiled, and many lived in *purdah* (isolated from public view) in some Muslim groups. However, by the 1980s many Muslim women were no longer wearing garments that covered their faces and hid their bodies, and they were often found in the workplace alongside men who were not their relatives. This situation caused sufficient consternation that a more fundamental approach toward Muslim women is being put into play in many places throughout the Muslim world now. In fact, some young women are actively seeking to resume the more traditional Muslim lifestyle.

The dietary laws for Muslims were developed by Muhammad and served partly to differentiate Muslims from those who practiced other religions, particularly Jews and Christians. The rules were quite simple:

1. Do not eat the flesh of carrion (animals found dead).
2. Do not consume blood in any form.
3. Stay away from all swine.
4. Do not eat food that has been given as an offering to idols.
5. Do not drink anything that has the power to inebriate.

Within Islam there are different groups, including the Shi'is, the Sunnis, and the Sufis, with each of these plus others being split into still more clusters. The Shi'is are a large minority group with much of its religious activities centered in Iran. The Sunnis are the group to which the majority of Muslims belong. Sufi Muslims are noted for their use of music and dance in their religious observances; the Whirling Dervishes of Kona, Turkey, are examples.

Seventh Day Adventist

Seventh Day Adventist is a group that had its origin in the United States in the mid-1800s when one of its founders, Ellen Harmon White, reported having visions and wrote about these visions and dreams for 70 years. Basically, this religion has roots in Protestantism, but it adds to this foundation the expectation of a second coming of Christ. The lifestyle espoused by Seventh Day Adventists included establishing the seventh day of the week, Saturday, as the holy day, with meal preparation and dishwashing chores being done either on the day before or the day following, thus leaving Saturday entirely free for dedication to their religion. The behavior code is based strongly on the Ten Commandments.

The dietary code of the Seventh Day Adventists is of particular interest in this chapter because of its thoroughness and its dedication to consuming a totally healthful vegetarian diet. This specific interest has led to considerable research that has added to the knowledge regarding this type of diet. Simplicity of foods is one of the basic premises on which Adventists have based their lacto-ovo-vegetarian diets. However, some followers have been more restrictive and have opted to eliminate eggs or milk (or both) from their diets, changes that greatly complicate the achievement of an adequate diet for people. Emphasis for protein sources is placed heavily on a variety of legumes, with nuts, cereals, eggs, and milk rounding out the protein requirement. Olive oil is recommended in place of animal fats, and whole-grain cereals are preferred over refined products. Alcohol, tobacco, tea, and coffee are prohibited because of their negative effects on health.

Key Terms

Hinduism

Avatar—Person so saintly that he is thought to be an incarnation of a deity.
Brahma—Creator god or universal spirit of Hinduism.
Brahmans—Highest caste in Hinduism; priests and teachers.
Devi—Hindu goddess, the wife of Shiva.
Ghee—Clarified butter; considered a sacred food by Hindus because it is from the cow, a sacred animal.
Kama—Hindu god of love.
Krishna—God celebrated as the eighth incarnation of Vishnu.
Kshatriyas—Second caste in Hinduism; warriors and rulers.
Mantra—Hindu incantation.
Manu—Source of Hindu laws on living, and ancestor of Hindus, progenitor of human race and source of Vedas.
Om—Sound chanted repeatedly for long periods to generate religious energy in Hinduism.
Shiva (Siva)—Destructive Hindu god.
Sudras—Fourth cast in Hinduism; menial workers.
Untouchables—All Hindus not born into a higher caste.
Vaisyas—Third caste in Hinduism; farmers and businesspeople.
Vedas—Four volumes of the collective wisdom on how Hindus must live.
Vishnu—Preserver god of Hinduism.

Buddhism

Bodhisattva—Semidivine, mystical being incorporated in Mahayana form of Buddhism.
Chorten—Tibetan religious (Buddhist) monument, often with some gold or silver gilding.
Circumambulation—Circling of a stupa or shrine by a Buddhist while meditating on the doctrines and offering food and flowers.
Kami—Supernatural beings (departed ancestors) in Shintoism in Japan.
Kutho—Kind or generous act that brings merit to help strive toward Nirvana.
Mahayana—Buddhist sect prominent in Tibet, Mongolia, and the Himalayas.
Pagoda—Several-storied shrine for Buddhists.
Stupa—Hemispherical mound with a central decoration, which serves as a shrine for Buddhists.

Theravada—Southern form of Buddhism based on a monastic approach; in Thailand, Myanmar (Burma), Sri Lanka, Cambodia, and Laos.

Judaism

Bar mitzvah—Maturity celebration for Jewish boy.
Bat mitzvah—Maturity celebration for Jewish girl.
Diaspora—Settling of Jews outside of Palestine.
Kashruth—Jewish dietary laws.
Menorah—Candelabra used in Jewish worship (usually with six or eight arms plus elevated center holder).
Shofar—Hollowed out ram's horn blown in the synagogue during Rosh Hashanah to call man to be aware of his shortcomings and to emphasize that God is the divine king.
Talmud—Authoritative body of Jewish tradition.
Torah—First five books of the Old Testament, the foundation for Judaism.
Yarmulke—Skullcap worn by Jewish men.

Islam (Muslim)

Five Pillars—Basic requirements of Muslim religion.
Hajj—Pilgrimage to Mecca; one of the Five Pillars.
Id al-Fitr—Three-day celebration marking the end of Ramadan; the Feast of the Breaking of the Fast.
Imam—Person who leads Muslims in their daily prayers.
Ka'ba—Black stone cube with a meteorite in its wall; shrine in the center of Mecca of importance to Muslims.
Khatib—Person who reads the Friday sermon.
Koran—Volume of writings (114 suras) given to the Prophet Muhammad by Allah (God) through the Angel Gabriel.
Mihrab—Niche in an interior wall of a mosque to indicate the direction of Mecca for worshipers during Salat.
Minaret—Slender tower with a balcony for the muezzin to call Muslims to prayer.
Minbar—Staircase topped with a pulpit in a mosque.
Mosque—Place of worship for Muslims.
Muezzin—Person who calls Muslims to prayer five times a day.
Muhammad—Arabian prophet who founded Islam in 622 CE.
Ramadan—Thirty-day fast in the ninth lunar month of the Muslim year.
Salat—Muslim daily prayer according to the Five Pillars.
Saum—Ritual of fasting; one of the Five Pillars.
Shahada—Creed that is one of the Five Pillars: "There is no god but God; Muhammad is the Messenger of God."
Zukat—Purifying tax; one of the Five Pillars.

Summary

Major religions have shaped the cultures and food practices of people around the world for many, many centuries. Among the religions that are practiced in the United States are Christianity, Judaism, Islam, Buddhism, Hinduism, and Seventh Day Adventism.

Hinduism is the oldest religion and includes the worship of several gods, notably Vishnu, Shiva, and Brahma, as well as the concept of castes. Hindus believe in repeated reincarnation. They frequently are vegetarians, a reflection of their reverence for life, and they also avoid alcohol.

Buddhism is a religion based on the Four Noble Truths and a carefully defined code of conduct. Among the directions for living are the avoidance of alcohol and, if a monk, not eating after midday. Animals are not to be killed to become a source of food, although it is approved to eat meat if the animal was not killed specifically to feed the person who might eat the meat. In China, Confucianism and Taoism blended with Buddhism, while in Japan the blend with Buddhism was Shintoism.

Judaism is a religion based on the Torah (particularly Genesis, Exodus, Leviticus, Numbers, and Deuteronomy) and the Talmud. This religion spread widely and contributed to the cultures of many different people scattered throughout Europe, Asia, and Africa prior to and after Christ. There are varying traditions, depending on the particular Jewish sect. However, the key holy traditions for all sects include Rosh Hashanah, Yom Kippur, and Passover, plus several others. Kosher food is required among Orthodox Jews, with the added stipulation that separate utensils and dishes must be maintained for meat dishes and dairy products. Pork is not a part of Jewish menus because it is from an animal that does have a cloven hoof but does not chew its cud.

Christianity also utilizes the Old Testament, but it adds to this the New Testament and a belief that Jesus was the son of God, which is in direct contrast to the Jewish interpretation of Jesus. The Roman Catholic Church was prominent in Europe, and the Eastern Orthodox Church represented Christianity in Greece and farther east. Protestantism split from the Roman Catholic Church. Catholics in years past have avoided eating meat on Fridays, but this is no longer required.

Islam is the youngest of the major religions, the product of the teachings of Muhammad, an Arabian prophet who lived in the 7th century. This religion is prominent among Arab populations, but also is the religion of many other people around the world today. Its foundation is the Five Pillars of Islam: Shahada, Salat, Saum, Zukat, and Hajj. Saum requires fasting, and Ramadan, the ninth lunar month, is a 30-day fasting period, which places strong demands on followers, particularly when this fast occurs in the heat of summer. The Five Pillars and all aspects of the lives of Muslims are described in the Koran and the hadith. Food prohibitions include avoiding eating swine, the flesh of carrion, blood in any form, food previously offered to gods, and alcohol.

The Seventh Day Adventist religion is significant in this chapter because of the dietary guidance, which is based on vegetarianism (usually lacto-ovo), whole-grain cereals, and legumes. Alcohol, tea, coffee, and tobacco are prohibited.

Study Questions

1. Give a brief description of each of the following religions: (a) Hinduism, (b) Buddhism, (c) Judaism, (d) Christianity, and (e) Islam.
2. Which three major religions view Jerusalem as a very important city for their faith, and why does each religion attach this importance?
3. Compare the dietary laws and food practices of the religions discussed in this chapter.

Bibliography

Barer-Stein, T. 1999. *You Eat What You Are.* 2nd ed. Firefly Books, Ltd. Ontario, Canada.

Cousins, L. S. 1997. Buddhism. In J. R. Hinnells, ed., *A New Handbook of Living Religions.* Penguin. London.

Goldman, A. L. 2000. *Being Jewish.* Simon and Schuster. New York.

Hinnells, J. R., ed. 1997. *A New Handbook of Living Religions.* Penguin. London.

Jackson, M. A. 2000. Getting religion—For your products, that is. *Food Tech. 54*(7), 60.

Lowenberg, M., E. N. Todhunter, E. D. Wilson, J. R. Savage, and J. L. Lubawski. 1974. *Food and Man.* 2nd ed. Wiley. New York.

Marcus, A. D. 2000. *The View from Nebo: How Archaeology is Rewriting the Bible and Reshaping the Middle East.* Little, Brown. Boston.

Panati, C. 1996. *Sacred Origins of Profound Things.* Penguin. London.

Simoons, F. F. 1994. *Eat Not This Flesh.* 2nd ed. University of Wisconsin Press. Madison.

Unterman, A. 1997. Judaism. In J. R. Hinnells, ed., *A New Handbook of Living Religions.* Penguin. London, England.

Walls, A. 1997. Christianity. In J. R. Hinnells, ed., *A New Handbook of Living Religions.* Penguin. London, England.

Weightman, S. 1997. Hinduism. In J. R. Hinnells, ed., *A New Handbook of Living Religions.* Penguin. London, England.

Welch, A. T. 1997. Islam. In J. R. Hinnells, ed., *A New Handbook of Living Religions.* Penguin. London, England.

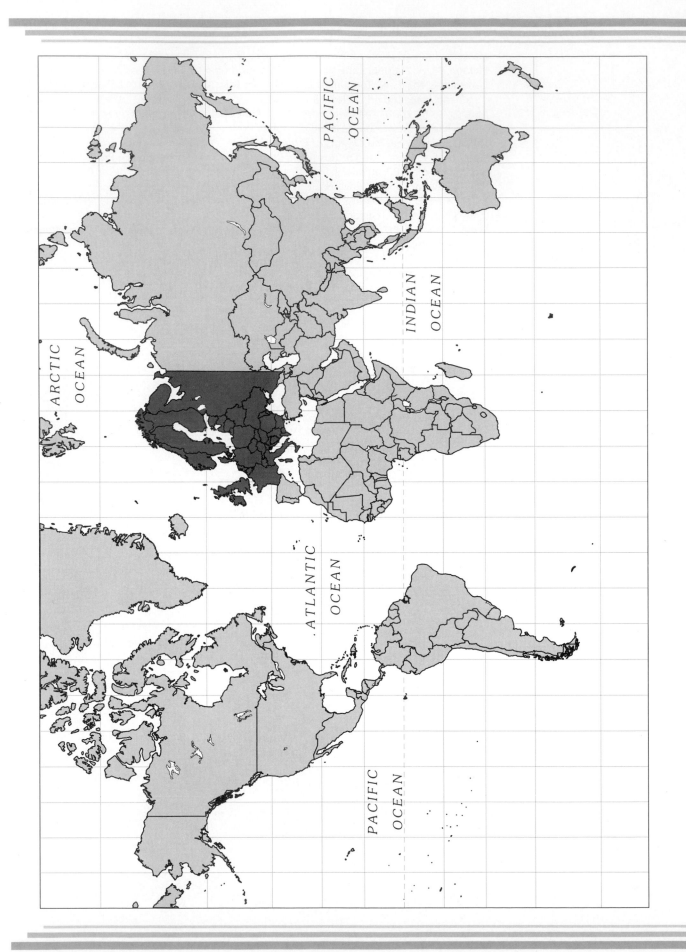

Part II

Europe: Roots of Our American Cuisine

4 British Isles

A Geographic Overview

The British Isles consist primarily of a very large island containing Scotland, England, and Wales, plus a somewhat smaller island, which is divided into Northern Ireland and Ireland. Although not actually a part of the European continent, the proximity to Europe and the long associations with it historically justify the inclusion of the British Isles here. This also is a very suitable spot for beginning our closer look at the various nations of the world, because many of the early settlers in the American colonies were from these islands, including the Pilgrims who sailed from Plymouth in southern England. And certainly we are all aware that the United States was a British colonial region before declaring independence in 1776 and subsequently winning freedom after the Revolutionary War.

The United Kingdom is actually not even as big as the state of Oregon, yet at one time it ruled over a vast empire that reached around the world, leading to the claim that "the sun never sets on the British Empire." From a food perspective, crops (especially wheat, barley, potatoes, fruits, and vegetables) can do well there because there is ample rain and the climate tends to be temperate, if a bit chilly. The land is generally suited to agriculture of various types, but the fields are rather small, probably due to centuries of a gradually increasing population that resulted in many villages situated fairly closely together, thus limiting farming areas. Even the mountains are on a rather small scale, with the highest in the United Kingdom being Ben Nevis (4,406 feet); the highest point in Ireland is only 3,800 feet.

Livestock production has been a part of the rural scene in the British Isles for centuries. Cattle are the dominant species in England, whereas sheep graze in large numbers in the highlands of Scotland and the rugged areas of Wales and

Figure 4.1 Sheep graze contentedly along the coast of the Dingle Peninsula in Ireland.

Ireland. The importance of beef in the British diet is highlighted by the famous Beefeaters, who guard the Tower of London to this day. Cheddar, Stilton, and Cheshire cheeses are justifiably famous, and so is their cream. Lovely sweaters and other apparel produced from the wool of all the sheep are valued in cold climates around the world. At home, the people of the British Isles have made mutton a major meat in their diet for centuries (Figure 4.1).

Perhaps as famous as Britishers' love of beef and mutton is the widespread consumption of fish. This certainly is not surprising in view of the convenient access to the surrounding ocean and the adequate supply of haddock, sole, mackerel, and other saltwater fish. Certain areas are especially noted for the fish caught there; salmon in Scotland, shrimp from the North Sea near the coast of Yorkshire, Dover sole, sea trout, and lobster around Dublin are just some examples of specialties.

History and Culture

Feasts of food, fancy clothes, music, and dances were all parts of life in "Merry England." The shopping list for the installation of Bishop Neville at York in 1467 included 104 oxen, 6 wild bulls, 1,000 sheep, 304 calves, 304 suckling pigs, 400 swans, 2,000 geese, 1,000 capons, 2,000 pigs, plus plenty of tarts and custards, all of which was to be washed down with bounteous amounts of ale and wine!

Various sights around England serve as enduring reminders of the long history of the British Isles. Stonehenge, the remarkable circle of huge stones constructed in the era around 1700 BCE, apparently for some form of worship, still stands to the south of London. Romans occupying England in the 1st and 2nd centuries built various structures that are still in evidence today—the baths at Bath (Figure 4.2), for example. Remnants of Hadrian's Wall, built to separate England's northern Brigantes from the lowland Novantae and Selgovae, can be seen around Chester and on to York today.

After the Romans, invasions of the British Isles by tribes from northern Europe and Scandinavia slowed the development of the region as a nation. However, a monarchy was in place by the 11th century, a tradition that still continues. Under William the Conqueror, who reigned for 20 years until his death in 1087, butchers, bakers, and grocers enjoyed some recognition in Britain, although the traditions were not refined then. People from the British Isles participated in the Crusades that were waged to attempt to free Jerusalem from the "Infidel." Perhaps the most renowned leader from England was Richard Lionheart, King of England, who led his forces on a 16-month expedition that ended in failure in Palestine in 1192.

A little over 400 years later, a religious contribution was made by England in 1611 when King James I published the King James version of the Bible, a version still held in great repute. For almost 100 years considerable turmoil existed between Parliament and the Crown, but both parts of the government survived. Scotland became united with England in 1707 during the reign of Queen Anne.

Figure 4.2 Romans built a public bath during their occupation of Britain; Bath is named for its famous legacy.

Great Britain's success in establishing the British Empire as a means of extending its trade throughout the world did much to add interest to the foods available for common folk in the British Isles. The British East India Company performed a major role in bringing India into the Empire. This dominance began about 1690 and continued until independence was granted to India and Pakistan in 1947. In Africa, Kenya was under British dominance from 1888 to 1963. Cecil Rhodes was instrumental in gaining the rights for the British South Africa Company to remove minerals from Rhodesia in 1889, and Britain was basically in control of Southern Rhodesia until 1923. Several changes of government led to the eventual formation of Zimbabwe in 1980, and Britain was no longer involved. The tip of Africa came under British control in 1806; gradual acquisitions and modifications resulted in the formation of South Africa, which still is a part of the British Commonwealth. Apartheid, the particularly contentious aspect of South Africa as a nation, ended in 1993. The Dominions of the British Empire today include Canada, Newfoundland, New Zealand, Australia, South Africa, and Ireland/Eire. Hong Kong reverted to China in 1997, 146 years after it came under British occupation.

As a result of the far-flung reaches of the British Empire, traders brought foods to the local British markets from all parts of the world (Figure 4.3). Exotic produce and spices were introduced. The introduction of tea, first from China

Figure 4.3 The houses of Parliament and Big Ben loom across the Thames, familiar symbols of the once far-flung empire.

and then from India, changed the beverage habits of not only Londoners, but also people throughout the British Empire. The traditions of afternoon tea and high tea can be found wherever the British ruled during the heyday of the Empire. The reverse trend also can be noted, because many people from the various Dominions have emigrated to the British Isles today, bringing with them their curries, chutneys, and other enriching food traditions to brighten the typical British table.

Food Patterns

The food patterns of the British are somewhat different, depending upon whether they are from the upper or the working class, for there is a class distinction that has persisted over the centuries. Time pressures have begun to erode the breakfast pattern that was the solid start for the day typically consumed by upper-class gentlemen. For countless years, the tradition for their breakfast would begin with oatmeal porridge, followed by either bacon or kippers (or other small fish) and eggs, accompanied by fried bread and perhaps a grilled tomato. Dundee orange marmalade always was available for topping the fried bread. Working-class men usually had a sturdy bit of bread and a hefty slice of meat or cheese. For both classes, plenty of strong, hot tea diluted with milk was the beverage. Upper-class ladies used to eat a leisurely breakfast in the middle of the morning, a light meal of cake and tea. Now, everyone is likely to eat lighter (and probably faster) at breakfast, with the trend moving toward the typical continental breakfast of a baked bread of some type and either tea or strong coffee.

Class distinctions may still persist for Sunday lunch (the noon meal that is the heaviest of the day). A large beef roast or perhaps mutton is likely to be featured in an upper-class home. Typically, the beef roast (usually cooked rare) is accompanied by Yorkshire pudding, oven-roasted potatoes, and a horseradish sauce to add excitement to the roast (Figure 4.4). Overcooked vegetables seem too often to be an item served more as a duty than an enhancement to the fare. Fish and chips are the favorite of the working class, and these often are bought away

Figure 4.4 Beef rib roast with horseradish sauce and a puffy Yorkshire pudding is a traditional meal in England.

from home, wrapped snugly in newspaper, and finally eaten with a generous sprinkle of vinegar. Incidentally, the chips are deep-fat fried potatoes cut in strips half an inch wide, and the fish is haddock, cod, or other white fish dipped in a batter of flour, egg, and beer, then fried.

Among typical favorites are Cornish pasties, hearty pastry turnovers filled with generous quantities of meat and vegetables. Their popularity stems from the ease of packing them for a lunch as well as from their flavorful heartiness at lunchtime. Another lunch favorite at home is cockaleekie soup, a Scottish soup made with stewed chicken, barley, and plenty of leeks. In Ireland, Irish stew and Irish soda bread are specialties that have migrated in various forms to the United States along with the many Irish immigrants who have enriched the American scene, particularly in New England.

Perhaps the most appealing tradition in British dietary patterns is afternoon tea. The long time that typically occurred between lunch and the very late dinners that were eaten in upper-class families made it almost imperative to have a snack of some type in the late afternoon, and teatime became the answer to this problem. Tea preparation requires that the teapot be preheated with boiling water, emptied, and then prepared with tea leaves (a teaspoon per cup plus one for the pot) over which boiling water is poured to fill the pot before the lid is replaced and a tea cozy (heavy cloth cover) is added to keep the tea hot. This ritual requires 5 minutes of patient waiting to allow the tea to brew in its mummy wrapping before it is ready to be poured and enjoyed. Other menu items vary considerably, from perhaps scones or cakes to some sherry, small sandwiches, and fancy cakes or even a trifle with a generous dollop of whipped cream garnished with berries.

After such generous fare the rest of the day, the British typically do not place much importance on the evening meal. Although tradition may be somewhat lacking regarding the menu for evening dining, there is a reasonable consistency to the pattern of young adults spending some time in the evening in a local pub, playing darts, quaffing ale, stout, or beer, and chatting with friends (Figure 4.5).

Christmas is the big holiday of the year in the United Kingdom, and a big holiday dinner is the tradition. Frequently, the dinner may feature turkey, but

Figure 4.5 Pubs are the center of the social scene and dining for many people living in the United Kingdom.

goose or a joint of beef (a large beef roast) is often preferred. Wassail (an alcoholic wine or ale beverage containing spices and perhaps baked apples) is a traditional beverage for toasting the holiday season. Accompanying the main course of Christmas dinner are such items as dressing, potatoes, (usually roasted, mashed, or simply boiled), and a vegetable (peas and brussels sprouts or other traditional favorites). To conclude the dinner, a flaming plum pudding with a brandy or other sauce is likely to be presented. The beauty of such a meal is that there are usually sufficient leftovers to feed the family for Boxing Day, the legal holiday that follows Christmas and honors service workers, such as the postman.

Key Terms

Biscuit—Flat cracker or cookie.

Bubble and squeak—Dish of leftover beef, potatoes, and vegetables that makes these noises while being fried together.

Crumpet—Similar to an English muffin, but somewhat thinner and more springy.

Finnan haddie—Smoked haddock poached in milk on a bed of onions.

Fool—Sweetened fruit puree blended with custard or cream; served cold.

Haggis—Scottish traditional pudding of oatmeal, variety meats, suet, onions, and seasonings boiled in a sheep's stomach; often served at dinners honoring Robert Burns, Scotland's famous poet.

Hot cross buns—Easter yeast buns containing cinnamon, allspice, and raisins and topped with a cross of candied orange peel or a strip of dough to represent the cross of Christ.

Irish stew—Stew of lamb cubes, potatoes, and onions simmered for a long time to tenderize the stew meat; frequently served with red cabbage in Ireland.

Jugged—Slow, moist heat cooking of meat in a covered clay pot.

Kippers—Herring prepared in the traditional Scottish way of splitting them and then salting, drying, and smoking them to preserve them.

Lemon curd—Egg yolk-thickened sweet filling flavored with lemon juice and rind; often used as filling for tarts and pies.

Mulligatawny—Curry-flavored rich soup made with a chicken or lamb base; reflecting British period in India.

Sally Lunn—Light yeast bread baked in a tubular pan, sliced in half, then topped with whipped cream or melted butter; originated in Bath, England (Figure 4.6).

Scones—Quick bread made from a dough that is rolled and cut into circles, then baked in a very hot oven; popular for teatime.

Shepherd's pie—Deep-dish meat pie made with cooked meat and onions, and topped with a crust of mashed potatoes before baking.

Shortbread—Very rich, flat, round cookie (biscuit, if using British vocabulary); often served with tea.

Steak-and-kidney pie—Hearty, savory pie containing pieces of beef steak and kidneys in the filling.

Toad-in-the hole—Sausages cooked in a quick-bread batter.

Treacle—Very thick molasses.

Trifle—Elaborate dessert made in a pretty glass bowl, which has been lined with lady fingers or slices of pound cake and then filled with layers of stirred custard, whipped cream, slivered almonds, and raspberries, and generously laced with sherry.

Worcestershire sauce—Pungent sauce made of soy sauce, vinegar, and garlic, and used quite universally at British tables; originated in Worcestershire, England.

Yorkshire pudding—Puffy pudding baked on meat drippings in a very hot oven; batter is a thin egg, milk, and flour mixture similar to popover batter.

Figure 4.6 Sally Lunn, a delicious yeast bread, originated here in Bath, England.

Recipes

Roast Beef

Standing rib roast, 6 lb, approximately
Preheat oven to 500°F.

1. Place roast in a shallow pan so that the ribs serve as the rack.
2. Roast 20 minutes at 500°F.
3. Reduce heat to 350°F and continue roasting until meat reaches desired interior temperature (145°F for rare, 160°F for medium, or 170°F for well done). Check doneness with thermometer. The time required is about 20 minutes per pound for rare, 25 for medium, and 30 for well done.
4. Remove from oven and reset oven to 400°F. Place meat on warm platter, and cover loosely with tent of foil.

Yorkshire Pudding (Serves 6–8)

2 eggs
1 c all purpose flour
1/2 tsp salt
1 c milk
2 tbsp roast drippings

1. Place eggs, flour, salt, and milk in blender and blend for 45 seconds, stopping twice to scrape sides with spatula.
2. Remove all but 2 tablespoons drippings from roasting pan.
3. When oven is 400°F, heat drippings in pan over direct heat until spattering.
4. Immediately pour batter over hot drippings and bake in 400°F oven for 15 minutes, then turn oven down to 375°F.
5. Bake 15 minutes more so that pudding is crisp and brown on surface. Cut into 6 or 8 portions and serve with roast beef.

Horseradish Sauce (Makes 1 1/4 cups)

3 tbsp prepared horseradish (squeezed in towel)
1 tsp white vinegar
1/2 tsp sugar
1/4 tsp dry mustard
1/2 tsp salt
1/2 tsp white pepper
1/2 c chilled whipping cream

1. Blend everything but the cream together in a bowl.
2. Beat cream until it will pull up into a peak.
3. Fold whipped cream with mixture completely. Refrigerate until ready to serve with roast beef.

Plum Pudding (Serves 12–16)

2 c sugar
2 c flour
2 c fine bread crumbs
2 tsp cinnamon
1 tsp nutmeg
1 tsp allspice
2 c ground suet
1 lb chopped raisins
1 lb chopped dates
1 lb chopped English walnuts
1 tsp baking soda
2 c milk

1. Mix sugar, flour, bread crumbs, spices, and suet in a bowl.
2. Stir in fruit and nuts.
3. Add milk and soda (dissolved in milk).
4. Place in metal molds and cover.
5. Steam 3 hours in covered steamer, adding water to steamer if necessary.
6. Pudding can be stored in freezer for up to a year or for a somewhat shorter time in refrigerator.
7. Reheat pudding thoroughly by steaming in mold until hot in middle.
8. Serve with sauce (see next recipe) or hard sauce.

Sauce for Plum Pudding (Makes 1 cup)

1/2 c sugar
2 tbsp flour
1 c boiling water
1 tsp vanilla
1 tbsp butter

1. Mix sugar and flour.
2. Add boiling water, stirring constantly.
3. Heat to boiling and until sauce is clear, stirring constantly.
4. Add butter and vanilla.
5. Serve hot over plum pudding.

*S*ummary

The British Isles were the source of some of the early American colonists who brought their food traditions to the United States and laid the cornerstone of American food preferences. The land and climate of England, Scotland, Wales, and Ireland shaped the agricultural products that formed the basic diets of the early Britishers—wheat, barley, potatoes, fruits, vegetables, livestock, and fish.

Such relics as Stonehenge, Hadrian's Wall, the St. James version of the Bible, and many castles trace the long history of Britain. The government has been a monarchy with a Parliament since the 11th century.

The British Empire extended all around the world at one time, but now is considerably reduced. The trade resulting from this extensive empire brought a wide range of food and other products to markets in the British Isles. Now, immigrants from India, South Africa, and other Commonwealth members add to the diversity, particularly in England.

Britishers tend to eat according to whether they are members of the upper class or the working class. The upper class eat a hearty breakfast, and a filling lunch is usually eaten by all. Teatime is an important tradition, with a fairly elaborate variety of savory items and sweets served for high tea. The evening meal is rather light. Hearty meat dishes and fish and chips, as well as tempting sweets and plenty of ale, stout, or beer, are familiar items. Many other dishes are also identified in this chapter.

Study Questions

1. Identify the location of the British Isles and name the countries that are found on the two major islands.
2. What two grains are grown in Great Britain in comparatively large quantities?
3. Describe the influence of the British Empire on the food patterns of people living in the British Isles.
4. Why are meat and fish so prominent in the British diet?
5. Identify three different desserts that could be considered to be British fare.

Bibliography

Bailey, A. 1969. *Cooking of the British Isles.* Time-Life Books. New York.
Bober, P. P. 1999. *Art, Culture, and Cuisine: Ancient and Medieval Gastronomy.* University of Chicago Press. Chicago.
Davidson, A. 1999. *Oxford Companion to Food.* Oxford University Press. Oxford, England.
Mercer, D. 1996. *Chronicle of the World.* D. K. Publishing. New York.
Palmowski, J. 1997. *Dictionary of Twentieth Century World History.* Oxford University Press. New York.
Pearcy, G. E. 1980. *World Food Scene.* Plycon Press. Redondo Beach, CA.
Viault, B. S. 1990. *Western Civilization since 1600.* McGraw-Hill. New York.

5 Scandinavia

Geographic Overview

When you think of Scandinavia, images of sunlit fjords and strains of Grieg's "Peer Gynt Suite" come to mind, but it also is realistic to add the somber, piercing paintings of Munch (particularly "The Scream") to round out the picture. The sharp contrasts found in the culture of Norway and its Scandinavian neighbors of Sweden and Finland are consistent with the extreme climatic shifts that result from the far-northern location of these countries.

A significant influence on life in Scandinavia is the change in the length of days and nights between midsummer and midwinter that results from the reality that Norway, Sweden, and Finland extend several degrees north of the Arctic Circle (Figure 5.1). This location has resulted in the romantic-sounding appellation of "Land of the Midnight Sun" and the frantic, night-long celebrations of Midsummer's Night at Rovaniemi, Finland, and other towns above the Arctic Circle in Norway and Sweden. Even as far south as Denmark, the long hours of daylight in summer are effective in fostering rapid growth of crops. Fortunately, the long days help to offset the comparatively short growing season for farmers. The opposite end of the extended daylight in summer are the very long nights and very brief hours of light during the winter, a situation that appears to present a psychological challenge to some people in the northern climes.

The four countries of European Scandinavia (Denmark, Finland, Sweden, and Norway) have long coastlines. Denmark consists of a peninsula (Jutland) that extends northward, with the North Sea on the west and the Baltic Sea and islands to the east. Finland is separated from the Scandinavian Peninsula by the Gulf of Bothnia, with the Baltic Sea lapping its southern coast. Sweden has a much longer coastline than Finland, for it extends considerably farther south to its tip before

Figure 5.1 Laplanders in the northern reaches of Scandinavia wear their distinctive costumes for special events, e.g., Midsummer's Night. *Photo by Wolfgang Kaehler/ ©Wolfgang Kaehler/CORBIS.*

its northwesterly reach toward Norway. By far the longest coastline (especially if the deep indentations of the fjords are included) is that of Norway, which is touched by the North Sea, Atlantic Ocean, and the Norwegian and Barents Seas!

Norway's physical geography is dominated by mountains, which has led to most residents living within a distance of little more than 10 miles from the coast. The steepness and ruggedness of these mountains have fostered a life dominated by the sea and small settlements since early days. Although Sweden does contain some mountains too, its terrain generally is far less precipitous than that of Norway. However, many lakes and forests are dominant features of much of Sweden. Similarly, Finland has innumerable lakes and vast reaches of forest; limited amounts of agriculture are found in the southern portion, which also is the region where most of the population lives.

Fish of various types play a significant role in the diets of people in all of the Scandinavian countries, which is not surprising in view of the easy access to the sea. Norwegians rely more heavily on fish than do other Scandinavians, perhaps because of their more rugged countryside and difficult farming conditions.

Agricultural crops are limited in Scandinavia by the climate and terrain. Denmark, the most southerly of these countries, has well over half of its land under cultivation, but only about 9 percent of the land in Sweden and Finland and less than 3 percent in Norway are dedicated to raising crops. Much of the farmed lands must be used to grow crops to feed to livestock. The remaining space is used to grow potatoes, sugar beets, turnips, and barley. Vegetables and fruits are grown in the southern areas adjacent to the cities.

The Danes are particularly noted for their animal products, including bacon, milk, cheese, eggs, and pork. Norwegians make some cheese, and they also may raise sheep or goats on their precariously steep hillsides. Limited numbers of livestock also are raised in Sweden and Finland. The small amount of good pasture for animals is reflected in the comparatively limited production of farm animals. However, the Laplanders in the northernmost reaches of Norway, Sweden, and Finland still rely heavily on their reindeer herds for their food, shelter, and even some clothing.

History and Culture

Evidence of inhabitants in Scandinavia dates back at least to the Bronze Age, but it is the period from around the era of the Vikings that is of particular interest in examining the various cultures of the world. The limited space for settlements and the inescapable presence of the sea combined to spur early Scandinavians to set forth in their small, but seaworthy boats to explore and conquer other lands.

As was noted in Chapter 4, the Scandinavians found the British Isles very tempting targets. They were within a reasonable sailing distance, and the resistance presented by the local people was unequal to the strength and ruthlessness of these tall plunderers from the north, who began to arrive near the end of the 8th century. Danes and Norwegians directed their conquests towards Britain, while the Swedes turned eastward to overrun Finland and venture into Russia, and even conducted trade along the Black Sea and in Constantinople.

Without doubt the most dramatic evidence of Viking seamanship was provided by Leif Ericsson near the beginning of the 11th century. Remains of the small settlement he built near the tip of Newfoundland around 1000 CE attest to the fact that the Vikings arrived in North America well ahead of Columbus. However, the Vikings did not establish enduring colonies.

The final invasion of England from the north occurred in 1066, but King Harold was able to repel the Vikings. Immediately, he was drawn to Hastings to protect England against William of Normandy, who invaded with his Norman soldiers (primarily Norsemen who had settled in Normandy and adopted the ways of the French). The death of Harold in the Battle of Hastings and the superior equipment and fighting techniques of the Normans established the Normans in England, and William became known as William the Conqueror. This event is the capstone of the Vikings in Europe.

Considerable intertwining of governance has occurred between the Scandinavian countries since the time of the Vikings. From time to time alliances through war or marriage have resulted in such combinations as Denmark and Norway, Norway and Sweden, and even the Kalmar Union (which united all three countries from 1397 to 1523). Sweden dominated Finland for much of the time from 1200 until the early 1700s, at which time Russia began to occupy Finland. Russian control was relinquished following the Russian Revolution of 1917. Finland's constitution was ratified in 1919.

One word basically summarizes religion in the Scandinavian countries: *Lutheran.* Although Catholicism predominated in this sphere prior to the Reformation, Martin Luther's message in the mid-16th century (particularly at the Diet of Worms in 1521 in Germany) quickly spread among Christians in Scandinavia. Eventually, Protestantism predominated, and the denomination selected was Lutheran (Figure 5.2). Despite the uniformity of the basic religion, church attendance among the majority of people is reserved for such special times as Christmas and Easter. The exception to the Lutheran choice is a small group of Russian Orthodox worshipers in Finland, the result of the extended relationship that Finland had with Russia in past centuries.

Holidays in the Scandinavian countries have seemingly as close a tie to the environment as to religion. Celebration of St. Lucia Day on December 13 in Sweden and Finland illustrates this point, for it marks the beginning of the Christmas season and brings considerable light and festivity to people who are already enduring the gloom of long winter nights. A young relative or daughter in the household wears a long white robe tied with a red sash and a metal crown of seven lighted candles with lingonberry sprigs entwined in it as she serves coffee and Lucia buns (*lussekatter*) to her family while they are still in bed. This brightly lighted celebration is a welcome prelude to the enthusiastic celebration of Christmas. This entire season serves as a warm, happy antidote to the darkness of the Arctic winter.

Figure 5.2 This Lutheran Church in Denmark is representative of the styles of churches in Scandinavia.

In Finland, the celebration of Christmas has been superimposed on an ancient celebration of the end of the harvest season and the start of the long, hard winter on the darkest day of the year (December 23). Food and fellowship were always the tradition at this celebration, but the Christmas tree became part of the scene about a century ago. Soon thereafter, the idea of Santa bringing gifts in his sleigh pulled by reindeer in Lapland captured the nation's children, too.

The Christmas tree is brought indoors on Christmas Eve in Sweden, and the tradition of decorating the tree then follows in many homes, a pleasant and social time following weeks of intensive baking and making of gifts. A big, festive dinner is a prelude to the exciting opening of gifts (often brought by Santa). A light meal is topped by a rice porridge *(risgrynsgröt)* and *lutefisk* (a very strong fish dish). The person who gets the whole almond that is hidden in the risgrynsgröt is the lucky one who will have a year of prosperity or will marry (if single). On Christmas Day a special service, the *julotta,* is held to celebrate the birth of Christ and also to remember departed loved ones. Several days of parties and hearty eating typically close the season's festivities in Sweden.

The day to decorate homes for Christmas in Denmark is December 23, when the tree is bedecked with lights and colorful decorations, including small Danish flags. The following evening, Christmas Eve, is the special time when Santa distributes gifts to the children in the family and a festive holiday dinner is served. Similar to the Swedish tradition, Danes serve *ris a' l' monde* (rice pudding complete with one almond that entitles the finder to a special gift). Christmas Day may include attendance at a Christmas church service, dinner, and time with family, friends, and new gifts.

Christmas extends over a prolonged period in Norway, with all preparations needing to be done by December 21, St. Thomas' Day. Christmas Eve dinner is identified with "twig meat," so called because lamb ribs are steamed on a rack made of twigs. *Gløgg,* a derivative of Vikings' mead, is a mulled, spicy beverage that traditionally is served. The singing of carols and exchange of gifts around the Christmas tree are key parts of the festivities. An almond ring cake occupies a prominent place on Norwegian Christmas tables, samples of which are given to all guests throughout the season until Epiphany on January 6. Final vestiges of

Figure 5.3 "The Little Mermaid" statue at the harbor in Copenhagen is perhaps the best known of Danish sculptures.

Christmas continue until January 13 (St. Knut's Day), which marks the end of the 20-day holiday.

Easter also is a time of celebration that is linked to the changing of seasons, for it is recognized as the celebration of the beginning of spring and the close of the long, dark winter. For those living at the Arctic Circle or farther north, this marks the return (if very briefly) of the long-departed sun and is surely a time of great rejoicing. Family holidays as well as celebrations of solitude mark this holiday time. Attendance at a church service also is part of the celebration for many.

Arts and crafts are an important part of the culture in Scandinavia (Figure 5.3). Although the folk art and contemporary arts and music today differ somewhat from country to country, they have certain commonalities. The simplicity of the designs, whether in such table appointments as silverware and china or in crystal, incorporates a feeling of quiet strength and elegance that is distinctive. Similarly, the folk art demonstrated in wood carvings painted in joyous colors and in tastefully and carefully crafted textiles express the appreciation of color and design of Scandinavian people.

The sauna is a distinctive part of Finnish culture. Its origins go back to early days when families living in the forests would have a log cabin where they could keep a fire going to have a warm place to gather and to bathe themselves. They were even used as a birthing room. The practice evolved into either keeping a special room in the home or a small cabin at a family vacation spot. The ritual involves making the room very hot by burning wood in the chimneyless room and then expelling the smoke before entering to bathe. An antidote to the extreme heat is available in winter when people race from the sauna to roll in snow or to jump in an icy lake!

The sauna is vital to people in Finland. The steam for this special custom is produced by throwing water on hot stones in a special, tightly closed room. A sauna is so important that sometimes it is built even before the rest of the house.

Food Patterns

Although there are subtle differences between the cuisines of the various Scandinavian countries, there are far more similarities. Coffee is the beverage of choice for breakfast and frequently throughout the day in all Scandinavian countries.

Generally, it is brewed to be quite strong, but sometimes it is combined with another ingredient, such as a liqueur.

Another pervasive part of the Scandinavian diet is fish. Herring and other sea fish are consumed in many different preparations, including pickled and smoked. Cod also is found on many menus. Perhaps the most familiar cod preparation is as lutefisk, a unique dish in which cod is soaked in lye for 2 or 3 days, then washed in running water for a similar length of time, and then boiled. Crayfish provide a special treat.

Bread is the backbone of the diets, with special preference given to rye bread. Particularly in Finland, but also in Sweden and Norway, rye bread is sliced carefully to serve as the base for open-faced sandwiches called *smørrebrød*. These are particularly popular for lunch, and they may actually be served most any time of day. However, breakfast likely will find rye or other breads or rolls being served with butter and cheese or jam. Porridge, cold meats, fish, and pastries are other possible breakfast items.

The main meal generally is quite hardy. Potatoes are common in Norwegian meals and are prepared in various forms. Often, they are a part of fish or meat stews. They also appear on tables throughout Scandinavia. Root vegetables, notably turnips and rutabagas, are well suited to the rigors of life in Scandinavia and are particularly appreciated by the Finns. Fresh fruits and vegetables are far more plentiful and utilized in the summer than in the winter, when they are difficult to obtain.

Probably the first image that comes to mind when thinking of Scandinavian foods is the smørgasbørd. Although this tremendous buffet originally was spread by Swedes, smørgasbørds are popular in all four countries. The actual menu for a smørgasbørd can be quite varied. Round balls of butter *(smör)* piled into a small pyramid are one of the many small plates of food arranged on a smørgasbørd in Sweden. In fact, their name supplies the first part of the term *smørgasbørd*. Although dark breads and *knäckebröd* (hardtack) accompany the plate of butter, they are only the beginning of the spread. Herring in many forms is featured promi-

Figure 5.4 Aebleskiver are doughnut like little cakes baked in a special pan. *Photo by Ted Streshinsky/ ©Ted Streshinsky/CORBIS.*

nently along with cold cuts, salads, an omelet (perhaps with mushrooms), other meats (usually pork or lamb) and fish, potatoes, and dessert. Nobody goes away from a smørgasbørd hungry.

The history of alcoholic beverages in Scandinavia goes back at least as far as the Vikings, who apparently drank plenty of mead to chase away the cold. *Akvavit* is a Scandinavian whiskey that originally was used as medicine in the 16th century. Beers are especially popular today. Scandinavian beers are respected and enjoyed on other continents too. Finland is noted for its production of vodka. Regardless of the type of spirit being consumed, a cheerful and hearty "*Skal*" is said by all to toast the convivial occasion.

In the dessert department, Danish pastry and cookies from these countries stand out. Apples may be featured in a cake, *aebleskiver,* or pastry (Figure 5.4). The berries from the Scandinavian Peninsula are extremely popular, particularly when cloudberries from the far northern areas are available fresh. Lingonberries appear in several different forms in meals throughout the year, adding a bright touch of color and heightening flavor in various dishes.

*K*ey *Terms*

Aebleskiver—Small Danish doughnuts prepared in a special pan.

Aquavit (Akvavit)—Aged whiskey made in Scandinavia and considered to possibly be the national Scandinavian drink.

Cloudberries:—Orange-yellow, plump berries that are similar in shape to blackberries; primarily available briefly from the far north in summer.

Crayfish—Freshwater crustacean; apparently introduced to Scandinavia via ships from Britain.

Fårikål—Thick lamb stew with cabbage; popular in Norway.

Fiskebeller—Norwegian fishballs.

Frikadeller—Danish meatballs.

Fruit soup—Dessert soup popular in Scandinavia; often made with various dried fruits that are readily available through long winters.

Gravet—Smoked salmon, a Norwegian delicacy.

Koldt bord—Literally, cold table; bread, butter and cold dishes that are the beginning part of a smørgasbørd.

Kringle—Nut-filled coffee cake from Denmark.

Lapskaus—Chunky and thick meat and potato stew.

Lefse—Norwegian flatbread.

Lingonberries—Mountain cranberry-like fruit particularly popular in Sweden.

Lutefisk—Cod soaked in lye until very soft (about 3 days), then rinsed in running water for 2 days and subsequently poached or boiled.

Rømmegrøt—Norwegian porridge of milk and sour cream thickened with flour and flavored with cinnamon and coarse sugar granules.

Sami—Nomadic reindeer herders (Laplanders) living in the arctic reaches of Scandinavia; shorter stature and darker coloring than the Scandinavians from the lower parts of this country.

Smørgasbørd—Very elaborate Scandinavian buffet with ample arrays of cold foods and hot dishes, as well as dessert choices.

Smørrebrød—Scandinavian open-faced sandwiches, usually with a base of rye bread and butter and artfully arranged toppings.

Spritsar—Swedish ring-shaped cookie often made at Christmastime.

Recipes

Fiskesuppe (Fish Soup) (Serves 6–8)

1/2 c sliced carrots
1/4 c finely chopped parsnips
1 medium onion, chopped
1 potato, peeled and chopped
3/4 lb boneless halibut or cod
1 bay leaf
1/4 tsp coarsely ground black pepper
3/4 tsp salt
4 c water
1/4 c finely sliced leeks
1 egg yolk, beaten
2 tbsp chopped parsley
4 tbsp sour cream (garnish)

1. Place water and all preceding ingredients in a 6-qt saucepan, cover, and heat just to boiling.
2. Simmer, covered, 10 minutes. Add leeks and simmer 2 more minutes.
3. Remove pan from heat; remove fish from pan and flake it.
4. Whisk a tablespoon of hot soup into beaten egg yolk and repeat until 4 tbsp soup have been blended smoothly with yolk.
5. Slowly pour yolk mixture into soup, stirring constantly.
6. Add parsley and flaked fish.
7. Reheat soup to serving temperature and adjust seasonings.

Smörrebröd (Open-Faced Sandwiches) (Optional)

Rye bread, thin or medium slices
Butter
Toppings (any or all of the following, or others): thinly sliced roast beef or cooked ham, shrimp, roast pork, paté, pickled herring, chopped or sliced hard-cooked egg, salami, gherkins or other pickles, bacon, sliced boiled new potatoes, sliced tomatoes, onions, cheeses, plus any other item needed to add flavor and beauty.

1. Spread butter evenly to the edges of slices of rye (or bread of choice).
2. Decorate each slice of buttered bread with filling of choice, being careful to make each as beautiful and tempting as possible.
3. Serve. (Heat those that need to be served hot.)

Karelian Stew (Finland) (Serves 4–6)

1/2 lb beef
1 onion, coarsely chopped
1/8 tsp allspice
1 tsp salt
1/4 lb mutton (or lamb)
1/4 lb pork
1/4 lb liver
Water to cover meat

1. Trim fat from meat and cut meat into chunks.
2. Arrange beef to cover bottom of oven-proof casserole dish.

3. Spread a third of onion and seasonings over beef.
4. Similarly, arrange a layer of mutton and liver topped with more onion and seasonings.
5. Top with a layer of pork, onion, and seasonings.
6. Brown the meat in a 475°F oven (uncovered).
7. Add water to cover meat.
8. Cover the casserole and continue braising the meat by reducing the oven to 350°F for 2 to 3 more hours until meat is tender.

Ärter med Fläsk (Pea Soup with Pork) (Serves 6–8)

2 c dried yellow split peas
4 c water
2 medium onions, chopped
1 carrot, chopped
1/4 lb chopped ham
1/4 tsp thyme
1/4 tsp marjoram
Salt to taste

1. Heat peas and water to boiling in covered pan.
2. Reduce heat, and simmer for 30 minutes.
3. Add vegetables, ham, and seasonings.
4. Continue simmering until peas and added vegetables are tender.
5. Adjust seasonings (if necessary) before serving.

Sillgratin (Serves 4–6)

1 tbsp butter
1 large onion, sliced thinly
3 large potatoes
2 herring fillets (in 1/2" diagonal slices)
Black pepper
1 tbsp fine bread crumbs
1/3 c light cream
1 tbsp butter

1. Saute onion in butter over medium heat until transparent.

2. Peel potatoes and slice thinly.
3. Beginning with a layer of potatoes, arrange layers of onion, fish, and end with a layer of potatoes in a 1 1/2-qt casserole.
4. Sprinkle black pepper and bread crumbs on top and pour cream over the surface. Dot with butter.
5. Microwave casserole on high for 1 minute.
6. Bake in preheated oven at 400°F for 1 hour (until potatoes are tender).

Lökdolmar (Serves 4)

3 large onions
1 tbsp butter
2 tbsp chopped onion
1/2 c mashed potato
1 1/2 tbsp fine bread crumbs
1/2 lb ground sirloin
2 tbsp cream
1/2 tsp salt
1/2 egg
3 tbsp butter, melted
2 tbsp fine bread crumbs

1. In a saucepan, cover peeled onions with water.
2. Bring to a boil and then simmer for 40 minutes, drain and cool.

3. Saute chopped onion in butter.
4. Combine sautéed onion, potato, crumbs, meat, cream, salt, and egg. (Note: Mixture may be sautéed to make Swedish meatballs.)
5. Pull off outer layers of cooled onion, cutting in half if very large.
6. Place heaping teaspoon of meat mixture on each piece of onion (excluding inner area).
7. Roll each onion leaf to encase meat.
8. Place seam down in a casserole containing melted butter after first rolling over to coat the top surface.
9. Bake in 400°F oven for 15 minutes.
10. Sprinkle with bread crumbs and bake 15 minutes more.

Frikadeller (Danish Meatballs) (Serves 4)

1/2 lb cooked ground meat
1/4 lb chopped bacon
1 onion, chopped
2 slices white bread soaked in water
2 eggs, beaten
1/2 tsp salt
1/4 tsp black pepper

1. Place meats and onion in a mixing bowl.
2. Squeeze water from bread, cut into cubes, and add to bowl.
3. Combine all ingredients and shape meat into small balls.
4. Fry slowly, turning frequently to brown on all sides. Cook until done in the center.

Länttulaatikko (Rutabaga Casserole) (Serves 4)

1 medium rutabaga, peeled and cut into very small cubes
1/2 tsp salt
1/2 c fine bread crumbs
2 tbsp cream
1/4 tsp nutmeg
1 egg, beaten
1/2 tsp salt

1. In a saucepan, heat rutabaga (covered with salted water) to boiling. Boil gently until tender (15 to 20 minutes).
2. Drain and puree.
3. Soak bread crumbs in cream, then mix with remaining ingredients.
4. Stir in pureed rutabaga and place in buttered 1 1/2-quart casserole.
5. Bake at 350°F for 1 hour.

Swedish Fruit Soup (Serves 4–6)

1/2 c dried apricots
1/2 c dried prunes
4 c water
2 tbsp cornstarch
2/3 c sugar
2" cinnamon stick
2 slices lemon
2 tbsp raisins
2 tbsp golden raisins
1 tbsp dried currants

1. Soak apricots and prunes in water for 30 minutes.
2. In a small bowl, mix sugar and cornstarch thoroughly.
3. Add this mixture and cinnamon and lemon to fruit.
4. Heat to simmering while stirring.
5. Simmer, covered, for 10 minutes, stirring occasionally.
6. Add raisins and currants, and simmer another 5 minutes.

Ris a' l' Monde (Serves 4–6)

1/2 c uncooked long grain rice
1 1/2 c milk
1/2 c sugar
2 tbsp sherry
1 c whipping cream
1/2 c chopped, toasted almonds
Berries (optional)

1. Combine rice, milk, and sugar in saucepan and heat to boiling while stirring.
2. Reduce heat to simmer until milk is absorbed, stirring constantly.
3. Remove from heat, stir in sherry, and chill.
4. Beat cream, then blend with rice and almonds.
5. Chill until served. Garnish with berries, if desired.

Spritsar (Cookies) (Makes 2 dozen)

1/4 lb unsalted butter
1/4 c sugar
2 egg yolks
1 tsp almond extract
2 1/2 c all purpose flour
1/4 tsp salt

1. Cream butter and sugar thoroughly until fluffy.

2. Beat in egg yolks and extract.
3. Add flour and salt gradually and stir until well mixed.
4. Use a pastry bag or tube with a star tip to pipe desired shape (S-shape about 2" high is typical) onto baking sheet.
5. Bake in oven preheated to 400°F until barely brown (10 to 12 minutes). Cool on paper towel.

Summary

The Scandinavian countries, their history, and their food patterns are shaped significantly by their extreme, northern location. Norway and Sweden form the Scandinavian Peninsula, which extends far north of the Arctic Circle. Neighboring Finland also has an extensive region into the Arctic. Denmark consists of a peninsula extending northward from Germany and also of islands in the Baltic Sea. The seas (Baltic, Atlantic, Norwegian, and Barents) influence the climate of the region and are a rich source of food. They also provided the pathway for Viking expeditions. The short growing season and very long winters fostered a diet not only of fish, but of pork, mutton, dairy products, and hardy vegetables that could be kept for several months.

Vikings influenced world culture by their forays into Britain and France. Leif Ericsson is credited with establishing an early 11th-century temporary settlement in Newfoundland on the North American coast.

Holidays also tend to reflect the northern influence. The celebrations around Christmas start with St. Lucia Day on December 13 and extend through St. Knut's Day on January 13, thus providing many warm, bright memories in the long period of winter darkness. Easter celebrations mark the return of the sun and herald the growing season that will follow a bit later. Celebration of Midsummer's Night, the longest day of the year, is a time of tremendous revelry, with huge bonfires and Maypole dances often extending throughout the bright night (the sun never sets in all parts of Scandinavia north of the Arctic Circle).

Folk art, clean and beautifully simple contemporary designs, and music are strong cultural contributions from Scandinavia. Food contributions are also noteworthy: smørgasbørds, smørrebrød, Danish pastries, and herring in innumerable preparations are some examples.

Study Questions

1. What parts of North America are at the same latitude as the northernmost and southernmost parts of Scandinavia?
2. Describe the influence of the Vikings on the world just before the end of the first millennium.
3. How has geography influenced the culture of Scandinavia over the past 11 centuries?
4. How has Finland's location affected its culture as contrasted with Norway?
5. Why is livestock more important in Denmark's agricultural scene than in Norway's?

Bibliography

Barer-Stein, T. 1999. *You Eat What You Are.* 2nd ed. Firefly Books, Ltd. Ontario, Canada.
Brown, D. 1968. *The Cooking of Scandinavia.* Time-Life Books. New York.
Butler, E. 1973. *Horizon Concise History of Scandinavia.* American Heritage Publishing, New York.
Jones, G. 1984. *A History of the Vikings.* (Rev.). Oxford University Press. Oxford, England.
Kagda, S. 1995. *Cultures of the World: Norway.* Marshall Cavendish. New York.
Lee, T. C. 1996. *Cultures of the World: Finland.* Marshall Cavendish. New York.
Lorenzen, L. 1986. *Of Swedish Ways.* Gramercy Publishing, New York.
Pateman, R. 1995. *Cultures of the World: Denmark.* Marshall Cavendish. New York.
Pearcy, G. E. 1980. *World Food Scene.* Plycon Press. Redondo Beach, CA.

6   Central Europe

Geographic Overview

Central Europe is not a precisely defined term, but in this chapter it will include Germany, Austria, Switzerland, and the Benelux countries of Belgium, the Netherlands, and Luxembourg. The Benelux lowlands hugging the northern shore of the European continent are all quite small and rather densely populated. Luxembourg, the smallest, is a tiny country tucked between France, Germany, and Belgium. Belgium, with its French speakers in the south and Flemish in the north, is a somewhat larger country that shares its borders with France, Germany, and the Netherlands (Figure 6.1). Like the Netherlands, Belgium is bordered by the North Sea. The Netherlands is unique in that 3,000 square miles of its land—some as low as 22 feet below sea level—have been reclaimed from the sea (Figure 6.2). This immense engineering effort is testimony to the work ethic and perseverance of the Dutch people.

A gradual rise in elevation is found in the European continent as it is viewed from the north toward the south. Much of the land in Germany, the Netherlands, and Belgium is well suited to growing crops. It also is a region with considerable population, which limits the amount of land actually available for farming. This situation has led to intensive farming to maximize the yields from the land that is being farmed. The latitudes of Central Europe are suitable for raising rye, barley, wheat, oats, such root crops as potatoes and sugar beets, vegetables, and fruits.

Progressing southward, the terrain rapidly becomes rougher, and soon the Alps become dominant, particularly in Switzerland and parts of Austria. Some livestock can be raised in the Alps, which has led to outstanding cheese production in Switzerland. Austria has another important geographic feature, the

69

Figure 6.1 Land is at such a premium in the Netherlands that houses are tall and very narrow, with canals interlacing in Amsterdam to serve as boat thoroughfares.

Danube River, which flows basically from west to east across the northern region. The other major river in Central Europe is the Rhine, which originates in Switzerland and flows northward to enter the North Sea in the Netherlands. Both of these rivers have been important through the ages for transport of goods and communication between people along their routes.

History and Culture

Strife pretty much typified the relationships between various parts of Central Europe as the people in the Middle Ages and later sorted out their political allegiance and dominance. In what is now Germany, Saxons ruled in the 10th century, followed by the Salian Dynasty, and then by the Hohenstaufen Dynasty until the middle of the 13th century. The Hapsburg Dynasty was in charge when the Protestant Reformation, spurred by Martin Luther in 1517, swept through this region. The result was that both Catholicism and Lutheranism could be practiced, depending on the decision of the current ruler. In northern Germany, a powerful family, the Hohenzollerns, began to amass an empire that was rivaled only by the vast Hapsburg Empire (Figure 6.3). Frederick William, the Great Elector, began his rule in 1640 and established a tolerant yet militaristic and well-governed regime. Somewhat later, Frederick the Great extended and strengthened his Prussian domain.

Figure 6.2 Much of the land now available for farming in the Netherlands has been reclaimed from the sea, which is kept out by dikes.

Figure 6.3 St. Stephan's Cathedral stands in the middle of old Vienna, where the Hapsburg Empire rivaled the Hohenzollerns.

To the south, the Hapsburg Empire encompassed not only Austria, but also Bohemia (Czechoslovakia), Hungary, and the northern part of the Balkan states. This meant that the Hapsburgs were governing not only Germanic peoples, but also Slovaks, Magyars, Slovenes, Rumanians, Italians, and Croatians—a truly formidable challenge!

Gradually, increasing freedoms were granted to the people by the rulers, particularly by Joseph II late in the 18th century. However, Francis I, the first emperor of Austria, undid much of the work accomplished by Joseph II. Hapsburg rule continued over the Empire until 1848, when the revolutionary spirit that was sweeping France and much of the rest of Europe fomented the unrest needed to overthrow the control of the Hapsburgs.

One outgrowth of this action was the formation of a German Confederacy. However, control of Germany involved Austria until 1871, when Prussia dominated the North German Confederation. Austria and Hungary then formed Austria-Hungary. The murder of the heir to this throne, Franz Ferdinand, and his wife in Sarajevo in 1914 plunged the world into World War I. Austria was created as a nation following the end of that war.

In the mid-19th century, King Wilhelm I of Prussia appointed Otto von Bismark as minister president, and he proved to be so strong militarily and politically that he was able to bring about formation of the German Empire in 1871. Germany agreed to back Austria in its Balkan crisis in 1914, which meant going against Russia and its support of the Serbs. Thus, Germany was quickly and deeply involved in World War I. The Weimar Republic that was established at the conclusion of World War I experienced the problems that other nations were undergoing as a result of the Depression, and the stage was set for the rise of Hitler and the Third Reich. World War II encompassed Europe, finally ending with the fall of Berlin and Hitler's suicide. The division of Germany that followed the close of World War II at last was erased when the Berlin Wall was torn down in 1989.

The disastrous impact of the two world wars of the 20th century may tend to overshadow some cultural developments that occurred at various times in Central Europe. It is important to recognize the musical geniuses from Germany and Austria who contributed so much to classical music literature: Bach, Handel, Beethoven, Brahms, and Wagner are among the German composers who are best known. Mozart and Johann Strauss are recognized as outstanding composers from Austria. The Brueghels, Rubens, and Van Dyck are famous Flemish painters. The Netherlands has also made significant contributions to the art world through the works of Rembrandt, van Gogh, and others.

Belgium and the Netherlands, despite their small size, were able to gain control over regions far from Europe. Belgium claimed the Congo in Africa in the late 1800s and proceeded to capitalize on its abundance of minerals, rubber, and ivory. The Netherlands established itself in Indonesia by acquiring it from Portugal, the earlier trading power. The Netherlands also established a presence in the western hemisphere in Brazil briefly and on the northern shoulder of South America. The lengthy involvement that the Netherlands had with the Dutch East Indies has had a lasting impact on Dutch food, where the exotic spices from Indonesia add a strong cosmopolitan flair.

Switzerland is unique among the nations in Europe. Its location in the center assured that it would serve as the crossroads for the continent. Its size and political interests contributed to its ability to maintain a neutral stance during the 20th century wars (Figure 6.4).

The Netherlands celebrates the Queen's birthday with the Queen riding through the streets of Amsterdam in a golden carriage drawn by fine horses, with multitudes of her subjects joyously cheering. The surprising part of this tradition is that the celebration occurs on the birthday of the Queen's mother in April, a time when the weather is far more suitable for this outdoor event. Celebration of the Christmas season is yet another time for festivities, beginning on December 5 with the arrival of Sinterklaas and his helpers in a boat. Gifts are brought by Sinterklaas and left by the fireplace. Householders leave carrots by the fireplace to help Sinterklaas feed the horses that help him on that special night. Another part of the Dutch Christmas is the Christmas tree. These are decorated imaginatively and then taken into a designated area in the streets on New Year's Eve for a huge midnight bonfire and fireworks to usher in the new year.

The celebration of Christmas in Germany has some similarities as well as some differences compared with the celebration in the Netherlands. Saint Nicholas Day celebration begins the evening before December 5. During that night, Saint Nicholas or a helper leaves nuts, candies, and apples in the stockings good children have hung, but bad children are greeted the next morning with a switch in their stockings! Another feature of Christmas is the Advent wreath, which has four candles; one is lit each week to mark the four weeks before Christmas. Also, an Advent calendar is a special treat as children open a window in it each day, with the last window on Christmas Eve featuring a picture of a Christmas tree. Fragrant evergreen boughs, considerable Christmas baking, and a lovely Christmas tree are other traditions of a German Christmas.

Germany has a special celebration in honor of the harvest each fall. This Oktoberfest is celebrated in Munich for more than 2 weeks in September and early October. Originally, the event was held to celebrate a wedding (Crown Prince Ludwig in 1810), but the revelry, abundant beer (Figure 6.5), and plentiful food became a tradition that draws people annually from around the world. Enthusiastic musicians in German "Oompah" bands add to the merriment.

Figure 6.4 Lucerne, with its famous covered bridges, has enjoyed the neutral state that Switzerland was able to maintain throughout two world wars.

Figure 6.5 Hops growing in Germany are an important component of famous German beers.

Food Patterns

Switzerland presents a surprising variety of foods for such a small country, doubtless the result of its much larger neighbors that spill their influences over the borders. Overtones of Germany are found in the northeast, of Italy along the southern region, and of France in the west and northwest. Yet there still are special dishes that are credited to Switzerland. A popular breakfast treat is muesli, a mixture of toasted oats, dried apples, and nuts that a Zurich doctor developed. The cheeses of Switzerland are notable and have served as the basis of two specialties: fondue and raclette. The original fondue was made using melted cheese diluted with wine. Then, long forks were used to dip bite-sized cubes of bread into the hot cheese mixture. This is still very popular, but variations of this, including dipping pieces of fresh fruit in melted chocolate, also may be found. Raclette again is based on melted cheese. However, the melted cheese is placed on a special plate with a sliced, boiled potato, a sweet gherkin, and pickled onions. Potatoes gain prominence in Switzerland's menus when they are parboiled, coarsely grated, and then fried like a pancake in sizzling butter until well browned on both sides. This traditional potato dish is called rösti. Switzerland also is known for its excellent chocolate candies.

A continental breakfast is a basic, light breakfast favored by many Europeans. This usually consists of coffee (or a variation, such as coffee with milk) and a bread or roll of some type. For many people, this is the means of getting through the first part of the day until more substantial food can be fitted into the day's activities. Certainly, this is true for many Belgians as well as other Central Europeans.

In the Netherlands menus are hearty, often featuring potatoes, soups, pork or other meats, fish, cabbage and other vegetables, and apples or other fruit for the one hot meal of the day. The other meals are considered to be "bread and butter" meals. These simpler meals may contain a variety of other items, such as an egg dish or other casserole, perhaps meat or fish, and some fruit, along with milk or buttermilk or coffee. Tea is a popular beverage for breakfast and again at teatime around 4:00 P.M. Coffee with milk or cream is the preference at "elevenses," the coffee break accompanied by a sweet touch at 11:00 A.M. After the evening hot meal, coffee may be served. *Borrel* (Dutch gin) or sherry and *bitterballen* (savory meatball appetizer) are favorites around 5:00 P.M. Special holiday treats include *pepernoten* (very hard Christmas cookies traditionally prepared for December 5 to be tossed mysteriously by the gloved hand of Black Peter, Sinterklaas's helper), *spekulaas* (rolled cookies flavored with cinnamon, nutmeg, cloves, and almonds and cut into doll or other shapes), *borstplaat* (fudge-like candy), *appelflappen* (fried, batter-dipped apple slices favored for New Year's celebration), and *oliebollen* (balls of yeast dough containing apples, currants, and raisins that are fried in deep fat and then sprinkled with powdered sugar to celebrate New Year's Eve). At any time of year, and especially when dining out, a favorite meal in Holland is *rijsttafel* (rice table), a multi-course meal of many hot and spicy foods as well as other milder items (usually prepared and served at the table by an Indonesian). This dining ritual is a result of the long association the Dutch traders of the Dutch East India Company had with the Spice Islands (today's Indonesia). Another special dish favored by people in the Netherlands is *hutspot*, a stew-like mixture of meat and vegetables in which the vegetables are mashed together, then served with the sliced meat.

Frederick the Great is credited with establishing the potato as a central part of the German diet when he required all peasants to grow potatoes in 1744. This ubiquitous vegetable has found its way into all parts of the German menu, even in the making of schnapps, a distilled liquor. Cabbage is another cornerstone of German food, most commonly in the form of sauerkraut, which is cabbage with salt added, and the mixture then is fermented. This tasty means of extending the useful food life of cabbage has been incorporated in a wide range of recipes, often being served with plump sausages or hearty roasts of pork, beef, or veal. These meats are served in generous portions and in various preparations throughout the day. Thin cutlets (often veal) are termed schnitzel (Figure 6.6). Schnitzel may be prepared breaded or plain, stuffed, in sauces, or even topped with such an item as a fried egg. Hearty stews of vegetables and meat plus barley or other cereal or dumplings are popularly called *eintopf*. The practice of mixing a sour taste with somewhat sweet flavors is represented by sauerbraten, which is a roast that has been marinated in a seasoned vinegar and wine with bay leaves and other herbs, simmered until very tender, and then served with a gingersnap-containing gravy and boiled red cabbage with apples. Baked favorites include *springerle* (popular picture cookies with anise flavoring), *lebkuchen* (gingerbread baked in picture molds), *stollen* (Christmas bread), and hearty dark breads such as pumpernickel and rye. Beers and Rhine wines are dear to the hearts of most Germans (and many other people as well).

Austrian cuisine is similar to that of Germany. However, there is a special fondness for coffee and something tempting to eat with it. The *Sachertorte* (Figure 6.7) is a lovely, layered chocolate cake with apricot jam spread between the layers and a chocolate glaze gracing the top and sides. *Apfel strudel* is another popular pastry. This treat is made by stretching a dough to cover a tablecloth (4 feet by 6 feet) so that it is almost thin enough to see through, brushing with melted

Vienna is noted for its elaborate desserts and pastries. Near the end of the 18th century, the court of Emperor Franz Joseph (known also for hiring Mozart as court composer) had such a vast and well-stocked kitchen that there were even small metal molds for shaping ice cream into individual servings.

Figure 6.6 Schnitzel is a thin cutlet, which has been breaded before cooking. Boiled potatoes are a common accompaniment in Vienna.

Figure 6.7 Sachertorte as it is served in the Sacher Hotel in Vienna, where this chocolate and apricot jam delicacy was created.

butter, and then spreading cinnamon-flavored chopped apples onto it before rolling the dough into a log and cutting it into 3-inch lengths for baking.

Key Terms

Apfel strudel—Austrian pastry made with extremely thin dough spread with melted butter and an apple filling, then rolled into a log, sliced into 3-inch lengths, and baked.

Appelflappen—Fried, batter-dipped slices of apple sprinkled with confectioner's sugar.

Borrel—Dutch gin.

Eintopf—Hearty German stew of meat, vegetables, and a cereal or dumplings.

Fondue—Swiss dish prepared by melting cheese with wine in a chafing dish and using long-handled forks to dip cubes of bread into the cheese mixture.

Hutspot—Hearty stew-like dish made in the Netherlands by simmering a large cut of meat with vegetables and then mashing the cooked vegetables before serving them with the sliced meat.

Lebkuchen—German gingerbread cookies baked in a picture mold.

Muesli—Breakfast cereal of toasted oats, nuts, and dried apples, developed by a Swiss doctor.

Pumpernickel—German dark, coarse bread made with unsifted rye flour.

Raclette—Swiss favorite consisting of melted cheese served with a sliced, boiled potato, sweet gherkin, and pickled pearl onions.

Rijsttafel—Rice table originating in Indonesia, but brought to the Netherlands by the Dutch East Indies Company; consists of highly spiced dishes and many other somewhat bland dishes, which are prepared at the table (usually in restaurants).

Rösti—Swiss dish of parboiled, grated potatoes sautéed in sizzling butter to make a pancake-like disk that is browned well on both sides.

Sachertorte—Austrian dessert; layered chocolate cake spread with apricot jam and topped with a chocolate glaze.

Sauerbraten—German dish; roast marinated in vinegar and wine and simmered with seasoning until very tender, then served with a gingersnap-containing gravy and red cabbage cooked with tart apples.

Schnitzel—German term for cutlets of veal or other meat cut thinly prior to cooking.

Sinterklaas—Name for Saint Nicholas in the Netherlands.

Springerle—Anise-flavored, German picture cookie popular at Christmas.

Recipes

Bitterballen (Dutch Appetizer) (Serves 4–6)

2 tbsp butter
2 tbsp flour
1/4 tsp salt
1/2 c milk
1 c chopped, cooked meat
1 1/4 tsp minced parsley
1 tsp Worcestershire sauce
1 egg
Fine bread crumbs
Oil for deep-fat frying

1. Melt butter, stir in flour and salt, then gradually stir in milk.
2. Heat, stirring constantly, until sauce boils. Chill.
3. Stir together sauce and remaining ingredients except for the bread crumbs and oil.
4. Roll mixture into 1" balls and coat each with bread crumbs.
5. Preheat oil to 400°F and fry balls until done (1 to 2 minutes). Serve hot with mustard, if desired.

Swiss Fondue (Serves 4–6)

12 oz grated Swiss cheese
2 tbsp flour
1/8 tsp white pepper
1 1/4 c dry sauterne
2 tsp kirsch
1/2 loaf French bread, cut into cubes

1. Toss the cheese and dry ingredients together.
2. Heat sauterne in a fondue pot or chafing dish.
3. Stir in cheese gradually until all is added and melted.
4. Stir in the kirsch.
5. Diners place a bread cube on long-handled forks and dip to coat them in fondue.

Sauerbraten (Serves 6–8)

Medium rump roast
2 c vinegar
2 c water
2 medium onions, sliced
20 whole cloves
4 bay leaves
20 peppercorns
1/2 green pepper, sliced
1/2 c gingersnap crumbs

1. Marinate the meat with the other ingredients (except gingersnaps) for 2 days in the refrigerator.
2. Remove meat from marinade and brown in oil in a Dutch oven.
3. Add marinade to cover pan about 1/2" deep.
4. Cover pan and simmer meat until fork tender (2+ hours).
5. Remove meat and thicken drippings with gingersnaps.

Rotkohl mit Äpfeln (Red Cabbage with Apples) (Serves 4)

1 medium onion, chopped
1 tbsp bacon drippings
1 head red cabbage, shredded
2 tart apples, pared and cubed
1/4 c vinegar
2 tbsp brown sugar

1. Saute onion in drippings.
2. Add other ingredients to skillet and cover.
3. Simmer 20 minutes, stirring occasionally and adding water as needed.

Pepernoten (Dutch Cookies) (Makes 4 dozen)

1 1/4 c flour
1 1/4 c self-rising flour
1/2 c brown sugar
2 tbsp water
1 egg yolk
1/4 tsp cinnamon
1/4 tsp nutmeg
1/4 tsp ground cloves

1/4 tsp anise or cardamom

1. Mix all ingredients to make a dough.
2. Make dough into 1" marbles and place 2" apart on cookie sheet.
3. Flatten balls slightly.
4. Bake in oven preheated to 350°F for 20 minutes (until hard).

Springlerle (Makes 4–5 dozen)

4 egg whites
5 egg yolks
2 c sugar
4 c flour
1 tsp baking powder
3/4 tsp anise oil

1. Beat egg whites until stiff.
2. Beat in yolks, one at a time.
3. Stir in sugar followed by flour and baking powder.
4. Stir in anise oil.

5. Roll on floured board 1/4" thick.
6. Carefully roll springerle rolling pin over dough firmly enough to print the pattern clearly and deeply.
7. Cut cookies apart and place on cookie sheets 1" apart. Store on counter uncovered for 24 hours.
8. Bake in oven preheated to 250°F for 20 to 30 minutes until firm but not browned.
9. With spatula, put cookies on a cooling rack. Store in tight jars.

Appelflappen (Serves 4–6)

1 c flour
Beer to make thick batter
2 Pippin apples
Oil for deep-fat frying
Confectioner's sugar (optional)

1. Stir enough beer into the flour to make a batter thick enough to coat apple rings.

2. Core and pare apples, then slice into rings 1/4" thick.
3. Heat oil to 375°F, dip each apple slice into batter to coat thoroughly.
4. Fry until browned on bottom, turn, and brown other side. Drain on absorbent paper towel.
5. Repeat until all slices are fried.
6. Sprinkle with confectioner's sugar.

Oliebollen (Serves 8–10)

1 loaf frozen bread dough
1/4 c dried currants
1/4 c raisins
1/4 c golden seedless raisins
1/4 c candied orange peel
2 tbsp lemon zest
Oil for deep-fat frying
Confectioner's sugar, optional

1. Thaw bread dough completely.
2. Knead fruits evenly into the bread dough.
3. Let dough almost double before punching down and squeezing off about 1/4 c dough for each ball.
4. Meanwhile, preheat oil to 375°F, fry the balls (a few at a time), turning as they brown.
5. Drain on absorbent paper towel.
6. Dust with confectioner's sugar.

Summary

Central Europe includes the Benelux countries of Belgium, the Netherlands, and Luxembourg, as well as Germany, Austria, and Switzerland. The northern part of this section of Europe is generally good for agriculture, but the rugged Alps toward the south present farming challenges. Particularly good crops in Central Europe include rye, barley, oats, potatoes and other root vegetables, and fruits; livestock is raised successfully in this region too.

Numerous wars have raged over this region, with the exception of Switzerland, which was even able to maintain neutrality in both world wars of the 20th century. The resulting interchange of cultures has blurred distinctions, but each of these countries still maintains some cultural uniqueness. The Netherlands in particular has introduced overtones of culture from its world trading dating back to the 16th century and its involvement with Indonesia. Traditionally Catholic Europe was rocked by the Protestant movement that highlighted Martin Luther in 1517. Still today, many Lutherans and Catholics practice the religions followed by their ancestors in Central Europe.

Central Europe set the stage for such prominent musical composers and artists as Bach, Beethoven, Brahms, Rembrandt, and van Gogh. Appreciation and support for these cultural pursuits were apparent in the period of the Hapsburgs and under other political regimes over the centuries. Contributions range from the very dramatic music of Wagner to the lighthearted joy of Johann Strauss.

Christmas celebrations vary a bit from one country to another, but usually include some version of Santa Claus and a Christmas tree. Often, the holidays extend for a month, which adds considerable brightness to a fairly long winter. Oktoberfest is a particularly uninhibited celebration centered in Munich, Germany, for 2 weeks, starting in late September.

Special dishes are a part of each of these countries. Tiny Switzerland boasts such treats as fondue, raclette, and chocolate candies. A restaurant meal favored in the Netherlands is rijsttafel (rice table). Holiday treats in the Netherlands include oliebollen, apelflappen, and spekulaas. Hutspot, a stewed dish in which vegetables are mashed at the end and served with sliced meat is another favorite throughout the year.

Germany's menus often feature potatoes, sauerkraut, and some hearty meat dish. Beer is a favorite beverage, and so are the Rhine wines that are produced from the grapes grown along this prime waterway of Europe. Austria adds some special dishes to the list of European favorites: strudel and Sachertorte.

Study Questions

1. Describe the key event that significantly altered religion in Central Europe in the 16th century.
2. Identify at least 5 musicians and artists from nations in Central Europe and briefly describe the cultural contributions each made.
3. Name at least 5 food crops that are particularly prominent in the food patterns found in Central Europe; explain why each type of food is part of the diet.
4. Define the following: hutspot; rösti; schnitzel; muesli; and rijsttafel.
5. Name and describe 2 Swiss dishes featuring cheese made in Switzerland.

Bibliography

Barer-Stein, T. 1999. *You Eat What You Are.* 2nd ed. Firefly Books, Ltd. Ontario, Canada.

Field, M., and F. Field. 1970. *A Quintet of Cuisines.* Time-Life Books. New York.

Halverbout, H. A. M. 1987. *The Netherlands Cookbook.* De Driehoek Publishers. Amsterdam. Cip-Gegevens Koninklijke Bibliotheek. Den Haag.

Hazelton, N. S. 1969. *The Cooking of Germany.* Time-Life Books. New York.

Palmowski, J. 1997. *A Dictionary of Twentieth Century World History.* Oxford University Press. Oxford, England.

Pearcy, G. E. 1980. *The World Food Scene.* Plycon Press. Redondo Beach, CA.

Solsten, E., and D. E. McClave, eds. 1995. *Austria: A Country Study.* Office of Federal Register, National Archives and Records Administration. Lanham, MD.

Solsten, E., ed. 1996. *Germany: A Country Study.* Department of the Army. Washington, D.C.

Sonnenfeld, A. (J. L. Flandrin and M. Montanari, eds.). 1999. *Food: A Culinary History.* Columbia University Press. New York.

Viault, B. S. 1990. *Western Civilization since 1600.* McGraw-Hill. New York.

Eastern Europe

Geographic Overview

Eastern Europe is surprisingly difficult to define geographically because there is no specific defining barrier, such as a river or sea, to distinguish Europe from Asia. The result is some ambiguity about what countries comprise Eastern Europe. For our purposes, the region covered in this chapter ranges from countries bordering on the Baltic Sea south to the Adriatic and Black Seas (Figure 7.1), as far west as the Czech Republic and as far east as Russia. This means that the Baltic states of Lithuania, Latvia, and Estonia in the far north, Poland, Belarus, Russia, Ukraine, Moldova, Romania, Slovakia, the Czech Republic, Hungary, Slovenia, Croatia, Yugoslavia, Bosnia-Herzegovina, Albania, Macedonia, and Bulgaria all are included in this chapter!

If you look on a globe, you will discover that the northern end of the Adriatic Sea is slightly north of the latitude of Montreal, which means that these countries are quite a ways north and therefore have limits on their agricultural production imposed by the shifts in daylight that occur between winter and summer at such a distance from the equator. Odessa in the Ukraine (which actually is quite a productive agricultural region) is at approximately the same latitude as Duluth, Minnesota, which is a city often mentioned in our winter weather reports as being a cold spot in the nation. In other words, the growing season is comparatively short in many of the countries in Eastern Europe.

On the positive side is the actual terrain. Much of the northern region has land that is flat enough to make crop-growing an excellent agricultural choice. In particular, cereal and root crops can thrive in the soil and climate of Poland, Hungary, Belarus, and most of the plains regions of Eastern Europe. The mountains that extend down the Balkan Peninsula significantly impact the agricultural op-

Figure 7.1 Yalta is a seaport on the Black Sea; it gained prominence when world leaders met in this Crimean Peninsula town near the end of World War II.

portunities. The rough terrain makes livestock more appropriate than crops in many areas of the Balkans. The countries of Slovenia, Croatia, Yugoslavia, Bosnia-Herzegovina, Macedonia, and Albania are especially rugged in terms of raising crops because of their mountains.

History and Culture

The Balkan Peninsula was settled by a people known as Illyrians prior to 700 BCE, and Greeks extended their influence into Albania beginning in the 7th century BCE. Rome came into conflict with the Illyrians and conquered the Balkans in 167 BCE. Under the Romans, this region flourished; one of the Roman emperors (Diocletian) was Illyrian and had his palace built in Split (what is now Croatia) on the Adriatic coast. Subsequently, the division of the Roman Empire resulted in some of the Balkans being a part of the Eastern Roman Empire (later known as the Byzantine Empire). By 1479, Albania and the other Balkan regions had fallen to the Turks and become part of the Ottoman Empire, a situation that persisted until the early 20th century. Throughout the 20th century, various occupations and conflicts raked the Balkans, which led to significant emigration to various other parts of the world, including the United States and Canada. The Balkan nations (most of which were joined in the Yugoslav Federation under Tito) were behind the Iron Curtain from the end of World War II until near the end of the 20th century.

Eastern Europe has seen invasions for many centuries. The Slavic tribes had originally been north of the Carpathian Mountains, the range that runs between Poland, the Czech Republic, Slovakia, and into Romania. Between the 6th and 9th centuries, they moved into the lands of Eastern Europe, westward from Berlin and south all the way down to Greece, mingling with the Illyrians, who were already in the Balkans. Beginning at the end of the 9th century, the Magyars (Hungarians now) took over the central basin region that included land as far south as Belgrade and also Transylvania (now Romania). The Turks attacked Eastern Europe from the southeasterly region, actually driving as far as Vienna and capturing much of Hungary. The Hapsburgs then defeated the Turks and claimed Bohemia (now the Czech Republic), Hungary, and Croatia, slowly following the Turks as the Ottoman Empire withdrew from the Balkan countries. Austria and Hungary shared control of a large domain in this region by 1867.

Poland has been carved up repeatedly by the nations that have waged their wars across its land. By 1795, Prussia and Russia claimed most of Poland, giving the remaining tidbit to Austria. This situation explains why the Poles were sup-

Figure 7.2 The central square in Warsaw, Poland, has been restored following the devastation of World War II and is a popular gathering place in the summer.

portive of Napoleon prior to his defeat at Waterloo in 1815. Poland once again became a nation at the end of World War II, but ended up behind the Iron Curtain until almost the end of the 20th century (Figure 7.2).

The Eastern Slavs lived in Russia from early times, successfully defending themselves from the Vikings and establishing agrarian lands and villages. They also ranged on forays as far away as Constantinople (today's Istanbul). Unfortunately for the Russian Slavs, Genghis Khan, the extremely powerful and ruthless leader of the Mongols (also called Tatars), began to attack. Russia was able to hold out against the Tatars until near the end of the 1250s, but Genghis Khan's grandson eventually defeated them. Russia finally freed itself from the Tatars early in the 16th century, and the reigns of the Ivans began. The next dynasty, that of the Romanovs, began in 1613 and continued until the Russian Revolution in 1917. Peter the Great began considerable progress toward developing Russia. Subsequently, Catherine the Great (Catherine II) exerted her strong influence in shaping the nation toward a more European focus and extended the boundaries of Russia significantly during her reign (1762 to 1796). Later efforts by Nicholas I to gain more territory resulted in the Crimean War (1853 to 1856). Russia and Turkey were the original opponents, but Turkey later was assisted to victory by French and English troops. The oppressive conditions under which peasants had lived for centuries in Russia and also the stress of World War I set the stage for Tsar Nicholas II's overthrow and subsequent murder during the Russian Revolution. The remainder of the 20th century saw a period of considerable Russian communist power and also tentative steps toward change.

Religion in Eastern Europe has undergone periods recently when great effort was made to prevent people from worshiping. Now, the various faiths are rebuilding strength in this sphere. The many waves of conquest throughout the region have resulted in a complex overlay of religions. The Byzantine influence resulted in the establishment of the Orthodox Church in this region, but the specifics vary a bit from one country to another. In Russia, the Russian Orthodox Church is regaining strength after many years of repression under the Soviet regimes that ruled following the Revolution. The preponderant religion in Bulgaria, Romania, and among the Serbs in the region formerly called Yugoslavia Federation is the Orthodox Church. However, Roman Catholicism predominates in Hungary (Figure 7.3), Slovakia, the Czech Republic, and Poland. In fact, Pope John Paul II, elected in 1978, is Polish. Albania has a large Muslim population, approximately 70 percent being Sunni. Bosnia-Herzegovina also has a significant Muslim following. Protestantism and Judaism can be found in Eastern Europe, but the numbers of followers are much smaller than either the Orthodox or Islam religions claim.

The Slavic languages are based on the Cyrillic alphabet that was developed by two monks, Cyril and Methodius, of the Byzantine church in the 9th century.

Figure 7.3 Catholic churches are prominent in Szent Endre and other Hungarian towns.

The literature from Russia and the various Balkan nations is written with this alphabet even now, which makes the reading of signs and travel information quite a challenge for visitors in these countries. The use of the Cyrillic alphabet in the Slavic regions stands in direct contrast to the use of the Roman alphabet by most of the northern and central parts of Eastern Europe.

One rather nomadic group that transcends national boundaries is the Roma (also called Romany and gypsies) that are scattered from Romania to Russia and indeed throughout Europe. Romania probably has the largest population of gypsies, but any attempt to get an accurate count appears to be impossible due to their nomadic lifestyle and ability to mingle and disappear. One of the particularly appealing contributions of the gypsies is their exciting and sometimes haunting folk melodies and spirited renditions of their music. Their fiercely independent spirit has enabled many of them to continue their wanderings around Europe and even to other distant parts of the world, despite the concerted efforts that various European countries have exerted to attempt to integrate the gypsies into the rest of the society and mores of the nations.

Some outstanding cultural contributions have been given to the world by the very gifted musicians, artists, and writers who have come from Eastern Europe. Among the famous musicians and composers are Chopin and Rubinstein from Poland, Dvorak and Smetana from the Czech Republic, and Liszt and Bartok from Hungary. This list must also include such renowned names as Tschaikovsky, Mussorgsky, and Rimsky-Korsakoff. Tolstoy and Dostoyevsky were great Russian writers. Bohemia, now the Czech Republic, gets the credit for originating the lively dance called the polka. The mazurka comes to us from Poland. However, dances of all types, ranging from folk dancing (Figure 7.4) to the formality of the wonderful ballet in Russia, are very important parts of the cultural heritage of this entire region.

Although religious activities were repressed during a significant portion of the latter half of the 20th century, religious holidays are the basis of some of the more important festive celebrations in the various countries of Eastern Europe. Christmas is a high point of the year for many people in the Christian religions, and so is Easter. Russian Orthodox Easter celebrations used to begin with *Maslenitas* a week before the start of Lent, but that week has evolved in many Orthodox

Figure 7.4 Folk dancing is a popular entertainment in Varna, Bulgaria.

homes as a single meal featuring *bliny* (small, thin Russian pancakes) served with a wide array of festive toppings. A particularly colorful and artistic feature of the Easter celebration in Russia and the Ukraine is the elaborately decorated hard-cooked eggs, which often feature intricate geometric designs. This practice apparently preceded the coming of Christianity in the Ukraine. The epitome of this art is the Fabergé eggs made for the royalty beginning in 1884. Two food traditions of Easter in Russia are *kulich* (a special yeast-leavened Easter cake containing candied and dried fruits, nuts, and liqueur) and *paskha* (pyramid-shaped cake containing pot cheese, eggs, cream, sugar, candied fruits, and nuts). Midnight services preceding Easter Sunday are the tradition in Orthodox celebrations. Incidentally, the use of the older Julian calendar in calculating Orthodox Easter means that Catholic and other western celebrations of Easter, which are based on the Gregorian calendar, may be in different months.

Christmas is a holiday in much of Eastern Europe, although the celebrations are somewhat simpler in nature than in other parts of Europe. However, religious holidays are only part of the scene here (Figure 7.5 and Figure 7.6). Most of the

Figure 7.5 Prague is a city that invites strollers to cross the Charles bridge.

Figure 7.6 The elaborate glockenspiel and amazing clock facing Wencelas Square in Prague provide a combination sure to attract a crowd on the hours.

countries have a celebration of their founding, and many have other traditional holidays as well.

Food Patterns

The Baltic countries have a food supply very similar to their neighbors, which translates into similarities in food patterns too. Popular dairy products include soured milk, sour cream, buttermilk, and soft cheeses. Root vegetables and cabbage (particularly in the form of sauerkraut) are standbys that are augmented in the summer by berries and other fresh fruits that can be grown in the cold climate of the Baltic region. A favorite dish in Lithuania is *kugelis*, which is a potato pudding.

Russian food maintains its distinctive foundation based on its climatic influence on available foods, but it also has overtones introduced from the west as a result of Peter the Great's interest in European ways. *Shchi* (vegetable soup containing cabbage) surprisingly is baked in the oven and then given a dollop of sour cream. *Ukha* is another popular soup made of fish and vegetables. Borsch (beet soup) is a vegetable soup featuring beets and cabbage, which is served very frequently, always topped with sour cream. *Kasha* (often buckwheat groats cooked in water until light and fluffy, but which could be another cereal grain) may have such added flavor as onions or mushrooms to make it a tasty starch in a meal. *Shashlyk* (the Russian version of Turkish shish kebabs), caviar, the elaborate dish *kulebiaka* (seasoned salmon loaf encased in a rich and artfully decorated pastry before baking), *pirozhki* (small, meat-filled pastries), and chicken Kiev (chicken breast with bits of butter implanted under the skin before frying) are other highlights of the foods found in Russia, Ukraine, and Belarus. Mention also needs to be made not only of vodka, but also of the *samovar*, the ubiquitous tea-making device introduced to Russia by the Mongols centuries ago. The tea essence contained in the teapot at the top of the chimney is poured into a cup and then diluted with the boiling water drawn from a spigot near the bottom of the samovar.

Sheep were domesticated and became an important part of the food supply in the Middle East because they could survive even when vegetation was sparse.

The Nile River has been providing water for irrigating crops in Egypt for centuries.

Caves dug into sandstone cliffs in Bamian, Afghanistan provided early homes, followed later by small houses made using sun-baked bricks.

Very high columns and stone beams in Karnak Temple outside Luxor, Egypt.

The Taj Mahal near Agra, India, is an architectural reminder of Mughal rule in the past.

Minoan fresco from one of the walls in Knossus' palace on Crete.

The Parthenon atop the Acropolis in Athens still retains a bit of its original sculptures on the cornice and many beautifully crafted columns.

One of the dominant features of the ruins of the ancient Turkish city of Ephesus is the two-story library facade.

This bas-relief in the ruins of the palace at Persepolis in Iran attests to the artistry of early Persians.

Machu Picchu, perched on a steep mountain in Peru, once was the home of many Incas.

Colorful spice markets are found throughout the Muslim areas of the world and also southeastern Asia.

This Masai mother and infant are outside their mud and thatch hut in Kenya.

Fanciful depiction of a multi-armed god protecting a wall along the entry into the Grand Palace complex in Bangkok, Thailand.

Conway castle in Wales faced the sea to protect the region from possible invasions in earlier times.

The temples of Angkor Wat near Siem Reap, Cambodia, attest to the grandeur of the early Khmer Kingdoms.

Hindu temples, such as this one in Kuala Lumpur, Malaysia, are adorned with numerous statues of deities.

This Buddhist temple is in Penang, Malaysia.

This Shinto shrine is surrounded closely by its neighboring buildings in Kyoto, Japan.

Orthodox and other Jews gather at the Wailing Wall in Jerusalem, Israel.

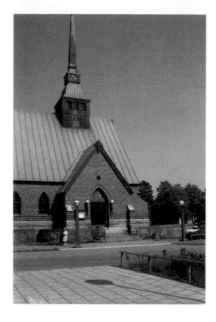

The Lutheran church is an important part of life in Finland and other Scandinavian countries.

This statue of a Greek Orthodox Patriarch beckons to worshippers in Athens.

The Blue Mosque in Istanbul, Turkey, is considered to be one of the most beautiful mosques because of its very graceful minarets and domes.

This mihrab in a mosque in Port Said, Egypt, shows worshipers the direction to face Mecca when reciting their prayers.

This minbar is the place in a mosque where the Khatib reads the Friday sermon and the imam leads prayers during the other days of the week.

Stonehenge was built in southern England around 1700 BCE.

The countryside in England's Lake District provided tranquil scenes for Beatrix Potter and several other British authors.

Tea accompanied by tempting cakes and small sandwiches all combine to brighten late afternoon in the United Kingdom.

Folk dancing in Rovaniemi, Finland, marks the longest day of the year when the sun never sets north of the Arctic Circle.

Private boats tied to the dock in Helsinki attest to the freshness of the fish and produce at this Finnish farmers' market.

This cathedral in Cologne is one of the finest in Germany.

Along the Rhine River, castles are interspersed with vineyards, which are the source of the grapes for famous Rhine wines from Germany.

Cows are raised in the Alps to provide the milk needed for making Swiss and other cheeses.

This castle on the shores of Lake Leman in Switzerland inspired Lord Byron's writing, "The Prisoner of Chillon."

The distinctive "onion" domes announce that this is an Eastern Orthodox cathedral in Odessa, Ukraine. © Dave G.Houser/CORBIS

Diocletian's Palace at Split, Croatia, on the eastern shore of the Adriatic Sea.

This bridge over the Mostar River was a famous landmark until it was destroyed during conflicts of the 1990s.

Churches and other public buildings in St. Petersburg reflect the European focus of Catherine the Great.

Eastern Orthodox church in Varna, Bulgaria, attracts worshippers and tourists.

Paprikas and garlic hanging outside a market are familiar sights in Hungary.

The hill town of Assisi in Italy's Apennine Mountains is best known for St. Francis and the lovely cathedral.

The Roman forum was the place for orators during the days of the Roman Empire.

The Ponte Vecchio with its small shops spans the Arno River in Florence.

The lovely golden mosaic façade and sculpture adorning St. Paul's Outside the Walls in Rome are examples of the wonderful art created by Italian artists over the centuries.

Mont-St-Michel, the 8th Century abbey, rises dramatically from the edge of the sea in Normandy, France.

The Pope's Palace at Avignon was the seat of the Catholic church from 1309 to 1377 CE.

The first day of the grape harvest in Bordeaux is a time for work as well as rejoicing.

Chenonceau is a unique French chateau in which part of the structure spans the Loire River.

The home of Monet at Giverney is surrounded by gardens, which provided the inspiration for many of his paintings.

Polish cuisine reflects the Italian influence brought by an Italian queen who married the king of Poland in the 16th century and also by a son of Catherine de Medici who had a brief reign in Poland late in that century. Russia, Germany, Austria, and Hungary added cosmopolitan touches to the Polish diet too. The result is abundant use of pork and beef, sour cream, bland cheeses, potatoes, beets, sauerkraut, honey, a variety of cereal grains (especially rye), butter, lard, and tea. A light breakfast in the morning is usually followed by a light lunch, with dinner usually being heavier and served in the late afternoon. Hearty soups, such as a vegetable and barley soup called *krupnik*, are popular and well suited to the Polish climate. Polish sausages called kielbasa are popular not only in Poland, but also in the United States, and they find their way into many Polish dishes. *Bigos* is a favorite dish made of cabbage, sauerkraut, onions, pimiento, pork, beef, sausage, and mushrooms, and seasoned with bay leaves, garlic, and tomato paste. It often is served on New Year's Day along with generous amounts of vodka. Beet soups *(chlodnik)* and other soups, often served with pierogi, are popular menu items. Pierogi are small pockets of dough that contain a filling such as mushroom, cheesy potato, or a sweet jam or fruit.

Czechs and Slovaks usually have a light continental breakfast with coffee as the beverage, a potato and meat casserole lunch, and maybe a meat (perhaps sausage) and potato supper or a sandwich. In general, the fare is rather simple, but hearty. The Czechs are fond of their beers, for which they are noted. The Slovaks generally choose wine, and *slivovitz* (potent plum brandy) is enjoyed by all. Dairy products, particularly sour ones; wheat and rye breads and other baked products; potatoes and other vegetables, including kohlrabi and cabbage; plus meats with plenty of gravy form the basis of the diets in both countries. Carp is traditionally served at Christmas, and herring also is eaten. *Knedliky,* flat circular dumplings made with potatoes or bread, are popular accompaniments to meat dishes. These dumplings are a popular dessert when made with fruit.

Paprika and goulash *(gulyás)* are culinary terms that immediately say Hungary, although how paprika got from the Americas to Hungary is a mystery. Goulash recipes vary widely, but they basically are a stew featuring braised meat seasoned with onion and paprika, and with varying amounts of liquid. The wine industry today is the result of the Roman occupation of centuries ago, and other conquerors also have left their marks on the Hungarian menu. Among the most common ingredients in the Hungarian kitchen are pork, sour cream, cabbage, potatoes, onions, green peppers, tomatoes, tea, coffee, wine, and paprika. Strudels and tortes with coffee are popular at a break during the day or as dessert at dinner. Whipped cream is a favorite means of adding calories to the already rich, sweet, and abundant desserts.

Romania, like Hungary, also has a cuisine that has drawn from the various conquerors that have passed through it during the past ages. An example of this is the seemingly pervasive *mamaliga,* a very thick cornmeal mush that can be cut into slices when cooled; mamaliga is closely related to the Italian dish *polenta. Ghiveciu* is a multi-ingredient dish: chunks of veal or pork, and then about eight different vegetables, are browned separately; the ingredients are then combined with some stock, tomato paste, and red wine plus green grapes in a pot *(güvec)* and then baked. This dish is from the reign of the Turks. Turkish coffee may be the choice of many Romanians. The ingredients frequently used in preparing Romanian meals include yogurt, sweet and sour cream, sheep's and goat's milk cheeses, cabbage and sauerkraut, eggplant, pork, veal, onions, leeks, black olives, and olive oil. *Dulceata,* a dish in which fruits are preserved in a heavy syrup, is popular, and so are pastries and cakes reflective of Austria and Turkey.

The food in the remaining regions of the Balkan Peninsula is similar to that of their neighbors, with considerable Turkish and Greek overtones. Dairy products generally are in clabbered forms and include local cheeses. Plums, apples, pears, peaches, and cherries are among the fruits that are grown there. The wide

Figure 7.7 A baker readies 3 pans of bread for baking in Bulgaria.

array of vegetables includes seasonal items like string beans, zucchini, tomatoes, eggplant, onions, and potatoes.

The food in Bulgaria draws heavily from its propinquity to Greece (Figure 7.7) and its occupation at one time by the Turks. *Musaka, sarma* (stuffed grape leaves), yogurt, feta-like cheeses, and *gyuvech* are examples of the Greek and Turkish influences. Also prominent are some of the hearty dishes from Hungary, although meat is used less abundantly. *Shopska salata* is a uniquely Bulgarian salad featuring tomatoes, unpeeled cucumbers, and a goat cheese called *sirene*. Hot red peppers are a product of the region that find their way into many main dishes. *Slivova* is a popular plum brandy dear to Bulgarians. Sausages and Bulgarian red wine are also favorites.

Breads are very popular, especially those made with wheat and rye; other cereals available include corn, oats, and rice. The usual meats are lamb and pork. Garlic, paprika, and caraway seeds are used generously in recipes. *Slatko,* a sweet fruit dish made by simmering selected fruits and sometimes blossoms in a thick syrup, is often an accompaniment to thick and very sweet Turkish coffee; these are popular with the Serbs. Croatians eat dishes that are similar to those originating in Austria and Hungary. Gnocchi (small dumplings made from wheat or cornmeal, or both) reflect the proximity to northern Italy. *Potika* is a Slovenian coffee cake filled between the many layers with nuts. *Srpska salata* (Serbian salad composed of raw peppers, onions, tomatoes, oil, vinegar, and chili) is a popular salad in Yugoslavia. Main dish pies include *zeljanica* (spinach and cheese pie) and *gibanica* (layered cheese pie).

In Bulgaria, ethnographers have recorded over 500 different shapes, sizes, and kinds of bread used to observe different customs. Custom even suggests that bran placed under the threshold of a home will prevent evil from entering.

𝒦ey Terms

Bliny—Small, thin Russian pancakes.

Borsch—Russian soup featuring beets and cabbage.

Cyrillic alphabet—Alphabet developed by Cyril and Methodius, Byzantine monks of the 9th century; used in Russia and many Slavic regions.

Dulceata—Romanian dish of simmered fruits in very heavy syrup.

Ghiveciu—Romanian casserole consisting of browned chunks of pork or veal, browned vegetables, tomato paste, red wine, and green grapes.

Gibanica—Yugoslavian layered cheese pie.

Gnocchi—Yugoslavian small dumplings of wheat or cornmeal, or both.

Gulyás—Hungarian stew made with chunks of braised meat, seasoned with onion and paprika, and varying amounts of liquid.

Illyrian—Group of people settling the Balkans prior to the Romans.

Kasha—Buckwheat groats (or sometimes other cereals) boiled in liquid until light and fluffy; popular in Russia and its environs.

Kielbasa—Polish sausage made of ground beef and pork, well seasoned with garlic.

Knedliky—Flat, circular potato or bread dumplings popular in the Czech Republic and Slovakia.

Kulich—Russian traditional yeast-leavened Easter bread containing candied and dried fruits, nuts, and liqueur.

Magyars—Ancestors of today's Hungarians.

Mamaliga—Romanian cornmeal mush similar to Italian polenta.

Paskha—Pyramid-shaped Russian Easter cake.

Pierogi—Polish dish consisting of small pockets of dough containing a filling (vegetable or sweet).

Pirozhki—Small Russian pastries filled with meat.

Roma—Nomadic group originating from India, but particularly numerous in Romania and spreading into most parts of Europe.

Samovar—Elaborate Russian device equipped with a chimney, a teapot for the essence of the tea, and a large area where the water is boiled for dispensing from the spigot.

Shashlyk—Russian version of shish kebabs.

Shchi—Cabbage-based soup made in Russia.

Slatko—Serbian dish made of fruit simmered with blossoms in a sweet sugar syrup.

Slivova—Bulgarian plum brandy.

Slivovitz—Plum brandy liqueur drunk by Czechs and Slovaks.

Tatars—Mongol invaders who originally gathered military might under Genghis Khan and who conquered Russia under his grandson's leadership.

Transylvania—Region in western Romania bounded by the Carpathian Mountains.

Zeljanica—Yugoslavian cheese and spinach pie.

Recipes

Bigos (Serves 8–10)

1 onion, chopped
2 tbsp butter
1 small head cabbage, finely shredded
3 c sauerkraut
6 mushrooms, sliced
2 c kielbasa (Polish sausage), diced
2 c cooked pork or beef, diced
2 bouillon cubes in 1 c water
2 Pippin apples, pared and diced
4 pitted prunes
1 c tomato paste
1 bay leaf

3/4 c red wine
1 clove garlic, crushed
Salt and pepper

1. Saute onion in butter.
2. Place all ingredients through the bay leaf in a 3-qt casserole.
3. Cover and bake for 2 hours at 300°F.
4. Add remaining ingredients and bake 30 minutes more.
5. Cool, then refrigerate for at least 2 days.
6. Reheat and serve.

Chlodnik (Serves 6–8)

1 lb cooked or canned beets, drained
1 cucumber, diced
1 pickle, diced
1/2 c diced radishes
1 garlic clove, crushed
1 qt yogurt
1 beef bouillon cube dissolved in 1 c beet juice
1 c cooked veal, cubed
2 hard-cooked eggs, sliced

1 tbsp chopped onion
Salt and pepper
1 tbsp chopped parsley
2 tbsp chopped dill

1. Cut beets in slivers.
2. Combine all ingredients except dill and parsley.
3. Chill.
4. Serve garnished with dill and parsley.

Ovocné Knedliky (Makes 12 dumplings)

1 1/2 tbsp butter
1/2 c cottage cheese
1 egg yolk
1/2 tsp salt
1/4 c milk
1 3/4 c flour
3 apples, chopped
Boiling salted water
3 tbsp melted butter
3 tbsp sugar

1. Cream first five ingredients.
2. Stir in flour until dough pulls away from bowl and is not sticky.
3. Roll dough on floured board into 9″ x 12″ rectangle and cut into 3″ squares.
4. Place spoonful of apple in center of each square and wrap into a ball.
5. Drop dumplings into 6-qt saucepan of boiling water.
6. Cook for 8 minutes; remove and drain thoroughly.
7. Pour a bit of melted butter and sugar over each dumpling.

Szekely Gulyás (Serves 4)

1/2 lb pork shoulder
1/2 lb pork ribs
1/2 tbsp lard
2 onions, chopped
1 garlic clove, crushed
1/4 tsp caraway seeds
1/2 tsp paprika
1/2 c water
1 tsp salt
1 qt sauerkraut
Water to cover
1 tsp flour
1 c sour cream

1. Brown meat (cut into 2″ pieces) in lard. Add onions and cook until golden.
2. Add all ingredients through the salt and simmer for 1 hour.
3. Add sauerkraut and enough water to cover. Simmer for 45 minutes.
4. Stir flour into sour cream, then stir mixture into the other ingredients.
5. Stir slowly while heating for 5 minutes to a simmer.
6. Serve with noodles.

Russian Borsch (Serves 4–6)

1/2 medium onion, chopped
1 tbsp fat
1/2 c diced potatoes
1/4 c diced carrots
1/2 c finely shredded cabbage
1/4 c chopped celery
1 qt beef bouillon
1/2 c canned tomatoes, pureed
1 1/2 tsp lemon juice

Salt and pepper
1 c diced beets with juice
1/4 c sour cream

1. Saute onion in the fat.
2. Add all ingredients except beets and sour cream.
3. Simmer until vegetables are done.
4. Add beets and heat to serving.
5. Serve hot with a dollop of sour cream.

Bliny (Serves 4–6)

1 pkg dry yeast
1/2 c lukewarm water
1/2 c buckwheat flour
2 c flour
2 c lukewarm milk
1/2 tsp salt
1 tsp sugar
1/4 c melted butter
1 1/2 c sour cream
3 eggs, beaten
Caviar or thinly sliced smoked salmon

1. Dissolve yeast in lukewarm water and let stand 5 minutes.
2. Meanwhile, mix flours and 2 cups of lukewarm milk.
3. Add yeast mixture, salt, sugar, and 3 tablespoons each melted butter and sour cream; add eggs. Beat vigorously until smooth.
4. Cover and let rise until light.
5. Preheat oven to 300°F and heat a nonstick skillet on the range until water sprinkled on it dances.
6. Pour three pancakes (about 3 tbsp each) on the skillet and fry for 2 1/2 minutes; brush top with melted butter and fry the second side.
7. Keep baked bliny in a dish in the oven until ready to serve topped with sour cream and caviar or salmon.

Nockerl (Serves 4–6)

6 eggs, separated
7 tbsp sugar
2 tbsp butter
1 tbsp milk
2 tbsp flour
1/2 tsp lemon zest
Powdered sugar

1. Preheat oven to 450°F.
2. Beat egg whites with electric mixer while gradually adding 6 tablespoons of sugar, and continue beating until stiff.
3. Meanwhile, heat 1 tablespoon of sugar with butter and milk until this browns slightly. Pour into soufflé dish and set in oven.
4. Beat egg yolks; stir in flour and lemon zest to blend.
5. Gently but thoroughly fold yolk mixture into whites.
6. Place four large dollops of mixture vertically in baking dish to fill the dish. Lightly sprinkle with powdered sugar.
7. Bake at 450°F for 4 to 5 minutes to lightly brown peaks.

Soft Custard Sauce for Nockerl (Makes 1 1/2 cups)

3 egg yolks, beaten
1/4 c sugar
1 c scalded milk
2 tsp kirsch
Berries for garnish (optional)

1. Combine yolks, sugar, and milk, and heat in top of double boiler.
2. Stir continuously until thick enough to coat a metal spoon.
3. Cool slightly. Stir in kirsch. Pour a spoonful onto each dessert plate, then spoon a large dollop of nockerl on top. Garnish with berries.

Mamaliga (Serves 4–6)

1 qt water
1 tbsp salt
2 2/3 c cornmeal
4 tbsp butter, melted

1. Bring water and salt to a boil.
2. Stir while slowly adding cornmeal and keep stirring until the mixture is smooth and beginning to thicken.
3. Cover and simmer for 10 to 12 minutes until water is absorbed.
4. Serve on a platter with melted butter, or let it cool and serve with dill, sour cream, black olives, and sliced hard-cooked eggs.

Summary

The countries of Eastern Europe include Lithuania, Latvia, Estonia, Poland, Belarus, Russia, Ukraine, Moldavia, Romania, Slovakia, the Czech Republic, Hungary, Slovenia, Croatia, Yugoslavia, Bosnia-Herzegovina, Albania, Macedonia, and Bulgaria. These countries have undergone numerous invasions by soldiers and marauders from many distant regions. The Illyrians preceded the Romans in the Balkans, and part of the region went with the Byzantine Empire after the division of the Roman Empire, while part was retained with the western part of the Roman Empire. Later, a large area came under the rule of the Ottoman Empire. Slavic tribes have been actively involved in the conflicts and the settling of the eastern part of Eastern Europe. The Magyars became the main group in the region of Hungary. The Tatars took over the eastern region, particularly in Russia. The Russian Revolution in 1917 and the two world wars greatly altered this region during much of the 20th century. The variety of religions, which include Orthodox, Muslim, Protestant, Jewish, and Roman Catholic faiths, can be cited as significant reasons for some of the unrest that still prevails, particularly in the Balkans. Use of both the Cyrillic and Roman alphabets adds to the difficulties in communication. The nomadic group that is concentrated in Romania, but which roams a good bit of Europe, is the Roma, who came centuries ago from India.

The cultural richness of this diverse and large region of Europe can be seen in the large numbers of musicians, composers, and artists who have made their homes in Eastern Europe, particularly in the countries of Russia, Poland, Czechoslovakia, and Hungary. Great literary works and a wide range of political ideologies and philosophies have also been created there.

The food patterns in Eastern Europe are influenced by the limited growing season for farm crops, although there are many excellent farming areas where wheat, rye, and other cereals, vegetables, and a variety of fruits can be grown. Great reliance in most of the countries is placed on hearty, relatively simple foods, with cereals, potatoes, cabbage, pork, and lamb or mutton being particularly common. In the areas where the Turks ruled for a time, various dishes reflect their influence. The same is true where Romans ruled.

Study Questions

1. Where are the following countries located: (a) Estonia, (b) Croatia, (c) Bulgaria, (d) Poland, (e) Slovakia, (f) Ukraine, (g) Russia, (h) Latvia, (i) Albania, (j) Hungary, (k) Bosnia-Herzegovina, (l) Lithuania, (m) Belarus, (n) Slovenia, (o) Moldova, (p) Macedonia, and (q) Yugoslavia?
2. Where do each of the following or their descendants live in the greatest concentrations in Eastern Europe: (a) Magyars, (b) Tatars, (c) Illyrians, and (d) Romas?
3. Why are both Orthodox and Roman Catholic believers living in various parts of Eastern Europe?
4. What was the avenue for spreading Islam to Eastern Europe?
5. What alphabet is used primarily in Russia? In the Czech Republic?
6. Generalize about the differences in the typical foods in Poland and those in Bulgaria. Explain some causes of these differences.

Bibliography

Barer-Stein, T. 1999. *You Eat What You Are.* 2nd ed. Firefly Books, Ltd. Ontario, Canada.

Cook, T. 1994. *Illustrated Guide to Prague.* Passport Books. Lincolnwood, IL.

Dydynski, K., S. Fallon, K. Galbraith, P. Hellander, and R. Klaskin. 1999. *Eastern Europe.* Lonely Planet. Oakland, CA.

Farley, M. P. 1990. *Festive Ukrainian Cooking.* University of Pittsburgh Press. Pittsburgh, PA.

Field, M., and F. Field. 1970. *A Quintet of Cuisines.* Time-Life Books. New York.

Heale, J. 1994. *Cultures of the World: Poland.* Marshall Cavendish. New York.

Höfer, H. 1996. *Budapest.* APA Publications.

Palmowski, J. 1997. *Dictionary of Twentieth Century World History.* Oxford University Press. New York.

Papashvily, H., and G. Papashvily. 1969. *Russian Cooking.* Time-Life Books. New York.

Pearcy, G. E. 1980. *The World Food Scene.* Plycon Press. Redondo Beach, CA.

Pettifer, J. 1994. *Blue Guide Albania.* W. W. Norton. New York.

Sheehan, S. 1994. *Cultures of the World: Romania.* Marshall Cavendish. New York.

Torchinsky, O. 1994. *Cultures of the World: Russia.* Marshall Cavendish. New York.

Viault, B. S. 1990. *Western Civilization since 1600.* McGraw-Hill. New York.

Ward, P. 1991. *Bulgaria: A Travel Guide.* Pelican Publishing. Gretna, LA.

8 Italy

Geographic Overview

Italy extends from the southern side of the Alps in Europe all the way down the boot-shaped Italian Peninsula to its very toe in the Mediterranean Sea and includes the large island of Sicily, which lies across the Straits of Messina. The northern region begins in the southern Alps and the Dolomites, with the Po River wending its way eastward more than 400 miles to empty into the Adriatic Sea. The Po Valley in the northern part of Italy is the major agricultural region, but there also is a good bit of farming done all through Italy. The olives, which are the source of Italy's famed olive oil, are seen growing in abundance on the trees that climb the sides of the Apennine Mountains that form the backbone of the entire peninsula.

The eruption of Mt. Vesuvius, which destroyed Pompeii (Figure 8.1) in 79 CE, and the ongoing rumbling and spewing of Mt. Etna on Sicily are evidence of the volcanic nature of southern Italy. Most of Italy is either on the coast or very close to the sea; the Tyrrhenian Sea lies on the west, the Mediterranean and Ionian seas to the south, and the Adriatic Sea is eastward. This large amount of water has a somewhat moderating effect on the climate, but the southerly location of much of Italy results in summers that can get uncomfortably hot. The winters are fairly mild, except in the northern, particularly the mountainous, area.

The land in the Po Valley provides the space for about a sixth of the agriculture of Italy; its flat fields are well suited to growing cereal crops, notably wheat but also corn and rice. Fruits and vegetables are grown in abundance in Italy, too. Its vineyards are the source of a wide array of wines. Animals are a very limited part of the farm scene, and even fishing is not a very large industry in Italy. However, meats of various kinds, fish, and dairy products (particularly cheese) are important in the diet, even if they have to be imported.

Figure 8.1 Pompeii is still being excavated from the deadly eruption of Mt. Vesuvius (visible through the arch) in 79 CE.

History and Culture

The land that presently is Italy has seen a seemingly endless parade of people from other regions since man's history began. The earliest group that developed a society and left its imprint was the Etruscans, who probably settled in the region now known as Tuscany sometime shortly after 1000 BCE. Within 300 years, they began moving southward until they encountered Greek settlements near Naples. A different (Latin) group founded Rome on the Tiber River in 753 BCE (according to legend), but the Etruscans seized Rome about 550 BCE and proceeded to instill their ways of speaking and writing (alphabet), as well as their skills in waging wars.

Dreams of expansion beyond the Italian Peninsula led to Rome's attempts to acquire land in North Africa and to the Punic Wars with Carthage (modern Tunisia) between 246 and 146 BCE. Roman expansion also is evidenced by the famous baths they constructed in Bath, England, and by Hadrian's Wall, which Hadrian built to keep out invaders from Scotland and the north in the 1st century CE. Rome's remarkable engineering achievements can still be seen at the Pont du Gard, an amazing aqueduct built in 19 CE in southern France near Nimes.

The zenith of the Roman Empire found Rome controlling vast reaches of the western world, but the power slowly eroded as the lifestyle began to focus on revelry and pleasures, which unfortunately included gladiatorial events at the expense of Christians and animals. In 330 CE, the governmental control was moved to Byzantium (renamed Constantinople), and the realm was split in two. By the late 3rd century, tribes from the north (Visigoths, Ostrogoths, Vandals, and Huns) caused chaos in the Roman Empire, but Diocletian and subsequent rulers restored order by the 4th century.

Between the 11th and 14th centuries, an extended contest between the landowning popes and the emperors kept Rome in turmoil. This allowed the rise of such city-states as Venice. Eventually, the papacy was transferred from Rome to Avignon in France, where the popes lived from 1309 to 1377. In the 14th century, Florence became the golden city in Italy as a result of the tremendous strength of banking interests and of cultural achievements fostered by the powerful Medici family. The center of enlightenment moved from Florence to Rome at the beginning of the 16th century. Various European powers, including Spain, France, and Austria, held sway in parts of Italy until the mid-19th century. Finally, Italy was united and Victor Emmanuel II was crowned. Subsequent political events have added to the problems Italy has had to face, probably the most difficult being the period of Mussolini's dictatorship prior to and during World War II.

Despite the seemingly endless conflicts that have occurred during Italy's history, some remarkable cultural achievements mark the creativity that appears to be almost inherent to Italians. In art, such giants as Leonardo da Vinci, Michelangelo, and Botticelli are but a few of the many gifted painters and sculptors from Italy. Musicians from Italy over the centuries have included such well-known people as Palestrina, Scarlatti, Paganini, Rossini, Verdi, and Puccini. Literary lights have included Ovid, Dante, Machiavelli, and the adventurer Marco Polo.

Architecture has been the forte of the citizens of the Italian Peninsula. Innumerable ruins are in evidence in Rome and various parts of the country. The Pantheon, Forum, Constantine's Arch, St. Peter's Basilica, and the Colosseum serve as magnets for tourists visiting Rome. Florence has the Ponte Vecchio, Giotto's bell tower, the Baptistry, and the Pitti Palace, to name just a few of the structures of architectural interest there. Of course, the city of Pisa is perhaps best known for its structural difficulties in the Leaning Tower. Venice presents yet another side of Italian architecture, with many palaces built along its canals and the Palace of the Doges and St. Mark's Cathedral that serve as centerpieces for its central piazza.

The numerous large and beautiful cathedrals, such as the remarkable ones in Milan (Figure 8.2) and at the Vatican, are impressive reminders of the power and wealth of the Catholic Church. This clearly is the dominant religion of Italy. In fact, the Vatican actually is a city-state set within the city of Rome. The Vatican (Figure 8.3) has been the Pope's residence for more than 600 years. Not only is the huge Basilica of St. Peter located in the Vatican, but so are the famous Sistine Chapel, with its ceiling painted by Michelangelo, and the remarkable art collection of the Vatican Museum. Huge throngs gather in the square designed by Bernini in front of the Pope's apartment adjacent to St. Peter's to receive the blessing of the current Pope. Swiss Guards are the traditional protectors of the Pope and the Vatican. The policies and statements emanating from the Catholic pope play an important and continuing role in everyday life of Italians. Mass, rosaries, and confession are central to Italian Catholics.

The ubiquity of the Catholic Church in Italy is reflected in the large number of holidays that are celebrated in honor of religious figures. Of course, Christmas and Easter are celebrated, and so are All Saint's Day, Feast of the Immaculate Conception, and St. Stefan's Day throughout Italy; various cities also celebrate their special saints on other days. Among the important features surrounding Christmas is the presence of *crèches,* many of which have been carved from wood and painted very long ago and which are prominently displayed to depict the

Figure 8.2 The large Catholic cathedral in Milan presents an exciting array of statuary icons to all who behold it.

Figure 8.3 The Vatican is actually a sovereign state within the boundaries of Rome and even issues its own postal stamps.

story of the Christ child's birth. Processions in many cities mark the Good Friday observances around Italy.

Food Patterns

Part of the love of the good life for Italians seems to include romance. Baci candy boxes in Perugia reportedly began when a girl working in the candy kitchen wrapped love notes to the store's owner in candies. He responded to this novel idea by ultimately marrying her and carrying on this romantic tradition for wrapping his candies.

"Love of the good life" seems to be the creed of many Italians, although the bursts of song from Venetian gondoliers and the cheers from opera-goers may be just a bit more muted today than in earlier years. Still, the highlight of Italian daily life has to be the food! Food and family are firmly implanted in the hearts of Italians. In contrast to the rushed pace of eating seen so often in northern countries, a meal in Italy is meant to be treasured and savored (Figure 8.4). Worldly concerns should not interfere with the concentration on the senses that good food requires. The result of this dedication to good food is a cuisine that has captured diners around the world. Perhaps part of the appeal is the relaxation that twirling long strands of spaghetti on a fork engenders. Who could possibly think that anything is more important than getting that last tempting strand ready to be transported in style to the mouth? And the tantalizing aromas that waft from dishes created with wonderful olive oil, garlic, tomato, balsamic vinegar, and maybe a bit of pesto and mushrooms simply require that they be eaten by the lucky diner. Don't forget the wonderful Italian breads, maybe washed down with a hearty red wine. Then, if there is still a bit of room for it, a *gelati* (ice cream) may be the perfect ending to a leisurely and sensually gratifying dining experience.

The choices available in the Italian cuisine are truly amazing. Creative ways of using the various flavorful ingredients that are available from the local farming efforts have fostered this broad menu. Underlying much of the diet is wheat, which is the basic ingredient for the pastas indigenous to Italian dining. Pastas may be made at home and used fresh, or they may be purchased from local shops, which feature a dazzling array of shapes, dimensions, and even a choice of color (spinach may be added to the dough to make it green). Ribbon-shaped pastas are used frequently in regions north of Rome, while tubular pastas may be the popular choice south of Rome. However, there really is not a strong regional preference; the choice is dependent upon the chef and the dish being prepared. The names of some of the pastas are spaghetti, ziti, penne, capellini, fusilli, lasagne, tortellini, cannelloni, ravioli, lumache, manicotti, tagliatelle, and macaroni.

Parmigiano (parmesan) doubtless is the best-known of Italian cheese, but there are others that are also used widely and are noteworthy. Romano, a sharp

Figure 8.4 Food important in Italy is featured in this lovely mosaic.

cheese made with sheep's milk, is also a very hard cheese for grating. Fontina is popular for use in fondue, while provolone and gorgonzola (a blue-veined, sharp flavor) are considered table cheeses. Pizza seems to call out for mozzarella, while ricotta (unsalted cottage cheese) is used in preparing blintzes and in other recipes suitable for cottage cheese. Mozzarella originally was made with buffalo milk, but the scarcity of this milk has caused most of this type of cheese to be made using cow's milk. Mascarpone is an unripened cheese that can be blended readily with liqueurs or a bit of honey and served along with fresh fruit (or candied fruit may even be stirred in).

Olive oils come from most parts of Italy and are generally of excellent quality. Although cooking in the south uses olive oil extensively, butter is the more common fat in northern Italy. Nevertheless, northerners use plenty of olive oil too. Northerners also contribute a special ingredient that has been adopted by gourmets in other countries too: balsamic vinegar, which is flavored with special herbs and aged according to carefully kept secrets. The prized balsamic vinegars are from the area of Modena in northern Italy. Like most foods, some balsamic vinegars are much more flavorful than some of the others; the fact that a vinegar is made in Modena does not guarantee the exciting flavors possible in a truly fine balsamic vinegar.

Among the best-known meats from Italy is prosciutto, the thin slices obtained from Parma hams. Parma hams are from the northern Italian region near Bologna, and they are made by salting and then drying for about 6 months, which results in a delicate flavor and a reddish color. Sausages are—not surprisingly—made in and around Bologna. Among the varieties are toscana (a rather fatty pork sausage made in Tuscany), salami, mortadello, and pepperoni. Veal is a very popular meat and is prepared in a variety of ways, including the popular veal scaloppini and *osso buco* (braised veal shanks).

The typical meal pattern in Italy begins with a continental breakfast of *caffe latte* (coffee with milk, usually the only milk drunk during the day) and a bread, perhaps with jam. The other two meals of the day are considerably more substantial. For starters, antipasto (before pasta) is served. Salami or other coldcuts, peppers or other pickled vegetables, and perhaps bruschetta (1/2-inch thick slices of Italian bread topped with olive oil, a hint of garlic, and sometimes a bit of tomato, then broiled), and olives might be found as the appetizing start before the pasta course. Some type of pasta or soup ordinarily follows the antipasto. The main course is likely to feature veal, but it may be some other meat, perhaps as a casserole dish. Braised vegetables (or vegetables cooked by another means) may serve as an accompaniment. Risotto, rice that has been cooked slowly often for an hour or more with special seasonings such as saffron, is a favorite dish in northern Italy; so is *polenta,* the cornmeal mush preparation that apparently was the antecedent to the polenta of the Balkans. Finally, fruit and cheese or some sweet may close the meal.

Espresso is a favorite Italian beverage. It is made most easily using an espresso machine. A dark-roast coffee bean, ground to a fine powder, is essential to preparing espresso. This special coffee is then brewed using steam under pressure to create espresso, which is served in a small cup (despite the fact that it may seem almost strong enough to not even require the cup). A fancy version of espresso is cappuccino, which is espresso wearing a hat of frothy hot milk.

A special Italian coffee cake called *pannetone* is an ideal accompaniment to either espresso or cappuccino. This rather coarse-textured but delectable, sweet, yeast bread is punctuated with candied fruits and raisins. The festive look of a slice of pannetone clearly explains why this is a favorite at Christmas (or any time of the year).

Key Terms

Antipasto—"Before the pasta" (hors d'oeuvre); wide variety of tidbits or appetizers, often olives, bread sticks, pickled vegetables, and other simple items.

Balsamic vinegar—Special herb-flavored vinegar, the best of which is made in the vicinity of Modena in northern Italy.

Bruschetta—Italian bread brushed with olive oil, garlic, and sometimes tomato, then broiled.

Caffe latte—Coffee with a generous amount of milk added.

Cannelloni—Ridged tubes of pasta that are designed to be filled with various stuffings for entrees or desserts.

Capellini—Angel hair (very thin, spaghetti-like pasta).

Cappuccino—Espresso topped with frothy white milk.

Espresso—Very strong Italian coffee made by brewing dark-roast, finely ground coffee with steam.

Etruscan—Group that settled in Tuscany and moved south, ultimately taking over Rome and contributing their alphabet, speech, and ability to wage war.

Fontina—Cheese well suited for making fondue; originally from Valle d'Aosta in northern Italy near Great St. Bernard Pass.

Fusilli—Wavy, spaghetti-like pasta.

Gelati—Italian ice cream.

Gorgonzola—Blue-veined cheese that originated in Gorgonzola near Milan in northern Italy and is now produced in the Po Valley.

Lasagne—Broad, ribbon-like pasta used in casserole dishes.

Lumache—Large, conch shell-shaped pasta suitable for stuffing.

Manicotti—Long, plain tube of pasta appropriate for stuffing.

Mascarpone—Unripened Italian dessert cheese made from fresh cream; may be flavored with honey, liqueurs, or candied fruit.

Medici—Powerful Florentine banking family; Cosimo, Lorenzo, and Catherine (who carried the excellence of Florentine cuisine to France when she married future King Henri II) are credited with influencing the artistic and culinary renaissance in the 15th and 16th centuries, particularly.

Mozzarella—Cheese used on pizzas, originally made from buffalo milk, but now often made from cow's milk.

Osso buco—Braised veal shanks simmered with herbs and wine until very tender.

Pannetone—Coarse, sweet yeast bread containing raisins and candied fruit.

Parmesan—Hard cheese often aged for more than 2 years; frequently grated over Italian dishes.

Penne—Tubular pasta cut on the diagonal into pieces about an inch long.

Pesto—Flavorful thick sauce made by pulverizing fresh basil and adding such ingredients as piñon nuts, parmesan cheese, garlic, and olive oil.

Prosciutto—Thinly sliced, well-cured Parma ham.

Ravioli—Rectangular pasta pouches stuffed with ground meat or cheese.

Risotto—Rice cooked for an hour or more, with saffron or other seasonings added.
Romano—Sharp, sheep's milk cheese; very hard cheese, ideal for grating.
St. Peter's Basilica—Very large cathedral in the Vatican city.
Tortiglioni—Spiral-shaped pasta.

Recipes

Manicotti with Ricotta Filling (Serves 4–8)

1 1/2 c ricotta
1/4 c chopped parsley
1/2 tsp salt
1 egg, slightly beaten
8 manicotti shells
1 c marinara sauce
1/2 c shredded mozzarella cheese
1/4 c grated parmesan cheese

1. Combine ricotta, parsley, salt, and egg; refrigerate.

2. Boil manicotti according to package directions.
3. Drain and cool in cold water.
4. Pour half of marinara sauce into 9" x 9" baking dish.
5. Stuff drained manicotti with filling and place on sauce in dish.
6. Moisten with remaining marinara sauce.
7. Scatter mozzarella on manicotti and sprinkle parmesan cheese over top.
8. Bake in preheated 350°F oven for 25 to 30 minutes.

Marinated Mushrooms (Serves 4–8)

2/3 c olive oil
1/2 c water
1/4 c lemon juice
1 garlic clove, crushed
5 peppercorns
1/2 tsp salt
16 small mushrooms

1. Simmer all ingredients except mushrooms for 15 minutes.
2. Add mushrooms; simmer another 5 minutes, turning as needed.
3. Cool and then store in refrigerator.
4. Drain before serving mushrooms.

Osso Buco (Serves 4–6)

1 c onions, chopped
1/4 c sliced carrot
1/4 c chopped celery
1 small garlic clove, minced
2 tbsp butter
3 to 4 lb veal shank, sawed to 2 1/2" lengths
1/2 c flour
Salt and pepper
1/4 c olive oil
1/2 c white wine, dry
2 tbsp chopped fresh basil
1 c beef bouillon
1/2 tsp thyme
2 c chopped tomatoes
4 sprigs of parsley
Grated rind of 1 lemon

1. Saute vegetables in butter in Dutch oven slowly for 10 minutes, stirring a bit.
2. Tie string around each bone, then roll in flour, salt, and pepper to coat.
3. Brown veal in oil in skillet.
4. Put browned veal on vegetables in Dutch oven.
5. Deglaze the skillet with wine, boiling briefly, then stir in the remaining ingredients and boil for 1 minute.
6. Pour this mixture over the veal in the Dutch oven.
7. Add more bouillon if needed to bring liquid halfway up the shanks.
8. Place covered Dutch oven in oven heated to 350°F and simmer for about 1 1/4 hours until tender. Check liquid and add, if necessary.

Saffron Risotto (Serves 4)

1/4 c minced onion
2 tbsp butter
1 c polished rice
3 1/2 c chicken bouillon
1/4 c dry white wine
Pinch of saffron, powdered
2 tbsp butter
1/4 c freshly grated parmesan cheese

1. Saute onions in butter, without browning, for 7 minutes.
2. Add rice and stir while heating until opaque.
3. Add half the bouillon and all of the wine, and boil until most liquid has been absorbed, stirring frequently.
4. Add half of remaining liquid and the saffron, and continue cooking slowly with stirring.
5. Add more bouillon as needed to soften the rice. Cook until rice is soft.
6. Use a fork to stir in the butter and parmesan cheese. (Rice should be creamy and very hot when served.)

Pesto (Makes 1 1/2 cups)

2 c basil leaves, packed
2 garlic cloves
2/3 c grated parmesan cheese
1/4 c piñon (pine) nuts
1/2 c olive oil
Pepper to taste

1. Place basil, garlic, cheese, and nuts in blender and blend on medium, scraping often with spatula.
2. Slowly add olive oil with blender set on medium and process until smooth.
3. Add pepper and blend in.
4. May be stored in refrigerator for up to 4 weeks or in freezer for 6 to 9 months.

Zabaione (Serves 4)

4 eggs, slightly beaten
1/2 c sugar
1/2 c marsala or sherry

1. Combine eggs and sugar in top of double boiler set over very hot water.
2. With a whisk, beat the eggs while very slowly adding the wine.
3. Continue beating while heating the double boiler for about 10 minutes until the mixture will mound.
4. Serve hot in sherbet glasses or small dessert bowls.

Summary

Italy is basically the boot-shaped peninsula that extends southward from the middle of Europe. It is bordered on the north by the Alps. The best agricultural land is the Po Valley in northern Italy, but farming is done throughout the rest of Italy too, despite the challenges the Apennine Mountains present along the length of the peninsula. Crops include wheat, corn, rice, olives, grapes (for wine), and fruits and vegetables, as well as some livestock and dairy products.

Italy's location and climate beckoned many people through the ages, the earliest actual society being the Etruscans in Tuscany. They later spread to the south and took over Rome. The Romans conquered a vast empire, which left the mark of the Romans in England, much of Europe, and around the Mediterranean. Northern tribes came over the Alps to finally lay waste to parts of the Roman Empire. By the 14th century, the Medicis in Florence and other enlightened people were fostering creative efforts in thought, music, art, and literature. Finally, the city-states that had sprung up in the peninsula were united (with the exception of the Vatican), and Italy was ruled by King Victor Emmanuel II. The 20th century was difficult because of the two world wars, particularly during World War II under Mussolini.

The importance of the Catholic Church is evidenced by the many large and beautiful cathedrals throughout Italy and by the many holidays that are held to honor Christ and special saints. The Vatican operates as an independent state, but is situated within Rome, and the Pope's actions are a dominant part of life in Italy.

Dining and excellent food are very much a part of life in Italy, and time is taken to savor the food experience. The most elaborate cuisine is that in the north around Milan. Also, Tuscany is the source of some delightful food. The cuisine often includes rice dishes and some corn (polenta is a favorite), but wheat in the form of pastas, pizzas, and breads dominates the menus. Olive oil and such cheeses as parmesan, Romano, ricotta, and mozzarella are essential ingredients in many recipes. Veal and pork, often in the form of flavorful hams and sausages, are the favored meats. Tomatoes, a wide array of vegetables, fresh herbs, and fruits also are eaten frequently. Antipasto usually begins every meal except breakfast. Pasta also appears at least once a day. Caffe latte is the breakfast beverage, wine accompanies other meals, and espresso or cappuccino are served in the evening and at many other times. Gelati, pastries, and pannetone or other cakes are often eaten with espresso.

Study Questions

1. Indicate the part of Italy where the following are key agricultural crops: (a) corn, (b) olives, (c) rice, (d) wheat, and (e) grapes.
2. Identify the type of creative work for which each of the following Italians is known: (a) Botticelli, (b) Machiavelli, (c) Leonardo da Vinci, (d) Verdi, and (e) Scarlatti.
3. Select a famous Italian artist, musician, or writer whose work you particularly enjoy. Search other references to find where this person was born, lived, and worked, and identify some of the works.
4. Describe what a typical day's menu might be if you were Italian.
5. Name 10 specific food items for which Italy is known.

Bibliography

Cronin, V. 1972. *Horizon Concise History of Italy.* American Heritage Publishing. New York.

De'Medici, L. 1996. *Tuscany: The Beautiful Cookbook.* Harper Collins. New York.

Kramer, M. 1988. *Illustrated Guide to Foreign and Fancy Food.* Plycon Press. Redondo Beach, CA.

Kubly, H. 1961. *Italy.* Time, Inc. New York.

Mayes, F. 1996. *Under the Tuscan Sun.* Broadway Books. New York.

Pearcy, G. E. 1980. *The World Food Scene.* Plycon Press. Redondo Beach, CA.

Pinder, D. 1998. *The New Europe: Economy, Society, and Environment.* John Wiley and Sons. New York.

Porter, D., and D. Prince. 1997. *Italy.* Macmillan. New York.

Root, W. 1968. *The Cooking of Italy.* Time-Life Books. New York.

Toor, F. 1953. *Festivals and Folkways of Italy.* Crown Publishers. New York.

9   France

Geographic Overview

France is bordered by Spain on the south and by Italy, Switzerland, Germany, and Belgium on the east. Along the west lies the Atlantic Ocean, with the English Channel forming the barrier in the north and the Mediterranean lapping the southern shores of France. Thus, France is in a key location in western Europe. The climate near the Mediterranean generally is quite mild—almost semitropical at times—certainly much less severe than in countries to the north. Rainfall throughout France is usually adequate for producing excellent crops.

France has portions of two mountain ranges, the Pyrenees along the border with Spain and the Alps, which loom over into France from Switzerland and Italy. Only a small fraction of the French landscape actually is mountainous. Much of the country is a highland area known as the Central Massif, which is ringed by two low-lying areas, the Paris Basin and the Loire Valley toward the northwest and the Rhone Valley eastward. The Seine River, which passes through Paris on its way toward the English Channel, and the Rhine River, which forms part of the border with Germany, are two other rivers that are among the geographic features of France.

France is one of the agricultural leaders in Europe, producing significant quantities of export commodities. The climate is very favorable for production of wheat, and also for corn, barley, and oats. The delta of the Rhone even serves as a site for production of rice for domestic use. In addition to such root crops as potatoes and sugar beets, domestic production of vegetables and fruits contributes a wide array of high-quality produce. The range of climates from north to south enables farmers to grow almost any fruits and vegetables except those that require tropical growing conditions. One of the particularly successful crops is grapes for wine (Figure 9.1). Although the varieties vary from one region of France to another, many areas are recognized as the sources of some of the world's leading

Figure 9.1 The climate in many parts of France is well suited to growing the grapes that are so vital to the nation's wine industry.

wines. Livestock include cattle and pigs for meat, poultry, and also dairy herds for milk, cream, and cheese. Although fishing is not a main industry, excellent fish are harvested from the surrounding waters for domestic consumption.

France is surprisingly diverse in its character in different parts of the country. Geographers often designate different regions as follows: The Ile de France is the area within a 50-mile radius of Paris. The Ardennes is the area north of Paris between Ile de France and the English Channel. Immediately west of Ardennes is Normandy, the region that includes the beaches where allies landed on D-Day in 1944 during World War II. Brittany is the peninsula that juts out into the Atlantic Ocean at the northwest corner of France. Just east of Brittany and south of Normandy is the Loire Valley, the region where royalty built their lovely, sumptuous estates. Continuing down the west side of France, the Atlantic coast region is home to some of the finest vineyards and wineries, as well as cognac. This is the region of Bordeaux. The Basque Country is just south of Biarritz, a posh seaside resort on the Bay of Biscay, and the Pyrenees provide a rugged southern border. Northward and inland is Perigord, the home of *foie gras* and truffles. The region

Figure 9.2 The thick, high walls and narrow windows served as a fortress for the people of Carcassone for several centuries.

of Languedoc-Roussillon is a marshy locale where the Rhone River forms its delta on its way into the Mediterranean Sea in the south of France. Carcassonne (Figure 9.2), a famous walled city founded by Visigoths in the 5th century, served as an almost impregnable fortress until the mid-17th century for the people living in the delta area. Now, the secure walls are invaded daily by throngs of tourists rather than by arrow-armed invaders.

The French Riviera is to the east of Marseille, and the famous region of Provence is just to the north. Avignon was the location of the Pope during the 14th century, when the rivalry existed with the Vatican in Rome. Burgundy is a large region in the east of France, while Alsace-Lorraine (just to the north) and Champagne (lying east of Paris) are other regions of France of importance in the production of wine and other products.

History and Culture

Evidence of early man in southern France is found in the caves at Lascaux (near Perigueux). The remarkable paintings of what appear to be animals such as deer, wild boar, and bulls were apparently done by people living in the Stone Age between 15,000 and 20,000 years ago. Jump now to a bit more than a century before Christ, and you will discover that the region around the caves and on to the north became part of the Roman Empire (Figure 9.3). The antecedent to the city of Paris was established in 52 BCE by the Romans on an island in the Seine, a spot that is part of Paris today. Along with many buildings in the region, the Romans left the Catholic Church firmly entrenched as a part of the local culture by the time they were defeated by the Franks and Clovis I in 511 CE. More than two centuries later, Charlemagne, who then was leader of the Franks, established his Carolingian dynasty and was even crowned Emperor of the Holy Roman Empire by the Pope in Rome in 800 CE. Although Charlemagne ruled over the areas that encompass both France and Germany today, his empire was divided after his death to define the boundaries that still are basically the same today.

The next landmark event after Charlemagne's rule was the conquest of England in 1066 by William the Conqueror. This set the stage for repeated contests between England and France, including the efforts of Joan of Arc to inspire the French to drive the English out of France. Her burning at the stake in Rouen in 1431 has been the subject of numerous plays and heated discussions over the intervening centuries.

Figure 9.3 The Pont du Gard aqueduct is a legacy from the Roman occupation of southern France in the days of the Roman Empire.

Figure 9.4 The palace at Versailles, clearly shows the opulence of the French monarchy, which led to the French Revolution.

Perhaps the best known monarchs of France are those beginning with Louis XIV (the Sun King), who ruled from 1643 to 1715. He was a powerful ruler who fostered a quite-luxurious court. This tradition of opulence (Figure 9.4) peaked during the reign of Louis XVI, who ruled from 1774 until the French Revolution of 1789, when he and his wife Marie Antoinette were imprisoned and ultimately submitted to the guillotine. The bloodshed that followed finally led to the emergence of Napoleon Bonaparte, who became the First Consul and Master of France in Paris in 1799. He led subsequent military attacks that were successful in northern Italy, but which led to his downfall when he had to retreat from Moscow in 1812 and then was defeated at Waterloo in 1815. The Franco-Prussian War later in the 19th century and both world wars in the 20th century were fought on French soil, which has taken a toll on both population and economy. However, France today is a vigorous and productive European nation.

As might be surmised from the many beautiful cathedrals in France and from such special places as the grotto at Lourdes, where the young Bernadette reportedly had 18 visions of the Virgin Mary, France is predominantly a Catholic country. The holidays also reflect the importance of Catholicism, although Protestants share some of these days, such as Christmas and Easter, which actually is celebrated on the Monday following Easter Sunday. Ascension Day, Whit Monday, Feast of the Assumption, and All Saints Day are other religious holidays. Not surprisingly, war events are also marked as holidays. These include Bastille Day on July 14, which celebrates the fall of the Bastille in 1789 at the beginning of the French Revolution, Victory in Europe Day (May 8 celebration marking liberation in World War II), and Armistice Day (November 11, the end of World War I).

Despite the many battles that have been fought in France during the past few centuries, the world is still the richer for the creativity of some of the French writers, musicians, architects, and artists. Voltaire, Balzac, Colette, and Victor Hugo are among the more prominent French writers. Composers from France include Saint Saëns, Debussy, Franck, Chausson, Fauré, Gounod, and Poulenc.

Paris has been like a magnet for creative people from many countries, not just for the French. For example, George Gershwin immortalized Paris with his "American in Paris" score, and Ernest Hemingway and such other notable writers as James Joyce gathered there to share the excitement of that unique city and its residents.

Architecture in France again shows creativity. The Gothic cathedrals featured pointed arches and stained glass windows, which were made possible by

Figure 9.5   The flying buttresses at the rear of Notre Dame provided the support necessary to build the soaring cathedral walls.

reinforcing the walls with exterior flying buttresses (Figure 9.5), as can be seen in Notre Dame in Paris. Numerous examples of Gothic cathedrals are found throughout France. The lovely castles and homes of royalty are found in several locations; the Loire Valley has such special ones as Chenonceau, which gained a unique feature when Catherine de Medici extended the palace by having a two-story gallery added across the river flowing beside the rest of the palace. The palace at Versailles outside of Paris is particularly well known for its Hall of Mirrors, where the treaty ending World War I was signed. In a totally different style, the Eiffel Tower was constructed in 1889 as a highlight for the Universal Exhibition; it still affords a commanding view of Paris. A less visible but nevertheless contemporary addition to Paris is the 1989 71-foot high pyramid designed by I. M. Pei to serve as the new entrance to France's most famous museum, the Louvre. A nearby museum, the Musée d' Orsay, is a converted train station now housing a fabulous collection of paintings by the Impressionists.

France contributed the Impressionist movement to the art world, a movement that has continued to be extremely popular among art lovers around the world. Pisarro was among the first of the French Impressionists. This group eventually included Cezanne, Gaugin, Manet, Degas, Monet, and Renoir, plus others, such as van Gogh, who came to France from other countries to paint with the French Impressionists.

There is yet another dimension to the contributions the French have made to the world, and that is the realm of haute couture (high fashion). Paris has been the focal point of elegant fashions and sometimes "far out" designs for many years, although Milan and other spots have challenged this dominance at times.

Food Patterns

The concept of French haute cuisine surprisingly stems from the Italian Renaissance figure Catherine de Medici, who brought her Florentine chefs with her when she moved to France as a bride to the future King Henry II in 1553. The elegance and

Even in the Middle Ages, a great French cook enjoyed such special privileges as carrying the first dish to the banquet table and occupying the coziest seat in the kitchen, by the chimney corner. He also had the right to carry a big wooden spoon as a symbol of his importance, and he could use that for tasting as well as to wave when scolding his assistants.

appreciation of fine food grew amidst the splendor of King Louis XIV. A cookbook written by Françoise Pierre de la Varenne, a famous chef of that period, added further refinement to French cooking despite the emphasis on gluttony in the royal court. Another famous French food writer is Brillat-Savarin (1755–1826), who wrote the classic *The Physiology of Taste*. Escoffier, perhaps the most famous French chef who was also a writer, wrote definitive books chronicling haute cuisine during his lifetime (1846–1935). It remained for Julia Child, in collaboration with Louisette Bertholle and Simone Beck, to bring widespread interest in French food to America in 1961 via their book *Mastering the Art of French Cooking*.

Sauces play a significant role in French cuisine. *Béchamel* (basic white sauce made with butter, milk, seasonings, and flour), hollandaise (emulsion of egg yolks, lemon juice, seasonings, and melted butter), béarnaise (similar to hollandaise except that vinegar, shallots, and seasonings are reduced, then used in place of the lemon juice), and *velouté* (similar to béchamel except a veal or chicken stock is used in place of milk or cream) are some of the basic French sauces.

Classic French cooking is time-consuming in its preparation and presentation, but is deemed by many appreciative diners in fancy restaurants around the world to be well worth the effort. The range of menu items is complete, from elaborate hors d'oeuvres to the most delectable and eye-appealing desserts possible. Some dishes, such as quiches, utilize flaky pastry. Soufflés and crêpes are other French creations that may be found at just about any point in a menu. Even the names of French creations heighten the drama of the food. Examples might be *quenelles* (dumplings made of pureed fish or other protein mixed into a cream puff dough and then poached), mousse (molded creation given its stability by using gelatin in the recipe), paté (finely mashed and seasoned spread of some type of meat), flan (baked custard), and *gâteaux* (cakes).

Provincial French cooking is less elaborate, but certainly as flavorful and delightful on the palate as the haute cuisine. As the name implies, provincial French cooking is food as it originates in the various provinces and which feature particularly fine ingredients from the immediate locale. The provincial foods of Brittany emphasize foods from the sea because of its peninsular setting. Normandy dishes feature milk, cream, and apples, all of which are abundant there. Quiche Lorraine is named for its origin in Alsace-Lorraine and is a tart with an open face revealing its flavorful custard and bacon filling. Burgundy boasts of *boeuf bourguignon*, its namesake beef dish utilizing beef stock, red wine from the region, onion, carrot, and little boiling onions with beef stew meat, all of which are braised together for up to 4 hours until the meat is extremely tender. Dishes originating in Provence are especially flavorful creations, stemming in large measure from the judicious use of the flavorful herbs that flourish in this region of southern France. Ratatouille is a wonderful vegetable medley that comes from Provence. *Cassoulet* is a delectable casserole starring white beans, carrots, and onions, plus duck and herbs, which was created in Toulouse in southwestern France. Bordelaise is the dark sauce that utilizes meat juices, bone marrow, tarragon, and shallots in combination with Bordeaux, the hearty red wine from the Bordeaux region. The fish stew called bouillabaisse is yet another famous dish from the Mediterranean coast of France.

Breakfast in France gets scant attention, usually being simply café au lait (coffee with milk) and a croissant or bread, maybe with jam, eaten in time to get to work by 8:00. Coffee break is not an established tradition, but dinner is important in the middle of the day, requiring at least an hour and a half to do it justice. The afternoon work schedule again is unbroken, leaving a good appetite when people depart from the job either to home or to a cafe for a bit of spirits and eventually a pleasing meal, which may be somewhat less elaborate than the midday meal.

Key Terms

Alsace-Lorraine—Eastern region of France bordering Germany.

Ardennes—Region north of Paris to the English Channel.

Béarnaise sauce—Sauce similar to hollandaise, but with vinegar, shallots, and seasoning used in place of lemon juice.

Béchamel sauce—Basic white sauce made with cream or milk and thickened with flour.

Boeuf bourguignon—French beef stew with vegetables and red wine.

Bordeaux—Western region of France that is home to some outstanding wines and cognac.

Bordelaise sauce—Dark sauce made with meat juices, bone marrow, tarragon, shallots, and Bordeaux wine.

Bouillabaisse—Hearty fish stew from the Mediterranean coast of France.

Brillat-Savarin—Author of *The Physiology of Taste.*

Brittany—Peninsula jutting from the northwest corner of France.

Burgundy—Region on the eastern side of France north of the Rhone Valley and southeast of Paris; also a wine produced in the region.

Café au lait—Coffee with milk, the most common breakfast beverage.

Carcassonne—Walled city founded by Visigoths and serving as a fortress in southwest France during the Middle Ages.

Cassoulet—Casserole dish from Toulouse made with white beans, onions, carrots, duck, and herbs.

Champagne—Region east of Paris where the sparkling wine is produced.

Crêpe—Thin French pancake.

Escoffier—Chef considered to be the definitive writer about French cuisine (1846–1935).

Flying buttress—External architectural feature to support the relatively thin and windowed walls of Gothic cathedrals.

Gothic—Style of cathedral featuring pointed arches and high, thin walls containing stained glass, and strengthened by flying buttresses on the exterior.

Hollandaise sauce—Sauce made of an emulsion of butter, egg yolks, lemon juice, and seasoning.

Ile de France—Region within a 50-mile circle of Paris.

Languedoc-Roussillon—Region in southern France that includes the marshy delta of the Rhone River.

Lascaux—Area in southern France where cave paintings from prehistoric people have been found.

Normandy—Northern region of France just east of Brittany and lying along the coast of the English Channel.

Perigord—Area north of the Pyrenees where truffles are found.

Provence—Region in southern France adjacent to the French Riviera.

Ratatouille—Highly flavorful medley of vegetables and herbs from Provence.

Soufflé—Baked foam of egg whites combined with a yolk and chocolate (or cheese or other flavoring) sauce.

Truffles—Dark, subterranean fruiting bodies of a fungus; especially rare and flavorful ingredient prized in French recipes.

Velouté sauce—Basic flour-thickened sauce made with a fish or chicken stock.

ecipes

French Onion Soup (Serves 6)

1 lb onions, thinly sliced
2 tbsp butter
4 tsp flour
1/2 tsp salt
4 c beef stock
6 slices French bread (1" thick)
Olive oil
Garlic clove, cut
1/2 c grated Swiss cheese

1. Slowly saute onions in butter in a Dutch oven for about 20 minutes to a golden brown.
2. Sprinkle flour and salt over onions. Stir while cooking for 3 more minutes.
3. Add the stock and simmer (covered) for 30 minutes.
4. Meanwhile, brush bread lightly with olive oil on both sides and place on baking sheet.
5. Dry the bread in 325°F oven until lightly browned on both sides.
6. Rub toast with garlic.
7. Ladle soup into oven-proof soup bowls, top with toast and then grated cheese.
8. Place bowls on baking sheet in 375°F oven and heat until cheese melts, then top-broil to brown the cheese a bit.

Sausage Soup (Serves 6–8)

3/4 lb smoked sausage (1/4" thick slices)
3 slices bacon, diced
1 large onion, chopped
4 1/2 c water
2 turnips, cubed
2 carrots, sliced
1 leek, sliced thinly
3 potatoes, diced
2 c shredded cabbage
1/2 tsp salt
1/4 tsp pepper

1 tbsp parsley, chopped

1. Brown sausage, bacon, and onion in Dutch oven over medium heat.
2. Remove fat; add water and heat to boiling.
3. Add turnips, carrots, leek, and potatoes.
4. Simmer 35 minutes, then add cabbage, salt, and pepper.
5. Simmer 5 minutes more; then serve garnished with parsley.

Quiche Lorraine (Serves 4–6)

1 c flour
1/4 tsp salt
1/3 c shortening
8 tsps water
4 strips of bacon
1/2 c chopped onion
2 eggs, beaten
1/2 c dairy sour cream
1/4 tsp salt
4 oz grated Swiss cheese (optional)

1. Stir flour and salt, then cut shortening into rice-sized grains with pastry blender.
2. Use fork to toss flour mixture while sprinkling water slowly all over mixture.
3. Stir to moisten all flour, then turn onto foil and form into ball.
4. Roll pastry to fit quiche pan and fit in pan.
5. Microwave bacon for 3 minutes or until crisp.
6. Crumble bacon and combine all other ingredients.
7. Pour into pastry and bake in 375°F oven until set (about 30 minutes).

Cheese Soufflé (Serves 4)

1/4 c butter
1/4 c flour
1/4 tsp salt
1 c milk
1/4 lb cheddar cheese, grated
4 eggs, separated
1/2 tsp cream of tartar

1. Melt butter in 1-qt saucepan.
2. Stir in flour and salt completely, then stir in milk until smooth.
3. Heat, stirring constantly, until mixture thickens and boils.
4. Add cheese, heating only if needed to melt cheese.
5. Meanwhile, beat yolks.
6. Stir spoonful of cheese mix into yolks; repeat three times.
7. Stir yolk mix into sauce; set aside to cool.
8. Beat whites with electric mixer until frothy, then add cream of tartar.
9. Continue beating until peaks just bend over.
10. Pour sauce at the edge of the whites and use rubber spatula to gently but thoroughly fold the sauce into the whites until there are no streaks of yellow.
11. Pour into soufflé dish and bake in preheated oven at 325°F for 55 minutes (until knife inserted in center comes out clean). Serve immediately.

Chicken Normandy (Serves 4–6)

1 frying chicken (in pieces)
2 onions, chopped
3 tbsp butter
1 tsp parsley
1/4 tsp thyme
6 tbsp cider
2 tbsp cream

1. Brown chicken in butter; add onions and brown.
2. Add seasonings and cider; cover Dutch oven and simmer until chicken is tender.
3. Remove chicken and keep warm while reducing juices to half and add cream. Serve over chicken.

Ratatouille (Serves 4–6)

2 garlic cloves, minced
1 large onion, chopped
3 tbsp olive oil
1 1/2 c diced eggplant
1 1/2 c diced zucchini
1 green pepper, very coarsely chopped
1 red pepper, very coarsely chopped
4 Roma tomatoes
1 tsp salt

1 tsp pepper
1 tbsp fresh basil, minced

1. Saute garlic and onions in oil until soft.
2. Add all other ingredients.
3. Simmer over moderate heat for 10 minutes while stirring.
4. Bake in a casserole in 350°F oven 30 minutes. Serve hot or cold.

Cherries Jubilee (Serves 4–6)

2/3 c red currant jelly
2 c canned dark sweet cherries (Bing) and juice
2 tsp cornstarch
1/4 tsp each ground cloves, cinnamon, and allspice
1/2 tsp grated lemon rind
2 tsp grated orange rind
1/4 c kirsch (cherry brandy)
2/3 qt vanilla ice cream

1. In chafing dish, melt jelly.

2. Drain cherry juice; blend with cornstarch until smooth.
3. Stir juice into jelly and heat to boiling while stirring vigorously.
4. Add spices, rinds, and cherries, and heat until cherries are hot.
5. Warm kirsch in very small pan, then pour onto hot cherry sauce. Immediately ignite with a long match without stirring.
6. Very carefully spoon onto each dish of vanilla ice cream.

Crêpes Suzette (Serves 6–8)

1 1/4 c flour
3 tbsp sugar
1 3/4 c milk
4 eggs
1/4 c Grand Marnier (or Cointreau)
2 tbsp melted butter (cooled)
1/4 lb butter
1/2 tsp grated lemon rind
2 tsp grated orange rind
1/2 c orange juice, strained
3 tbsp sugar
1/4 c Grand Marnier (or Cointreau)
2 tbsp dark rum

1. In a blender, blend flour, sugar, milk, eggs, liquur, and 2 tablespoons melted butter for about 40 seconds, stopping and scraping sides; blend until smooth.
2. Heat 5" skillet (nonstick coating) until water drop skips and evaporates immediately.

3. Pour 2 tablespoons batter into pan and immediately tip it to coat bottom. Pour any excess batter back with remainder of batter.
4. Heat skillet until edges of crêpe brown a bit; flip and cook for 1 more minute.
5. Stack baked crêpes on plate.
6. Repeat steps 2 to 4 with rest of batter. (Freeze extras.)
7. Melt 1/4 lb butter in chafing dish, then add rinds, juice, and sugar.
8. Heat to reduce to 1/2 cup sauce.
9. Using a serving spoon in one hand and a fork in the other, transfer a crêpe to the chafing dish and moisten both sides of it, fold it into quarters, and place it at edge of chafing dish. Repeat with all crêpes to be served.
10. Pour liqueur and rum into center of chafing dish. Ignite with a match if it has not flamed.
11. As soon as flame ceases, spoon sauce over crêpes and serve.

Summary

The geography of France is well suited to raising a wide variety of crops in most regions. Cereals, particularly wheat, thrive in the relatively level terrain of the country. Produce is grown close enough to the cities to provide an abundance of fruits and vegetables in season. Grapes for producing wines are grown in several regions, with the varieties varying according to the specific growing conditions of each locale. Livestock for meat and dairy products are important aspects of France's agriculture. Some fishing is done to add to the food supply.

The numerous unique regions in France include Ile de France (surrounding Paris for 50 miles), the Ardennes, Normandy, Brittany, the Loire Valley, Bordeaux, the Basque Country, Perigord, Languedoc-Roussillon, French Riviera, Provence, Burgundy, Alsace-Lorraine, and Champagne.

France was part of the Roman Empire for more than 500 years. Romans left buildings and a strong Catholic Church behind when they were defeated by the Franks and Clovis; eventually, Charlemagne not only ruled France, but also was crowned Emperor of the Holy Roman Empire in 800 CE by the Pope in Rome.

William the Conqueror invaded England in 1066. Tempestuous relations between England and France persisted for a very long time. The splendor of court life during the reign of Louis XIV and continuing to Louis XVI was shattered with the storming of the Bastille and the French Revolution in 1789. Ten years later Napoleon became Consul and Master of France and began his military attacks that resulted in a retreat from Moscow in 1812 and defeat at Waterloo in 1815. Subsequently, France has survived the Franco-Prussian War and World Wars I and II.

France has provided a setting that inspired considerable creative accomplishments in all of the arts: literature, music, painting, and sculpture. Architectural contributions include the Gothic cathedrals and their flying buttresses, as well as lovely castles and palaces. In addition to tours of these buildings, excellent museums make it possible to view many of the art works.

Food has been a passion in France, particularly among royalty and the well-to-do. This has led to the development of haute cuisine, which emphasizes complex preparations and very carefully crafted presentations to please the eye as well as the palate. Provincial French cooking is less elaborate, but still exciting for diners. Sauces, soufflés, crêpes, mousse, paté, flan, and gâteaux are just some of the dishes created by the French. A wide vocabulary of culinary terms has been developed by the French and adopted by many serious cooks and professional chefs throughout the world.

Study Questions

1. Identify the region where each of the following are produced: (a) champagne, (b) Bordeaux, (c) burgundy, and (d) truffles.
2. What contribution(s) did each of the following people make: (a) Escoffier, (b) Monet, (c) Debussy, (d) Brillat-Savarin, (e) Renoir, (f) Victor Hugo, and (g) Gounod?
3. Why are flying buttresses necessary for large Gothic cathedrals?
4. How is a soufflé prepared?
5. Name five sauces used in French cooking and describe each one.

Bibliography

Child, J., et al. 1961. *Mastering the Art of French Cooking.* Alfred A. Knopf. New York.

Claiborne, C., et al. 1970. *Classic French Cooking.* Time-Life Books. New York.

Evans, E. S. 1966. *France: An Introductory Geography.* Frederick A. Praeger. New York.

Kramer, M. 1988. *Illustrated Guide to Foreign and Fancy Food.* Plycon Press. Redondo Beach, CA.

LaCroix, P. 1963. *France in the Middle Ages.* Frederick Ungar Publishing Co. New York.

Mayle, P. 1989. *A Year in Provence.* Vintage Books. New York.

McKay, J. P., B. D. Hill, and J. Buckler. 1999. *History of Western Society.* Houghton Mifflin. Boston.

McWilliams, M. 1998. *Illustrated Guide to Food Preparation.* 8th ed. Plycon Press. Redondo Beach, CA.

Pearcy, G. E. 1980. *World Food Scene.* Plycon Press. Redondo Beach, CA.

Porter, D. and D. Prince. 1998. *France.* Macmillan. New York.

Viault, B. S. 1990. *Western Civilization since 1600.* McGraw-Hill. New York.

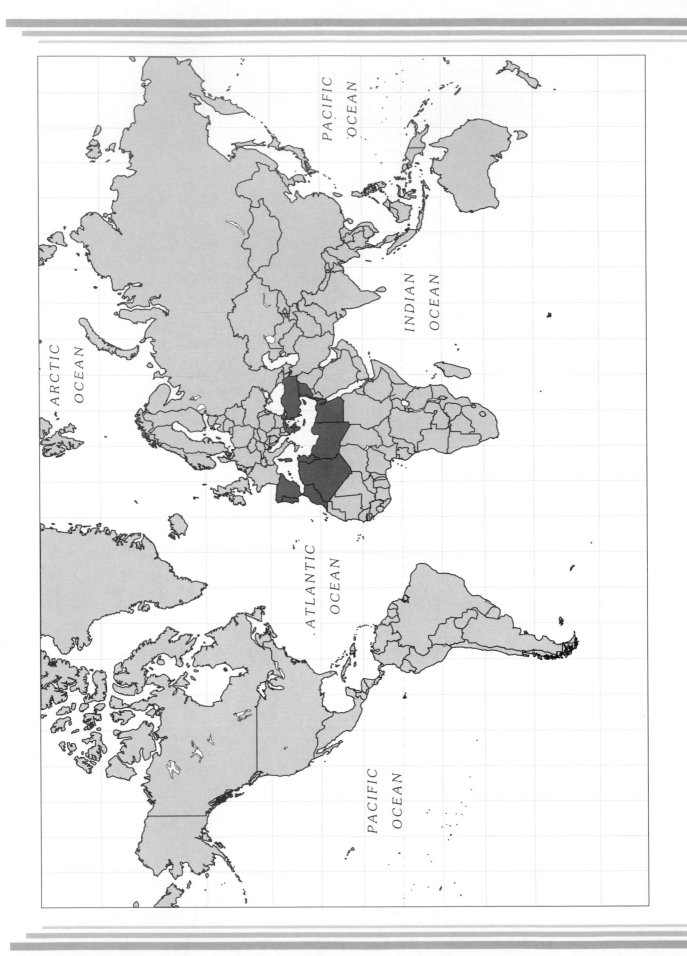

Part III

Enriched by the Mediterranean Sphere

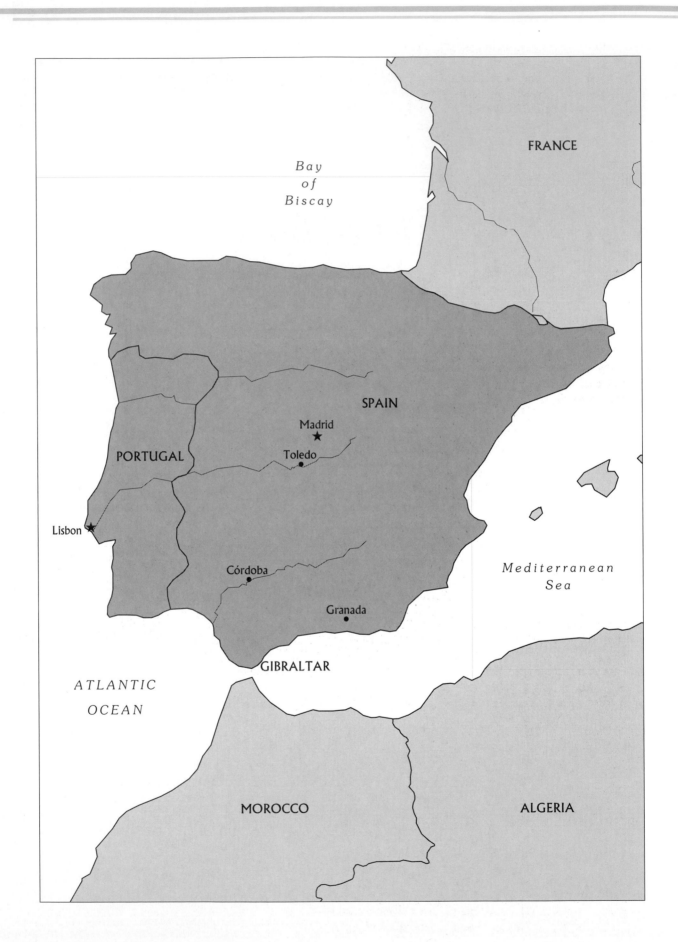

10 The Iberian Peninsula

Geographic Overview

Although the Iberian Peninsula actually is a part of Europe (the southwestern corner) and has a significant amount of land bordering the Atlantic Ocean, it nevertheless shares many commonalities with the various countries surrounding the Mediterranean Sea. Another reason for considering this region along with others in the domain of the Mediterranean is that the rugged Pyrenees Mountains form an extremely effective geographic barrier that promoted development of cultures that were quite different in France than in Spain despite the shared border. In fact, the proximity of the tip of this peninsula (Figure 10.1) to the continent of Africa made interactions with Africa somewhat easier than with other countries on the European continent.

Spain and Portugal are the only two countries on the Iberian Peninsula, and Spain is by far the larger, about five times larger than Portugal. Portugal is tucked along the Atlantic Ocean shoreline from the Gulf of Cadiz northward for more than 300 miles and extending eastward in a rectangular shape about 200 miles. The south-facing shoreline of Portugal along the Gulf of Cadiz is a famous resort area known as the Algarve. Lisbon, the capital, is on the Atlantic about a third of the way north in the country at the mouth of the Tagus River. The other river emptying into the Atlantic is the Douro, which is where the famous home of port wine, Oporto, is located.

Spain is centered by the Spanish Meseta, which is a rather barren and large plateau about 2,000 feet high, and is ringed by mountains that rise to 11,000 feet and more in the Sierra Nevada in Andalusia (southern Spain) and in the Pyrenees. Green Spain on the north and northwest of the peninsula has sufficient rain to keep it verdant, whereas the climate is dry and hot in summer in much of the

Figure 10.1   The Rock of Gibraltar serves as an imposing sentinel on the northern side of the strait linking the Atlantic Ocean and the Mediterranean.

rest of Spain. Winters can be a bit harsh on the Spanish Meseta, although snow generally is seen in Spain only in the mountains.

The result is that agricultural efforts in both Spain and Portugal are hindered by terrain and weather. However, wheat can be grown in the northern Meseta regions, and some rice is grown where irrigation is possible. Corn, potatoes, apples, and rye are other crops. In Portugal and southern Spain wine grapes are grown, and both countries are noted for some distinctive wines (Portugal for its port and rose wines and Madeira, and Spain for its sherry and many fine wines from various parts of the country). The Mediterranean climate and the somewhat rocky soil of the southern part of Spain also are well suited to growing olives and oranges. The production of olives and olive oil is a large business. Livestock production is primarily sheep and pigs, with sheep being particularly well suited to rugged lands such as that of the Basques in the Pyrenees. Cork trees in both countries also are a source of income from the land, albeit an inedible crop.

*H*istory and *C*ulture

The history of Portugal and Spain, like its geography, is somewhat intertwined. Actually, early destiny of the peninsula was shaped by the Romans, but when their empire collapsed, the peninsula gradually underwent invasions from different directions. Germanic tribes ventured in from Europe, and the Moors successfully began taking over much land in 711 CE when they crossed over from North Africa. Christian attempts to rid the continent of the Moors and their Islamic influence began in the northern part of the Iberian Peninsula, with the result that Portugal became a nation state in 1139, according to the declaration of King Afonso Henriques.

Portugal's numerous voyages of discovery began in the first half of the 15th century with sea voyages that reached the Azores and later in the century rounded the Cape of Good Hope at the southern tip of Africa. Prince Henry the Navigator was the first Portuguese leader to show support and interest in developing the trade possibilities along the west coast of Africa (Figure 10.2). Among the famous Portuguese who explored and claimed distant places for their country were Magellan (leader of the first circumnavigation of the world from 1519 to 1522, but who was killed in the Philippines), Bartolomeu Dias (who sailed around the Cape of Good Hope in 1488), and Vasco da Gama (credited with opening trade routes to India with his voyages in 1498 and 1502).

Considerable wealth came to Portugal from Brazil (1500 to 1822), Goa (next to India) from 1510 to 1960, and Macao (1557 to 1999) over many years following the navigational exploits of the early explorers. Brazil became independent in 1822, Goa was annexed to India in 1960, and Macao reverted from trading post status to China in 1999, thus ending the imperial phase of Portugal's history.

Spain remained in the grip of the Moors for about 350 years as the Christians gradually drove the Muslims from Toledo in 1085. Around this time, El Cid (actually named Ruy Diaz de Vivar) became a Spanish hero for his military exploits despite that he sometimes fought for the Moors and sometimes for the Catholics. He is best known for freeing Valencia from the Moors in 1094.

The Catholics finally defeated the Moors at Granada in 1492 and forced them back to Africa. This defeat left the Catholic monarchs Ferdinand and Isabella in power. Under their dominion, extensive voyages of discovery were sponsored; Columbus was launched almost immediately on his voyage of discovery that resulted in his finding the "New World." From the Spanish perspective, the voyages of Columbus and subsequent adventurers (Cortés and Pizarro) brought back great riches, resulting in Spain becoming a powerful and wealthy nation.

The Inquisition wrote a sad chapter in Spain's history during this same period, for Jews, Moors, and all other non-Catholics were required to either convert to Catholicism or leave the country. The result was severe torture or displacement, or both, for those who were the targets, and the country lost large numbers of bright and creative people—a tragedy for all, which extended to the Spanish-dominated regions of South America and continued on both continents well into the 18th century.

Meanwhile, although its trade relationships were being maintained with its empire over the centuries, Portugal itself was undergoing numerous upheavals, including domination by Spain. In fact, Spain launched its attack on England with its Armada sailing from the port of Lisbon in 1588. A war for independence from Spain was waged in Portugal from 1640 to 1668. Numerous attempts at various types of government marked the period following Spanish dominance. Antonio Salazar was politically active in the 20th century, beginning with his title of finance minister in 1928 and continuing with his title of prime minister of Portugal in 1932 until his retirement in 1968.

Spain lost much of its power in Europe by the end of the 16th century. Its famed Armada of 133 ships was defeated when it tried to invade England in 1588,

Figure 10.2 Portugal still owns the island of Madeira in the Atlantic Ocean.

a financial as well as a psychological blow to Spain's image. Actually, Spain was viewed in Europe almost as a pawn during the 17th and 18th centuries, as the Hapsburgs and the Bourbons and later even Napoleon used Spain to their own advantage at different times.

A civil war raged within Spain from 1931 to 1939, further adding to the stresses the nation faced. From this period, Franco emerged as the dictator, and he continued to hold power until his death in 1975, even though a king had been named in 1969. Both Spain and Portugal were able to remain neutral in World Wars I and II, aided significantly in this position by the geography of the peninsula. This same geography, notably the Pyrenees where the Basque population lives, has enabled the Basque separatist movement to continue for an extended period to the present. Other developments have caused Spain to evolve into basically a democracy with a parliament and a king.

Despite the frequent exchanges and interactions between Spain and Portugal, each nation has maintained its individual language, Portuguese being the language in Portugal (and also Brazil) and Castilian being the official Spanish language. There are other major dialects spoken in different parts of Spain, including Catalan, Galician, and Basque. A unique characteristic of Castilian is the practice of speaking with what seems to be a lisp, or *th* sound, rather than an *s* when a soft *c* or *s* is followed by the letters e, i, or z. Rumor has it that this practice was adopted when the region was ruled by a king who lisped.

By far the dominant religion in both Portugal and Spain is Catholicism. This is not surprising in view of the early rule by Romans who were Catholic and also as a continuing result of the long period of the Inquisition. The Muslim influence spread by the conquering Moors centuries ago was expunged when the Christian forces of Ferdinand and Isabella ultimately drove the Moors out of Spain in 1492. However, the role the Islamic religion played during the reign of the Moors is evident from the remnants of mosques that remain in both countries. The occupation by the Moors in Portugal was confined largely to the southern portion and for a comparatively short time, but still Arab characteristics are seen.

What started as a Portuguese tradition to honor their favorite saint, St. Anthony, on Saints Day has evolved into an intense competition. Each year, ever-taller and more elaborate thrones are built and paraded through the streets so the thrones can be presented to St. Anthony.

The most amazing reminder of the Moslem presence in Spain is the huge mosque at Cordoba. This mosque dates from 758 CE and has been modified many times by various builders, the most lavish of whom was al Hakam II. He added a fancy *mihrab* (prayer niche) and *maqsura* for the caliph in the 10th century. The remarkable aspect of this imposing mosque is that the Catholics, who subsequently came into control of the mosque after defeating the Moors, built their own cathedral within the inner portion of the mosque. It is a somewhat curious sight to encounter an Italianate cathedral within the depths of the 850 granite columns that serve as the supports for the roof of the mosque.

The architectural heritage of the Moors is seen throughout southern Spain. One of the most exciting sights is the Alhambra at Granada. This royal complex was built atop a hill overlooking the main part of Granada and appears as a most graceful reminder of the delicacy of line and the ornamentation that marked the buildings during the Moorish occupation of Spain (Figure 10.3). The only jarring note within the walled complex is the palace that King Charles had constructed later in a much heavier style in 1526. A particularly refreshing and lovely estate called the Generalife is connected to the Alhambra by way of a short path and lovely gardens.

One of the distinctive notes in many Portuguese and Spanish buildings is the tiles that add artistic touches throughout many homes and public buildings. These painted ceramic tiles are one manifestation of the love of beauty shared by the people occupying the Iberian Peninsula. Styles of painting, subjects, and colors vary with the time in history and the skill and artistry of the tile painters. Decorated ceramic dishes, vases, figures, and pots are all part of the cultural heritage.

A unique part of Portuguese culture is a form of blues from Lisbon; this music is called *fado*. Fado is a heartfelt vocal accompanied by a classical guitar

Figure 10.3 The Lion's Court in the Alhambra features the center fountain, which is supported by several lion statues.

and an acoustic guitar, or both. Fado has also been the subject of paintings. One of the most famous Portuguese writers was Eca de Quieros. Jose Mulhoa was an artist of some renown from Portugal.

Among the names of Spanish artists that spring to mind are Velázquez, Murillo, and El Greco, painters from the 16th and 17th centuries. Actually, El Greco was born in Crete, but generally is considered a Spanish painter because he painted in Spain for the rest of his life after he arrived in his 30s. Goya also was a prominent Spanish artist, but he painted during the late 18th and early 19th centuries. Picasso, Miró, and Dali are prominent among 20th century artists born in Spain, but who did much of their work in France and other places because of the civil unrest in Spain during their lives. A 20th century architect who showed a very creative style was Gaudi, who is particularly noted for his unfinished Church of the Holy Family and numerous remarkable homes and other buildings in Barcelona. The most familiar Spanish writer is Cervantes (1562–1635), who wrote *Don Quixote* and so clearly portrayed human dignity and innate goodness through this character and his faithful companion Sancho Panza.

Music seems to be an inherent part of the Spanish soul, and some wonderful musicians contribute particularly to the cultural heritage of Spain. The names of artists such as Segovia and Casals have been known to concert-goers around the globe during the 20th century. Other well-known performers today include Placido Domingo and Alicia de Larrocha. Flamenco, thought to have been brought by the gypsies in the 1500s, is a dance that has captured the essence of Spain. Its exciting rhythms and melodies skillfully played on the guitar to accompany the song provide high drama to the gypsy-like dances. Stamping feet, clapping, and a sense of urgency or sadness add to the flavor of flamenco.

Bullfighting is a key national sport in both Spain and Portugal. Some feel that this is definitely an artistic element on the Spanish scene. Certainly, matadors execute almost dance-like, artistic movements as they battle the bull. There also is considerable color in the traditions surrounding the fights, including the initial parade to present the *picadors* on horseback, the *banderillos* marching on foot, the matador, and the bull. A famous tradition related to bullfighting is the Running of the Bulls in Pamplona, a hazardous festivity featuring bulls running unfettered through the town in pursuit of people who risk their good health and sometimes their lives as they attempt to keep out of the reach of the stampeding bulls' horns.

Holidays in Spain and Portugal are reflective of the strong Catholic faith of the people. In addition to Christmas and Easter, many local celebrations are held honoring the various saints. Parades with elaborate floats and with penitents carrying crosses are seen at religious celebrations in Seville and some other cities in Spain.

Food Patterns

The extensive trading that the Portuguese did with distant parts of the world—South America, Macao in the Far East, Goa and India, and along the coast of Africa from the Atlantic around the Cape of Good Hope and the Indian Ocean—meant that exotic foods became a part of the meals when the adventurers brought back their discoveries. Corn, tomatoes, pineapples, potatoes, pumpkin, squash, beans, and coffee are examples of the foods from afar that became part of the culture of Portugal. Tea and a wide array of spices are yet other additions resulting from the voyages the Portuguese traders made in their caravels, which were sturdy vessels with lateen sails (triangular sails extended on a spar and flying from a rather low mast), launched by Prince Henry the Navigator to meet the challenges of sailing along the African coast. Added to these new foods was an abundance of salted, dried cod. This preserved fish fared well for use on long sea voyages and served as a mainstay for the Portuguese at home.

The typical food patterns of the Portuguese are generally quite simple. Breakfast is frequently a cup of coffee with milk (or hot chocolate) plus some bread and jam. Milk usually is only consumed at breakfast in one of these beverages and in the form of cheese at other times of day. It is not considered to be a beverage that is consumed alone. Lunch and dinner are quite substantial meals that more than make up for the slim breakfast menu. Although there is plenty of food, Portuguese meals are actually quite hearty and simple. This may reflect in part that many of the women work alongside their men, which limits the time available for preparing meals.

Pork (Figure 10.4) and fish are the most important sources of protein in Portuguese meals. Pork sausages of various types are very popular. Smoked ham is another form of pork that is common. Fish are available from the sea, but perhaps the most abundant fish included in meals is salted, dried cod. *Bachalhau* recipes are abundant in Portugal, with the salted, dried cod combined with greens, other vegetables, and seasonings adding an individual touch from the cook.

Figure 10.4   Many varieties of ham and sausages are very popular meats in Spain and Portugal.

Potatoes are a particularly important vegetable and may be served with other starch-rich foods, particularly with rice. Vegetables are almost always cooked rather than served raw. Kale, which is abundant, is the main ingredient in *caldo verde*, a soup featuring pork sausage, potatoes, garlic, and julienne slivers of kale. Eggs are served in many different ways, one of the favorites being caramel flan for dessert. Crusty breads are available and really enjoyed at meals. Wines from Portugal are popular as the beverage at meals, and coffee and tea also are often served.

The food in Spain tends to be more adventuresome and somewhat fancier than the dishes commonly served in Portugal. Probably the most familiar dish served in Spain is *paella*, a rice and meat dish that is prepared in a wide, shallow pan with sloping sides. The meat is first cooked in the paella pan until browned and then is set aside while the vegetable ingredients are sautéed. Rice and liquid are added before the meat is arranged on top. The assembled dish is baked on the floor of the oven for about 30 minutes to absorb the water in the rice and to blend the flavors while the meat finishes cooking. Saffron is always an ingredient in paella. The orange to yellow color of the rice in paella is the result of using saffron (the orange to yellow stigmas of purple crocus). This also adds to the flavor of the dish.

Another national tradition is *cocido*, which varies greatly from place to place but consists of three courses: clear soup, a platter of cooked vegetables, and an array of boiled meats. This is often consumed for the midday meal around 2:30 P.M. Appetites for this meal generally are quite large, for breakfast at around 7:00 A.M. probably was simply a cup of coffee with milk and a *churro* (a spiral-shaped fried bread similar to a doughnut). Spaniards typically have a long rest period for much of the hot afternoon. This is followed with more work before stopping that day's work to enjoy drinks and *tapas* (little plates of food served at bars) to help control appetites until dinner is served, usually at 10:00 P.M. or later. The Spanish people thrive on their late dining hours and sociable evenings. Life is not meant to be rushed in this warm climate.

Sopa de ajo (garlic soup) is a specialty in the central part of Spain. Sangriá (a wine-fruit punch) also is a favorite beverage; wines from various parts of Spain are a part of all meals except breakfast in Spain.

*K*ey Terms

Churro—Spiral-shaped quick-bread similar to a doughnut.

Cocido—Meal consisting of three traditional courses (soup, cooked vegetables, and boiled meats), the specific ingredients being quite variable.

Cortés—Spanish explorer in Central America, particularly Mexico, in the 16th century.

Diaz, Bartolomeu—Portuguese navigator who sailed around the Cape of Good Hope (southern tip of Africa) in 1488.

El Cid—Spanish military hero who fought many battles for both the Moors and the Catholics, and freed Valencia from the Moors in 1094.

Flan—Baked custard dessert, usually served with caramel in it in both Spain and Portugal.

Franco—Spanish dictator for about 40 years in the 20th century.

Inquisition—Period when Spain required non-Catholics to convert or leave the country; torture sometimes was part of the imprisonment process in Spain, Peru, and Portugal.

Magellan—Portuguese navigator who led the first circumnavigation of the world from 1519 to 1522; he died in the Philippines during the trip.

Meseta—High central plain in Spain.

Moors—Islamic invaders from Africa (Morocco).

Paella—Traditional rice dish containing saffron and topped with cooked vegetables and meats.

Pizarro—Spanish explorer who conquered Peru in the 16th century.

Prince Henry the Navigator—Portuguese leader who sponsored voyages of exploration aboard caravels to very distant places.

Saffron—Orange to yellow spice; the stigma of purple crocus.

Sangria—Red wine with fruit juices.

Sopa de ajo—Garlic soup popular in Spain.

Tapas—Small plates of tidbits of food designed for nibbling while having a drink in the late afternoon or early evening.

Vasco da Gama—Portuguese navigator who opened trade routes to India in 1498 and 1502.

Recipes

Gazpacho (Serves 4–6)

1 c water
1 c bread crumbs (no crust)
2 c peeled, chopped tomatoes
1/2 medium cucumber, chopped
1/2 garlic clove, crushed
1/2 onion, coarsely chopped
1/2 green pepper, coarsely chopped
1 tbsp olive oil
2 tbsp red wine vinegar

Salt and pepper to taste

1. Mix all ingredients in bowl.
2. In a blender, puree about 2 cups of mixture until smooth.
3. Transfer puree to another bowl and keep repeating until all of the mixture is pureed.
4. Adjust seasonings, then chill for 2 hours or more. Serve chilled.

Sopa de Ajo (Serves 4)

1/4 c olive oil
2 garlic cloves, minced
1 1/2 c French bread crumbs (no crust)
1/2 tsp paprika
Pinch cayenne pepper
1/2 tsp salt
3 c water
4 poached eggs (optional)

2 tsp chopped chives (optional)

1. Saute garlic in olive oil for 2 minutes (do not brown).
2. Add bread and stir while heating to golden.
3. Stir in spices and water.
4. Poach eggs in separate pan while simmering soup.
5. Serve soup and add egg. Garnish with chives.

Caldo Verde (Serves 6–8)

1 lb potatoes, peeled and sliced
5 c water
1 1/2 tsp salt
1/4 lb chorizo (sausage with garlic)
1/4 c olive oil
1/4 tsp black pepper
1/2 lb kale leaves, julienne cut

1. Boil potatoes in salted water until tender.
2. Meanwhile, simmer chorizo in water for 15 minutes, then drain and slice 1/4" thick.
3. Place potatoes in a bowl and mash with a fork.
4. Put potatoes back in pan, stir in olive oil and pepper, and heat to boiling.
5. Add kale and boil for 4 minutes.
6. Add chorizo and simmer for 2 minutes.

Cocido Madrileno (Serves 8–12)

1/2 c dried chickpeas (garbanzo)
5 qt water
1 large stewing hen
1 lb beef brisket
1 lb boneless ham
2 carrots, pared
2 leeks
1 garlic clove, crushed
1/2 lb chorizo
Cabbage (cut in 6 cored wedges)
6 potatoes, pared

1. Soak garbanzos according to package directions for 12 hours.
2. Drain and place garbanzos in a large stock pot and add water, hen, and brisket. Simmer for 2 hours.
3. Add ham, carrots, leeks, plus seasonings, and simmer for 30 minutes.
4. Meanwhile, simmer chorizo for 15 minutes in water, then drain and slice 1/4" thick.
5. Add chorizo, cabbage, and potatoes; simmer for 30 minutes.
6. Serve broth first, followed by a platter of vegetables and then a platter of meats.

Paella (Serves 6–8)

6 pieces chicken
1/4 c olive oil
16 raw shrimp, shelled (or 2 raw lobster tails and 8 shrimp)
1/2 lb chorizo (garlic flavored sausage)
3 strips bacon, diced
1 large onion, finely chopped
1 tsp minced garlic
1 sweet red pepper in julienne strips
1 large tomato, finely chopped
1 can garbanzos or cooked beans
6 c water
3 c long grain rice (uncooked)
1 tsp salt
1/4 tsp ground saffron
Salt and pepper to taste
6 uncooked hard-shelled, small clams
6 raw mussels
Lemon for garnish

1. Carefully brown chicken in 1/4 cup of olive oil, removing from skillet when well browned.
2. Simmer seafood for 3 minutes. Meanwhile, simmer sausage for 5 minutes in water, drain, and slice 1/4" thick.
3. In a skillet, sauté sausage, bacon, onion, garlic, red pepper, tomato, and beans, stirring while heating until thick enough to pile lightly.
4. Preheat oven to 400°F while heating water to boiling. Put rice, 1 teaspoon salt, sautéed vegetables, and saffron in an oven-proof, two-handled, 14" skillet or paella pan.
5. Pour boiling water over rice and stir well. Heat again while stirring to bring mixture to boiling.
6. Remove from heat and then arrange the seafood and chicken on top.
7. Place pan very low in the oven and bake at 400°F until water is absorbed (25 to 30 minutes). Garnish with lemon and serve from pan.

Churros (Serves 4–6)

2 c water
1/2 tsp salt
2 c all-purpose flour
Oil for deep-fat frying
Sugar
Cinnamon (optional)

1. Boil water in 2-qt saucepan.
2. Immediately remove from heat and add flour and salt in one addition. Beat hard to form a dough mass that pulls away from the sides.
3. Cool to room temperature; begin heating the oil to 400°F.
4. Use the star disc with a metal cookie press, which is filled with the dough.
5. Press 6" lengths of dough into the hot fat.
6. Fry until pleasingly browned (5 to 7 minutes), turning occasionally.
7. Drain on paper towels and sprinkle with sugar.

Sangria (Serves 6–8)

1/2 c brandy 1/4 c Curaçao or Cointreau (orange-flavored liqueurs) 1/2 c lime juice 2 c orange juice	1 bottle chilled red wine (Spanish) 1. Mix everything but the wine and refrigerate in a large pitcher for at least 3 hours. 2. Add the wine. Stir before serving.

Summary

The Iberian Peninsula and its countries of Portugal and Spain form the southwestern tip of Europe, a region that is shut off from the rest of the continent by the Pyrenees Mountains. Other mountain ranges also ring the central plateau, the Spanish Meseta. The climate is quite varied, which permits the production of a variety of crops ranging from cereals in the central and northern regions to oranges and olives in the southern region.

The Romans left their mark on Spain and Portugal, to be followed by the Germanic tribes from the north. The Moors invaded from Morocco in 711, bringing Islamic followers to the previously Catholic peninsula.

The proximity to the sea fostered the remarkable voyages of exploration by sea that reached around the world. Prince Henry the Navigator encouraged voyages along the coasts of Africa. King Ferdinand and Queen Isabella (who reigned immediately after the defeat of the Moors in 1492) sponsored the voyages of Columbus. Both countries were able to establish colonies and trade routes that brought considerable wealth and power to Spain. The lengthy period of the Spanish Inquisition resulted in the ouster of Jews and Moors who refused to bend under painful pressure to adopt the Catholic religion. This resulted in the loss of many bright and creative people and cost Spain dearly in manpower and material goods.

Portugal became a nation when it gained independence from Spain in 1668. Antonia Salazar was prominent in governing Portugal in the 20th century. Franco was the dictator who ruled Spain following its civil war, fought from 1931 to 1939. He was in power until he died in 1975. Presently, Spain is ruled by a monarchy and an elected parliament.

The language in Portugal and also in its former colony of Brazil is Portuguese. Spain has a number of dialects, but the formal language is Castilian Spanish. The distinctive feature of Castilian is the lisp-like character that results from pronouncing the letter *s* as *th* if the s precedes an e, i, or z.

The dominant religion in both Spain and Portugal is Catholicism. Most Muslims were either driven out by the war that ended in 1492 or were forced out by the Inquisition. The Inquisition also removed the Jewish believers, although some Jews were invited back when the Spaniards became aware of the importance of the abilities the Jews brought to Spain.

The Moors left a lasting array of highly creative and artistic buildings, including the mosque at Cordoba and the Alhambra in Granada. Portugal's contributions to the arts include the fado, a unique form of blues. Spain has had many artists and writers, including Velázquez, Murillo, El Greco, and the more recent artists such as Picasso, Miró, and Dali. Cervantes, the author of *Don Quixote*, and Gaudi, the imaginative Barcelona architect, also were Spaniards. Spain also is noted for its flamenco dancing and exciting music.

Bullfighting and the running of the bulls in Pamplona add to the color that represents Spain today. The deeply moving religious holiday celebrations, particularly the parades with floats and the participation of penitents carrying crosses during Holy Week in Seville, are clear evidence of the importance of the Catholic beliefs in Spain and in Portugal.

Foods are quite imaginative on the Iberian Peninsula because of the wide array of ingredients that are available, but Portuguese foods tend to be somewhat simpler than the fare in Spain. Both countries have a simple breakfast pattern: coffee with milk and some bread and jam or churros. The two other meals of the day are much more substantial. The combination of a big meal in the early afternoon and the heat of the day (particularly in summer) has fostered the tradition of a long break in the afternoon, followed by more work and then some drinks and tapas with friends before finally eating a late dinner (often 10:00 P.M. or even midnight in Spain). Sausages and salted, dried cod are staples in the Portuguese diet. Paella and cocido are national dishes in Spain. Soups, wines, olives and olive oil, oranges, and tapas are items that invoke the essence of Spanish food.

Study Questions

1. What contributed to Portugal's rise in power and wealth during the 15th through 17th centuries?
2. Briefly describe the contribution of each of the following: (a) Vasco da Gama, (b) Dali, (c) Prince Henry the Navigator, (d) Gaudi, (e) King Ferdinand and Queen Isabella, (f) Magellan, (g) Velázquez, (h) El Greco, (i) Cervantes, and (j) Picasso.
3. Describe at least two buildings in Spain that were built by the Moors.
4. What was Spain trying to accomplish by its Inquisition? Where did its practices occur? What were some of the results of the Inquisition?
5. Describe the meal pattern that is typical in Spain.
6. Briefly define the following: (a) cocido, (b) paella, (c) tapas, (d) saffron, and (e) churros.

Bibliography

Barer-Stein, T. 1999. *You Eat What You Are.* 2nd ed. Firefly Books, Ltd. Ontario, Canada.

Feibleman, P. S. 1969. *The Cooking of Spain and Portugal.* Time-Life Books. New York.

Hilliard, C. B. 1998. *Intellectual Traditions of Pre-Colonial Africa.* McGraw-Hill. New York.

Inman, N., ed. 1996. *Spain.* Dorling Kindersley, Ltd. London.

Irving, W. 1953. *The Alhambra.* Macmillan. New York.

Kohen, E. 1992. *Spain.* Marshall Cavendish Corp. New York.

McKay, J. P., D. H. Bennett, and J. Buckler. 1999. *A History of Western Society.* Houghton Mifflin. Boston.

Michener, J. A. 1968. *Iberia.* Random House. New York.

Palmowski, J. 1997. *Dictionary of 20th Century World History.* Oxford University Press. Oxford, England.

Pearcy, G. E. 1980. *The World Food Scene.* Plycon Press. Redondo Beach, CA.

Symington, M. 1997. *Portugal with Madeira and the Azores.* Dorling Kindersley, Ltd. London.

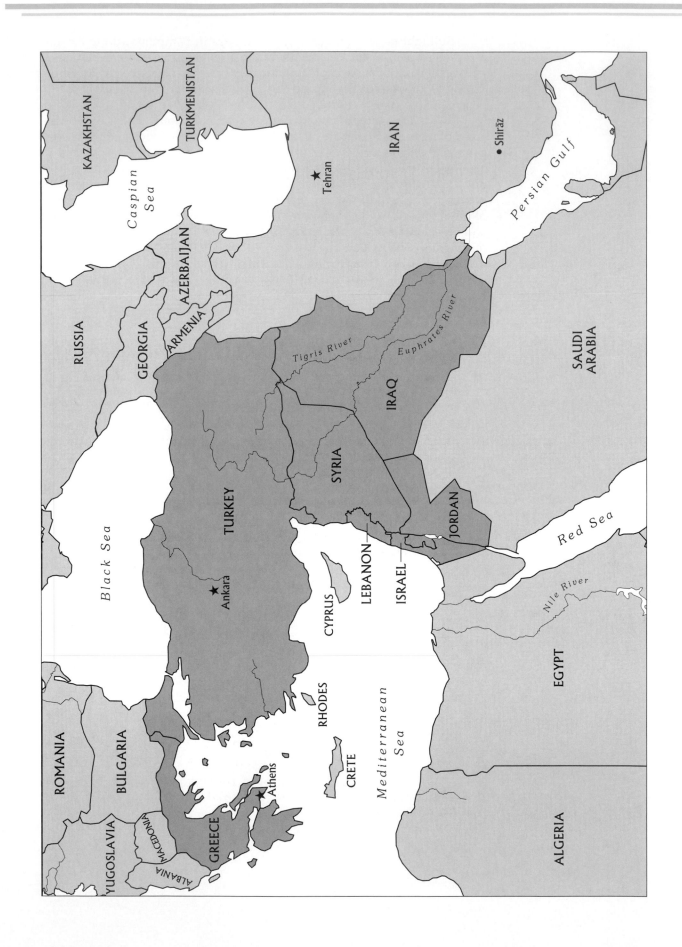

11 Greece, Turkey, and the Levant

Geographic Overview

The Mediterranean Sea provides the common denominator between Greece, Turkey, and the Levant, although there are some distinct differences in the terrain and the people that create the uniqueness of each country. Greece is part of the Balkan Peninsula, but the rugged terrain has served to maintain Greece as its own nation, one with a remarkable heritage from a time when the Greeks represented the epitome of culture and learning.

Geographically, Greece seems to be poorly suited to agriculture, for over half of the land is barren, supporting only stunted vegetation interspersed among many rocks and large rock formations. Nevertheless, Greece does a surprisingly good job of providing its own food, and even exports some. Wheat, corn, and rice are the favored cereal crops, although the sparse rainfall limits production. Grapes (consumed as wine, fruit, or leaves) and olives are important crops that figure prominently in the diets of the Greek people. Olive oil is used generously in cooking, and Greek olives are favorites. Citrus fruits and vegetables are other crops suited to the land and climate. Sheep can be raised successfully in this rocky land and are important in the diet both as meat and as a source of dairy products. Feta cheese is a product of ewe's milk. Fish is available from the sea to round out the sources of protein.

Turkey is adjacent to Greece, a proximity that has fostered considerable unrest at various times in history between the two countries. Turkey is quite a unique country in that it straddles two continents: Europe and Asia (Figure 11.1). A waterway from the Aegean (consisting of the Dardanelles, the Sea of Marmara, and the Bosporus) leads directly into the Black Sea, forming a division not only between the continents, but also between parts of Turkey. This situation linking

Figure 11.1 Muslim woman preparing the land for spring planting in central Turkey.

waterways and creating a pathway between Europe and Asia has placed Istanbul (formerly called Byzantium and Constantinople) in the path of armies and traders over the centuries (Figure 11.2). This unique country has almost 2,500 miles of shoreline, including the Aegean, Marmara, Black, and Mediterranean Seas. It also has very high mountains in the east, with Mt. Ararat rising 17,000 feet. The Taurus Mountains near the Mediterranean in southern Turkey are more than 12,000 feet high. The central Anatolian Plateau is large and quite barren, but it is a region where wheat is grown successfully. Corn, fruit, tobacco, and nuts are grown in abundance along the plains facing the Black Sea in the northern part of the country. The land bordering the Aegean provides grapes, figs, olives, cotton, and tobacco in quantities adequate for exporting as well as for home use. The land along the Mediterranean in the southern part of Turkey produces citrus, sesame, bananas, oil seeds, olives, and cotton when irrigation appropriate to the particular crop is provided.

Turkey's neighbors in Asia include Syria, Iraq, and Iran. Iraq and Iran are quite a distance east of the Mediterranean and do not share the climatic influence of that sea. Hostilities have isolated these countries for many years, but they have had and continue to have influence on the rest of the world because of their abundant supply of oil. Iran is noted for its beluga caviar, which is harvested from the Caspian Sea on its border. Iran's high mountains limit land for agriculture, and a fairly dry climate adds to the problems. Iraq is noteworthy as the land where the Tigris and Euphrates rivers flow together and form the Shatt-al-Arab before flow-

Figure 11.2 Istanbul's position straddling the continents of Europe and Asia means extensive coastline. Hagia Sofia and other mosques and minarets add their distinctive touch to the city's skyline.

Figure 11.3 The Dead Sea, the lowest place on earth, lies in an extremely arid region east of Jerusalem and north of Jordan.

ing into the Persian Gulf. Much of Iraq is desert, and Iran also has areas where agriculture is quite difficult.

Syria, Lebanon, and Israel all have some Mediterranean seacoast, but very arid conditions exist in much of these lands. Military concerns have limited agricultural development, although Israel has been able to develop its agricultural potential very effectively in meeting the challenge to feed its people. Mountains are a part of the landscape in these three countries and also in neighboring Jordan. Israel and Jordan border the Dead Sea, which is the lowest spot on earth (1,286 feet below sea level). Although some agricultural efforts are very successful when irrigation is available, water is a dear commodity because of the hot and dry desert climate that dominates the Levant (Figure 11.3). Olive trees are productive in this region of the world, and citrus, papaya, eggplant, dates (Figure 11.4), tomatoes, and various vegetables also are grown under irrigation. The primary livestock is sheep, which are well adapted to the terrain of this area, but cattle and chickens are also raised.

Figure 11.4 Dates grow well in the hot, arid climate of the Levant, and they have the added advantage of being able to be stored for long periods after harvest.

History and Culture

The country that is now Greece has a long and complicated history dating back beyond the early Bronze Age of 3000 BCE. Minoans and Myceneans left their marks on the region before 1200 BCE, and Homer described the Trojan War around 750 BCE. City-states, notably Sparta and Athens, were developed and protected against many invaders, sometimes successfully and sometimes not. The defeat of the Persians under Xerxes paved the way for the Golden Age of classical culture, beginning in 475 BCE. This was the period when the Parthenon and other classical structures were built on the Acropolis. Unfortunately, the Peloponnesian Wars between city-states (Athens and Sparta) led to a decline. Then, the Macedonians took over, followed by the Romans in 146 BCE.

By the 5th century, other invaders began to challenge the people living in the region of modern Greece. Goths, Franks, and Venetians were all fighting there at various times. The Crusaders also went through Greece. Finally, the Ottoman Turks gained control and ruled for almost 400 years, from the late 1400s to the 19th century. A strong surge of nationalism culminated in the Greek War of Independence, which was fought from 1821 to 1829. This laid the groundwork for the establishment of the country of Greece. However, animosity toward Turkey has not been resolved completely and remains in evidence in the contest for control of some Aegean islands and the divided island of Cyprus.

The history of Turkey shares some common threads with Greece, but has a unique record of its own. The early settlers in the central part of what is now Anatolia were the Hittites, who lived near modern-day Ankara (capital of Turkey today). The Hittites were advanced for their day (1700 to 1200 BCE), leaving behind written records, metal sculptures, and rock carvings that can be viewed today in a museum in Ankara. After the Hittites, smaller states formed, the most noteworthy being Phrygia and Lydia. Greeks traded with these states, but the Persians gained control until the region was liberated by Alexander the Great in 334 BCE. Rome interacted with the people in Anatolia, and Constantine claimed the city of Byzantium for the capital of the eastern part of his empire in 330 CE. The name was changed to Constantinople and finally to Istanbul in 1453 (by the Ottomans).

The Byzantine empire fell to the Turkish tribes in 1071, bringing Islam into what then was predominantly a Christian realm. The rulers of this new Turkey were Seljuks. It was this new political entity that inspired the First Crusade at the urging of Pope Urban II. Eventually, three additional Crusades also invaded the western region of Turkey and proceeded south to Jerusalem, leaving evidence of these Christian invasions along their routes. Mongols conquered the Seljuks in the 13th century, and finally Osman, an Anatolian, established the Ottoman Empire, which grew and ranged westward as far as Vienna, where the Hapsburgs halted their advance in 1529 and again in 1683. The Ottoman rule was Islamic and maintained a powerful stance in Turkey, with the actual empire being broken up at the end of World War I. Kemal Ataturk became the leader of Turkey and is credited with making many of the changes that form the foundation of modern Turkey.

In the Levant, Phoenicians evolved into powerful traders with other Mediterranean regions by 1000 BCE. On land, trade routes wended their way in ancient times between Egyptian settlements in Africa, Mediterranean ports in Antioch, Tyre, and Gaza, and on through either Petra in what is now Jordan or Palmyra in modern Syria. They extended onward to reach the civilizations of Babylon on the Euphrates or Kuwait and Bahrain on the Persian Gulf. Trade was very much alive from as early as the 5th century BCE. Names from the Bible spring to life in the history of this region of the world: Moses, King Solomon, David, the Queen of Sheba, and many others.

Farther to the east, the Persians established their control and expanded their empire under Cyrus the Great and controlled much of the area of Turkey and the Levant until Alexander the Great overturned their control. The destruction of Persepolis in the region of Fars in southern Iran in 330 BCE by Alexander marked the end of an era in this part of the world.

The Middle East has been the subject of numerous wars and battles because it is there, particularly in Jerusalem, where three major religions—Judaism, Islam, and Christianity—all come together in an emotional and passionate way due to the significance of the area for each religion. Thus, the Crusades in the Middle Ages were launched to free Jerusalem from the Muslims in the name of Christianity. When the powerful sultan Saladin (who ruled much of the Middle East) recaptured Jerusalem in 1187, Richard the Lionhearted from England, Frederick Barbarossa of the Holy Roman Empire, and Phillip Augustus of France launched the third of the Crusades. The fourth of the Crusades (1202 to 1204) was a religious disaster, for the capture of Constantinople made a schism between the Roman Catholics and Eastern Orthodox Catholics that remains today.

Actually, the Crusades were but a part of continuing religious arguments in the Levant. David, the son of King Saul (who united the Israelites around 1050 BCE), began building Jerusalem to be the capital of his kingdom. Solomon, his son, had a temple built for the Israelites to worship their God. Two factions developed after Solomon split Israel into a northern section, with Samaria as its capital, and a southern section called Judah. People who lived in Judah were the first people to be called Jews.

When the Romans took the land in 63 BCE, the Jews were not allowed to practice their religion in their own way. This led to the dramatic standoff at Masada, where the Jews who fled from conquered Jerusalem gathered on a mountain plateau high above the Dead Sea in 70 CE. It took the Roman army of 15,000 almost 2 years to build a ramp up the most vulnerable side of the fortress and break down the wall to enter the site, where less than 1,000 Jews had held out. The Jews all committed suicide to escape being captured alive by the Romans, thus ending a particularly sad and dramatic episode in the history of Israel. Another revolt in 132 CE resulted in the Romans scattering the Jews along the shores of the Black Sea, throughout the Greek islands, and around the Mediterranean Sea, an action referred to as the diaspora. Many Jews fled as refugees to northern European locations of their own choosing to escape the Roman actions.

This region was known as Palestine following Roman rule, a time when Christianity was gaining support. The Byzantine Empire was followed by the rule of Muslims, which eventually triggered the Crusades. Possession of Jerusalem passed back and forth between Christians and Muslims for a couple of centuries, but the Mamelukes from Egypt, who were Muslims, ruled for about 250 years. The Ottomans, who succeeded the Mamelukes, were fairly tolerant of religions and gradually allowed Jews to return and gather more presence in Palestine. The culmination of the gradual return of Jews was the establishment of the nation of Israel in 1948. When the British withdrew from the region and Israel declared its independence, four Muslim nations (Egypt, Jordan, Iraq, and Lebanon) attacked, only to have Israel gain more land than it had originally, including half of Jerusalem. Syria and Egypt attacked Israel in 1967, but Israel emerged six days later with the Golan Heights, Sinai Peninsula, all of Jerusalem, and the West Bank of the Jordan added to its territory. The attack on Yom Kippur in 1973 by Syrian and Egyptian troops, plus numerous other skirmishes, have been the result of festering disagreements over land in dispute since 1967. Peace negotiations are gradually making progress, and the Palestinians, who were headquartered in Lebanon for many years, have begun to move toward having their own nation. Lebanon is finally able to begin rebuilding, but tensions, both political and religious, remain high throughout the Levant.

Religion varies considerably between Greece, Turkey, and the countries of the Levant. Greece is almost entirely a nation of Greek Orthodoxy, which branched centuries ago from the Roman Catholic doctrines. However, people in Greece are free to observe any religion they please. The new year marks the Feast of St. Basil, a Byzantine tradition in which a special sweet bread called vassilopita, containing one coin, is eaten; the person who gets the coin will have a lucky year. Greek Independence Day is celebrated March 25, a holiday that marks the struggle against the Ottomans and also the religious event of the Feast of the Annunciation. Several other religious holidays are celebrated, with the Easter celebration keyed to the celebration of Orthodox Easter. The feasting for Greek Orthodox Easter includes red-dyed Easter eggs and lamb roasted on a spit.

In Turkey, most of the Muslims are Sunni and carefully follow the teachings of Muhammad, according to the writings in the hadith (Figure 11.5). However, some Turks are Shiite Muslims, the group that pays special attention to Ali (son-in-law of Muhammad) and believes in hidden meanings in the Koran. Sacrifice and martyrdom are part of this branch of Islam. Turkey has been rather broadminded in its expectations for practicing Muslims, with women often not being required to cover their heads, and both sexes sometimes having an alcoholic beverage despite its prohibition. Another sect of Muslims in Turkey is Sufism, which is a somewhat mystical interpretation of the faith. The Whirling Dervishes, such as those in Konya, are examples of this Muslim sect.

Israel has a predominance of Jews, but there are different approaches to Judaism. Orthodox Jews practice the faith as it has always been practiced, with its strong adherence to observing the Sabbath, following of kashruth (Jewish dietary laws), celebrating all holy days, and separating men and women at worship (head covering and prayer shawls for men and head coverings for all married women). Hebrew is the language used in Orthodox services, but the language of the country is used by Reform Jews in their services, and they also are less strict in dietary and clothing practices. Degrees of strict adherence underlie the various Jewish groups in Israel. These differences sometimes lead to political problems.

Figure 11.5 The Blue Mosque in Istanbul draws many Muslims throughout the week and at prayer five times each day.

Within Israel, there are also Christians from different Protestant groups, Catholics, and Muslims. This diversity is not surprising in view of the history of the region and the focal point that Jerusalem and Israel represent.

The diversity of religions has inspired the building of quite different structures of worship in this part of the world, and nowhere is it more apparent than in Jerusalem. The Christian part of old Jerusalem contains the Church of the Holy Sepulchre, while the Temple Mount is in the Muslim Quarter. The Temple Mount includes the Dome of the Rock, which is the most important spot in Jerusalem for Muslims because it contains the spot where Muhammad is believed to have departed from earth to enter heaven. The Western Wall, or Wailing Wall, is a stone wall forming part of the Temple Mount and dates back to 20 BCE when King Herod was having the retaining wall for the Second Temple built. The Wailing Wall is all that remains as a result of the Roman destruction of the Second Temple in 70 CE. Because of its history and religious significance, the Wailing Wall is a very important site for Jews to pray (men at one section and women at the adjacent part of the wall).

Evidence of the Crusades can be found throughout the Levant, and some of the buildings actually present a picture of the results of the battles. At the Krak de Chevalliers in the western part of Syria, the architectural style is clearly that of the Crusaders from England, but within its lovely little chapel is the *minbar* (stairway always found in Muslim mosques), silently revealing the fact that the Crusaders ultimately lost their fortress to the Muslims. On the island of Rhodes, the Order of St. John's built walls to protect the old city, creating the appearance of a European walled city as a reminder of the Crusades.

In Istanbul the Hagia Sophia has been turned into a museum today, but its architecture is testimony to the scale the Byzantine Emperor Justinian chose for this huge example of domed religious architecture. Both nature and man have attacked this monumental edifice over the ages, with nature in the form of an earthquake causing the vaulted dome to fall only 20 years after the completion of the Eastern Orthodox church in 537. When the dome was repaired in 563, sturdy (but not very artistic) buttresses were added, providing the necessary support for the gigantic dome (rising 55.6 meters above the floor). Catholics in the fourth Crusade did considerable damage to the building, only to be driven out by the Byzantines, who then lost to the Ottomans in 1453. The numerous transitions throughout its history have left some mosaics from the Byzantines and a minbar plus other evidence of the Muslim religious observances that occurred for centuries prior to the transition to the status of a museum.

A far more beautiful mosque that remains active even today is the Blue Mosque, with its six intricate and delicate minarets standing very close to the rather awkward vastness of the Hagia Sophia. Although the Blue Mosque is probably the most beautiful of the mosques in Istanbul, it has plenty of competition for the honor. Indeed, the city seems to be a panoply of minarets when viewed from the deck of a ship traversing the Bosporus.

Central Turkey afforded yet another approach to providing places of worship for the various religions. Cappadocia, an almost unearthly region of formations called *tufa* (marshes that contained volcanic ash of a consistency that was carved over the eons by wind and erosion into weird shapes, some resembling mushrooms) provided the isolation and material needed by Christians escaping from Romans. These formations have been carved into numerous small chapels and caves, where these early worshipers lived and created paintings and altars in security from persecution.

A few palaces and public buildings, or at least their ruins, remain in this part of the world, and they illustrate various phases in the history of the region. The Persians, under Darius the Great in 518 BCE, built a remarkable palace in southern Iran at Persepolis. Although Alexander the Great burned it in 330 BCE, some beautiful bas-reliefs and stone carvings still remain, attesting to the lovely, unique artistic style of these early craftsmen. In Greece on the Peloponnesus, the famous Lion Gate is the very weathered remnant of the art of the Myceneans around 1250 BCE. This style is totally different from that of the Persians. In Jordan the ruined trade city of Petra is best known for the Treasury (Khasneh), which is a rose-colored façade and rooms carved into a dramatic cliff at the end of a narrow gorge. The façade bears evidence of the influences of the Greeks and Romans, which is not surprising, since these ancient artisans doubtless had contact with these cultures because of the trade that passed through this strategic point in the desert. Other interesting ruins are found in Baalbek in Lebanon and Palmyra in Syria.

Greece's contributions to both art and architecture are legendary. The Parthenon probably is the most famous building or ruin, and its simplicity and detail have inspired many buildings and designs throughout the world. Among the most famous of the art works are the Elgin Marbles, which have inspired extensive and heated arguments regarding the benefits and appropriateness of allowing them to continue in their protected but expatriate address in the British Museum in London. The Caryatids (women's draped figures, beautifully carved) that support the porch roof of the Erechtheum on the Acropolis are other transported art that is cherished by the world.

Istanbul features not only mosques, but also palaces. The most famous, the Topkapi, is now a museum, but it provides a clear perspective on how the court life of the Ottomans was conducted. Built by Mehmet the Conqueror from 1458 to 1465, the harem quarters, vast kitchen complex, and living quarters as well as administrative rooms are indicative of the total power of the ruler. The Dolmabache Palace presents a marked contrast, for it was not built until the mid-1800s when the Ottomans were influenced greatly by European, particularly French, ornateness. Ataturk, considered to be the founder of modern Turkey, lived in this palace, which now is a museum.

Music and art from this part of the world have not generally become widely popular in the western world, but the intensity and compelling rhythms and haunting melodies do capture attention. Israel's *klezmer* music is probably the most familiar type of music from this region, although its origins may belong to Eastern Europe. Certainly, Israel is alive with this energetic and exciting music. There also are many famous concert soloists who claim Israel as home. Love of music and the ability to pursue highly polished performances on their instruments are hallmarks of these special performing artists.

There is yet another distinctive cultural separation within the Greek and eastern Mediterranean countries, and that is the alphabet that is used. The diversity found in the alphabets is another factor that makes communication difficult. The Greeks still use the Greek letters in their signs and some of their writing, while many other countries in this region rely heavily on the flowing Arabic script, and Hebrew adds still another dimension for Jews in Israel. The dissimilarity in appearance as well as in vocabulary makes it far more difficult to read even simple signs in this part of the world than in Europe, where the commonality of the letters and the similarities of many of the essential words in the different Romance languages facilitate at least superficial understanding.

Food Patterns

Many similarities exist in the food patterns of people in the various countries considered in this chapter. The overarching Mediterranean climate characterized by limited rainfall and heat plus the generally rocky terrain results in an abundance of such foods as olives, eggplant, onions and other vegetables, wheat, lamb and

Challah, the traditional bread served in celebration of Rosh Hashanah, represents the cycle of life and the beginning of the Jewish new year. The dough may be shaped as ladders to help people reach great heights or hands to help people be inscribed in the book of life for the coming year. Before baking, seeds are sprinkled on top to symbolize fertility and plenty.

mutton, and legumes. The ways in which these ingredients and others are used may vary a bit between countries, but there are commonalities that label the food patterns throughout the region as Mediterranean. Perhaps the single cause of the differences is the particular religion or religions practiced in a country; Muslim and Jewish dietary laws play an important role (see Chapter 3), and this is especially evident in Israel because of the predominantly Jewish population. In the other countries except Greece, Muslim dietary laws are the foundation of the diet (Figure 11.6). Greece does have some followers of each of these religions, but the major religious group is Greek Orthodoxy, which allows more freedom in food preparation.

The typical dietary pattern is a light breakfast fairly early in the morning (often just tea or coffee and a baked bread or other baked item), a rather hearty lunch (that seems to beg for a subsequent nap on hot afternoons), and a late supper. Snacking is an acceptable means of stretching the time between the day's three meals. Particularly in Greece, a very late dinner and considerable revelry before retiring is the preferred schedule for those who have enough energy (Figure 11.7).

Pita, or pocket bread, is quite universal throughout the region, but the character of the bread may vary from fairly thick and hearty to quite thin and rather crisp. These breads commonly are purchased from a local baker, or else the home-made dough is carried to a bake shop where it is baked for the customer. In Syria it is not unusual to see freshly baked, unwrapped rounds of pita cooling on staircases or even on the hoods of parked cars. The basic ingredient of these breads is refined wheat flour. *Lavosh*, or Armenian cracker bread, is a very thin, crisp, bread-like variation of pita that is found less often but is sometimes eaten.

Phyllo (also spelled *filo*) is a very thin pastry from this region. The thin sheets of dough usually are brushed with oil or melted butter, then stacked to the desired depth. Chopped nuts, sweetened rosewater, and honey are interspersed with the sheets of dough before baking to make the ubiquitous dessert called *baklava*. There are many different but quite similar versions of this popular dessert. In fact, some bakeries have as many as 10 or more versions, some of which resemble shredded wheat in appearance and others that are twisted or cut to add variety to the choices available. Phyllo also is the basis of some appetizers or main dishes, such as *spanakopite*, a pastry that contains spinach.

Legumes are found in many Middle Eastern dishes (Figure 11.8). The chickpea, or garbanzo, is particularly popular. When chickpeas are soaked and ground into a paste, then seasoned and formed into balls or other shapes, they are fried into *fulafel*. Another use for garbanzos is to make hummus, a dip made by dilut-

Figure 11.6 Muslim dietary laws form the basis of what many people eat in the Middle East.

Figure 11.7   Street vendors in Greece and Turkey sell these hearty, crusty circles of bread to people wanting a snack.

ing a puree of cooked garbanzos with *tahini,* lemon juice, and garlic, and finally pouring a bit of olive oil on top before dipping bits of pita into it. Black or broad beans often are soaked with chickpeas for a couple of days before being cooked until tender. This preparation is finished by adding garlic, olive oil, lemon, tomato, and cilantro; the finished dish is called *foul.*

Tahini is a very common ingredient in this cuisine. A rather simple blend of ground sesame seeds, lemon juice, and sesame oil, tahini can be made at home or purchased in finished form to save some time in preparing the array of foods that often is expected, particularly at the midday meal.

Cracked wheat may be used in such dishes as *kibbeh* and *tabouli* or even used as the basis of pilaf. Partially cooked and dried cracked wheat is called *bulgur* (sometimes *burghel).* Kibbeh can be made by grinding lamb and finely ground cracked wheat together to make a thick paste that can be pressed into the shape of an egg shell, which then is stuffed with a filling, pressed closed, and deep-fat fried. Tabouli is quite a different dish, although it too is made with bulgur. The bulgur in tabouli (a salad) is soaked with water and then combined with minced mint and parsley, diced tomatoes, olive oil, and lemon juice.

Figure 11.8   This wide array of legumes is available not only in the market at Iraklion on the island of Crete, but in Turkey and other countries of the Middle East.

Figure 11.9   Moussaka as it is served in the shadow of the Acropolis in Athens, Greece.

Whether they are called *dolmas* or *dolmades*, stuffed grape leaves are a dish that is treasured throughout this region. Credit for their origin is not certain, but some say the Greeks, and others say the Persians, are responsible. Rice usually is at least part of the stuffing, often combined with lamb or other ground meat and various spices. These may be served either hot or cold, frequently with yogurt.

Shawarma, which is prepared by closely packing layers of chicken and fat into a solid that can be grilled vertically on a rotisserie, is available from street vendors in Greece and many other locations in the Middle East. Another popular way of preparing meat is the kabob, or kebab, which is marinated lamb or chicken and sometimes vegetables grilled on skewers. Turkey is thought to be the origin of this dish.

Eggplant is a particularly common vegetable, one which the Greeks have elevated to prominence in a dish called *moussaka* (Figure 11.9), a casserole creation featuring ground or small pieces of lamb, onions, tomato sauce, and eggplant slices. Olives also find their way onto the table, either as ingredients or as side dishes. These may be processed in various ways to alter the texture and flavor of the olives.

Feta cheese is used frequently by the Greeks. Yogurt is used to an extent in the region. *Lebneh* (Figure 11.10) is a soft cheese that is made by draining yogurt to reduce the whey content. After draining for about half a day or longer, the desired firmness can be achieved.

Turkey grows tea near the Black Sea, and the leaves are used to make the ever-popular beverage. It is served in rather short glasses without handles, even though the beverage is extremely hot. Sugar is available, but milk and cream are not. Often, the tea is flavored with mint. Turkish coffee provides an experience quite unlike the brew in the United States. The beans for Turkish coffee are roasted very dark and ground to an extremely fine powder, which is used to make the coffee. The long-handled, narrow-necked device used to make this beverage is called a *tanaka*. The finished beverage is served in a demitasse cup. The coffee grounds do settle a bit in the cup, but the beverage seems to be almost chewy with the grounds. The coffee usually is very sweet and flavored with cardamom.

Although Muslims may not drink alcoholic beverages, *raki* is the aperitif chosen by many people in Turkey. It turns milky when water is added. The alcoholic beverage that serves a similar purpose in Greece is *ouzo*. *Retsina*, a pine-pitch and anise-flavored beverage, is also popular. Wines may be available, particularly in Greece.

Figure 11.10   Lebneh is offered for sale in this market in western Turkey.

Key Terms

Baklava—Baked dessert made of multiple layers of phyllo brushed with butter and with honey or rosewater (or both) plus chopped nuts.

Bosporus—Narrow channel that separates Europe from Asia between the Sea of Marmara and the Black Sea.

Bulgur—Partially cooked and dried cracked wheat.

Byzantium—Early name for the city now called Istanbul.

Dolmas—Stuffed grape leaves usually containing rice and often other ingredients; may be served hot or cold.

Falafel—Dish made by forming a paste of soaked chickpeas and seasonings, shaping into balls or other shapes, and frying in deep fat.

Feta—Soft cheese made from ewe's milk.

Foul—Mixture of cooked chickpeas and black or broad beans that have been soaked together for at least 2 days before being cooked; served with topping of garlic, olive oil, lemon, tomato, and cilantro.

Kabob (kebab)—Meat and sometimes other items grilled on a skewer.

Hummus—Dip made with pureed, cooked chickpeas, tahini, lemon juice, garlic, and olive oil.

Kibbeh—Deep-fat fried, egg-shaped shell of finely minced lamb and cracked wheat paste encasing a filling of another meat.

Lavosh—Armenian cracker bread; basically a very thin version of pita.

Lebneh—Soft cheese made by draining whey from yogurt.

Levant—Lands at the eastern end of the Mediterranean Sea.

Moussaka—Eggplant casserole usually containing lamb, onions, tomato sauce, and eggplant slices.

Peloponnesus—Peninsula extending off the southwestern region of Greece.

Phyllo—Extremely thin dough that is formed into large sheets and serves as the main ingredient for desserts and some main dishes.

Pita—Pocket bread that is common throughout the Middle East.

Shawarma—Thinly sliced chicken layered tightly with fat and formed into a solid that is grilled vertically on a rotisserie and sliced off in very thin slices.

Spanakopite—Main dish consisting of many layers of phyllo, spinach, and various other ingredients according to taste.

Tabouli—Salad containing soaked bulgur, minced parsley and mint, diced tomatoes, olive oil, and lemon juice.

Tahini—Paste of finely ground sesame seeds, sesame oil, and lemon juice.

Recipes

Avgolemono (Greek) (Serves 4–6)

3 c chicken broth
3 tbsp uncooked rice
2 eggs
2 tbsp lemon juice
Salt to taste

1. Simmer broth and rice for 15 minutes until al dente.

2. Beat eggs and lemon juice thoroughly, then stir while adding 1/2 cup hot broth to the eggs.
3. Add egg mixture to broth and rice. Stir constantly while heating slowly until mixture coats spoon. Be sure not to boil it.
4. Salt to taste and serve immediately.

Baba Ghanouj (Makes 1 1/2 cups)

1 eggplant (1 lb)
2 tbsp tahini
5 tbsp lemon juice
1/2 garlic clove, minced
1 tsp salt
1/4 tsp black pepper
1 tbsp cold water

1. Prick eggplant skin in many places with a fork, then broil it until skin blisters all over.
2. Cool, then peel, slice, and chop pulp.
3. Puree and mix in the rest of the ingredients.
4. Serve as dip for vegetables, lavosh, or flat bread.

Kibbe Naye (Serves 4–6)

1 1/2 c fine bulgur
1 lb finely ground lamb
1/8 tsp allspice
1/8 tsp freshly grated nutmeg
1/8 tsp cayenne
1 tsp salt
Black pepper
Oil for deep-fat frying

1. Cover bulgur with water; soak 10 minutes.
2. Drain in sieve, squeezing out extra moisture with hands.
3. Combine bulgur, lamb, and seasonings, kneading until smooth.
4. Form into meatballs and deep-fat fry. Use a stuffing in the kibbe (meatballs), if desired.

Dolmades (Makes 30–40)

30 to 40 grape leaves (in brine)
2 qt water
2 onions, finely chopped
1/2 c olive oil
3 garlic cloves, minced
2/3 c cooked lentils
1/2 c uncooked long grain rice
1/2 bunch parsley, chopped
2 medium tomatoes, chopped
2 tsp dried mint
Dash ground cloves
Salt and pepper
Juice of 2 lemons

1. Rinse leaves well; soften in scalding water for 3 minutes.
2. Saute onions gently in 3 tablespoons of olive oil in a skillet until translucent.
3. Remove from heat and stir in garlic, lentils, rice, parsley, tomato, mint, cloves, salt, pepper, and 3 tablespoons of olive oil.
4. Put a layer of grape leaves on the bottom of a saucepan containing 2 tablespoons of olive oil.
5. Using a leaf at a time, put a teaspoon of rice mixture in the center at the bottom of the leaf. Fold both sides over the filling, and roll from bottom to form log.
6. Place log in prepared saucepan, seam side down.
7. Repeat with remainder of leaves and stuffing mixture.
8. Pour remaining olive oil, lemon juice, and enough water to cover the leaf logs by 1 1/2 inches. Put a plate over the leaves to hold them in place.
9. Cover pot and simmer over low heat for 50 to 60 minutes until rice is done.
10. Serve either warm or cold. Yogurt is good on the side.

Moussaka (Serves 6–8)

2 lb eggplant
Salt
1 lb ground lamb or beef
2 onions, chopped
1/4 tsp pepper
1/2 tsp oregano
1/4 c red wine
1 c grated mozzarella cheese
1/2 c soft bread crumbs
1 lb canned plum tomatoes, drained and quartered
2 tbsp olive oil
3 tbsp flour
1 1/2 c milk
Dash of nutmeg
1 egg, beaten
1/4 c parmesan cheese

1. Pare eggplant and slice 1/2" thick. Salt on both sides and drain on paper towels, pressing to get water out.
2. Sauté meat, adding onions in time to brown lightly too.
3. Add pepper, oregano, and wine, and simmer to remove excess liquid.
4. Remove from heat; stir in cheese and 1/4 cup crumbs.
5. Blot eggplant and saute both sides in hot oil.
6. Scatter rest of crumbs over bottom of 9" x 13" greased baking pan; place alternating layers of eggplant, meat, and tomatoes, ending with eggplant.
7. Sprinkle remaining cheese on top.
8. Stir flour into oil and then stir in milk; heat to boiling while stirring constantly.
9. Carefully blend in nutmeg and egg and pour over top of casserole, then sprinkle with parmesan cheese.
10. Bake at 350°F for 50 minutes.

Spanakopite (Greek Spinach-Cheese Pie) (Serves 6–8)

1 onion, chopped
1/4 c chopped green onions
2 tbsp olive oil
1 pkg frozen chopped spinach, thawed and drained
2 tsp dry dill weed
1/4 c parsley, finely chopped
1/4 tsp salt
1/4 tsp white pepper
2 tbsp milk
1/2 lb feta, finely crumbled
4 eggs, beaten
16 sheets (1/2 lb) phyllo
1/4 lb butter, melted

1. Saute onions in oil; add spinach, cover, and cook for 5 minutes.
2. Add dill, parsley, salt, and pepper; heat while stirring to evaporate liquid.
3. Stir in milk and cool.
4. Add cheese and eggs, beating to combine.
5. Cover 9" x 13" x 2" baking pan with 8 sheets of phyllo; brush each sheet with melted butter.
6. Spread spinach mixture over sheets, cover with 8 more sheets of phyllo, and then brush with butter.
7. Bake at 300°F for 1 hour until crisp and lightly browned.
8. Cut into squares and serve warm or at room temperature.

Hummus bi Tahini (Chickpea and Garlic Dip) (Makes 2 1/4 cups)

2 c canned chickpeas
3 garlic cloves, minced
1/4 c tahini
5 tbsp lemon juice
1/2 tsp salt

2 tbsp water (or enough for dip consistency)

1. Drain chickpeas; add garlic and mash to a paste.
2. Beat in remaining ingredients.

Tabouli (Serves 4–6)

3/4 c bulgur
2 c cold water
2 bunches parsley, destemmed and finely chopped
1/2 bunch fresh mint leaves, finely chopped
4 tomatoes, diced
1 bunch green onions and tops, chopped
1/2 c lemon juice
2 tbsp olive oil
Salt and pepper

1. Soak bulgur for 15 minutes in water; drain and squeeze out the water. Discard water.
2. Combine drained cracked wheat and vegetables.
3. Add lemon juice and oil, then toss the salad. Salt and pepper to taste.
4. Store overnight in refrigerator to allow flavors to blend if time permits. Stir to serve.

Turkish Delight (Makes 12 pieces)

1/4 c cold water
2 tbsp unflavored gelatin
1/2 c rosewater
2 c sugar
1/2 c orange juice
1/4 c lemon juice
Powdered sugar

1. Soften gelatin in cold water.
2. Boil rosewater and sugar to 255°F.
3. Stir in gelatin until dissolved; add orange and lemon juices and stir.
4. Pour into a buttered square pan and cool until firm.
5. Cut in squares and roll each square in powdered sugar.

Honey Cake (For Rosh Hashanah) (Serves 8–10)

1/2 c chopped dried apricots
1/4 c rum
2 eggs
1 c honey
1/3 c oil
Zest and juice of 1 orange and 1 lemon
1/3 c sugar
1/2 tsp salt
1/3 c apricot jam
1 3/4 c all purpose flour
1/4 c cake flour
1/2 tsp baking soda

1/2 c slivered almonds

1. Soak apricots in rum.
2. Combine eggs, honey, oil, citrus, sugar, salt, and jam in a bowl.
3. Add flours and soda, and stir.
4. Stir in rum drained from apricots, then fold in apricots and almonds.
5. Bake in two greased 5" x 9" loaf pans at 350°F for 40 minutes or until toothpick inserted in center comes out clean.

Potato Latkes (For Hanukkah) (Serves 4–6)

3 large potatoes, pared and cubed
2 tbsp non-dairy margarine, melted
1 tsp kosher salt
2 tsp sugar
Oil

1. Cover potatoes with water and boil in covered saucepan for about 15 minutes until tender.
2. Rice or sieve to make 3 cups riced potatoes.
3. Add margarine, salt, and sugar.
4. Mix well and cool.
5. Make eight balls from mixture.
6. Heat waffle iron and brush with oil.
7. Place one ball in middle of iron and close lid. Bake 4 to 5 minutes.
8. Repeat to bake others.

Hamantaschen (For Purim) (Makes 5 dozen)

1/2 c butter
1/2 c sugar
3 eggs
1 tsp orange zest
2 c flour
1 1/2 tsp baking powder
1 tbsp poppy seeds
3 8-oz cans poppy seed filling

1. Cream butter and sugar.
2. Beat in 2 eggs and orange peel.

3. Carefully but thoroughly stir in flour, baking powder, salt, and poppy seeds.
4. Divide dough in quarters on floured board and roll each quarter 1/2" thick.
5. Cut into 2 1/2" circles and put 1 tsp poppy seed filling in center of each. Fold edges toward middle to make a triangle with a bit of filling showing.
6. Pinch seams to seal and brush with last egg.
7. Bake on foil-lined sheet for 10 minutes at 375°F.

Matzo Farfel Kugel (For Passover) (Serves 6–9)

Oil
1/4 c finely chopped nuts
4 matzo farfel
Boiling water
Salt and pepper
4 eggs, separated
1/2 c unsalted margarine, in pieces
1/2 c golden raisins
1/2 c diced apples
1 tsp cinnamon
2 tsp sugar

1. Brush 8" x 8" baking pan with oil and scatter nuts in it.

2. Soften farfel in colander by pouring boiling water over it.
3. Combine softened farfel, salt, pepper, egg yolks, margarine, raisins, and apples.
4. Beat egg whites until peaks just bend over and immediately fold into farfel mixture.
5. Transfer to prepared pan and sprinkle with mixture of cinnamon and sugar.
6. Bake at 350°F for about 45 minutes until golden brown.

Note: *Matzo* is unleavened bread made from flour and water, and baked at a very high temperature. Matzo can be crushed finely to make *matzo meal*. When matzo is broken coarsely, it is *matzo farfel*.

*S*ummary

Greece, western Turkey, Lebanon, and Israel near the coast have a climate moderated by the Mediterranean Sea, but inland from the sea, the remainder of the Levant and eastward as far as Iraq and Iran is very hot in the summers except for the mountainous regions. The rugged terrain and limited rainfall of the whole area make agriculture difficult except where irrigation water is available. Wheat, olives, grapes (in some areas), eggplant, onions, and other vegetables are produced in this region. Sheep are adapted well to this type of landscape, but some pigs, cattle, and fowl also are raised. Fishing generally is somewhat limited as a source of food for most of the area. Despite the difficulties, trade routes have extended across these several lands since long before the time of Christ.

The region that is now Greece was invaded by the Persians and later by the Romans, followed by Goths, Franks, Venetians, Crusaders, and the Ottomans. Turkey also was in the path of various conquests, which resulted in changes in religions from largely Christian (Eastern Orthodoxy) to predominantly Muslim, with others living there too. The Seljuks (who were Muslims) captured Byzantium, which caused Pope Urban II to call for a Crusade (the first) to liberate the region from what he viewed to be infidels. Subsequently, three other Crusades passed through western Turkey. Then came the Mongols; the Ottomans finally seized power to create the strong Ottoman Empire that ruled for centuries, finally being displaced at the end of World War I when Ataturk was able to lead the modern state of Turkey. Jerusalem and the surrounding lands that were called Palestine long ago have been the scene of many religious disagreements because Christianity, Judaism, and Islam all have sites of great significance in Jerusalem and the surrounding area. These places today include the Dome of the Rock, the Wailing Wall, and the Church of the Holy Sepulchre. Historical arguments over the region have involved Romans and later the Crusaders. Even today, negotiations are continuing to attempt to resolve territorial issues. Religious problems are not a great concern in Greece; much of the population is Greek Orthodox. Turkey has many Sunni Muslims, but other religions are able to operate there too.

Architectural structures, some standing and some in ruins, are prominent in this region of the world. Examples are the Parthenon and other structures on the Acropolis in Athens, Hagia Sophia and the Blue Mosque in Istanbul, the Treasury in Petra, Jordan, and such palaces as the ruins at Persepolis in Iran and the Topkapi Palace and the Dolmabache Palace in Istanbul.

Food patterns throughout this region have some strong similarities. The most common ingredients are wheat, lamb and mutton, eggplant, olives, various vegetables, and legumes. Muslim avoidance of pork and alcohol and the Jewish dietary laws influence food practices in families adhering firmly to these dictates. Phyllo is the key ingredient in several desserts and main dishes. Pita is the most common type of bread, although lavosh and Arab flat bread also are very popular. Several different legumes are used, but the most common is the chickpea. Tahini is a ubiquitous paste made with sesame seeds and their oil with lemon juice added. Bulgur is used in a variety of dishes, including tabouli. Other common foods are dolmas (or dolmades), kebabs, shawarma, feta, lebneh, Turkish coffee, raki, ouzo, and retsina.

Study Questions

1. Identify the countries that border on (a) Turkey, (b) Israel, and (c) Syria.
2. Compare the architectural style of the Parthenon with that of the Blue Mosque.
3. What was the purpose of the Crusades? Were the Crusaders successful in their fight? What were some of the effects of the Crusades?
4. Describe at least one dish in which the following ingredient is significant: (a) phyllo, (b) bulgur, (c) eggplant, and (d) sesame seed or sesame oil, or both.
5. Identify similarities and differences between Muslim and Jewish dietary rules.

Bibliography

Barer-Stein, T. 1999. *You Eat What You Are.* 2nd ed. Firefly Books, Ltd. Ontario, Canada.

Browning, I. 1997. *Petra.* Chatto and Windus. London.

DuBois, J. 1993. *Israel.* Marshall Cavendish. New York.

Facaros, D., M. Davidson, and B. Walsh. 1993. *Greek Islands.* Cadogan Books. London.

Hassig, S. M. 1993. *Iraq.* Marshall Cavendish. New York.

Humphreys, A. and N. Tilbury. 1996. *Israel and the Palestinian Territories.* Lonely Planet. Oakland, CA.

Humphreys, A., P. Hellander, and N. Tilbury. 1999. *Israel and the Palestinian Territories.* 2nd ed. Lonely Planet. Oakland, CA.

Kramer, M. 1988. *Illustrated Guide to Foreign and Fancy Food.* 2nd ed. Plycon Press. Redondo Beach, CA.

Lorentzen, C. R. and P. C. Pihos, eds. 2000. *Let's Go Greece.* Let's Go Press. Cambridge, MA.

McKay, J. P., B. D. Hill, and J. Buckler. 1999. *History of Western Society.* Houghton Mifflin. Boston.

Mesulam, S. and E. S. Daniel. 2001. *Let's Go Turkey.* Let's Go Press. Cambridge, MA.

Packard, D. P. and M. McWilliams. 1993. Cultural Foods Heritage of Middle Eastern Immigrants. *Nutr. Today, 28*(3).

Pearcy, G. E. 1980. *The World Food Scene.* Plycon Press. Redondo Beach, CA.

Shahbazi, A. S. 1976. *Persepolis Illustrated.* 25th Shahrivar Printing House. Tehran.

Sheeban, S. 1993. *Turkey.* Marshall Cavendish. New York.

Stewart, D. 1965. *Turkey.* Time, Inc. New York.

Uvezian, S. 1999. *Recipes and Remembrances from an Eastern Mediterranean Kitchen.* University of Texas Press. Austin, TX.

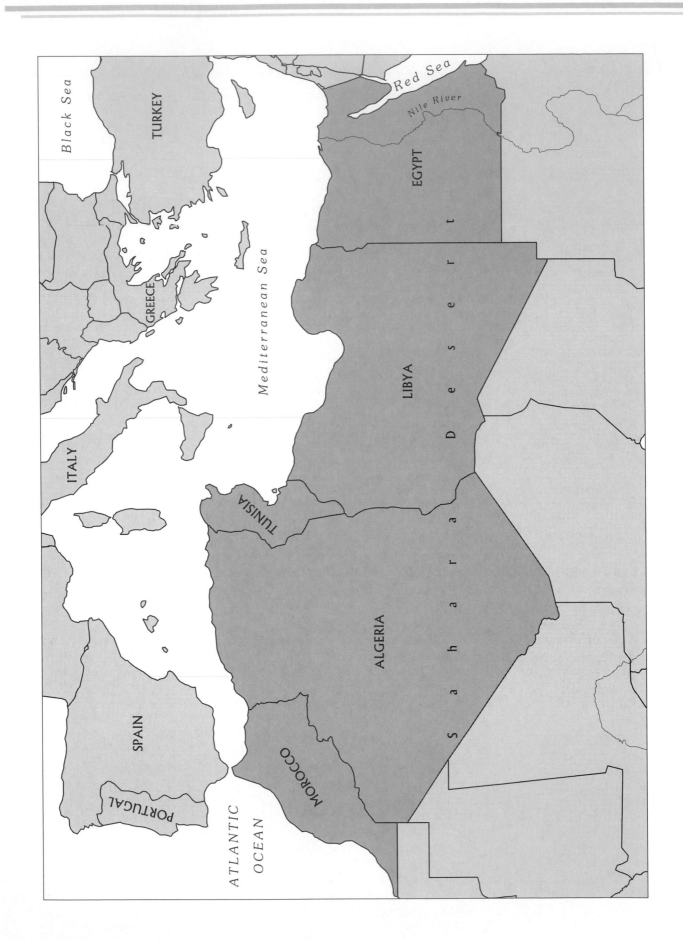

12 North Africa

Geographic Overview

Five countries extend across North Africa from the Sinai east of the Suez Canal to the western shoreline of Morocco overlooking the Atlantic Ocean. They all share the Mediterranean Sea's southern waters. Egypt is on the northeastern point of Africa. Just to the west of Egypt is Libya. Tunisia is a small country that is sandwiched between Libya and neighboring Algeria; it has considerable shoreline as a result of the continental protrusion into the Mediterranean. Algeria is the largest country in this group. Morocco is a bit larger than Tunisia, but it has the distinction of containing four mountain ranges: the Rif in the north, and the Middle Atlas, High Atlas, and Anti-Atlas mountains. The High Atlas are so high that they may have some snow in a few spots throughout the year, which is surprising in view of the intense heat of the Sahara Desert that is such a dominant feature of these countries. Mountains extend into Algeria and Tunisia, although they are considerably lower than the High Atlas of Morocco.

Immediately along the shores of the Mediterranean Sea, all of these countries derive a bit of a respite from the heat and also have some arable land that is of significance in feeding their people. However, temperatures soar in large regions of these lands, particularly in summer. Winter temperatures are generally comfortable. The very dry conditions promote chilly nights.

Adequate water is the universal problem throughout North Africa. The only river of any significance is the Nile River in Egypt. The Nile has long provided Egyptians with some farmland. In years past, its annual flood deposited silt to enrich fields all along its course from the south of Egypt to its delta leading into the Mediterranean. The construction of the Aswan Dam in southern Egypt was completed in 1971, a feat that eliminated the annual floods and altered the environment. Considerable controversy regarding the advantages and detrimental effects of the

151

Figure 12.1 Dovecotes, such as this one near Port Said, Egypt, are a useful source of food (pigeons) for farmers.

Some farmers along the arid northern coastlands of Africa maintain dovecotes (Figure 12.1) that provide stylish homes for the birds and ultimately tasty fowl for family dinner tables. Bastila, a favorite specialty of Morocco, features pigeon as the main ingredient.

Aswan Dam continue to rage and may never be settled. The steadier supply of water along the Nile enables farmers to raise as many as three crops per year rather than the single crop that was possible before construction of the dam. However, the Nile Valley is very narrow (from about 2 to 14 miles wide) and provides a comparatively small amount of land for feeding the ever-increasing population of Egypt.

Agriculture in all of these North African countries is severely limited by lack of rainfall and the vast expanses of the Sahara Desert, where only a few oases afford a bit of water for the nomads of the region. Sheep, goats, and camels can be raised in some parts of this forbidding landscape, but only a small amount of beef is produced. Cereal crops raised in Egypt and the other countries of this region include wheat, millet, and some corn and rice as well as broad beans and vegetables. Some fruits add to the local foods. These crops are produced in the northern regions of these countries and in some of the valleys in the mountains of Morocco. These limitations on agriculture account for the need to import many different foods in this region of the world.

History and Culture

The history of Egypt, accentuated with its dramatic remnants of the glorious structures dating from 5,000 years ago, has captured the world's interest beyond that of any other part of the world. Even young children are well acquainted with pictures of the pyramids and the sphinx at Giza, which were built by rulers in the Fourth Dynasty between 2650 and 2500 BCE. There were 31 dynasties that ruled before Alexander the Great conquered Egypt in 332 BCE. Then, a general of Alexander, Ptolemy I Soter, assumed the role of king and established the Ptolemaic Dynasty. The Ptolemy rulers were in power until 30 BCE, when Cleopatra (the last of the Ptolemaic rulers) and Mark Antony committed suicide as Octavian captured Alexandria. Egypt then came under Roman rule, but the governance was shifted to Constantinople when the Empire was divided. At this time, the official religion was Christianity. However, Arabs brought the Muslim religion to Egypt when they invaded in 640 CE. Saladin established his dynasty in Egypt and then proceeded to capture Jerusalem in 1187. The Mameluke sultans ruled Egypt for 300 years before it became part of the Ottoman Empire in 1517. The French occupied Egypt for a mere 3 years at the end of the 18th century, just long enough for some of Napoleon's soldiers to be accused of shooting off part of the nose of the sphinx. The British also occupied the country for half a century (1882 to 1936), and they returned to help drive out the Germans and Italians during World War II. Since then, Egypt has been ruled by its own leaders.

The cultural heritage of Egypt is great. The engineering feat of building the pyramids is considered a wonder even today. The architectural features of the temples from ancient Egypt and the style that characterized the art of the early Egyptians are admired and sometimes serve as the stimulus for architecture and design today. The golden funeral mask of King Tutankhamen and many of the items found in his tomb have been exhibited in cities around the world, attracting huge crowds wherever they are shown. The financial resources required to move the temples at Abu Simbel (Figure 12.2) to a safe height above the level of Lake Nasser (created by the Aswan Dam) were raised from all over the world—a further indication of the intense interest that people of other nations have in the early cultural history of Egypt. Egyptian culture is even evident in Paris today through the display of one of its obelisks in the Place de la Concorde and the pyramid-shaped glass entrance that architect I. M. Pei added to the Louvre as part of his renovation of this noted museum.

The sturdy buildings of the pharaohs, the highly decorated tombs and temples they built, and the hieroglyphics (translated by such scholars as Champollon when the Rosetta Stone [Figure 12.3] was found and studied) are still viewed as objects of wonder by people today. The amazing thing is that these achievements date back more than two millennia before Christ! Such antiquity of culture is not only a matter of pride for today's Egyptians, but also is embraced by people throughout the world.

Religion occupies a prominent position in the lives of many Egyptians, with Islam being the religion of about 90 percent of the people. Most of the remaining people are Christians, many of them Coptics. The Coptic Christians were formed at the time that the Byzantine Empire was being overthrown, and this small group in Egypt remained rather isolated from other forms of Christianity. There are monasteries along the Nile in northern Egypt that provide places of retreat and meditation for Coptics, and there is a Greek Orthodox monastery (St. Catherine's) in the Sinai desert in eastern Egypt, dramatically positioned below Mt. Sinai, the mountain where Moses is reported to have received the Ten Commandments. A small population of Jewish people also is found in urban areas. However, the dominance of the Muslim faith is evident in the myriad mosques, the calls to prayer throughout the day, and the holidays that are celebrated.

For much of the period of the early civilizations around the Mediterranean Sea, all of the northern coast of Africa except Egypt was viewed as being one region, Libya. No divisions were noted for what now are the countries of Tunisia, Algeria, and Morocco. This region was known to the seafaring Phoenicians, who used the tip of the semi-peninsula in the middle of the northern shore of Africa as

Figure 12.2 The temples at Abu Simbel are imposing sights despite their being moved up above the site where Ramses II built them originally.

Figure 12.3 The Rosetta stone, which enabled scholars to interpret the hieroglyphics of ancient Egypt, is on display in the British Museum in London.

a port for their trading ventures. This port was named Carthage, and a bit of its ruins can be seen near Tunis today.

Carthage was the point in Africa that was closest to Rome, which was of significance to the Romans as they were establishing their ever-widening domain in the millennium prior to Christ. Following their conquest of Carthage in 146 BCE, they began to develop the northern part of the present country of Libya as an important source of wheat and other grains, establishing the necessary wells and irrigation needed for agriculture. This area of Africa was part of the western Roman Empire, and Egypt was in the eastern domain when the division was made in 395. Christians and Jews were living in this western region along the coast. Inland in the desert and mountain areas were native peoples called Berbers. They maintained control over the desert and its caravan routes, and also ruled in the mountains, and even defeated the invading German Vandals when they ousted the Romans and took over the Roman forts and settlements along the coast in the north.

Arab invasions began in the middle of the 7th century, bringing Islam with them. However, not all Muslims believed in belonging to a single sect, and division and fighting set the tone for the ensuing centuries in Tunisia, Algeria, and Morocco, the region known collectively as the Maghreb. Shiite Muslims (followers of the descendants of Ali, the prophet's son-in-law), from what is now northern Algeria, sought to conquer Egypt to widen their religious base. The result was that they founded Cairo in 972. However, their homeland in Algeria reverted to Sunni (based on descendants of the fifth caliph) beliefs. Then, Arabs (Shiites) from the southern part of Egypt invaded the Maghreb in large numbers, ultimately remaining as settlers throughout the region and replacing the Berbers as the majority.

The Berbers were extremely competent fighters, who accepted Islam. Their religion assumed considerably more importance in their lives when a chieftain founded the Almoravid dynasty, following his *hajj* to Mecca, and expanded control from Morocco and Algeria, establishing Marrakesh as the capital in 1069. Expansion of the Moors into Spain to conquer the Christian lands there was accomplished by the end of the 11th century. Eventually, the Christians in Spain and political pressures from the east of the Maghreb resulted in the downfall of the Berber's Almoravid regime.

Morocco was under the control of successive regimes until the middle of the 19th century. The remainder of the Maghreb was the domain of Barbarossa, a Turkish pirate who raided ships plying the Mediterranean off the Barbary Coast of Algeria and Tunisia. He and his brother formed an alliance with the Turks, who supplied 6,000 troops and the assistance needed to overthrow the Spaniards in Algiers in 1529 and to regain control of Tunis a few years later. Although Spain again took Tunis, by 1574 the Ottoman Turks and the Barbary pirates were in control of Algeria, Tunisia, Libya, and the Mediterranean in that region. Ottoman control lasted until the end of the 18th century in Algeria and Tunisia, and until the 20th century in Libya. However, throughout the centuries the desert nomads, dubbed the Bedouins, pursued their wanderings relatively free of political shifts.

Control of Algeria was wrested by the French in 1830; Algeria became a French protectorate at that time and remained so until independence from France was finally accomplished by a 6-year war that ended in 1962. Morocco and Tunisia also were taken over by the French as protectorates, Morocco from 1881 to 1956 and Tunisia from 1912 to 1956. Libya was invaded by Italy in 1911 when the Italians and Turks went to war. The Italian control of Libya was a period of intense cruelty by the Italians against the Arabs. Finally, Libya became an independent nation in 1951 following the end of World War II, parts of which were fought across the Libyan terrain. Subsequently, the regime of Muammar Qaddafi has resulted in serious problems of terrorism that have echoed around the world, leading to isolation of Libya from the world's other nations.

The teachings of Islam dominate the lives of the people throughout North Africa today and have also influenced the cultural heritage of this region. The early art of Egypt and some paintings found on rocks in the desert in Tunisia and Libya provide evidence of the creative efforts of pre-Islamic inhabitants. However, the art of today generally is restricted to calligraphy, utilizing the very beautiful script of Arabic writing. In the mosques, decoration is provided by some artistic Arabic lettering of passages from the Koran, carefully crafted designs in hand-woven rugs covering the entire floor inside, and beautiful architecture, particularly in the design of the minarets. Exotic simplicity perhaps describes the architecture of North Africa.

Doorways and courtyards afford the aesthetic highlights of many public buildings and also of homes. Privacy and a certain quality of mysticism are achieved by the use of limited, high windows blended with the decorative arches that beckon visitors to enter. Interiors feature seating on huge cushions, low tables for dining, and *kilims,* or carefully knotted and handcrafted carpets, to adorn the floors and walls. The *casbah* (also called *medina)* is the old, walled part of North African cities. In no other way is immersion in the culture accomplished faster than by wandering through this realm and shopping in the various *souks* (the cluster of stalls featuring spices, gold, and many other items for sale).

Clothing choices are quite varied in this part of the world. Many women wear modest garments designed to avoid showing their bodies and even their faces if they are from families following traditional practices. In some families, adolescent girls begin to don the long, off-white robes worn in Tunisia, called *safsari,* or dark ones, such as those worn in Libya and Egypt, and a headpiece with a veil that covers all of the face except the eyes. However, traditional dress for women is not the rule for many women in this region, particularly in the cities. Men often wear the *burnous* (or *burnoose),* which is a dark, long, cape-like garment with a hood. Other men may wear white robes and a cloth over the head secured by twisted rope, and a few choose the red fez for their heads. In the cities, business men often wear western-style clothing. The overall effect on the street is a dazzling and exotic look into a different part of the world.

Even the calendar of Islam differs from that of the western world, for the Islamic calendar is based on 12 lunar months. The result is that the calendar is 10 days shorter each year; the timing of the religious holidays is shifted 10 days each year, bringing the fasting of Ramadan (the 9th month) at various seasons of the year. When Ramadan falls during the heat of summer, the hardship of avoiding drinking from sunrise to sunset is extremely great in these torrid regions.

Daily life is influenced by Islamic traditions throughout this region. Since Islam is almost the universal religion of the people, the day marked as the holiest of days is Friday. Of course, prayer five times daily is also practiced during the rest of the week. From the age of puberty onward, males and females generally tend to be separated in public and in school beyond the elementary grades. Secular entertainment is not the usual choice for leisure hours. Actually, the time devoted to religion, work, and family leaves little opportunity for other activities.

Food Patterns

Meals in North Africa commonly are eaten at low tables while sitting on cushions scattered on the floor. In the past, the men usually ate before the women and children, but this pattern is not always followed now because of the lack of space in city apartments. The tradition of a meal begins with hand-washing (often in rose-scented water). A small, narrow glass of very sweet green tea with mint serves as the opener, with usually two more glasses of mint tea to follow. The serious eating is done using the first three fingers of the right hand. The left hand is never used, for to do so is considered bad manners. All diners remove a bite of food from the platters in the middle of the table, dip it in any desired sauce that is provided, and then quickly put it in their mouths. This process continues until the food is gone or the diner is satisfied. Little conversation occurs while people are dining, for this is serious business that is worthy of full attention. When the meal is finished, diners again rinse their hands with water.

Throughout this region, brass and copper serving trays (often with flowing designs), sturdy copper cooking pots, uniquely shaped coffee pots, pottery bowls, and skewers for shish kebabs are standard equipment in most kitchens. Emphasis is on large trays and pots because of the family-style service. Morocco has a unique type of cooking and serving container called a *tagine,* which is also the name of the stew that traditionally is prepared in it. The tagine is a round pottery bowl that has a conical-shaped pottery cover.

Breakfast often is simply coffee and some bread or cereal product. Coffee (usually sweet and strong) and very sweet, minted green tea appear at frequent intervals throughout the day. These are important sources of fluid in the heat of these countries, where consumption of sodas and especially of alcoholic beverages is not an accepted part of the culture. However, men sell water by the cupful on the city streets, particularly in the squares and parks where people gather. Milk (goat, water buffalo, or ewe's) is not widely used as a beverage, although *leben* (similar to buttermilk) is used a bit, and so are some cheeses.

Meats are included in special meals and occasionally at other times, but the expense limits their use. Since strict Muslims need to have their meats from animals that have been sacrificed according to a prescribed ritual, markets are likely to have live chickens, lambs, and other sources of protein available for purchase so that the householder can assume that responsibility. Lamb, goat, and camel may be included in the diet, but pork is prohibited in both Islamic and Jewish dietary laws, which leaves too few customers for this meat. Meats may be eaten in the form of shish kebabs, but they often are included in casseroles or stews augmented with vegetables.

Vegetables and legumes are usually at least a small part of the diet in all of North Africa. Eggplant, onions, cabbage, spinach, potatoes, cauliflower, and okra are quite common, and carrots, cucumbers, and sometimes tomatoes are also used. Fruits available include large quantities of dates, oranges, limes, and even some pomegranates, olives, bananas, and grapes. Legumes are used extensively; *ful* (beans simmered slowly) and *tamiya* (fried bean patties) are favorite ways of eating legumes, but beans also are often basic ingredients in soups and stews.

Bet tai (or *bettawa*) is the name of the classic large disc of leavened wheat bread that is popular in Egypt and the other countries of North Africa. Variations abound in this basic staple food, including *fenugreek* to contribute the flavor of anise, and corn, millet, or sorghum as supplemental types of flour. The influence of the French in the Maghreb can be seen in the extensive use of baguettes and croissants. *Burghul,* the cereal product made by boiling and drying cracked wheat, is a popular food that may be used uncooked in salads after soaking or as an ingredient in a variety of casseroles and stews. Rice also is used in main dishes. However, couscous is the dominant cereal used (except for breads). The Berbers are acknowledged as the originators of couscous, which commonly is made from dry wheat flour into which water is drizzled while the mixture is manipulated manually into very small pellets. These pellets then are steamed in an uncovered steamer (with a perforated bottom) placed atop a boiling pot of stew until the couscous is light and fluffy. The finished couscous sometimes is combined with stew ingredients, or it may be served as a separate dish.

Oils are used fairly extensively in North African meals. Olive oil is poured generously over various dishes (both main and side) as a type of garnish. Sesame oil also is popular for this purpose, while peanut oil often is the choice for cooking. Sometimes, clarified butter may be used. The consumption of oils is of importance in the diets of people in this region. Sweets also are very popular, especially desserts made with honey, such as baklava.

Although much of the diet of the people in North Africa is similar to that of those living in the Levant, there are some dishes uniquely characteristic to one or more of the countries in the Maghreb. Perhaps the most unique dish is *bastila* (or *pastilla*), which is Morocco's fabulous flaky-crusted pigeon pie. *Harira* is a hearty legume, meat, and vegetable soup seasoned with cinnamon, saffron, ginger, turmeric, and lemon that traditionally ends each fast day in Morocco during Ramadan. Pastries that have been boiled in honey *(mahalkra* or *shebakia),* dates, other fruit, and coffee round out this meal.

Key Terms

Bastila—Flaky-crusted pigeon pie flavored with ginger, cumin, cayenne, saffron, and cinnamon, and dusted with confectioner's sugar; Moroccan specialty.

Berbers—Natives of the mountains of North Africa noted for their fighting skills and horsemanship.

Bet tai—Disc-shaped, yeast-leavened, wheat flour Arab bread, usually about 14 inches in diameter.

Burghul—Granular cereal product made by boiling and drying cracked wheat.

Burnoose—Dark, cape-like, hooded garment worn by Arab men, particularly in Morocco.

Casbah—Walled part of Arab city in North Africa.

Couscous—Cereal product made by drizzling water on wheat flour and rolling it into small pellets, which are then steamed until fluffy.

Harira—Hearty soup containing legumes, meat, and vegetables, and seasoned with spices and lemon; important for suppers during Ramadan.

Maghreb—Countries in the northwestern part of Africa: Morocco, Algeria, and Tunisia.

Medina—Old native quarter of a North African city.

Moors—Inhabitants of northwestern Africa (mixture of Arabs and Berbers) who invaded Spain in the 8th century.

Safsari—Robes worn by women in North Africa to cover their bodies and veil their faces.

Shiite—Branch of Islam practiced by those who follow Ali, the prophet's son-in-law.

> **Souk**—Arab marketplace featuring specific types of shops, such as spice shops and gold shops.
>
> **Sunni**—Branch of Islam practiced by those who follow the descendants of the fifth caliph.
>
> **Tagine**—Stew prepared in a round pottery bowl topped with a conical lid (bowl and conical lid also called tagine), a unique product of Morocco.

ecipes

Bastila (Morocco) (Serves 6–8)

4 1-lb Cornish hens or pigeons
5 tbsp butter
1 c chopped onion
2 tbsp chopped cilantro
1 tbsp chopped parsley
1 tsp ground ginger
1/2 tsp ground cumin
1/2 tsp cayenne
1/4 tsp turmeric
1/8 tsp saffron
1/8 tsp cinnamon
1 c water
1 1/2 c blanched almonds
1/2 tsp cinnamon
2 tbsp sugar
6 eggs, beaten together
10 sheets phyllo (16" x 12")
1/2 c melted butter
3 tbsp oil
2 tbsp confectioner's sugar
1 tbsp cinnamon

1. Brown fowl (washed, patted dry) in butter in large skillet until browned on all sides.
2. Remove fowl; brown onions, add herbs, spices, and water, and heat to boiling.
3. Add fowl to skillet, cover, and simmer for about 1 hour until tender.
4. Brown and chop almonds, then stir in sugar and cinnamon.
5. Skin and debone fowl and cut meat into 2" strips.
6. Pour 1 1/2 cups liquid from skillet (reserve it), then quickly reduce the remaining liquid to 1/4 cup in the skillet.
7. Return liquid to skillet, add eggs, and heat while stirring until eggs form soft curds.
8. Overlap 6 sheets of phyllo on board, forming a circle; fold two sheets in half and put in center of phyllo circle.
9. Sprinkle almond mixture in a 9" circle in center of phyllo; spread half of egg mixture over it.
10. Arrange all fowl in a circle to make a layer, then cover with rest of egg and two folded sheets of phyllo.
11. Brush exposed phyllo with melted butter; fold each leaf of protruding phyllo over circle and brush each phyllo lightly with butter; fold over the next phyllo to completely enclose the pie.
12. Heat remaining butter and oil in large skillet until very hot. Carefully slide the bastila into the hot fat to brown for 2 to 3 minutes on each side.
13. Top with mixture of confectioner's sugar and ground cinnamon; slice into wedges.

Harira (Morocco) (Serves 4–6)

1/2 lb lamb stew meat
2 tbsp olive oil
1/2 tsp ground ginger
1/4 tsp turmeric
1/4 tsp ground cinnamon
1/2 c chopped onion
2 medium tomatoes, coarsely chopped
1 lb canned chickpeas, drained
2 tbsp cilantro, chopped
Salt and pepper
1 qt water
1/4 c orzo (or rice)

2 eggs, beaten lightly
2 tsp lemon juice
Sprinkle of cinnamon

1. Brown meat in hot olive oil, then stir in ginger, turmeric, cinnamon, onions, tomatoes, chickpeas, cilantro, water, salt, and pepper.
2. Simmer 1 hour.
3. Add orzo and simmer another 10 minutes until orzo is tender.
4. Beat in eggs, lemon juice, and cinnamon. Serve.

Brik bil Lahm (Tunisia) (Serves 4)

1/2 c chopped onion
1/2 lb ground lamb
2 tbsp chopped cilantro
1/8 tsp ground saffron
Salt and pepper
1 tbsp butter
2 tsp grated parmesan cheese
4 sheets phyllo (16" x 12")
4 eggs
lemon garnish

1. Thoroughly mix onions, lamb, cilantro, saffron, salt, and pepper; brown in butter in a skillet, being sure to break into small pieces.

2. Remove from heat and stir in cheese.
3. Brush sheet of phyllo with butter; fold sheet of phyllo in half and again in half to make a rectangle 8" x 6", and then fold 2" over to make a 6" square.
4. Make a mound of 1/4 of lamb so it will be in center of a triangle if the dough is folded over to make a triangle.
5. Make a well in the mound and crack egg into the well.
6. Moisten the edges of phyllo, then fold dough over to make a triangle enclosing the filling. Be sure to press dough firmly to seal.
7. Fry in very hot olive oil for 2 to 3 minutes per side.
8. Repeat to make 4 briks.

Djedje Tagine (Morocco) (Serves 4–6)

1 chicken fryer, in pieces
3 tbsp butter
1 c water
2 medium onions, chopped
1/2 tsp ground ginger
1/8 tsp cumin
1/8 cayenne
1 lemon, sliced (seeds removed)
1/4 c chopped parsley
1/4 tsp black pepper
1 7-oz jar pitted whole green olives
2 tbsp flour
2 tbsp cold water

1. Brown pieces of chicken in butter in Dutch oven; add water, onions, ginger, cumin, cayenne, lemon, parsley, and pepper.
2. Simmer, covered, for 45 minutes.
3. Meanwhile, drain olives. Cover olives with water in a saucepan and heat to boiling. Drain and boil again in water to cover.
4. Add olives to chicken and stir, then transfer to serving platter.
5. Thicken remaining liquid with flour mixed with cold water to make a smooth paste. Stir while heating slowly to thicken. Add water if necessary to make 1 1/2 cups.
6. Pour over chicken and olives, and serve.

Tunisian Doughnuts (Makes 12)

2 eggs
1/4 c salad oil
1/4 c orange juice
1 tsp orange zest
1/4 c sugar
2 c flour
3 tsp baking soda
2 c water
2 c sugar
2 tbsp lemon juice
1/2 c honey
1 tsp orange zest
Oil for frying

1. Beat together eggs, oil, orange juice, orange zest, and sugar until smooth.
2. Stir in flour mixed with soda and continue beating until very viscous. Cover for 30 minutes.
3. Boil water, sugar, and lemon juice in small saucepan to 230°F.
4. Add honey and zest, and simmer 6 minutes.
5. Preheat deep-fat fryer oil to 360°F while shaping doughnuts.
6. Divide dough into 12 and roll each piece into a ball into which a hole is punched with a finger.
7. Fry doughnuts for 5 minutes without crowding them, turning to brown them evenly on both sides. Drain on paper towels.
8. Dip each doughnut in warm syrup and serve.

Couscous with Lamb (Algeria) (Serves 6–8)

2 1/2 c water and 2 1/2 tsp salt
1 tbsp olive oil
2 c couscous
1 1/2 lb lamb stew meat
1 medium onion, minced
1/4 c olive oil
1/2 tsp ground cinnamon
1/8 tsp cumin
1/4 tsp black pepper
4 c water
2 c canned chickpeas, drained
4 carrots, pared and sliced (2" slices)
1 1/2 lb turnips, pared and quartered

1. Pour salt water and olive oil over couscous; gently lift and rub couscous between palms of hands until water has been absorbed. Cover for 20 minutes.

2. Brown lamb and onion in olive oil, cinnamon, cumin, and black pepper in a Dutch oven or bottom of couscoussier.
3. Add water and chickpeas, then place cheesecloth-lined colander or top part of couscoussier on top and seal the two parts with aluminum foil to trap steam upward through the couscous.
4. Boil to generate steam and slowly add couscous, a cup at a time, while rubbing pellets between hands. Steam 20 minutes after all couscous is added.
5. Add vegetables to bottom of pot; sprinkle cinnamon and salt water over couscous and fluff a bit.
6. Steam couscous and boil vegetables for 20 minutes. Serve couscous mounded on a large platter with meat, vegetables, and some of the juices over it.

Summary

North Africa is comprised of Egypt, Libya, Tunisia, Algeria, and Morocco; the latter three often are referred to as the Maghreb. All have shoreline on the Mediterranean and large desert regions (the Sahara) as well as some mountain ranges, the best known being the Atlas ranges. The very dry climate and heat have shaped the agricultural patterns so that some crops are raised in the northern regions and along the Nile and wherever irrigation is possible. Meat sources raised in the region include sheep, goats, camel, some beef, and poultry. Wheat and some other cereals are grown with irrigation, and so are some vegetables and fruits.

Egypt was the site of an advanced and artistic civilization that included hieroglyphic writing more than 2,000 years before Christ. Artifacts and architectural monuments from this period are admired around the world today. Additional historic mementos of subsequent Phoenician and Roman conquests are also in evidence all along the shores of North Africa.

Religion shifted from that of the early Egyptians to a Christian era that gave way to the dominant Islamic beliefs and practices of modern North Africa. There are still some Coptics, other Christians, and Jews scattered throughout these countries today, although they definitely are the minority in all of these countries.

In addition to the early Egyptians, other groups lived throughout this expanse of northern Africa. The Berbers in the mountains and valleys of what is now Morocco were early settlers. Bedouins managed to survive the rigors of desert life by practicing a nomadic lifestyle, which still can be found today in some regions of the Sahara and its borders.

The Moors, the name given to the mixture of Arabs and Berbers living in the region of Morocco, invaded Spain by way of the Strait of Gibraltar during the 11th century and controlled much of that peninsula until late in the 15th century. Their advanced culture and architectural designs left structures and traditions that still remain a significant part of Spain. The similarities between southern Spain and Morocco are very evident today despite the changes that have ensued in the 500 years since the days of the Moors in Spain.

Phoenicians, Greeks, and Romans interacted with people in North Africa as they traveled through the Mediterranean Sea in search of trade and conquest. Piracy based from North Africa was the pattern of the day during the late 16th and 17th centuries when the Ottoman Turks were in control of much of the region. Eventually, France gained control of Algeria, Morocco, and Tunisia during the 19th and part of the 20th centuries. Italy controlled Libya for much of the first half of the 20th century.

The cultures of these countries today are largely a reflection of their Islamic heritage. Mosques are adorned with lovely calligraphy that is based on the Koran. Privacy and quiet are fostered by building designs that feature lovely doorways and interior courtyards. Clothing is modest; some women wear long robes and veils that reveal only the eyes. Some segregation of sexes occurs after the age of puberty. Dining may be separated by sex in some families, and eating with the right hand is the accepted practice, usually while seated on cushions surrounding a low table. The food patterns are quite similar to those found in the Middle East, although couscous, bastila, and tagine are particular favorites in North Africa.

Study Questions

1. Identify three distinctive geographic features that are important to North Africa and describe the influence that each of these features has had in shaping the region.
2. Describe the cultural impact of Islam on Egypt, using architecture or other features.
3. Cite at least one aspect of today's life in North Africa that can be traced to the presence in the past of each of the following: (a) Phoenicians, (b) Romans, (c) Ottoman Turks, (d) Arabs, (e) Christians, (f) Italians, and (g) French.
4. Define (a) Maghreb, (b) tagine, (c) Berber, (d) Moor, (e) Bedouin, (f) couscous, and (g) bulghur.
5. Compare some of the dining traditions of Morocco with those in France, and explain why they are different.

Bibliography

Barer-Stein, T. 1999. *You Eat What You Are.* 2nd ed. Firefly Books, Ltd. Ontario, Canada.

Bowles, P. 1992. *Morocco.* Harry N. Abrams. New York.

Brander, B. 1966. *River Nile.* National Geographic Special Publications. Washington, D.C.

Budge, E. A. W. 1979. *Tutankhamen.* Bell Publishing. New York.

Crowther, G, and H. Finlay. 1992. *Morocco, Algeria, and Tunisia.* Lonely Planet Publications. Berkeley, CA.

Desroches-Noblecourt, C. 1965. *Tutankhamen.* Doubleday. Garden City, NY.

Field, M., and F. Field. 1970. *Quintet of Cuisines.* Time-Life Books. New York.

Haag, M. 1994. *Illustrated Guide to Egypt.* Passport Books. Lincolnwood, IL.

Malcolm, P. 1993. *Libya.* Marshall Cavendish. New York.

Neubert, O. 1972. *Tutankhamen and the Valley of the Kings.* Mayflower Books. London.

Paliouras, A. 1985. *Monastery of St. Catherine of Mount Sinai.* St. Catherine's Monastery at Sinai. Sinai, Egypt.

Pearcy, G. E. 1980. *The World Food Scene.* Plycon Press. Redondo Beach, CA.

Reader, J. 1997. *Biography of the Continent of Africa.* Vintage Books. New York.

Stewart, D. 1977. *Pyramids and Sphinx.* Newsweek. New York.

Tompkins, P. 1971. *Secrets of the Great Pyramid.* Harper and Row. New York.

Wright, C. A. 1999. *A Mediterranean Feast.* William Morrow. New York.

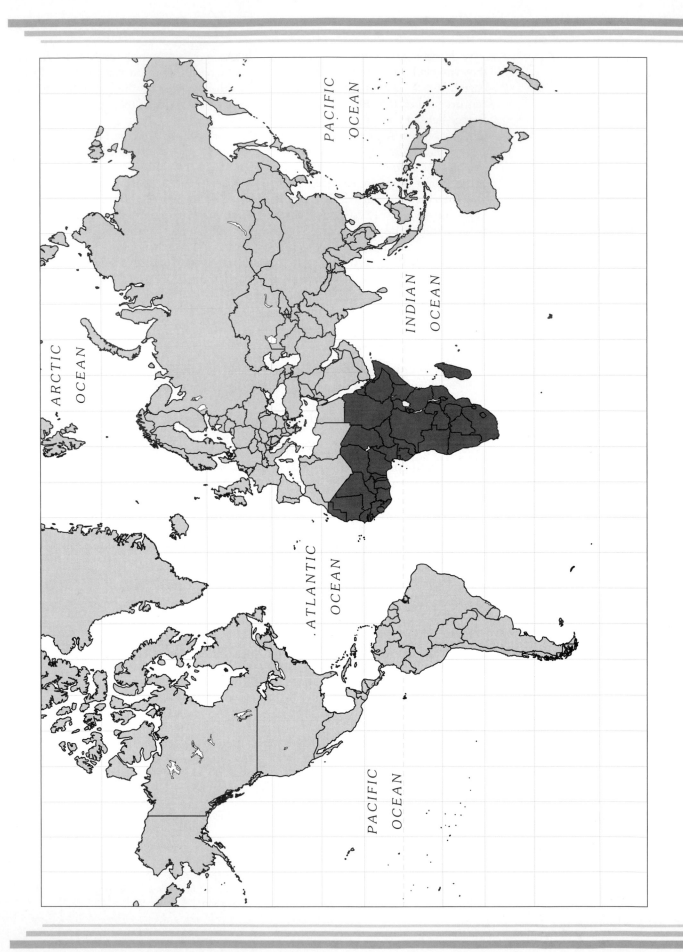

ARCTIC OCEAN

PACIFIC OCEAN

INDIAN OCEAN

ATLANTIC OCEAN

PACIFIC OCEAN

Part IV

Heritage from Sub-Saharan Africa

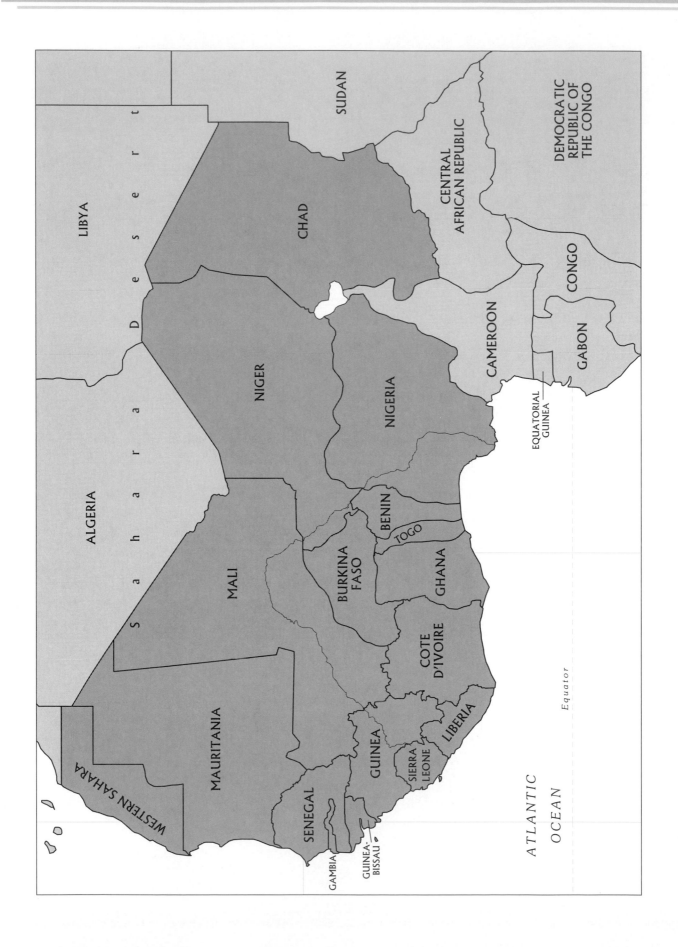

13 West Africa

Geographic Overview

Geographically, West Africa is viewed as being the countries south of the Sahara that constitute the large western bump of the African continent. In terms of the theory of plate tectonics, continental drift, and the hypothesized super-continent called Pangaea, West Africa would account for the void that created today's Caribbean. Most of these nations (Gambia, Guinea, Sierra-Leone, Ivory Coast, Ghana, Togo, Benin, and Nigeria) have at least some shoreline on the Atlantic Ocean, but Chad, Niger, Mali, and Burkina are isolated from the sea. The Niger and Volta rivers are long, navigable rivers that provide limited transportation of some crops and goods in the various countries they traverse.

In general, the coastal strip is fairly narrow before the rise to the continental plateau that comprises much of the African continent south of the Sahara. This plateau has considerable breaks in it, which limit the usefulness of the terrain for farming. However, subsistence farming is possible in parts of these West African countries. The rainfall in parts of West Africa creates an equatorial rainforest, while farther north the rainfall begins to dwindle, reducing the amount of crops that can be grown until the edge of the desert completely eliminates agriculture. The broad strip of land north of the rainforest and up to the southern edge of the Sahara (the Sahel) includes grassy savanna to semi-desert.

Although much of the agricultural effort is basically subsistence farming, food exports are also a source of some national income. Among the export crops are peanuts, palm oil, cocoa, kola nuts (for cola beverages), coffee, bananas, sugar, and pineapples. Livestock can also be raised successfully in areas that are free of the tsetse fly.

The tsetse fly is not the only health hazard found in the difficult climatic conditions in West Africa. The intense heat of the tropics and the rainfall patterns also create unfortunate opportunities for parasites and bacteria to propagate and infect the population, sometimes with conditions that are debilitating to life threatening. Productivity is sometimes seriously impacted by the prevalence of disease outbreaks, while intermittent recurrences of malaria and other tropical health problems are ongoing problems that sap the population's energies. A high rodent population adds to the sources of health problems in West Africa.

History and Culture

The history of the African continent extends back to very early man in various regions. Evidence of farming in the Sahel goes back as far as 6,000 years ago. Relics (Figure 13.1) of early farming include bones from cattle herds, hoes, scythes, pottery, and remnants of crops of yams, millet, and rice. Stone village remnants found in the Sahel of West Africa have been dated at about 1200 BCE. The early settlers centered around the Niger River and Lake Chad, both suitable regions for developing agriculture. The tools that could be made from iron began to improve farming there by about 450 BCE. Perhaps the earliest town of significance was Jenné-Jeno in Mali, which was flourishing before 500 CE. In fact, the Bantus began to migrate from Central Africa eastward and southward, which was a migration significant to the development of the rest of Africa.

The social history of West Africa is extremely complex because the region consisted of numerous tribes, none of which was numerically dominant enough to reign over its neighbors for long periods. The result was the development of

Figure 13.1   Ankle bracelet c 1500–1600 CE Africa. *Pitt Rivers Museum*, Oxford.

many languages and familial traditions that tended to sometimes foster disagreements and battles. Among the established empires were the following:

- Empire of Ghana, from about the 5th to the 11th century,
- Empire of Mali, which dominated trade from Senegal to Egypt from the 13th to the 15th century,
- Empire of Songhai, which detached from Mali from the 14th to 16th century and included the fabled trading outpost of Timbuktu.

Other smaller domains existed to the south of these empires, but played lesser roles in trade than did the Ghana, Mali, and Songhai empires.

European nations have a long history of intertwining with Africa, a history that developed along the western coast (Figure 13.2) from the interests of Prince Henry the Navigator when he sent Portuguese ships in the early 1500s to explore opportunities for shipping African gold via Portuguese vessels. The result was that the Portuguese were able to ship valuable cargo from Senegal and other ports by sea, thus avoiding the costly and uncertain trade routes via camel across the Sahara. Belgium, England, and France quickly became interested in trading with and colonizing West Africa too. This imperialistic frenzy culminated in the Berlin Conference of 1884–85 when the concerned European powers essentially carved up Africa without any input from the affected populations of Africa! Belgium ended up with the Congo, Germany had Togo and Cameroon, Portugal received Guinea-Bissau and some islands in the Atlantic, England had a bit of the coastline of West Africa as well as much of the regions of East and South Africa, while France got the rest of West Africa and the remainder of the central part. Germany lost its holdings as a result of World War I, and the remainder of the countries in West Africa were able to achieve independence at different times following World War II. This independence has led to considerable conflict both between and within nations, which has extracted a haunting human toll.

Figure 13.2 c 900 BCE The Nok people of West Africa, A Western African Terracotta head. *Dorling Kindersley.*

The specter of slavery immediately comes to mind when examining the history of West Africa. A portion of its coastline in Benin and Nigeria was once even termed the Slave Coast. Slaves had been a sad consequence of such conquerors as Alexander the Great and various Roman leaders, to cite a few who claimed slaves as part of their booty long before the use of slaves apparently began in West Africa. In fact, prior to the arrival of the Portuguese, conquered Africans were being sold to other Africans or were taken to the home territories of the victors and used to perform heavy labor. However, slave trade increased markedly after the Portuguese traders developed their markets along the West African coast and acquired slaves to carry to Brazil to provide labor for the sugar plantations.

Several European nations who were building their colonial holdings in the western hemisphere had a seemingly insatiable need for slave labor to work the cane, tobacco, cotton, and other fields being cropped to the benefit of the controlling nation. During the 17th and 18th centuries, four European colonial powers (Spain, England, Holland, and France) were heavily involved in transporting slaves to work in South American regions and the Caribbean as well as in their domains in Southeast Asia. Slaves were shipped out from ports in the western part of Africa (most frequently from the island of Goree near Dakar, Senegal) and also overland across the trade routes to the east. American ships eventually were involved in the slave trade too. The impact of the use of African slaves in the South is well known as the cause of the Civil War in the United States. Thus, the African slave trade has had a lasting and significant effect on both sides of the Atlantic. Despite the fact that the slave trade itself was abolished across the Atlantic by a series of treaties in the early part of the 19th century and ended totally in 1830, the practice of slavery persisted well beyond that time. Abolition occurred in such distant places as India in 1843, the United States in 1865, and Saudi Arabia in 1962. Many, but certainly not all, of the slaves affected were the natives of West and Central Africa.

Religion in West Africa appears to have been essentially that of animism prior to the arrival of the message of Islam in the Sahel by the 14th century. Muslims adapted Islam somewhat, incorporating some overtones of nature and spirits to retain some of their earlier culture. Many Muslims live today in the Sahel across West Africa (Figure 13.3), the exact number being impossible to determine. Christians from Europe brought their message to West Africa, and this faith was accepted particularly in the southern coastal regions of West Africa. Again, converts to Christianity retained some aspects of their traditional beliefs when they also accepted the faith of the Christians. Estimates of religious affiliations are that the southern region along the coast of West Africa is predominately Christian, and the northern part is mostly Muslim, giving a division of about half and half to these two major religions.

Most of the people living in West Africa prior to the early part of the 20th century lived in rural circumstances (Figure 13.4), and many still live on land that they farm to support their families' food and living requirements—often at subsistence level. However, urbanization is developing in some places, a trend that has tended toward a two-class system. This is particularly apparent in Nigeria, where the oil boom of the late 1960s and 1970s brought sudden wealth to a limited number of people and left a trail of problems when the oil bubble burst and profits were severely diminished. The problems confronting comparatively rich Nigeria and the other countries of West Africa are large and seemingly impossible to solve in the near future. Such accepted things as safe water for drinking and enough calories to eat are basics that are not available to many people, especially when weather problems reduce the harvests from their land.

Oral traditions have been passed from generation to generation over the centuries in West Africa. The spoken word in the form of elaborate storytelling has enriched the heritage of innumerable people for whom access to education and to libraries has often not been possible. The Yoruba living in southwestern Nigeria are an ethnic group with a long and rich history of storytelling as a means of shaping and retaining their cultural uniqueness.

Figure 13.3 Potter in the Muslim section of Yacouba Village, Nigeria, Africa. *Dorling Kindersley/Gales.*

The African spirit is truly amazing. The cultural heritage is handed down from generation to generation, even though reading and writing may not be a part of many of their lives. This explains the great value placed on story-telling in West Africa. The history and imagination of West Africans have been captured in the stories they tell, not only to each other but also to the world. The story of Br'er Rabbit is an example of stories thought to have originated in Africa.

Figure 13.4 Carving and decorating gourds; the bottom of a beautifully painted gourd. *Powell Cotton Museum.*

Figure 13.5 Meals usually are cooked in a single pot over a fire.

Music is another forte of West Africans. Singing, which usually includes spirituals if the vocalists are Christians, has provided a rich heritage and pleasure for all people, both performers and the audience. Instrumental music also is a part of West Africa's cultural traditions; drums of various pitches produce exotic and exciting rhythms that are unique and lasting.

Adornment plays a significant role of identity for the many tribes of West Africa. The dances that these tribes perpetuate as part of their lasting traditions usually feature dancers with remarkable masks appropriate to the dance and tribe. African masks are a key part of the artistic culture from West Africa. Other artistic achievements are the fabric designs and the large bead and shell necklaces.

Food Patterns

The foods that thrive in West Africa on family farms have formed the foundation of the diet in this part of the world. Two of the most important crops, maize and cassava, were promoted heavily by slave traders in previous centuries because they could be shipped with the slaves to feed them on the long ocean voyages. Both maize and cassava are still mainstays of diets today. In addition, sorghum, wheat, rice, millet, plantain, greens, legumes, groundnuts (peanuts), and yams are key components of meals. Eggs, milk in various forms, chicken, and small amounts of beef, goat, sheep, or wild game are sometimes included in the diet.

The dish that forms the backbone of the diet for many people in West Africa is *fufu*. This is made by pounding or grinding a starchy vegetable or cereal until it becomes pasty and then boiling with added water to make a very thick product. No single recipe is used for fufu. The starch source may be manioc (cassava), yams, millet, rice, plantain, or other starchy foods. Fufu is eaten by scooping up a bite of the cooked paste in the right hand (left hand is used for toilet chores), forming it into a ball, and then dipping it in some type of spicy sauce.

Cooking likely is limited to recipes that can be boiled in a single pot (Figure 13.5) or to something that is fried. Ovens are not available in many homes. Frying is a popular method of cooking, usually done in palm oil or peanut oil. The palm oil is likely the type that is a reddish color; the higher cost of peanut oil limits its use.

Vegetable mixtures cooked in a pot are varied according to the vegetables that may be available at the particular moment. Often, a bit of meat or egg is added if it is available, but the cost of these protein foods limits the frequency and the amount used. To add excitement to these dishes, a variety of seasonings and sauces is used. Preference seems to run toward hot, hotter, and hottest! Peppers and chilies are essential in West African cooking. Seeds, particularly sesame, are used generously too. Not surprisingly, salt is a noticeable ingredient, which is helpful in replacing the body's salt lost in perspiration in the very hot days typical of West African weather.

Fruits are available in the tropical parts of West Africa. Bananas, papayas, mangoes, pineapples, melons, and citrus are among the most common. However, there also are some more exotic tropical fruits that may be eaten on special occasions.

Peanut butter (called groundnut butter) finds many uses as a dip, spread, or ingredient in a range of dishes. Chopped peanuts also are used to add texture and nutrients to some stews. Other popular dishes are *yassa* (a dish made with meat or chicken that has been marinated in a lemon sauce), *gari foto* (a stew of hard-cooked eggs, onions, and tomatoes), and *jollof* rice (layers of meat, tomatoes and other vegetables, and steamed rice simmered together).

Key Terms

Berlin Conference of 1884–85—Meeting at which European colonial powers divided the African continent without including Africans in their decisions.

Empire of Ghana—Dominant power in West Africa from 5th to 11th century.

Empire of Mali—Empire dominating trade from Senegal to Egypt from the 13th to the 15th century.

Empire of Songhai—Dominant empire in West Africa (including Timbuktu) after splitting from Mali in the 14th century into the 16th century.

Fufu—Starchy paste produced by pounding and boiling manioc or other rich source of starch and then dipping each bite in a spicy sauce.

Gari foto—Stew of hard-cooked eggs, onions, and tomatoes.

Goree—Island just off the coast of Dakar, Senegal, from which vast numbers of slaves were shipped to the Americas and Caribbean islands.

Jenné-Jeno—Very early town (before 500 CE) in Mali.

Jollof rice—Dish comprised of layers of meat, tomatoes and other vegetables, and steamed rice.

Niger River—One of the longest rivers of the world, it traverses much of West Africa, running northward before turning east and south; it has an interior delta and one at the coast.

Sahel—Broad band of land across West Africa between the Sahara and the lush vegetation along the southern coast.

Tsetse fly—Vector for sleeping sickness, a serious disease in parts of West Africa.

Yassa—Dish made with lemon-marinated chicken or meat.

ecipes

Banana Fritters (Serves 4–6)

6 ripe bananas
1 c flour
1/4 c sugar dissolved in 1/4 c water
1/2 tsp ground nutmeg

1. Mash bananas with fork until smooth.
2. Stir in other ingredients, adding a little water if needed for a consistency like pancake batter.
3. Fry like pancakes, turning once.

Fish Stew and Rice (Serves 4–6)

1/2 onion, chopped
2 tbsp oil
3 tbsp tomato paste
2 carrots, sliced
1/2 lb cabbage, shredded
1/2 pkg frozen okra
2 yams, cubed
1 1/2 lb fish (deboned), cubed

4 c water
2 tsp salt
3 c cooked rice

1. In Dutch oven, saute onions in oil until golden.
2. Add tomato paste, vegetables, fish, water, and salt.
3. Simmer for 1 hour, covered.
4. Meanwhile, cook rice.
5. Ladle stew over mound of rice.

Fried Chicken with Peanut Butter Sauce (Serves 4–6)

1 chicken fryer, cut in pieces
2 tbsp peanut oil
3/4 c chopped onion
1 tomato, diced
2 tbsp tomato paste
1 tsp salt
1 tsp paprika
1 bay leaf
2 c water
1 c peanut butter

1. Brown chicken in oil in Dutch oven.
2. Add onions, tomato paste, seasonings, and water. Cover and simmer for about 45 minutes until chicken is almost tender.
3. Remove chicken. Blend chicken stock into peanut butter to make a smooth sauce.
4. Return chicken to pan and pour peanut butter sauce over it; cover and simmer until chicken is very tender.

Jollof Rice (Serves 4–6)

1 small frying chicken, in pieces
2 tbsp oil
1/3 lb ham, cubed
2 onions, chopped
1 tsp salt
1/4 tsp pepper
1/2 tsp ground allspice
2 1-lb cans tomatoes
1 6-oz can tomato paste
1/4 lb green beans
3/4 c water
1 c rice

2 c water
1 tsp salt

1. Brown chicken in oil in Dutch oven.
2. Add ham, onions, seasonings, tomatoes, paste, beans, and water.
3. Cover and simmer for 1 hour, stirring occasionally.
4. Meanwhile, simmer rice in salted water for 15 minutes, covered.
5. Spoon rice over vegetables and chicken, cover, and simmer 10 minutes.

Lamb Gumbo (Serves 6)

2 lb cubed lamb stew meat
2 tbsp peanut oil
1/2 c minced onion
3 tbsp flour
1 6-oz can tomato paste
2 red peppers (seeds removed), diced
1 1/2 tsp salt
4 c water
1 10-oz pkg frozen okra
1 c whole wheat flour
1/2 c water
Salted water

1. Brown lamb in oil in Dutch oven.
2. Add onion and flour, stirring and heating to brown flour.
3. Add tomato paste, peppers, salt, and water.
4. Cover and simmer for 1 hour.
5. Add okra and simmer until soft.
6. Meanwhile, make whole wheat balls: Mix flour and water together, then cook (covered) in top of a double boiler for 30 minutes.
7. Scoop balls of dough and drop in boiling, salted water for 10 minutes.
8. Drain balls and serve with the lamb gumbo.

Bananas, Black-Eyed Peas, and Shrimp (Serves 4–6)

2 c dried black-eyed peas
1 qt boiling water
1/2 chopped onion
1 tomato, chopped
1 tbsp crushed, dried red peppers
2 tbsp tomato paste
1/2 lb canned shrimp
3 large bananas (1/4" slices)
1/2 tsp salt
1 c oil

1. Rinse black-eyed peas, then boil for 2 minutes and let them soak without heat for 2 hours.
2. Simmer peas until tender.
3. Add vegetables and boil very gently for 15 minutes.
4. Add tomato paste and shrimp, and simmer for 15 minutes.
5. Meanwhile, sprinkle bananas with salt.
6. Deep-fat fry bananas to a golden color. Drain well on paper towels.
7. Serve bananas with the peas.

Summary

West Africa includes Gambia, Guinea, Sierra-Leone, Ivory Coast, Ghana, Togo, Benin, Nigeria, Chad, Niger, Mali, and Burkina. The latter four countries are without access to the sea, but the other nations have coastlines on the Atlantic. Rainfall ranges from heavy enough to support equatorial rainforests in the southern areas to extremely arid approaching the Sahara toward the north. Subsistence farming is found in much of the region, but a few crops, such as peanuts, cocoa, kola nuts, and bananas, are raised in sufficient amounts to be exported. The tsetse fly is a hazard to animals and people in some regions. Tropical illnesses, parasites, and rodents add to the health hazards for people in West African countries.

Evidence of agriculture in West Africa dates from more than 6,000 years ago, with iron tools being used around 450 BCE. The Bantus appear to have gradually migrated eastward and southward from the eastern edge of West Africa over the next 1,500 years. The empires that developed in West Africa included Ghana (5th to 11th century), Mali (13th to 15th century), and Songhai (14th to 16th century).

The coast of West Africa was visited by the Portuguese ships of Prince Henry the Navigator in the 1500s. This led to trade via the Atlantic to compete with the camel routes through the Sahara. European nations carved up Africa at the Berlin Conference of 1884–85, establishing control of various West African countries by England, France, Germany, and Belgium. This situation evolved slowly into the establishment of independent nations.

Slavery had been a fact in various nations long before the practice in the Roman Empire, but it became a tragedy for people living in West Africa during the era of colonialism. Slaves were bought in various West African ports and shipped under the flags of Portugal, Spain, England, Holland, and France to their respective colonies in the Americas and Caribbean. Those slaves who survived the terrible conditions during the ocean voyages were sold at slave markets to work in the fields or on plantations of their masters. The slave trade was abolished in most countries by the mid-1800s, but many people continued to live in slavery for some time after that.

Religion is varied in West Africa. The people living just south of the Sahara most frequently are Muslims, but Christianity is found in the southern parts of the region. Some of the aspects of their earlier religion have been incorporated into the Muslim and Christian practices of West Africans.

Storytelling is a rich cultural tradition of West Africa. Music features exciting rhythms from drums and also includes songs. Dances, often with costumes and masks, are another cultural expression of the region.

The food traditional to West Africa is based on extensive use of cassava, maize, rice, plantain, legumes, yams, sorghum, wheat, and rice. Limited amounts of meat, chicken, eggs, and milk may be consumed too. Recipes that can be cooked in a single pot over an open fire form the basis of the diets of many people. Frying is also a common means of cooking food. Root vegetables and various tropical fruits such as bananas and pineapples are served frequently.

Study Questions

1. Compare the typical foods in the diets of West Africans with those from North Africa. Why are these diets different?
2. Identify at least three factors that have influenced the dishes West Africans usually eat.
3. Why was Prince Henry the Navigator interested in West Africa?
4. Did slavery have its beginnings in West Africa? If not, identify some earlier domains where slavery existed.
5. What are the two most common religions in West Africa, and where is each predominant? Why does this difference exist?

Bibliography

Appiah, K. A. and H. L. Gates, Jr., eds. 2000. *Africana*. Basic Books. New York.

Barer-Stein, T. 1999. *You Eat What You Are*. 2nd ed. Firefly Books, Ltd. Ontario, Canada.

Burenhult, G. 1994. *Traditional Peoples Today*. Harper Collins. New York.

Coetzee, R. 1982. *Funa—Food from Africa*. Butterworths. Durban, South Africa.

Devere, J. 1980. *Black Genesis: African Roots*. St. Martin's Press. New York.

Else, D., A. Newton, J. Williams, M. Fitzpatrick, and M. Roddis, eds. 1999. *West Africa*. 4th ed. Lonely Planet. Oakland, CA.

Levy, P. 1993. *Nigeria*. Marshall Cavendish. New York.

Pearcy, G. E. 1980. *The World Food Scene*. Plycon Press. Redondo Beach, CA.

Reader, J. 1997. *Africa: A Biography of the Continent*. Vintage Books. New York.

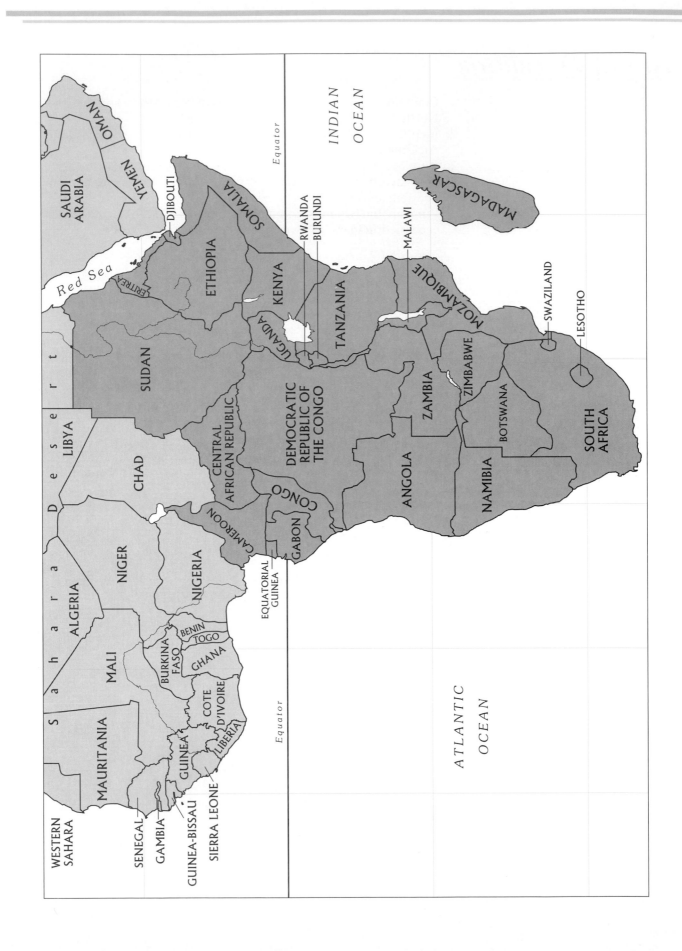

14 East and South Africa

Geographic Overview

The whole continent of Africa is so vast that it is difficult to grasp its total extent. Perhaps the fact that its area is greater than the combined areas of the United States, China, Europe, India, New Zealand, and Argentina will help to establish a sense of its size. The area of the United States is somewhat smaller than the part of Africa lying south of the equator. Obviously, the geographic details of such a huge area as that encompassed in the eastern and southern parts of Africa cannot be pinpointed; only a broad-brushed examination is feasible here. The countries included in this chapter are Sudan, Eritrea, Djibouti, Ethiopia, Somalia, Kenya, Tanzania, Uganda, Rwanda, Burundi, Gabon, Cameroon, the Democratic Republic of Congo, Angola, Zambia, Malawi, Mozambique, Zimbabwe, Botswana, Namibia, and South Africa.

These areas of Africa are mostly high plateaus, but there are some outstanding geographic features. Mt. Kilimanjaro in Tanzania near the border of Kenya towers to a height of 19,340 feet. Second in height is Mt. Kenya, which rises to an impressive 17,058 feet. The Great Rift Valley extends from Jordan in the Middle East, south and west to end in Mozambique, its depth varying greatly at various points along its length, but overall giving a fairly deep depression in contrast with the rest of the landscape of the African continent. The rivers of note in this part of Africa include the Zambezi with its remarkable Victoria Falls, the Congo, and the Limpopo. The Atlantic Ocean lies on the west and the Indian on the east, with the two confronting each other where they meet at the Cape of Good Hope in South Africa.

Figure 14.1 Elephants and other wild game in eastern and some parts of southern Africa are important now as a means of bringing tourists to the region to help the economy, whereas earlier people used the animals primarily for meat.

The climate of South Africa is temperate (much like Southern California) because of its distance from the equator. However, the other countries of this region generally have considerable heat and extremes in rain or drought, depending on the time of year. In areas of high elevations, the temperatures are more comfortable, despite the location in the Tropics. However, the low coastal regions are very hot and steamy.

Agricultural efforts have been quite varied in this part of Africa. The original inhabitants basically were subsistence farmers or herdsmen. In regions receiving enough rain, crops could be raised in quantities sufficient to feed their families. Where rainfall was inadequate, there still was sufficient vegetation available to raise livestock (cattle, goats, and sheep). In East Africa, Europeans who came as settlers introduced other crops to grow as export commodities. Coffee and tea were planted in Kenya, for example. The traditional crops of the subsistence farmers include corn, legumes, sweet potatoes, potatoes, millet, sorghum, and bananas. Wild game animals sometimes served as sources of meat in earlier times, but their primary role today is to bring in tourist dollars, which help indirectly to feed people living in parts of Africa, particularly south of the equator (Figure 14.1).

History and Culture

Some of the very earliest traces of man have been unearthed in the Olduvai Gorge in Tanzania, attesting to the presence of early hominids in Africa more than 1.5 million years ago. The climate in much of Africa south of the Sahara appears to have been favorable to survival, with adequate food available for the picking and hunting. Petroglyphs, such as those in Botswana at the Tsodilo Hills and in Zimbabwe at Matobo National Park, Domboshawa, and Ngomakurira, afford glimpses of the animals these people confronted in the early Stone Age. However, little else remains to provide information about the developments of early civilizations until comparatively recent times. During the times of early Egypt, Africa to the south of Egypt was referred to as the land of Punt. Queen Hatshepsut was one of the Egyptian rulers who sent expeditions to Punt to bring back such goods as ivory, myrrh, and human slaves.

Perhaps the most successful settlements where structures are still in evidence today were Aksum and Great Zimbabwe. Aksum was carved in the highlands of northern Ethiopia, where the climate was cool and wet at the time of year that the nearby Red Sea coast of today's Ethiopia was at its hottest and driest. The abundant crops and the energies of the people fostered a society that peaked in the 4th and 5th centuries CE. The Red Sea afforded trading opportunities with Egypt, the Arabian Peninsula, and countries on the eastern end of the Mediterranean. Aksum residents developed a language that was not only spoken, but also written. Their stone churches left permanent evidence of their civilization.

Great Zimbabwe was built later, its Great Enclosure being constructed in the 14th century in what is now the country of Zimbabwe. Actually, this site of civilization was occupied and developed during the three centuries leading up to the construction of Great Zimbabwe's Great Enclosure. The amazing stone structure called the Great Enclosure defined an ellipse that was more than 90 yards wide and was about 250 yards in total length. Imagine the amount of stone that had to be placed to construct this wall, which was 5 yards thick and as much as 10 yards high! Among the artifacts that have been unearthed during the archaeological explorations of Great Zimbabwe are shards of Chinese and Persian wares, mute evidence of the trade that obviously existed during the zenith of Great Zimbabwe.

Much of the development of the eastern and southern regions of Africa stems from a combination of the climatic and trading influences. A migratory procession of Bantus slowly moved into these regions when rains and weather favored agricultural production of crops and livestock, notably cattle. The demands of the slave traders for slaves added to the impetus for Bantus and others to move into the new regions to avoid this threat.

Portuguese traders were in the forefront in opening trading in the southern reaches of Africa. The Cape of Good Hope was so named by Bartolomeu Dias, leader of the first Portuguese expedition to round the southern tip of Africa. Vasco da Gama returned 9 years later in 1497 and continued his voyage of exploration all the way to India, a voyage which revealed the strong presence of Arabian and Indian traders already along the west coast of Africa.

Foreign probes into Africa were triggered not only by interest in trade, but also by religion. Christians believed that there was a Christian kingdom ruled by the mythical Prester John, who was rumored to have a distant and rich Christian domain somewhere in the depths of the African continent beyond the Sahara. The Portuguese were highly motivated to find and join forces with Prester John, both to defeat Islamic forces they had encountered as a result of Vasco da Gama's voyage and to secure the riches that could be obtained by trading along the east coast of Africa. The Dutch and then the French and English were attracted to Africa as the slave trade and the Middle Passage (transport of slaves by sea from Africa to the various colonial possessions) became economically significant in the 16th century. Even after abolition of the Atlantic slave trade in the 19th century, the slave trade flourished in the eastern and southern parts of Africa and continued eastward from the east coast for much of the remainder of the century. Throughout Africa, the introduction of cassava and maize by the early European slave traders left at least the lasting benefit of these two important food crops that provided so much sustenance for people throughout much of Africa.

The Cape of Good Hope was a logical site for establishing a provisioning post to facilitate the trading voyages the Dutch wished to make to the various ports in India and beyond. This need led to the settling of the land that is now South Africa, beginning at its southern shore, which is about as far south of the equator as Greece is north of it. Successful development of such a post required agricultural efforts by the new settlers.

The Bantu farmers (originally from north of the equator) had not traveled nearly that far south in their expansion, because their major crops of millet and sorghum grew much better farther north than in the Cape region. This left the land relatively available to the Dutch settlers who arrived in Table Bay in 1652, and they worked hard to achieve good harvests. The native Khoisans raised cattle and moved them around as necessary for adequate grazing lands. This arrangement worked well at first, but the increasing need for farmland as new Dutch settlers (called Boers) arrived began to restrict the grazing land and inexorably moved the original inhabitants of the Cape from their land.

The Dutch East India Company, the trading company that started the development of what is now Cape Town, had intended only to be able to restock ships at its new port. However, employees who left the company to settle in Cape Town, and new arrivals from other countries, began to crowd the surrounding farmland to the point that expansion to the east and into the interior regions had to occur, a movement that eventually led to the migration dubbed the Great Trek, which took place between 1835 and 1839. Participants in this migration were called *Voortrekkers* (or *trekboers)*, and this movement is commemorated at a memorial built near Pretoria, the capital of South Africa (Figure 14.2).

Not surprisingly, conflicts were frequent between the whites (who were usurping much of the good land previously available to the original inhabitants) and the blacks. The Afrikaners (farmers of Dutch heritage) faced daunting times as they developed their farmlands in the interior, but the problems confronting the blacks were also overwhelming. Nevertheless, it was the language of Afrikaans which eventually gained status alongside English as the language of the country. The various black languages were ignored.

Many different groups of blacks migrated over many centuries into South Africa as well as into Botswana and Zimbabwe. Some of the more predominant groups included the Zulu, Ndebele, Xhosa, Sotho, and Tsonga. A particularly strong leader of the Zulus was a chief named Shaka, who ruled from 1816 until he was killed in 1828.

Adding to the racial complexities was a group termed the coloreds, which included Indians, Malays, and offspring of interracial marriages. This occurred

Figure 14.2 The former home of South African statesman Paul Kruger in Pretoria, South Africa, is maintained as a museum now.

Customs vary widely from tribe to tribe, sometimes contrasting sharply with traditions in America. An example is the custom of the Tswana, who live between the Kalahari Desert and the mountains of southern Africa. Their tradition is to marry a cousin in order to be certain that the children of the marriage belong to the husband's family. The groom pays a dowry to the bride's family (usually cattle).

commonly in the early days when very few white women settled in the region, causing the white settlers to reach out to other racial and cultural groups for sociability.

The final straw in this rather volatile milieu was the diverse backgrounds of the whites: Dutch Boers and British. Their inability to utilize each other's strengths and their clashes in philosophy, land, and governance resulted in the bloody Boer War at the end of the 19th century. The governmental stance that emerged from this war led to the divisive policy of apartheid, with its tragic treatment of blacks and coloreds. At least the 20th century saw the abolition of apartheid, and a black president was elected. The situation in South Africa has undergone a significant transformation. The mineral riches of this nation, particularly diamonds and gold (Figure 14.3), should fuel the strengthening of this new governmental approach in the 21st century.

South Africa suffered under its white rulers for a very long time, but also gained some benefits in terms of development and organization. At the Berlin Conference in 1884, the rest of eastern and southern Africa also was handed over to various European nations. The Congo was awarded to Leopold of Belgium, with the result that huge numbers of people died while the rubber and other riches of the region were being shipped to Belgium. Britain received the Sudan, Kenya, Zimbabwe, Botswana, and South Africa. Germany received Tanzania, and Italy gained Somalia. The results in these countries generally were far less damaging than in the Congo, but national freedom became the goal of these countries. The various nations achieved independence at different times during the 20th century. However, evidence of the British remains wherever they established their organization and administration, leaving a legacy that generally has aided in moving forward after independence.

Missionaries were very active during the colonial period in Africa; they represented various Christian denominations as they brought their messages of the Bible and their faith. They also brought education to many people who had never had an opportunity to receive an education. In some aspects, the missionaries and their congregations melded their beliefs and practices well, but the Africans sometimes retained their beliefs in mysticism, the use of mediums, and magic as well as occasionally their practice of polygamy. Nevertheless, the overall interaction was viewed as successful and helpful to the people the missionaries reached.

Muslims also were practicing their faith in some parts of Africa, particularly along the eastern coast, and some Hindus were worshiping the faith they brought

Figure 14.3 Gold and diamond mines have long provided their riches to some people in South Africa.

with them from their homes in India. Although there are many Africans practicing the Lutheran, Anglican, Dutch Reform, Methodist, Roman Catholic, and other religions brought by the missionaries, there still is a strong belief in animism among many people in this region. There is special veneration of ancestors and a strong interest in communicating with them, often with the assistance of a medium. Beliefs in potions and spells may also be quite strong among these people.

Music plays a role in the various countries of Africa. For instance, the marimba and a variety of drums and rattles are utilized in music from Zimbabwe. Horns from some of the wild animals sometimes find a role in making music. Missionaries also encouraged singing religious songs, a heritage which continues today. Other creative directions in Africa include storytelling, a particularly effective art among the populace where educational opportunities have been rather restricted. In South Africa attention has been directed toward developing authors and poets. Zimbabwe also has some excellent sculptors who produce uniquely lovely native sculptures. Native dancing is yet another creative art that affords considerable pleasure and creativity to the dancers and that sometimes can be seen by tourists.

Some annual festivals illustrate the importance of the relationship between the people and their daily routines. In Zimbabwe the festival "Making the Seeds Grow" begins with the elders of the village meeting with a medium, an event that is held prior to the beginning of the rainy season. An evening bonfire forms the setting for feasting and dancing. The following day there are preparations for the growing season that will be coming, including gathering seed, which a medium then treats with special remedies to help ensure protection against pests once they are planted. The "Rainmaking" celebration is held just before the rains are to begin. It is a village event usually held in a sacred place at night with the intent of making ancestral spirits happy to help bring the desired rain.

Circumcision of both adolescent boys and girls is a ritual that is practiced to mark the passage into adolescence in some tribal groups. When this procedure is done to girls, the event is held with privacy. However, the ritual passage this marks for males is celebrated in public by Masai villages in Kenya and also in many other tribal villages in Africa.

Food Patterns

Food patterns in the various countries of the region have been influenced significantly by their colonial rulers, but the food habits and preferences of their ancestors still play an important role in the diets of these countries. An illustration of the influence Europeans exerted is the extensive use of cassava and maize throughout much of Africa south of the Sahara. British food patterns have implanted their overtones on food habits as much as England has determined the side of the road on which drivers will proceed. Tea is a clear example of a dietary pattern brought by the British to South Africa, Kenya, and other areas where they established colonies.

However, the crops that can be grown in the various regions and also the suitability of the climate for raising livestock have shaped the diets. Traditionally, tribal societies in the eastern and southern parts of Africa count on women for growing and harvesting their field crops, with children and adolescent males tending to the grazing livestock during the day. Women also are the ones ordinarily responsible for preparing the two meals each day.

Breakfast in the villages consists of a porridge made with a cereal and water, and boiled over a fire of twigs and grasses. It may be served in a communal pot

Olive groves thrive in southern Spain, providing an abundant supply of olives and olive oil.

This view of Toledo, Spain, from across the Tagus River still closely resembles El Greco's famous painting of the scene.

Moors built the Alhambra in Granada, a palace complex that still reveals its architectural splendor.

Bullfighting is a sport that attracts crowds because of its pageantry and excitement.

Paella is considered by many to be the national dish of Spain.

Long strings of garlic bulbs hang decoratively in markets until they are purchased to make sopa de ajo or many other favorite dishes.

Spectacular rock pinnacles around Meteora, Greece provide ideal sites for monasteries and monks seeking solitude.

The Lion's Gate guards the entrance to the remains of Agamemnon's Palace in Mycenae in the Peloponnese of Greece. © Chris Hellier/CORBIS

This sparkling white Greek Orthodox church is situated atop the dramatic cliff that rises from the sea, forming part of the walls of Santorini's extinct volcano.

Blue dolphins cavort in a mural on a wall in Knossus' palace in Crete, a delightful remnant of the Minoan culture.

Muslim women in Antalya and throughout Turkey seem to be crocheting continually whenever they sit to rest.

These Muslim women enjoy a bit of sociability along with productivity as they process wool manually to produce the yarns needed for making Turkish carpets.

Hagia Sophia was built originally to be a gigantic Christian cathedral, but it subsequently was converted to a mosque, minarets were added, and now it is a museum.

Greek-built ruins are found in abundance at Priene and various other sites along the western region of Turkey.

People still live in the caves of Cappadocia, Turkey, which were carved from the volcanic ash (tufa); earlier residents and worshippers were Christians who fled to escape persecution.

Bedouins with their herds of sheep and goats live a nomadic life in Iran near Persepolis.

The ruins of the palace of Darius, center of the Persian Empire, at Persepolis, Iran.

Bas-relief in the ruins of the palace at Persepolis depicting people in a court procession.

Temple at Baalbek in eastern Lebanon preceded Christian worship in the Middle East.

Krak de Chevalliers in Syria was built by English crusaders as a fortress, but eventually it fell to Muslims.© Michael Nicholson/CORBIS

A camel and its native rider survey the Roman ruins at the desert town of Palmyra, Syria.

Crusaders established a strongly-protected island fortress on the island of Rhodes, as evidenced by its large gate at the harbor.©Wolfgang Kaehler/CORBIS

The Dome of the Rock on the Temple Mount in Jerusalem has deep religious significance which has led to seemingly never-ending conflicts between Jews and Muslims as each group seeks control of the same spot.

The Treasury, which was carved out of a rose-colored cliff, greets travelers as they emerge from a narrow canyon to the open area and the ruins of the ancient town of Petra, Jordan.

Baklava and mandarin oranges are for sale in markets and stalls throughout the Middle East.

Phyllo is folded into triangles encasing the filling in spanikopite which is served on the small tray to the right of the feta cheese in this array of appetizers and homemade bread at a party in Athens, Greece.

Mykonos is the Greek island where this man is slicing shawarma (tightly packed layers of chicken and some fat skewered and barbecued vertically on a rotisserie).

Bedouin men warming themselves beside their fire outside a practical home in a cave in the Sinai Desert in eastern Egypt. (Photo courtesy of Ruth MacFarlane)

St. Catherine's monastery is situated dramatically at the base of a precipitous mountain in the middle of the Sinai Desert in Egypt, a setting which gives its monks the isolation they seek in pursuit of their religion.

Shish kebabs are a familiar menu item in Tunis, Tunisia.

Water from the Nile enables farmers at Luxor, Egypt, to irrigate crops throughout the year.

Goats are herded in Egypt and other countries along the northern reaches of Africa where some grazing is possible. (Photo courtesy of Ruth MacFarlane)

The sphinx and pyramids at Giza near Cairo are perhaps the best-known monuments built by the early Egyptians.

The temple of Karnak, with its avenue of sphinxes leading to the entrance, is a remarkable illustration of the building capabilities of early Egyptians.

The interior of King Tut's tomb is smaller than the other tombs in the Valley of the Kings near Luxor, Egypt, but it has yielded wonderful treasures for museums and it still amazes visitors with its painted walls and sarcophagus.

The head of a giant sculpture captures the regal quality of the Pharaoh as he appears to welcome people to Luxor Temple in the middle of Luxor, Egypt.

The Nile River transports its life-giving waters the length of Egypt and welcomes felucca owners to sail on it; Kitchener's Island and the mausoleum of the Aga Khan (atop a hill in the distance) are sights in Aswan, Egypt.

Only a few ruins mark the site of the port of Carthage on the Mediterranean shore near Tunis, Tunisia.

This Muslim woman is wearing a sifsari in Tunis, Tunisia.

Camels are well suited to the hardships of desert life in Morocco and other countries in North Africa and the Middle East.

The ruins at Volubilis in Morocco provide mute evidence of the earlier invasion by the Romans.

One of the King's guards protects the palace in Rabat, Morocco.

The casbah in Fez, Morocco, presents such amazing contrasts as this stylishly tailored man, complete with his fez on his head, and a burro patiently hauling goods to a shop deep within the twisting streets of this old part of the city.

Live chickens can be purchased in the souk in Fez, Morocco.

Bread dough is brought to this neighborhood baker in Morocco to be baked in his oven and then is carried back home to be eaten.

Honey-sweetened pastries and dried fruits are featured wares in this merchant's shop.

Elaborate, ornate doorways are typical of the style of public buildings in Rabat, the capital of Morocco.

Water men in their "lampshade" decorated hats look for customers to buy cups of water to quench their thirst while shopping in Jemaa-El Fna Square in Marrakech, Morocco.

or ladled into bowls or *calabashes* (dried hard shell of a gourd). The men may eat together in the tribal council, in which case a young girl will deliver the porridge to her kinsmen. Women and children eat inside or outside their huts. The porridge usually is made from corn that has been ground into a meal, which accounts for the South African name "mealie meal" to designate the meal they make from *mealie* (their name for corn). Zimbabweans term their rather stiff corn porridge *sadza,* while Kenyans call it *ugali.* Despite the name, this porridge made from maize is a cornerstone of native diets, and other dishes prepared later in the day frequently rely on cornmeal or corn kernels (dried or fresh, depending on the season). Beer is even made from corn in some homes. In Kenya, this beer is called *pombe.*

The other meal of the day also includes cornmeal in some form as a significant part, but vegetables and sometimes meat are added for variety. Usually, these ingredients are cooked along with the porridge in a one-dish meal (Figure 14.4), which again is served from a large pot or from calabashes. Fingers are the preferred tools for eating. People eat together, but men commonly eat before women and children.

Some insects and small creatures are considered delicacies among some groups in these regions of Africa. Termites, for example, are a treat to some Africans living south of the equator and are eaten either roasted or even raw! Other insects also are collected as special treats in the diet. Field mice are another source of protein for some people.

Safe water is one of the significant problems for rural Africans, particularly in the tropical areas. Often, it must be carried some distance and then stored in jugs or calabashes (Figure 14.5) for subsequent use. Boiling is necessary to help assure safety. Added to the problems of food safety is the lack of refrigeration in many villages. The practice of boiling the ingredients in a common pot to make porridges and stews certainly is of great value in helping to maintain health.

Milk is not a prominent part of the diet after children are weaned, although some people do use a bit of milk in cooking. The Masai in Kenya are noted for keeping cattle and for their practice of combining blood from the animals with some milk, which then is drunk promptly, thus avoiding safety problems. By using their cattle in this way, and only occasionally using them for meat, they are able to get maximum dietary benefits while generally maintaining the size of their herds.

Root vegetables are very important in the African evening meal. Cassava is used in abundance and is nutritionally valuable as a good source of starch. In order to avoid the potentially poisonous effect of fresh cassava, the root must be pretreated carefully by soaking it for a few days before boiling it for at least 10 minutes and then squeezing out the liquid. The remaining pulp of the cassava is then ready to beat or to work in a mortar and pestle to make a soft dough.

Figure 14.4 Remains of a one pot meal in a village in Botswana.

Figure 14.5 A calabash full of water hangs outside this native hut.

Kenyans call this cassava dish *fufu*. Pumpkins, various types of squash, sweet potatoes, and potatoes are also used extensively.

Other ingredients for meals may include meat of various types. Barbecues (*braaivleis*) are popular; barbecued pieces of meat are called *sosaties.* However, some people have a particular animal as a totem, and meat from this animal must absolutely not be served to a person with this totem. Otherwise, the meat may be either domestic or sometimes a wild animal (or the aforementioned small rodents). The fruits vary with the season, but are popular when they are available. In the tropics there may be considerable variety. Coconut is popular; its liquid is used in cooking and its meat is used in a variety of ways.

Key Terms

Afrikaans—Language spoken by Afrikans (South African farmers of Dutch heritage); one of the official languages of South Africa.

Aksum—Early, well-developed settlement in the highlands of Ethiopia of importance in the 4th and 5th centuries CE.

Bantus—Very large group of Africans originally from west and central regions of Africa, who spread eastward and south prior to colonial days.

Boer—South African of Dutch descent.

Braaivleis—Barbecues in the southern countries of Africa.

Calabash—Dried hard shell of a gourd suitable for holding liquids or foods.

Cape of Good Hope—Region at the southern tip of the African continent.

Dutch East India Company—Trading company that established Cape Town as a post to restock its ships plying between the East Indies and Holland.

Fufu—Starchy paste or dough made of cassava and popular in Kenya.

Great Rift Valley—Vast depression in the earth extending from Jordan south and west to Mozambique.

Great Zimbabwe—Settlement in Zimbabwe featuring the Great Enclosure built of stone in the 14th century.

Mealie meal—South African name for cornmeal (*mealie* means *corn*).

Pombe—Kenyan beer.

Prester John—Mythical Christian leader of a domain deep in Africa.

Sadza—Zimbabwean name for a stiff cornmeal porridge.

Sosaties—Barbecued pieces of meat on a stick.

Trekboers—Boers who made the Great Trek to settle the interior of South Africa.

Ugali—Kenyan name for a stiff cornmeal porridge.

Voortrekkers—Boers who used oxen and covered wagons to make the Great Trek between 1835 and 1839; also called trekboers.

*R*ecipes

African Beef Stew (Serves 4–6)

1 lb beef stew meat (1" cubes)
1 onion, chopped
1 tbsp oil
3 plantains, cut in quarters
2 tbsp lemon juice
3 tbsp tomato sauce
1/2 tsp salt
1/4 tsp ground sage
1/4 tsp pepper

Water to cover

1. In a Dutch oven, saute meat and onion in oil until browned.
2. Rub plantain pieces with lemon juice, and add to meat.
3. Stir while heating slowly for 5 minutes.
4. Add remaining ingredients, then simmer (covered) for 2 hours.

Vegetable Stew (Serves 4–6)

1 c dried beans
4 c water
1/2 lb cubed lamb stew meat
1 onion, chopped
2 potatoes, pared and cubed
2 stalks celery, 1" slices
3 carrots, pared and sliced
1 c corn
1 tsp curry powder

1 tsp salt
1 c boiling water

1. Boil beans in water in a Dutch oven for 2 minutes. Let stand without heat for 1 hour.
2. Simmer beans for 1 hour.
3. In frying pan, brown meat and onion in oil.
4. Add meat, onion, and other ingredients to beans and simmer for 1 hour.

Chicken in Peanut Butter Sauce (Serves 4–6)

1 frying chicken, cut in pieces
1/4 c oil
1 6-oz can tomato paste
1 1/2 c water
1 tsp salt
1/2 tsp pepper
1/4 c peanut butter

1. Brown chicken in oil; discard oil.
2. Dilute tomato paste with water, and pour over chicken.
3. Cover and simmer 30 minutes.
4. Add seasonings and peanut butter; simmer 20 minutes.

South African Chutney (Makes 3 cups)

1/4 lb dried pears, chopped
1/4 lb dried apricots, chopped
1/4 lb dates, chopped
1/4 lb dried apples, chopped
1/4 lb golden raisins
2 c water
1 c cider vinegar
1 c brown sugar
1/4 tsp chili powder

1/4 tsp ground nutmeg
1/4 tsp ground ginger
1/2 clove garlic, crushed

1. Soak fruit in water in covered bowl overnight.
2. Transfer to a big pan and add the rest of the ingredients.
3. Stir while bringing to a boil, and then simmer 1 1/2 hours to thicken, stirring occasionally.

Fufu (Serves 4)

1 lb cassava
Water to cover

1. Peel cassava and soak for 4 days.
2. Cut out the core.
3. Put in a saucepan and add water to cover.

4. Bring to a boil, then turn down heat and simmer 10 minutes.
5. Pound in a mortar using a pestle until the cassava makes a soft dough.
6. Serve with stew.

Lamb Sosaties (Serves 4–6)

1 c vinegar
1 onion, thinly sliced
12 dried apricot halves, chopped
1/2 tsp curry powder
2 tbsp brown sugar
2 c water
Leg of lamb or chops in 1″ slices, cut to make pieces for barbecuing
2 tbsp cornstarch
1/2 c cold water

1. Make marinade by boiling vinegar, onion, apricots, curry powder, sugar, and water for 3 minutes.
2. Pour cooled marinade over lamb, adding water if necessary to cover lamb.
3. Refrigerate for 2 days.
4. Thread lamb onto skewers and barbecue.
5. Stir cornstarch and water mixture into marinade and bring to boil while stirring.
6. Serve lamb with thickened marinade and chutney.

Peanut Butter Soup (Serves 4–6)

1/2 lb lean ground beef	2 tbsp peanut butter
1 1/2 qt water	2 tbsp lemon juice
1 onion, chopped	
2 cloves garlic, pressed	
1/2 tsp coarse grind black pepper	
1 1/2 tsp salt	
1 stick cinnamon	
2 cardamom seeds, ground	

1. Simmer all ingredients except peanut butter and lemon in a saucepan for 1 1/2 hours.
2. Stir 1/2 cup stock into peanut butter, then add peanut butter and lemon juice to the soup.
3. Simmer for 5 minutes.

Mashed Plantains and Chicken Stew (Serves 4–6)

1 frying chicken, cut in pieces	Salt and pepper
1 onion, sliced	
1/4 c oil	
2 tomatoes, chopped	
2 potatoes, peeled and cubed	
Salt and pepper	
2 c water	
3 plantains, peeled and quartered	
Water	

1. Brown chicken and onions in oil in a Dutch oven.
2. Add tomatoes, potatoes, seasonings, and water, then simmer (covered) for 1 hour.
3. Meanwhile, steam plantains on a rack in a steamer until tender.
4. Mash plantains and season with salt and pepper.
5. Serve chicken stew over plantains.

Summary

The countries included in this discussion of eastern and southern Africa include Sudan, Eritrea, Djibouti, Ethiopia, Somalia, Kenya, Tanzania, Uganda, Rwanda, Burundi, Gabon, Cameroon, the Democratic Republic of Congo, Angola, Zambia, Malawi, Mozambique, Zimbabwe, Botswana, Namibia, and South Africa. The terrain includes much of the Great Rift Valley, a high plateau, some high mountains, low tropical seacoasts, varying agricultural conditions ranging from very humid to arid, and a dramatic tip (the Cape of Good Hope) where the Atlantic and Indian Oceans meet very far south of the equator. Farmers can raise some commercial crops, such as tea and coffee, while many subsistence farmers are able to grow barely enough for their families. Some livestock are raised, and wild game is occasionally eaten. The wildlife are valued more for the ability to attract tourist dollars than as a meat source for the continent.

Traces of very early man have been found in such places in Africa as the Olduvai Gorge in Tanzania. Much more recently, evidence of the early Ethiopian city of Aksum, dating from the 4th century, and Great Zimbabwe, with its Great Enclosure, built in Zimbabwe in the 14th century, provide historical perspectives too. Portuguese traders opened up the coasts of Africa in their quest to find a sea route to the East Indies. After rounding the Cape of Good Hope, they discovered that Arab and Indian traders were already exchanging goods with the people along the east coast of Africa.

Colonization by the Dutch with its Boer farmers at the Cape began the settlement by Europeans in the southern part of Africa. Bantus were migrating into eastern and southern regions from their roots in the western and central parts of Africa. Eventually, considerable conflict erupted, particularly in South Africa, where the British and the Boers (Dutch settlers) were attempting to establish authority over what is now South Africa and the neighboring regions. Belgian colonization of the Congo also resulted in considerable loss of life among the natives. Added to this situation was the ongoing problem of slavery and the slave trade for more than 200 years. The various African nations have now gained their independence, although considerable unrest still is found in some of them. The end of apartheid in South Africa and the free elections that followed are beginning to bring a period of greater tranquility and productivity there.

Missionaries worked extensively in these countries to bring Christianity. This still is often mixed with animistic practices by many African natives. There also are other religions, particularly Muslim, the result of the Arab influence. Immigrants from India have also brought Hinduism to a limited extent. Music, especially with drums and percussive instruments, is popular in Africa. Also, dancing is a traditional cultural heritage. Storytelling is another favorite way of keeping tradition alive from generation to generation.

Women traditionally prepare the two meals that are served in many families. A thick porridge, usually made of cornmeal, is commonly served for breakfast. The evening meal also is likely to feature a cornmeal or cassava dish as a source of starch. Some meat and plenty of vegetables may be cooked together to make a stew when these items are available. Fruits are also popular. Meals prepared in a single pot are well suited to regions where good water and a regular stove may not be readily available. Insects and small field animals may be found in some diets. Milk is sometimes consumed when it is available, but lack of refrigeration in living quarters can make this a very hazardous item.

Study Questions

1. Why were the Portuguese so eager and persistent in their efforts to explore the coasts of Africa?
2. Compare the problems of establishing colonial settlements in the Congo with those in South Africa.
3. What were some of the problems that Bantu farmers had to overcome in growing crops in the equatorial regions? Why did they halt their southward migration before they got to the coast of South Africa?
4. What are some of the vegetables commonly eaten in eastern Africa?
5. Describe the way in which a village family might eat for a day in Zimbabwe.

Bibliography

Abrahams, C. 1995. *Culture and Cuisine of the Cape Malays.* Metz Press. Welgemoed, South Africa.

Barer-Stein, T. 1999. *You Eat What You Are.* 2nd ed. Firefly Books, Ltd. Ontario, Canada.

Coetzee, R. 1982. *Funa—Food from Africa.* Butterworth. Durban, South Africa.

Hopkinson, T. 1964. *South Africa.* Time, Inc. New York.

Kiley, D. 1976. *South Africa.* B. T. Batsford. London.

Kingsolver, B. 1998. *Poisonwood Bible.* Harper Flamingo. New York.

Pateman, R. 1993. *Kenya.* Marshall Cavendish. New York.

Pearcy, G. E. 1980. *The World Food Scene.* Plycon Press. Redondo Beach, CA.

Reader, J. 1997. *Africa: A Biography of the Continent.* Vintage Books. New York.

Sheehan, S. 1993. *Zimbabwe.* Marshall Cavendish. New York.

Swaney, D. 1999. *Zimbabwe, Botswana, and Namibia.* 2nd ed. Lonely Planet. Oakland, CA.

Van Wyk, M., and P. Barton. 1996. *Traditional South African Cooking.* Central News Agency, Ltd. Johannesburg.

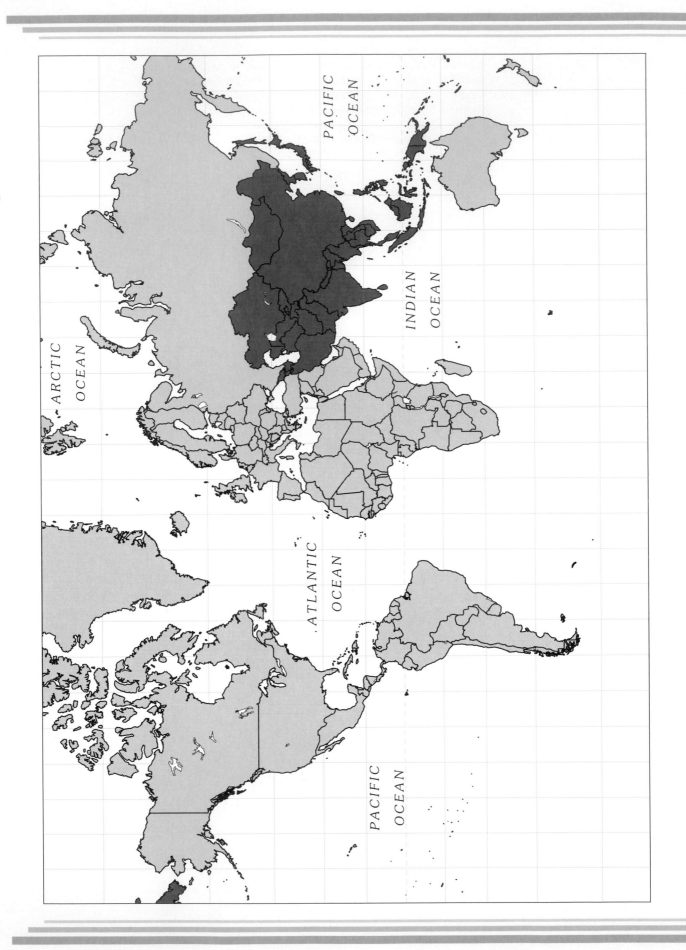

Part V

Food Treasures from the Orient and the Pacific

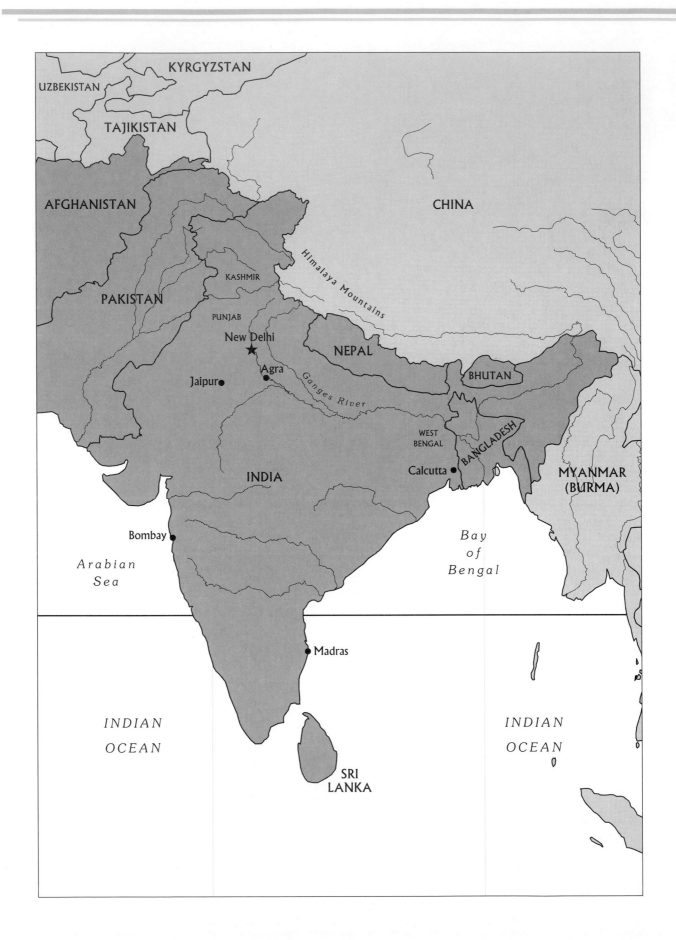

15 India and Its Neighbors

Geographic Overview

India is described as a subcontinent of Asia, with the Himalayas still being shoved ever higher on the northern reaches of the country as its plate subducts under the main plate of Asia. The result of this slowly evolving shift is a protective barrier that served as a deterrent to invaders from the north in centuries past. Mt. Everest, the highest mountain in the world, stands more than 29,000 feet and is still growing. Other Himalayan peaks of over 20,000 feet are found all along this imposing range that touches on not only India, but also its northern neighbors—Afghanistan, Pakistan, Nepal, and Bhutan—as well as Tibet on the northern slopes (Figure 15.1). The other countries surrounding India are Bangladesh to the east and Sri Lanka, the island nation to the south.

Traversing between the eastern and western parts of northern India and Pakistan is the Indus River, which empties into the Arabian sea on the west after flowing many miles through Pakistan. The Ganges, considered to be the holiest of rivers, and also the Brahmaputra, flow eastward into the Bay of Bengal soon after entering Bangladesh on the east of northern India. These rivers plus lesser rivers in the north are fed by the melting snows of the Himalayas as well as by the heavy rains that pelt the region during the monsoon season (Figure 15.2). Trading via rivers in India is not generally practical, and the extensive shoreline of the peninsula comprising southern India also presents challenges to trade because of the very limited number of good ports. Nevertheless, such ports as Bombay and Madras are able to accommodate a considerable amount of freight via ships.

India has rather diverse agricultural areas. The Himalayan foothills in the north have long been the source of excellent tea, which flourishes in the relatively cool and adequately moist climate. Some of the most favorable conditions for

193

Figure 15.1 Mt. Everest and other high Himalayan peaks dominate the land along India's northern border.

farming are found on the Indo-Gangetic plain, for the seasonal flooding helps to bring fresh soil to support the crops that are grown there. The monsoon rains are well suited to raising rice, beginning with the flooding of the fields (Figure 15.3), followed by the gradual drying as the crop matures. The Thar Desert, south of the Indus River, is hostile to farming. Wheat, some barley, sorghum, and millet are other cereal crops that are grown in some parts of India. Legumes are important crops, particularly because of the vegetarian food patterns of many people in India. Cooking oils are available from cottonseed, peanuts, rape seed, and sesame grown in the country. In addition to various fruits and vegetables, coconut and some spices are also grown in southern India, south of the vast Deccan Plateau. Buffalo milk is the dairy product commonly used; cows are sacred and thus are not generally considered a source of food, but some people do consume their milk. Some beef is consumed in India, although lamb is more popular, particularly in the north.

History and Culture

Early in the history of southern India, a dark-skinned people called the Dravidians appear to have made their way beyond the Deccan Plateau into the hospitable region at the southern tip of India (Cape Comorin). There they were

Figure 15.2 High stilts lift these homes in India above the threat of monsoon flooding.

Figure 15.3   Rice paddies flooded from the monsoon will later dry to produce a good rice harvest.

generally isolated from the struggles that often marked the development of northern India. Their language, Tamil, was distinctly different from the Aryan languages that evolved in northern India. The Tamil also migrated to the island of Sri Lanka, just off the tip of India.

In the Indus Valley, farming communities began to evolve as early as 4000 BCE. This led to trading and an advance in civilization that even included development of seaports and a form of writing with pictographs. Aryans invaded from north of the protective mountains and ravaged the existing civilization in the Indus Valley before they began to settle in the region around 2000 BCE. Although civilization appeared to take a step backward at that time, there were Aryan priests who carefully created the Vedas, the four books outlining Hinduism, over the course of 10 centuries prior to 500 BCE. This religious documentation established the caste system and other significant aspects of Hinduism that are very much a part of life in India today. The Aryans are credited with bringing the language of Sanskrit to India and to Hinduism. Gautama Buddha, who was born about 567 BCE in India, developed his version of religion, which is Buddhism. Thus, India was the spiritual home of two major religions that are still practiced today.

Numerous small political units evolved as a result of conflicts in India, and eventually India even felt the impact of Cyrus the Great when his Persian troops defeated the people in the Indus Valley and the Punjab in 531 BCE. Persian dominance contributed to the culture of the region while also exacting its toll in the form of troops for wars as far away as Greece. Subsequently, Alexander the Great invaded India for a couple of years, but left in 323 BCE. This led the way to the formation of the Mauryan Empire, a unifying force for India. Ashoka, the Mauryan king from 272 to 236 BCE, was a powerful convert to Buddhism who played a major role in promoting the spread of this religion.

The Gupta Empire reached across northern India during the period from 320 to 750 CE. Although this was a Hindu empire at that time, much evidence of Buddhism, such as *stupas* (dome-shaped religious mounds) and statues (Figure 15.4) coexisted with the art associated with Hinduism. During the reign of the Gupta monarchs, art and literature flourished. Astronomy and mathematics also were major interests (Figure 15.5). This golden period ceased when the Huns invaded.

Muslim invaders pushed their way into parts of western and northern India over a period of about 200 years and stayed to become a part of the religious scene of the country. The barbarous attacks of Genghis Khan in central Asia drove many well-educated and artistic Muslims to seek refuge in India, which added to the cultural richness of the region. A gradual decline in political leadership left the way open for the invasion of Babur, a Mongol descendant of Genghis Kahn,

Figure 15.4 This giant Buddha carved in a sandstone cliff in Bamian, Afghanistan, has looked down on centuries of attackers in the region (including Genghis Khan), but it was destroyed by the Taliban in 2001.

who created a powerful and culturally rich empire in northern India. This Mughal Empire ruled much of India from 1524 to 1707 and left such cultural richness as the Taj Mahal and other artistic accomplishments (see Chapter 1). Although the religion of the Mughals was Muslim, Hinduism and Buddhism continued to flourish throughout India, gaining strength after the fall of the Mughals.

European influence began to be felt along the seacoast of India. Portugal established trading posts at Bombay, Goa, and some other ports along the Arabian Sea in western India. The British, Dutch, and French also began a vigorous trade with India during the 17th century. However, it was the British who eventually controlled India. They brought their excellent administrative abilities and helped to establish the foundations of business, education, and government that are still a part of India today.

Significant changes have taken place since independence from England was achieved in 1947. A particularly dramatic change was the creation of Pakistan as a

Figure 15.5 The observatory built centuries ago attests to the scientific interests of rulers in Jaipur in northwestern India.

separate Muslim country and subsequently the formation of Bangladesh from what was East Pakistan. The extensive shifting of Muslims from India to Pakistan and of Hindus from Pakistan to India that occurred as a result of this cleavage of a once united land resulted in incredible bloodshed. This continues even today in the disputed region of Kashmir, the lovely northern tip of India.

In view of the lengthy history of India and its unique background that melds influences from diverse religions and a variety of ethnic backgrounds, it is not surprising that India presents a very rich cultural heritage. Caves near Ajanta in western India still are enriched by the wall paintings done by Buddhist monks over the eight centuries prior to 600 CE. Artistic cave paintings then were done in the same region near Ellora, the paintings a blend of Buddhist and Hindu art. Later artistic expression can be found throughout many parts of India where numerous statues of Buddha and many ornate and intricately decorated Hindu temples attest to the highly developed artistic skills of the people living in India over the centuries. The Mughals left some intricately executed and delicate structures, such as the Taj Mahal, and also some sturdily built yet beautiful palaces and forts in Rajasthan in northern and northwestern India. The love of detailed art is evident in many creations in this nation.

India is a densely populated country that faces the challenging problems associated with feeding, educating, and governing so many people. The diversity of populations within the country complicates matters still further. Since becoming a nation free of the rule of the British Raj, there have been several changes in the leadership of the government, some of which have been accompanied by violence. Despite such problems, the nation continues to develop as a significant part of the world community.

Music also is a passion for many Indians. The style of Indian music is distinctly different from American forms and is based on individual creativity as well as on melodies learned by rote from gurus or teachers of music. The instruments also are quite varied and include several types of stringed instruments that can be bowed, plucked, or tapped, and also drums and wind instruments. The sitar is an Indian stringed instrument that has gained some popularity in the United States. To the western ear, Indian music seems to often have a rather sing-song quality and a meandering style that captures the unique magic of the Indian people.

The official languages of India are Hindi and English, but there are many different dialects. English serves as the unifying mode of communication between speakers of these many dialects. Considerable literature has been created in India over the centuries. Tamil and Sanskrit were early languages for literature, but contemporary literature usually is written in the languages of the country. Also, storytelling is an ancient art that remains a popular part of the culture today.

India is a land that embraces holidays and practices elaborate traditions to celebrate them. The calendar is quite full of religious holidays because of the many religions in India. The religious holidays associated with Hindu, Buddhist, Muslim, and Christian beliefs are all a part of the celebrations in India. *Holi* is the popular festival of spring, and it is celebrated by tossing purple-colored powder or water at any hapless person who comes within range that day. The greatest celebration of the fall is *Divali*, which celebrates Lord Krishna's triumph over a demon and the return of Rama from his exile. Independence is also marked by a day of celebration on August 15.

Yet other dimensions of India's culture are mysticism, meditation, and physical tests of concentration. Levitation demonstrations, walking on hot coals, and snake charming are sights that can still be seen in India. Another exotic aspect of India is the presence of tigers, elephants, and other wild game in the northern part of the country. Clearly, this is a different world than the one familiar to Americans.

India's neighbors have their own distinctive cultures, although each has some overtones of the culture of its large neighbor. Nepal lies just on the northeast shoulder of India and borders on Tibet along its northern edge, thus sharing part of the Himalayan range with Tibet (Figure 15.6). The southern part of Nepal actually is low enough to be home to some wild tigers and elephants, but much of the country is very mountainous. Population pressures have led to deforestation and serious erosion in populated areas, but much natural beauty—spectacular mountain peaks, tree-sized rhododendrons alive with their red blooms, and even wild orchids—sets this country apart from most others. Of cultural interest are the Durbar Squares in Kathmandu, Patan, and Bhaktapur in the Kathmandu Valley. The Hindu and Buddhist religions are melded in this setting, uniting earlier centuries with today. Two Buddhist stupas in the Kathmandu Valley keeping watchful eyes over the scene are Swayambhunath and Bodhnath. A Hindu Shiva shrine, Pashupatinath, is the scene of ritual bathing, cremation, and religious devotions in Kathmandu Valley. The *ghats* (cremation pedestals) amidst the worshipers and wild monkeys create a picture that lingers long in memories. Also not to be forgotten is a glimpse of the Living Goddess, a prepubertal girl considered to be an incarnation of Shiva's consort. She lives in seclusion and comfort in the Kumari Bahal (an 18th century structure in Kathmandu) during her reign, which ends when she enters puberty. The Pokhara Valley to the west provides a look at rural life (Figure 15.7) and the village agricultural scene. The towering mountains beckon mountain climbers, who are aided by local Sherpas, the mountain people in the region.

Bhutan is a small kingdom a bit east of Nepal, affording yet a different cultural flavor. Its state religion is Mahayana Buddhism, and this sets the tone for a somewhat contemplative, unhurried lifestyle that is very much in touch with nature. The careful control of tourist traffic and the small population create an unusually tranquil setting in today's world. Even the style of the buildings, although quite massive, is pleasing and harmonious. The country's slogan, "Gross national happiness," and its alternative name of "Land of the Thunder Dragon" clearly capture Bhutan's essence. Among the sights of Bhutan are the many *dzongs* (thick-walled, very large and sturdy stone buildings with windows placed high from the ground), prayer flags frantically waving their messages heavenward in the winds, and the precariously perched Taksang, or Tiger's Nest, Buddhist monastery high on the cliffs of the Paro Valley.

Nepal, India, and Bhutan lie along the southern side of the Himalayas and have provided refuge for many Tibetans who fled over the mountains when the Chinese invasion forced the Dalai Lama to flee in 1979. The Buddhist monasteries in these countries have been instrumental in providing safe harbors and a spiritual home for these refugees for more than 20 years.

Figure 15.6   Many Tibetans have remained in their Himalayan homeland, and countless others have left for freedom south of the Himalayas in Nepal, India, and Bhutan. (Photo courtesy of Eileen Welsh).

Figure 15.7 Villagers living in the Pokhara Valley in Nepal lead unhurried lives.

Bhutan's architecture and religious features have much in common with Tibet, which is not surprising, since they are very close neighbors, being separated more by the precipitous mountain peaks than by their religious beliefs. The outstanding building in Tibet is the Potala in Lhasa, the home of the Dalai Lama before his flight to Dharamsala, India, in 1959. The Dalai Lama's summer palace, the Norbulinka, affords another glimpse of this earlier life in Tibet. The most holy place of worship in Tibet is the Jokhang Temple, which has an endless parade of pilgrims prostrating themselves as they circumambulate the holy site. All through Tibet, as well as in Bhutan and Nepal, whirling prayer wheels seem to constantly be in motion in the hands of devout Buddhists. Larger prayer wheels also are whirled by the faithful as they pass outside the temples.

Pakistan presents quite a contrast to these mountain kingdoms, for it clearly is a Muslim country. The traditions and clothing are conservative, following the teachings of the Koran. This is a land that presents contrasts between the rural populace who struggle to eke out a subsistence and the urban dwellers who live a modern existence. Pakistan has nuclear capability and remote areas where camels, goats, and sheep graze. Cities range from Peshawar, with its frontier (close to Afghanistan) costumes and character, to Lahore and its remaining mosques and monuments from the Mughal Empire, and on to Karachi and its bustling urban life and seaport.

Bangladesh became an independent nation in 1971 when it declared itself free of West Pakistan; India sided with Bangladesh and quickly defeated West Pakistan when it sent its army against the former East Pakistan. This rather young nation has a precarious existence because of its very dense population and its physical position at a very low elevation at the head of the Bay of Bengal, which leaves it devastated by floods when monsoon conditions are especially vicious. Tidal waves and heavy rainfall are a continuing threat to humans, animals, and crops. The problems of an adequate food supply sometimes seem insoluble.

Sri Lanka is India's other immediate neighbor. Its location just off the tip of southern India gives it quite a different character. Parts of the island are dry, while other parts have adequate rainfall, and crops are able to thrive. The culture in Sri Lanka is a mixture of ethnic groups and religions. The dominant ethnic groups are the Sinhalese (of Aryan heritage) and Tamils (descendants of Chola and other Indian invaders from many centuries ago). Hindu and Buddhist followers are prominent in Sri Lanka and are often quite intertwined. Islam and Christianity also have followers here. The racial problems underlying Sri Lanka's current scene are between Sinhalese Buddhists and the Tamils in the northern part of the island. Some reminders of British rule still are in evidence, although the British left in 1948. Remnants of much earlier cultures go as far back as the third century BCE and include water reservoirs as well as Buddhist and Hindu artifacts.

Food Patterns

The food patterns throughout the region of India and its neighboring countries reflect the religions that dominate the lives of the populace. Vegetarianism is quite common, partly because of economic factors and partly because of religious dictates. Legumes and cereals are the major components of most meals. If meat is included, it is usually in small quantities. Buddhists and Hindus avoid beef and also usually pork. Eggs are sometimes used. Milk in various forms, often clabbered, and from different animals may be consumed. Fruits and vegetables are eaten, although somewhat sparingly. Perhaps the most unique and compelling part of dishes typical of this part of the world is the imaginative and pervasive use of a wide variety of spices and seasonings (Figure 15.8). These additions bring basic ingredients into an exciting whole.

Food availability and economic factors exert a significant impact on the dietary intake of many Indian families. Over the centuries, the traditionally available cereals have been rice and wheat, the two cereals that are particularly well suited to the agricultural conditions in India and have therefore served as the main components of meals. The other cornerstone of Indian diet is the legume family, which includes the ubiquitous lentils and a wide array of beans. These legumes and cereals not only conform to religious requirements, but also have the advantages of being comparatively inexpensive and able to be stored for long periods without refrigeration. Even today, large numbers of Indian families have no way to keep foods safely chilled. They also may not have enough money to buy even the basic food needed for an adequate diet. Added to these difficulties is often the serious problem of obtaining safe drinking water. For large numbers of Indians, eating is a daily challenge.

Considering the array of invaders who have forced their way into India over the centuries, the uniqueness of Indian food is surprising. There are overtones of Persian and European contributions to the Indian cuisine, but the special ways in which Indians prepare and season their traditional dishes are very much the result of their own ideas. In fact, it can be argued that Indians have given more to the culinary world than they have taken from the cuisines of other cul-

Figure 15.8 Muslim woman shops for other food behind a spice stall in Kabhul, Afghanistan.

tures. Among the spicy seasonings and flavors featured generously in Indian cookery are turmeric, ginger, cinnamon, mint, dill, coriander, cumin, pepper, cardamom, saffron, poppy seeds, cloves, chilies, fennel, mace, and nutmeg. The use of this wide range of flavoring ingredients requires judicious blending into recipes if the results are to meet the critical expectations of Indians. They rely heavily on the right seasonings to lift what could be a rather bland diet into a higher realm of excitement in eating. The term Indians use to designate a blend of spices is *masala*. Many different blends are used, but a basic blend (generically dubbed *garam masala*) usually contains cardamom, cloves, cumin, cinnamon, nutmeg, saffron, and other spices that are ground together thoroughly and then stored for use in many different dishes. Sometimes, spices are ground with herbs, water, and vinegar to make a wet masala that will be used immediately in preparing a particular dish. Whether a masala is comprised of a skillful blend of dry spices or is a wet masala is not important to the success of a dish; it is the pleasure in the mouth provided by the masala that is the final test.

The word *curry* seems almost synonymous with Indian food, and certainly a chutney must be at least one of the accompaniments served to highlight this central dish. Surprisingly, the curry powder that is sold in American markets is not the seasoning used to make Indian curries. Instead, each recipe for curry includes a complex list of spices to achieve just the right flavor for the particular curry being prepared. Indeed, use of spices is considered to be an art in Indian kitchens, and the truly fine food of India is prepared in private homes rather than in commercial restaurants. Recipes for curry are extremely varied and may feature shrimp or other seafood, mutton or lamb, vegetables, or other imaginative ingredients. Chutneys also afford considerable leeway for the creative cook. They may feature fruits cooked with spices to a thick, sweet product, or they may be quite spicy or even sour. The individuality of chutneys is truly amazing.

Lentils are a favored legume, and they appear in many different forms. They can be cooked and pureed with various spices or other ingredients to make *sambar,* which frequently is served with *idlis* (rice cakes) to add flavor to the meal. A usual part of the evening meal is *dal,* which is commonly a fairly bland puree of lentils of varying consistency, ranging from very thin to a bit pasty. Other legumes, including various peas called *gram,* are familiar ingredients in dishes for the evening meal.

Ghee, which is clarified butter that has been cooked down a bit and poured from the milk solids, adds a distinctive flavor when used in cooking and is the preferred fat to use if it can be afforded. Peanut oil and other oils also are used and are certainly less costly than ghee. Vegetable shortenings are another type of fat used in India.

The general name for breads is *roti.* There are some interesting kinds of roti, such as *chapati, paratha, naan,* and *puri.* Chapatis are whole wheat bread made by rolling a 2-inch ball of dough into a 5-inch circle and then baking it on a hot griddle, much like baking a pancake. Paratha is a bread similar to the chapati, but it is rolled into somewhat larger rounds, and more ghee is used in its preparation, both in the dough and in frying it on the griddle. Naan is baked in a *tandoor,* a deep, jar-shaped clay oven heated by a charcoal fire. The naan dough is patted into an oval shape, then slapped against the upper wall of the tandoor for baking. (Incidentally, the chicken or other meats that may be roasted in a tandoor will be just as tasty as the delicious naan!) Puris are deep-fat fried, 5-inch rounds of whole wheat bread dough, which puff up in the middle during frying.

Samosas are popular in India, not only for their delicious flavors, but also because of their convenience. They are pastry tightly enclosing any of a variety of fillings, which then are fried. Since the fillings are sealed inside the pastry, samosas make a very portable and tasty snack or dinner item (Figure 15.9).

People in India and some of the surrounding countries enjoy winding off a meal by chewing on a betel nut or its leaf, or both. In India, *paan* (a betel nut

Figure 15.9 Indians sharing lunch on a balcony overlooking a street in New Delhi, India.

wrapped in a betel leaf) may be seasoned with other ingredients and chewed at the close of a dinner. Betel nuts also often are chewed between meals. There is a distinctive deep red color in the betel nuts, which quickly stains the teeth and lips a very noticeable shade. The suggestion is that betel aids digestion, and some people credit betel with additional therapeutic qualities that have yet to be proven.

Key Terms

Betel nut—Nut from a climbing pepper that is chewed for its digestive qualities; it has a deep red juice.

Chapati—Pancake-like, grilled whole wheat bread popular in India.

Chutney—Chunky and flavorful sauce often served as accompaniment to curry.

Curry—Hearty and well-seasoned, stew-like dish featuring meat or legumes and served with several accompaniments.

Dal—Puree of lentils or other legumes, usually rather blandly seasoned.

Dravidians—Early people of southern India.

Garam masala—Basic mixture of spices usually prepared in quantity and used as desired to season many different dishes in India.

Ghee—Clarified butter that has been cooked down a little to add flavor; expensive, but preferred fat for cooking in India.

Idlis—Rice cakes.

Naan—Oval-shaped whole wheat bread baked by sticking it to the wall of a tandoor.

Paratha—Whole wheat bread circles about 7 inches in diameter, made with ghee in the dough and fried in ghee on the griddle.

Potala—Seat of Tibetan Buddhism and the former home of the Dalai Lama.

Puri—Deep-fat fried rounds of whole wheat bread that puff in the middle during frying.

Roti—Indian word for breads.

Sambar—Spicy puree of lentils, which often is served with idlis.

Samosa—Fried pastry enclosing a filling.

Sinhalese—Descendants of Aryans living in Sri Lanka.

Stupa—Covered mound, often containing a relic of significance in Buddhism.

Taj Mahal—Mausoleum built by Shah Jahan in Agra, India, to honor the memory of his favorite wife, Mumtaz.

Tamils—Descendants of early invaders of Sri Lanka.

Tandoor—Thick-walled, deep, jar-shaped clay oven used for roasting meats and baking naan.

Recipes

Chapatis (Serves 2–6)

1 c whole wheat flour
4 tsp ghee (or clarified butter)
1/2 c warm water 110°F (plus more as needed)

1. With a fork, mash ghee into flour to a mealy texture.
2. Gradually add measured amount of water, stirring hard between additions.
3. Very gradually add (while mixing) just enough more water to make a dough that will form a firm ball.
4. Knead vigorously on a floured board until dough surface is very smooth.
5. Very lightly grease the surface of the dough ball, then let it rest at least half an hour.
6. Shape dough into balls, using about 2 tablespoons per ball, and then roll or pat each into a 5″ circle.
7. Heat griddle until a drop of water dances on it.
8. Bake first side of chapatis until the top edges begin to brown; flip and bake the second side for a minute. (Use a spatula to keep from sticking during baking.)

Beef Biryani (Serves 4)

1 onion, sliced thinly
1 1/2 tbsp oil
1 green chili, minced
2 garlic cloves, crushed
1″ ginger root, minced
1 c long grain rice
1/4 tsp ground turmeric
1 lb beef tenderloin, 1″ chunks
2 tsp curry powder
1/4 tsp garam masala
3 tomatoes, thin wedges
2 bay leaves
2 cardamom seeds
1/4 tsp saffron
4 cloves
Chutney, if desired to serve with this dish

1. Stir-fry onions in oil, adding chili, garlic, and ginger just as onions begin to turn golden. Continue to cook for about 2 minutes.
2. Prepare rice according to package directions, but with turmeric.
3. Add beef to onion mixture and stir-fry for 5 minutes, stirring every minute or so.
4. Add curry, garam masala, and tomatoes to beef mixture; stir together and heat gently for 8 minutes.
5. Add bay leaves, cardamom, saffron, and cloves to rice; stir gently to mix.
6. Layer rice and beef mixtures in a baking dish, ending with rice.
7. Bake in preheated 375°F oven for 15 minutes.

Dal (Serves 4–6)

1/2 c lentils
2 c water
1 tsp grated ginger
1 tsp crushed garlic
1/4 tsp turmeric
2 green chilies, chopped
1 tsp salt
1 tbsp oil
1 onion, thinly sliced
1/4 tsp mustard seed
4 dried red chilies
1 tomato, chopped
Cilantro and mint, chopped

1. Boil lentils with water, ginger, garlic, turmeric, green chilies, and salt until very soft (about 20 minutes).
2. Puree, adding water if needed to achieve desired consistency.
3. Heat oil in frying pan, then add onion, mustard seed, dried chilies, and tomato; saute until onion is tender.
4. Pour over lentils to serve, garnished with coarsely chopped cilantro and mint.

Ghee (Makes about 1 cup)

1 lb unsalted butter

1. Melt butter in large saucepan, stirring to keep it from browning.
2. Heat rapidly until the surface is covered with white foam.

3. Immediately reduce heat while stirring.
4. Simmer, uncovered, for about 45 minutes without stirring. (Solids on bottom are golden brown.)
5. Very carefully pour off ghee through a filter of linen or cheesecloth. Repeat if any solids are in the filtered ghee.

Garam Masala (Makes 1 cup)

5 sticks cinnamon (3" each)
1/4 c cardamom seeds
1/2 c cumin seeds
1/2 c black peppercorns
1/4 c coriander seeds

1. Spread spices on jelly roll pan and bake at 200°F for 35 minutes, stirring occasionally.
2. Crush cinnamon between layers of linen towel, using a hammer.
3. Mix spices together, then grind together.
4. Store tightly sealed for up to 6 months. Use as needed.

Khir (Milk and Rice Pudding) (Serves 4–6)

1 qt milk
3 tbsp long grain rice
1/2 c sugar
1/4 c blanched almonds, chopped
1/8 tsp cardamom seeds, crushed
1/2 tsp rosewater (optional)
2 tbsp toasted, sliced, blanched almonds

1. Bring milk quickly to a boil in a heavy saucepan and immediately reduce heat to simmering.

2. Simmer milk for 30 minutes, stirring occasionally.
3. Add rice and stir often while simmering for the next 30 minutes or until rice is completely soft.
4. Add sugar and chopped almonds; heat while stirring until pudding is thick enough to coat the stirring spoon.
5. Add rosewater and cardamom and stir, then pour into a dish; chill for 4 or more hours. Garnish with toasted almonds.

Mango Chutney (Makes 1/2 cup)

1 mango
1 hot red or green chili
1 tbsp coriander, finely chopped
2 tsp salt
1/8 tsp cayenne pepper

1. Thoroughly wash mango before cutting flesh (with skin) away from its seed, and then slice fruit into very thin slices.
2. Discard chili seeds; slice into thin rings.
3. Add other ingredients and mix well; refrigerate for 1 hour (or 1 day maximum).

Mulligatawny Soup (Serves 6–8)

Stewing chicken in serving pieces
6 c water
2 tsp salt
1 c canned tomatoes
1 onion, chopped
1 garlic clove, crushed
1/2 tsp coriander seeds
1 tsp cumin seeds
1/2 tsp ground ginger
1 bay leaf
3" cinnamon stick
12 peppercorns
2 tsp peanut oil

2 tbsp lemon juice
1 c coconut milk (or half and half)

1. Stew chicken in water and salt for 30 minutes, then add tomatoes, half the onion, garlic, and seasonings.
2. Simmer 30 minutes more.
3. Remove chicken and strain stock.
4. In same pan, brown remaining onion in fat; return chicken and strained stock to pan.
5. Add lemon juice and coconut milk, and heat to serving temperature.

Naan (Makes 6 ovals)

3 1/2 c flour
1 tbsp sugar
1 tbsp baking powder
1/2 tsp baking soda
1/2 tsp salt
2 eggs, beaten
1/2 c plain yogurt
1/2 c milk
1/4 c ghee

1. Combine dry ingredients in mixing bowl and stir well.
2. Beat eggs and yogurt into dry ingredients.
3. Stir while slowly pouring milk in. Mix thoroughly to combine all ingredients.

4. Knead dough vigorously, adding flour to board and hands to prevent sticking while kneading until dough is very smooth.
5. Grease dough ball surface with ghee and let rest 30 minutes.
6. Preheat oven (and baking stones, if available) to 450°F.
7. Grease palms with ghee, then flatten one-sixth of dough into 10" circle. Repeat with other five parts of dough.
8. Stretch each into an oval and arrange on cookie sheets to bake on the hot tiles in oven.
9. Bake for about 6 minutes until firm on surface, then broil for a minute to brown the surface a bit.

Saag Aloo (Greens and Potatoes) (Serves 4–6)

1 lb spinach
1 tsp black mustard seeds
1 tbsp oil
1 onion, thinly sliced
2 garlic cloves, crushed
1" ginger root, minced
1 1/2 lb potatoes (1" pieces)
1 tsp chili powder
1 tsp salt
1/2 c water

1. Wash spinach and blanch in boiling water. Pour into strainer to drain well, pressing to force water out.
2. Fry mustard seeds in oil in skillet until they pop; add onion, garlic, and ginger, and fry for 5 minutes more.
3. Add potatoes, chili powder, salt, and water to skillet; stir-fry for 5 minutes.
4. Add spinach, cover, and simmer for 15 minutes until potatoes are done.

Samosas (Serves 4–6)

2 c flour
1/2 tsp salt
1/4 c butter
3/4 c plain yogurt
Filling of choice
Vegetable oil for frying

1. Mix flour and salt, then cut in butter to consistency of coarse meal.
2. Stir in yogurt until dough forms a ball.
3. Wrap tightly in foil; refrigerate for 1 hour or more.
4. Roll a fourth of dough on floured pastry cloth to 1/16" thick.
5. Cut 4" circles, and cut each in half.
6. Moisten edges, place teaspoon of filling in middle; fold dough edges over filling to form a triangle, pressing edges to seal. Refrigerate up to a day before frying.
7. Fry in deep fat at 375°F for about 4 minutes to brown both sides and heat filling.

Shrimp Filling for Samosas (Fills 4–6 samosas)

1/2 c minced onion
1 garlic clove, crushed
2 tbsp oil
1/2 lb shrimp, deveined and chopped
1/4 c tomatoes, diced
1/2 tsp salt
1 tsp coriander seeds, crushed

1 tsp cumin seeds, crushed
1/8 tsp red pepper, crushed

1. Stir-fry onion and garlic for 6 minutes.
2. Add remaining ingredients and continue stir-frying for 5 minutes.
3. Store in refrigerator until needed for filling pastry.

Summary

Southern Asia includes the very large country of India, plus its neighbors: Pakistan, Nepal, Bhutan, Tibet, Bangladesh, and Sri Lanka. The major rivers in this subcontinent of Asia include the Indus, Ganges, and Brahmaputra. Particularly productive farmland for India is found in the Indo-Gangetic plain, but the Thar Desert and the Deccan Plateau are quite limited in terms of agriculture. Particularly prominent crops in India are wheat, rice, peanuts, and a fairly wide assortment of fruits and vegetables; some livestock is also raised.

India's very long history revealed that Dravidians settled in the south, developing their language, Tamil. Somewhat later, Aryans came from the north. The writing of the Vedas was done by Aryan priests, who laid the written foundation of Hinduism. Gautama Buddha was born in Hindu India, but he gradually developed Buddhism, a somewhat mystical religion that has incorporated some aspects of Hinduism and gathered many worshipers in many countries.

Over the centuries, there have been many changes of power in India, among them Persian invaders, Alexander the Great from Greece, the Mauryan Empire, the Gupta Empire, Muslim invaders, and the Mughal Empire. Subsequently, European influences spurred by trading with this exotic region established trading posts, and eventually Great Britain governed India before granting Indian independence in 1947.

Indian love of art is reflected in its architecture, which shows the style in favor during the various ruling periods. Music is another aspect of Indian culture that is distinctly different from western music. The instruments, meandering compositions, and rhythms evoke feelings of mysticism and nature. Storytelling and dancing are other expressive cultural outlets that are popular in India.

Religion plays a major role in the year's holiday calendar and also in the dietary patterns of the people. The various religions practiced in India contribute many holidays to be celebrated. Similarly, the avoidance of meat that is a part of some religions accounts in part for the vegetarian dietary pattern that is followed broadly in this region. Economic considerations and available commodities reinforce vegetarian food choices.

India's neighbors are uniquely different from each other and from India. Pakistan was created as a Muslim nation when India was partitioned, and the Hindus were concentrated in India. Muslim traditions present a contrast, both in traditions and attitudes. Nepal melds Buddhism and Hindu traditions, in contrast to Tibet, which is Buddhist even though its Dalai Lama had to flee from the Potala to Dharamsala in India when the Chinese took over in 1959. Bhutan is an idyllic Buddhist kingdom, in sharp contrast to the poverty and food shortages that Bangladesh must solve. Sri Lanka is still attempting to halt frequently violent conflicts stemming from the Tamil drive to be a separate state on the island.

The foods of India concentrate on legumes and cereals, which are the basis of the vegetarian diet. Wheat and rice are the favored cereals, and lentils of various types and also dried beans and peas are used in many different ways. Creative use of spices has made the flavors of Indian cuisine exciting and different from western food. This uniqueness depicts Indian food ways, which have been altered only a little by the various invaders who have dominated their land at different times. Among the words in Indian menus are *ghee, naan, samosas, curry, chutney, paratha, roti,* and *puri.*

Study Questions

1. Where are each of these countries located, and what geographic features influence the lives of people living in them: (a) India, (b) Bangladesh, (c) Sri Lanka, (d) Bhutan, (e) Tibet, (f) Nepal, and (g) Pakistan?
2. Select one of the empires or periods in India's history and describe it by discussing the following: (a) when, (b) rise to power and fall, (c) influence on the region then and/or subsequently.
3. Describe an Indian work of art, work of literature, dance, or music performance. Visit art galleries, libraries, music stores, or live performances, if possible, to select the work you are describing.
4. Define (a) ghee, (b) naan, (c) masala, (d) tandoor, (e) chapati, and (f) curry.
5. Identify 10 spices used in Indian cooking. Why do you think spices are so important in Indian cooking?

Bibliography

Barer-Stein, T. 1999. *You Eat What You Are.* 2nd ed. Firefly Books, Ltd. Ontario, Canada.

Hoefer, H. 1990. *Insight Guide: Asia.* APA Publications. Singapore.

Neal, W. C., and J. Adams. 1976. *India.* 2nd ed. Van Nostrand. New York.

Pearcy, G. E. 1980. *The World Food Scene.* Plycon Press. Redondo Beach, CA.

Rau, S. R. 1969. *Cooking of India.* Time-Life Books. New York.

Schulberg, L. 1968. *Historic India.* Time-Life Books. New York.

Sheehan, S. 1994. *Pakistan.* Marshall Cavendish. New York.

Sinclair, T. 1995. *India.* Guidebook Co. Hong Kong.

Srinivasan, R. 1992. *India.* Marshall Cavendish. New York.

Wanasundera, N. P. 1991. *Sri Lanka.* Marshall Cavendish. New York.

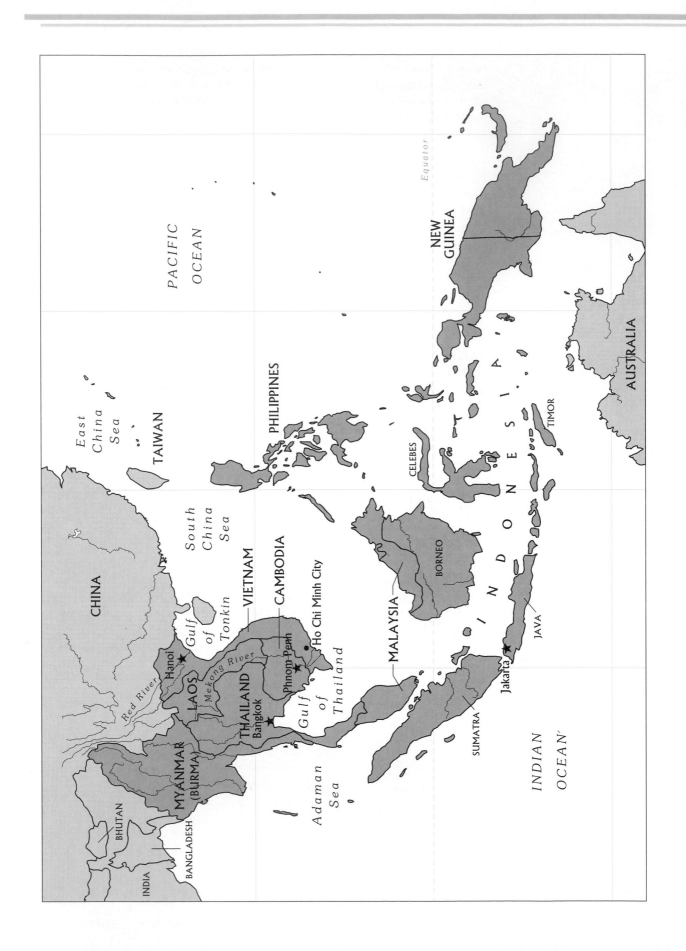

16 Southeast Asia and Its Islands

Geographic Overview

The southeastern part of the Asian continent (Figure 16.1) and the related islands considered in this chapter begin with Myanmar (formerly Burma, which lies to the east of India and Bangladesh and extends southward along the eastern shores of the Bay of Bengal), Thailand and the three countries of the Indochina Peninsula (Cambodia, Laos, and Vietnam), and the western part of Malaysia (Figure 16.2). These countries are all part of the continent. From the tip of the Malay Peninsula, Singapore actually is an island connected to the continent by a causeway. The eastern part of the nation of Malaysia encompasses part of the northern edge of Borneo, a large island lying to the east of Sumatra. Indonesia is a very scattered country consisting of many islands, some large and others quite small. Sumatra, Java, Bali, Borneo, and Sulawesi are some of the larger and more familiar islands in this nation. To the north of Sulawesi and east of Vietnam is the group of islands comprising the nation of the Philippines. Actually, there are many other islands scattered in clusters in the Pacific and at various distances east of Indonesia. Among these are the Solomon, Gilbert, Fiji, Samoa, Society, and Marquesa island groups, the latter two lying east of the international date line. These various islands appear to have been settled over many centuries as adventurous seafaring people set their courses into unknown seas and eventually brought their culture to the Hawaiian Islands. Although this chapter encompasses a vast amount of ocean, the dietary patterns and the foods available in this extensive geographic reach are closely related.

The countries on the continent have highland and somewhat mountainous terrain in their northern areas and give rise to rivers that serve as important links to the marketplaces within each country. The Irrawaddy River in Myanmar, the

Figure 16.1 Pagodas and temples dot the landscape while a flock of birds wheels overhead and cattle graze on scraggly brush near Pagan, Myanmar (formerly Burma).

Chao Phyra in Thailand, and the Mekong River in the Indochina Peninsula are major rivers that have important seaports at their mouths, enabling these countries to participate in international trade in their cities of Yangon, Bangkok, and Ho Chi Minh City, respectively.

These countries experience monsoons, which bring the rain needed for growing their rice and other crops. The hottest part of the year is the dry season, particularly the spring months, for the monsoons begin in the summer and help to alleviate the intense heat (Figure 16.3). However, these countries are sufficiently close to the equator that they are not really cold at any time, with the exception of high elevations. Myanmar has mountains in its west and north, the highest mountain being over 19,000 feet. Much of the land in the central part of these countries is sufficiently flat to make farming quite successful. In fact, farming is the primary way of life in many regions of these nations. The crops in addition to rice include a wide array of fruits and vegetables. Tropical fruits, such as mangoes, coconuts, papayas, durian, bananas, rambutan, breadfruit, and pineapple, are available throughout this region. Meat, poultry, and fish also are raised for food.

Similarly, the islands are generally able to grow reasonable crops. Of course, seafood is available for the catching in the various island groups (Figure 16.4). The sea complicates the food situation because foods not raised on the island must be brought in either by sea or air. This added cost limits what may be available to people with limited incomes. The various islands raise coconuts, bananas, and some other fruits, as well as a wide range of spices in quantities sufficient to

Figure 16.2 Cambodians fish in the Mekong River at Phnom Penh near a grove of banana trees.

Figure 16.3 In Cambodia, these two bullocks stand at attention outside their owner's farm, with its house on stilts to avoid the monsoon waters.

generate good income for some people. The close proximity of the islands to the equator promotes crop production throughout the year, thus providing food for the islanders as well as for export.

History and Culture

Some evidence of early cave dwellers has been found in the hills on the eastern edge of Myanmar in the northern region. Later settlers came from southern Tibet and developed a civilization in the 8th century, only to be defeated by the Shans and the Mons. The region around Pagan eventually became the First Burmese Empire and was ruled for a time by King Anawrahta, who brought Buddhism to his kingdom. The First Burmese Empire came to an end in 1287 when Kublai Khan and his forces destroyed it, causing the Mons to shift south and the Shans to move to the west. Almost 300 years later, the Second Burmese Empire governed from 1551 to 1752, with territory being taken from what is now Thailand to in-

Figure 16.4 Ancient fish traps still function in this inlet on Huahini in the Pacific's French Polynesia.

crease its holding. Traders from Europe and Arabia were active during the latter part of this period. In fact, France supported the Mons in overthrowing the government in 1752. The Third Burmese Empire lasted until 1885, during which time Siam (the earlier name for Thailand) brought much of its highly developed culture (Figure 16.5) to Burma, the influence of which is still evident today. The British cast a greedy eye (and also military force) on Burma and finally gained control over it in 1886, after three wars between the two nations. The imperialism of British rule was unacceptable to Burmese nationalists, who wanted independence. This struggle was led by Aung Sun, but the Japanese took over during World War II, and the British regained control briefly after the war until independence finally was achieved in 1948. This story still does not have a happy ending, because a very repressive and backward-thinking regime has hung onto its power despite the efforts of Aung Sun's daughter, Aung San Suu Kyi (who has been under house arrest for many years following her return to Burma in 1988), and of others who want democracy. Education is close to nonexistent, with universities being closed all of the time except for examinations. The isolation achieved by the current regime has trapped Myanmar in a time warp remote from the rest of the nations of the world.

The history of Thailand involves interactions between people in neighboring countries and shifts of power back and forth, depending upon who emerged victorious from the battles. Among the early settlers were the Yunnan immigrants from southern China, who arrived in the northern part of Thailand and established a kingdom in 1238. Even earlier, the Mons had been pressing in from their base in Burma and made contact with the Khmers, who were coming in from the east from their domain in Cambodia. The Khmers built a city called Sukhotai in northern Thailand, which operated as the capital of the region. Hinduism was the first religion, but Buddhism soon became dominant. The result is that the ruins of Sukhotai have a Hindu temple (Wat Phra Phai Luang) at the city's edge and numerous Buddhist temples and *chedis* (lotus bud-shaped stupas). Wat Mahathat, a particularly lovely temple ruin, and Wat Sra Sri (the temple on two islands in a lake) are restored highlights of the old Sukhotai. After Sukhotai lost its power in the 14th century, Ayutthaya was established by Rama Tibodi I farther south on the Chao Phyra River. This center was the capital of Thailand for more than 400

Figure 16.5 The unique and graceful lines used in designing the Grand Palace in Bangkok, Thailand, were transported to Burma by Thai artisans when Burma conquered Thailand in the 18th Century.

years until Burmese invaders destroyed it in 1767. Subsequently, the capital of Thailand was established in Bangkok, where its exotic Grand Palace eventually was built and remains the most remarkable sight in the city. Although Siam had contact with European traders and other foreigners, it did not actually become a part of any other nation's colonial empire. Instead, it remained comparatively free of cultural influences from others and retained its unique and complex cultural styles.

Cambodia had a culturally distinguished past that culminated in the building of the vast complex at Angkor Wat between the 9th and 11th centuries in northern Cambodia near Siem Reap. Somewhat later, Jayavarman VIII, a strong Buddhist king, had Angkor Thom and many other wats built quite close to Angkor Wat, resulting in an amazing collection of ruins from this fruitful period of Khmer rule. After invaders from Thailand defeated the Khmers in 1594, an extended period of weak rule followed, with the capital being moved south to Phnom Penh. Thailand and Vietnam basically were in control of the region until the French arrived in the latter part of the 19th century. The French controlled Cambodia from the 1870s until 1954, except for a period of Japanese occupation during World War II. Finally, independence was achieved, but stability was not the result. Traumatic years were to follow as the regime of Lon Nol and the Khmer Rouge jousted for control. The Pol Pot regime exacted a terrible human toll, which led to the Vietnamese invasion to liberate Phnom Penh in 1979. The extensive damage caused by landmines is slowly being eliminated as the result of prolonged programs to clean out the minefields in the country, but many people throughout the country bear mute physical testimony to the damage these explosives have caused. The country is moving very slowly toward normalcy, but the terrors of the past leave haunting memories in its people. How hard it is to reconcile today's Cambodia with the glories of the Khmer domain at the time of Angkor Wat.

Laos, like the rest of the countries in the southeastern region of the Asian continent, acquired early settlers from China to the north. Finally, Fa Ngum became the ruler of Lan Xang in 1353. The capital of his Buddhist kingdom was established at Luang Prabang in northern Laos. Two centuries later the king moved the capital to Vientiane toward the south, where it still remains. By the 18th century, Thailand had control over parts of Laos, and Burma controlled the northern part around Luang Prabang briefly before losing this region to Thailand. During the 19th century, many Laotians were moved to Thailand, and the French were beginning their move to gain what was to become French Indochina. The country that now is Laos was defined geographically by the French, in concert with Britain and China. The Japanese occupation of Laos in 1941 actually provided a small opportunity for more local control, but France quickly returned after the war in 1945, only to be driven eventually from French Indochina as resistance to them and the desire for freedom set war in motion. Events during this period were stormy. The ultimate result was that communism infiltrated into Laos, heavy bombing and loss of life occurred during the Vietnam War, and thousands of Hmong from northern Laos were in refugee camps in Thailand for many years. Many of the Hmong, who were mostly from the northern hill region of Laos, have emigrated to the United States.

Vietnam, with its long seacoast, attracted Chinese settlers many centuries ago. The excellent farming available in the deltas of the Red and Mekong rivers and the opportunity for trade from prospective seaports were driving forces for these settlers. Even today there is a strong imprint on all aspects of life in Vietnam of the early and also later Chinese immigrants and the rule of China for more than a millennium. One of their particularly important contributions was the development of dikes and canals to control floods and assist farmers. They also brought a panoply of religions: Taoism, Mahayana Buddhism, and Confucianism.

After 900 CE, Vietnam began to exert its strength against its neighbors in the Indochina Peninsula. However, France became involved in this peninsula and its governance when the French East India Company and also French missionaries arrived. Cochin China was the name applied to the Mekong Delta area that they shaped politically. Cambodia became a French protectorate in 1865, and French influences could begin to be seen throughout the major cities of Cambodia, Laos, and Vietnam until World War II. After the war, the division of Vietnam into North Vietnam and South Vietnam set the stage for what was to evolve into the Vietnam War that created a tragic situation for the people living in both parts of Vietnam and for many nations elsewhere because of the international presence fighting on both sides. By the end of the 20th century, unification of Vietnam seems to have improved understanding on the part of people from both the former North and South Vietnams; strengthening economic factors finally are beginning to improve the lives of people living in Vietnam.

Malaysia occupies the Malay Peninsula's southern half and shares a border with Thailand on the north. Its western shoreline borders the Indian Ocean. A particularly significant geographic factor in Malaysia's history was the Strait of Melaka, which not only separated the island of Sumatra from the Malay Peninsula, but also afforded a place for early trading vessels from Europe, India, and China to be protected from bad weather while also providing opportunities for trading. Indian traders brought religions with them to Melaka (now spelled Malacca) along with their trading goods. The trading activity caused some friction with Thailand (then Siam) even before European trade arrived. Portugal claimed the Straits of Melaka in 1511, bringing Christianity in the form of Roman Catholicism to the region. However, the Dutch soon were sailing on the western side of Sumatra, a route that precluded the need to land at a Portuguese port on the way to Java, an important island south of Sumatra and the Asian mainland. Nevertheless, the Dutch wrested Melaka from the Portuguese in 1641. By the time the British claimed the island of Penang just off the northern coast of Malaysia in 1786, no other significant trading was taking place along western Malaysia.

Politically, there were several Malay states, basically all protected by Britain until the Japanese invasion in 1943 during World War II. After the war, Malaysia was organized to include the peninsular region and also Sarawak and Sabah, two former British colonies on the island of Borneo (Figure 16.6). This final arrangement was completed in 1963. Singapore, which arguably should be part of Malaysia, opted to become its own republic in 1965.

This federation of 13 states, not surprisingly, has an extremely varied population. A few of the original peoples of the Malay Peninsula and of Borneo can still be found, but modern Malays plus Chinese and Indians who are permanent residents represent the largest part of the population today. Britain has continued to maintain commercial ties with Malaysia, which results in a detectable British overtone in the country. This cultural milieu is evident in the clothing worn by people in the city and also is evident in the mosques, temples, and churches. Al-

Figure 16.6 Kuala Lumpur, the capital of Malaysia, retains some British influence despite the fact the British no longer are in charge.

though the official language is Bahasa Malaysia, many languages are spoken on the street, and newspapers in several languages are available.

Indonesia is geographically even more far-flung than Malaysia. Its more than 13,000 islands are spread for more than 3,000 miles from the Pacific Ocean on the east to the Indian Ocean on the west, and they range for more than 1,000 miles from Asia to Australia. This reality inevitably settles down to more significance being placed on some of the larger islands, while smaller (sometimes uninhabited) islands are pretty much ignored. The islands were the destination of Arabian and Chinese traders for more than 1,000 years before the Europeans began to explore possible routes to reach the exotic spices available there. Marco Polo was aware of the trading riches that were to be found in Java in the 13th century. Europeans paid huge prices to Arab traders, which clearly provided them the incentive to find another way to the source, bypassing the Arab profiteers.

The Portuguese did sail beyond Melaka as far as Macao on the edge of the Chinese mainland, but they left the Indonesian islands to the Dutch. In fact, the Dutch settled in Java and many other islands as they established control of this valuable source of spices in the 16th century and held not only Java, but also Bali, Sumatra, Borneo, and Sulawesi (Celebes) and others. The Dutch extracted a considerable amount of wealth from these ports during the almost 300 years they were in control. However, the Japanese seized the region during World War II, bringing an end to Dutch power in the region.

The focus on the role that trade played during the colonial era overlooks the fact that Bali and some of the other islands had been inhabited for many centuries and had developed cultures that built lovely temples and created beautiful sculptures that are still enjoyed today. It also minimizes the warlike behaviors that often existed between islands (Java and Bali, for example) and even between groups living on one island. Difficulties between islands and groups persist today in serious conflicts between Timor and the Indonesian government in Jakarta and also in the riots against the Chinese businesses in Jakarta. Nevertheless, this federation of islands remains as Indonesia.

Various other Pacific island groups also contribute to the cultural richness of this region. An example of these island groups is the Society Islands in which such familiar island states as Tahiti, Moorea, and Bora Bora are found. Captain James Cook, the British explorer, visited Tahiti in 1769, but after Bougainville's claim, it was the French who eventually controlled these islands. The original islanders had developed their own culture long before the arrival of the Europeans, and a few petroglyphs remain, as do some of the dances and food patterns. However, French overtones are very evident in French Polynesia today, the result of being a French protectorate in 1842, a French colony in 1880, and now an overseas territory of France (Figure 16.7). The language is French, financial matters are

Secret societies play an important role in communities on such Pacific islands as the Solomons, Fiji, New Caledonia, New Hebrides, and Vanuatu. Wealth is a requirement for belonging to one of these societies. To belong to a secret society is considered to be a distinct honor, but the inner workings of these groups remain totally secret and are known only to members. The best known is the Dukduk Society of the Tolai people.

Figure 16.7 A whimsical reminder of the relationship with France are bread boxes long enough for the delivery of French Baguettes along a bakery route on Moorea in French Polynesia.

under French supervision, and France has the ultimate legal authority, although many governmental affairs are handled by the islanders. There are 14 islands included in French Polynesia, some of volcanic origin, while others are atolls composed of coral reefs and motus barely above sea level. The beauty of the region and easy availability of food and simple housing create an idyllic setting for an unpressured lifestyle, one that has resisted change. *Pareus* (wraparound garments) are the favored garment, being both convenient and easy to market because a single size fits all.

The Philippines had contact with other groups of people perhaps as long ago as 5000 BCE when people arrived by sea from what is now Vietnam. Arrivals from the Malay Peninsula as early as 300 BCE added to the mix of people living on some of the islands in the Philippines. Trade with Arabia, India, and China clearly flourished by the 7th century CE. Islam arrived with some of the Arab, Islamic Malaysian, and Sumatran traders in the southern islands of the Philippines during the 15th century, but the situation changed when Europeans began to arrive in 1521. Ferdinand Magellan, the Portuguese explorer, was the first European in the Philippines, an honor that led to the loss of his life at the hands of some natives less than 2 months after his first landfall. Spanish expeditions were sent to the Philippines after Magellan's ship finally returned to Europe in 1522. Their purposes were to convert the natives to Catholicism and to gain wealth through trade. This move served to halt the spread of Islam. Plans for developing the Philippines as a Spanish possession included creating Manila as the capital. Over the centuries, Spain did little to develop the Philippines once the Catholic conversion was accomplished in the north. However, the Islamic regions in the south generally did not convert to Catholicism.

Spain's dominance of the Philippines was not accepted without protest from other European powers, for Portugal, the Dutch, and British all attacked at various times. In fact, the British actually were in charge of the Philippines for a little less than 2 years in the 18th century. The Spanish-American War that was being fought halfway around the world from the Philippines caused Admiral Dewey and his ships to be sent to attack the Spanish fleet at Manila. This resulted in the United States taking over the Philippines, not with the greatest of respect for the local people. A strong desire for independence eventually led to an agreement that would have resulted in independence in 1945. The obviously bad timing of this transition was delayed by the Japanese invasion and occupation during World War II, but the Philippines became independent in 1946. Since that time, efforts to establish a truly effective government have tended to veer in various directions, but finally seem to be coalescing to begin to meet the needs of the citizens.

The religious landscape in Southeast Asia and the Pacific Islands reflects the various waves of traders and missionaries who brought religious messages to the people of the region. Buddhism is the dominant religion in many of the countries on the continent: Myanmar, Thailand, Laos, Cambodia, Vietnam, and Singapore. Hinduism is practiced by most people on Bali (Figure 16.8) and by some in Malaysia and Singapore. Islam was embraced in Malaysia, Indonesia, the southern Philippines, and somewhat in Singapore. Catholicism found some followers where the French were involved, notably in Vietnam; Spain's Catholic priests were very effective in converting many in the Philippines. In the Pacific, islanders have often been receptive to the efforts of missionaries, whether Protestant, Catholic, or Mormon. The religion that is dominant in these various countries has a strong influence on many aspects of their cultures, particularly on the holidays and how they are celebrated. Singapore and Malaysia have a range of religious holidays throughout the year because of the importance of more than one religion to significant numbers of citizens.

Christian holidays are celebrated in the Philippines. Malaysia and most of Indonesia plus the southern region of the Philippines celebrate Islamic holidays.

Figure 16.8 Hinduism is the dominant religion on the island of Bali.

The practice of fasting during Ramadan and the breaking of the fast are events of tremendous religious importance. In contrast, Bali's predominantly Hindu population has elaborate Hindu celebrations that feature food displays arranged artistically, if somewhat precariously, atop the heads of lovely young Balinese women (Figure 16.9), young men carrying images, and villagers in festive attire as they wend their way to the temples for blessings. Thaipusam is the Hindu day of penance, marked by parades.

Buddhist holidays are celebrated in the many Buddhist countries of this region. Festival of Lights is a joyous celebration of the end of the 3 months of Buddhist Lent, which fortuitously occurs at about the end of the rainy season. This celebration is especially elaborate at the Shwedagon Temple in Yangon, Myanmar, where its lights add to the splendor of the amazing number of shrines encircling its central pagoda.

Lunar New Year celebrations are traditional throughout most of the countries in Southeast Asia. Because of their tie to the lunar calendars of the area, they occur in January or February, but not on January 1. The celebrations differ in various

Figure 16.9 Hindu women on Bali march with massive trays of fruit atop their heads as they celebrate a festival day.

countries, but they often involve intensive cleaning in preparation and the wearing of new clothes on the actual holiday. Fireworks are likely to be a noisy and bright feature of the night. Harvest festivals also are held in many of these nations, with the colorful rituals being somewhat variable from country to country. Independence is cause for celebration in this region, which is not at all surprising considering their relatively recent emergence from colonial subservient status.

Throughout Southeast Asia, the artistry and creativity of the people can be seen in the beautiful and imaginative crafts they make. Thailand has evidence of its abilities in the carvings, statues, and architecture as well as its amazing array of silks in many colors and its dazzling jewelry featuring precious and semiprecious stones set in gold and silver in original designs. Myanmar has patterned its artistic styles after those of the Thais, a deliberate move when Burma brought some of the Thai craftsmen to Rangoon as captives after its incursion into Siam. The elaborate use of gold leaf and many Thai designs are in evidence in Myanmar in temple decorations and also in their unique puppets (Figure 16.10). Puppet shows feature wonderfully imaginative characters that bring the tales of Rama and other familiar personalities to their audiences.

The carvings and art seen in Cambodia and in Laos (Figure 16.11) are clearly similar to those in Thailand, yet they have a bit stronger, more primitive character than the graceful quality of Thai art. The wood carvings and other arts found in Bali are often very intricate, revealing qualities similar to Thai art, yet even more fanciful in their execution. Such work is distinctively different from the carvings seen in the Pacific islands of Polynesia, where the work is less detailed, yet conveys the spirit of the artist or carver. Of course, Paul Gauguin painted his interpretation of Polynesia, paintings that have been admired around the world, but his work is that of a European and not representative of local art. Nevertheless, he immortalized lovely scenes of Polynesia and its people.

Dance is a form of art found throughout this region. Many folk tales have been transmitted from generation to generation throughout Southeast Asia, proving to be a very effective way of preserving stories and passing on the culture. The costumes worn by the dancers are often elaborate to create a feeling of mysticism and fantasy befitting the myths that are conveyed through the dances and their musical accompaniments. A particularly amazing part of Thai and Cambo-

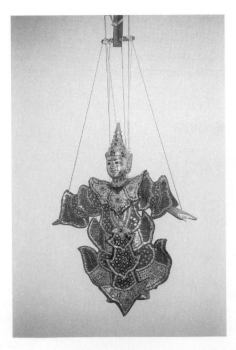

Figure 16.10 Gold-embellished Myanmar puppet resembles the designs found in Thailand.

Figure 16.11 This black Buddha on the temple near Luang Prabang, Laos, reveals a somewhat less delicate style than is found in similar works in Thailand.

dian dancing is the graceful backward bending of fingers to which incredibly long curved nails are added. The hands are used to convey part of the story's message. Hands are an important part of Polynesian dancing too, but the whole hand rather than one extended with artificial nails is featured. Added to the hand action is the seemingly impossible hip movement in Polynesian dancing. Music for the dances and also music for its own sake can be heard throughout the nations of this region. The groups usually have drums, flutes or similar instruments, variations of strings, and unique percussion. Gamelan groups play many folk melodies on their various gongs, providing lovely music for the dancers.

Certain garments and customs set some of the people in the various countries of Southeast Asia a bit apart from the typical scenes found in cities around the world. The creamy yellow paste that is smeared generously on the cheeks of Burmese children and women, a cosmetic called *thanaka,* immediately tells the traveler that this is Myanmar. Presumably, this paste will help prevent burning under the scorching Burmese sun. The *longyi,* which is a length of cloth like a sarong, is wrapped around the lower torso and legs by both men and women in Myanmar and tucked in at the waist, but it can be hiked up as needed for walking or for cooler comfort on the legs. Monks throughout Southeast Asia are wrapped in saffron-colored robes.

Most of the rural people in the rest of the region dress quite simply to accommodate the demands of working in flooded rice paddies, threshing rice, and herding water buffalo or oxen. Simple, widely flaring straw hats provide shade for field workers. Filipinos have beautifully embroidered, tailored shirts to be worn over pants by men for dressy occasions, while the women wear rather elaborate dresses with uniquely puffed sleeves. Thai, Malay, and Indonesian women are likely to wear garments of colorful silks, often rather tailored and with a fairly long skirt.

The style of eating varies a bit by countries too. People in Myanmar, Thailand, Malaysia, Indonesia, Cambodia, Laos, and southern Vietnam may choose to eat using the fingers of the right hand rather than silverware, while northern Vietnamese prefer chopsticks. The difference indicates the strong Chinese influence over northern Vietnam. However, many people opt for silverware rather than fingers today.

Food Patterns

Rice is the cereal grain used universally in the nations of Southeast Asia, the type varying from north to south within the various countries. Long grain, fluffy rice is popular in Vietnam and Malaysia. Sticky rice, often used to make sweet desserts, is preferred in the north of Thailand and among its neighbors. An appetizing example of this use is the Thai dessert featuring glutinous rice cooked in coconut milk accompanied by slices of fresh mango. Rice in these countries is likely to be included in at least two meals a day, either in a mixed dish or served separately with various sauces or other accompaniments to round out the meal, depending on the country or the available food. It may be the basis of the dramatic cone *(nasi tumpeng)* that is prepared in Java for religious ceremonies and decorated colorfully with strips of such foods as shredded beef, peanuts, slivers of red chilies, and chopped hard-cooked egg arranged to lead to the tip of the cone and its topping of green coriander. Fried rice is also popular.

The versatility of rice and its suitability as an agricultural crop have made it a staple used in numerous dishes and in various applications. For example, rice can be made into a vinegar, and it can be fermented to make wine. It can be made into delicate, edible rice paper in which fillings can be wrapped and then fried, and it can be used to make noodles. It may appear at breakfast as a rice gruel called *congee*.

The other cereal that makes an appearance in these countries is wheat, which is used to make a variety of breads and noodles. The breads may be round, flat breads reminiscent of the breads of India; others reflect French influence in the form of baguettes or other popular French breads and baked goods of nations formerly run by the French.

The meats served in these countries are influenced greatly by religious dictates of the dominant religions (see Chapter 3). Pork is avoided in Malaysia and most of Indonesia because of the dominance of Islam, whereas beef is shunned in Bali with its dominant Hindu population. Nevertheless, chicken, duck, fish, pork, beef, and eggs are popular. Many Buddhists throughout Southeast Asia generally avoid meats and even fish. This has fostered extensive use of soy products as a source of protein. Tofu and *tempeh* (fermented soybean curd) appear in many dishes throughout these countries. Mung beans and other legumes also are used extensively as meat substitutes, either replacing meats and fish or reducing the quantities served. Peanut oil is the preferred cooking oil in much of this region. Its flavor adds to the dishes.

Fruits and vegetables are used generously throughout the region. In addition to the fruits and vegetables familiar in the United States, there are exotic tropical fruits such as rambutan, mangosteen, carambola (star fruit), jackfruit, breadfruit, and coconut. Vegetable greens and various peppers are traditional ingredients. Thai cookery is noted for its generous use of chilies and peppercorns, making some dishes among the most fiery experiences you can find.

Creative use of spices and herbs can be found not only in Thailand, but in Malaysia, Indonesia, and pretty much throughout Southeast Asia. Curry variations are popular, and they are prepared using such spices as turmeric, peppers, ginger, and saffron. Other flavoring ingredients used in the region include lemon grass, coconut milk, mint, coriander, garlic, green onions, and chives. Various sauces are characteristic of the region. Vietnam features *nuoc mam* (fermented, salted fish sauce) and *nuoc cham* (chili peppers, lime or other citrus juice, garlic, onions, and vinegar condiment), both of which are virtually used as staples. *Nam pla* (a fermented fish sauce) and a dried shrimp paste called *kapi* are popular ways of adding some salt at the table in Thailand (Figure 16.12). Soy sauces are used throughout the area and are particularly popular among people of Chinese de-

Figure 16.12 Nam pla and kapi are Thai sauces used to add salt and flavor to fried fish.

scent. Filipinos are fond of *bagoong* (salty, fermented shrimp paste) and other sauces featuring soy or salty anchovy paste (*patis, toyo,* and *hipon* sauces).

The various conquerors and traders who played significant roles in the history of Southeast Asia have left their marks on the foods that are favored in the different countries. For example, Myanmar, Malaysia, and Indonesia often feature curries and *satays* (Indian version of shish kebab), which is not surprising considering the proximity of India and the trade that existed. The Philippines reflect their Spanish involvement in such dishes as flan and *adobo,* a dish featuring chicken and pork in which Spanish seasonings intersperse with vinegar and soy sauce that are characteristic of the area. French breads are familiar fare in Cambodia, Laos, and Vietnam, where the French ruled before the war. Thailand, which really never was conquered by countries other than immediate neighbors, has developed its own somewhat unique cuisine, especially favored because of its use of seasonings and its careful attention to beautiful presentations of food to delight both the eye and the mouth.

The foods that are dominant in the diets of the Pacific Islanders are somewhat different from those in Southeast Asia. The islands are excellent sources of breadfruit (Figure 16.13), taro (Figure 16.14), coconut, pineapple, banana, papaya, yams, and cassava. The meats include pork, chicken, and seafood. Coconut is crucial to preparing many Polynesian dishes. The young coconut (one forming for 6 months on the tree) can be scraped out with a spoon and eaten that way. It is sometimes fed to babies. Usually, coconuts remain on the tree for a year so that they ripen and develop the familiar hard brown shell. Coconut cream and co-

Figure 16.13 Breadfruit thrives on the islands in French Polynesia.

Figure 16.14 Taro grows with very useful large leaves and a large edible starchy tuber to provide an important staple food in Polynesia.

conut milk can be made using grated fresh coconut, and these are included in many recipes. The liquid that can be drained by puncturing the eyes of the coconut is coconut water, which can be drunk but is not a cooking ingredient. Coconut milk or cream requires that the flesh of the coconut be pared to get rid of the brown skin; chunks of the white flesh are then put in a blender with an equal amount of hot water and blended for a minute on high. This puree has to be strained through cheesecloth, which then is squeezed to get the coconut milk to drip out. With less water, the coconut milk will be more creamy. Fortunately, canned coconut milk is available and saves considerable time.

Poe (spelled *poi* in Hawaii) is the starchy paste prepared by boiling and pounding peeled taro root to make a thick paste. Liquid can be added to achieve the desired consistency. Poe seems to be an acquired taste for some people, who describe it as a clone of library paste. However, Polynesians may flavor their poe with fresh fruits for added flavor.

Ti leaves sometimes are used to wrap meat or fish before steaming it. This imparts a bit of flavor. Banana leaves are also used in this way. Many different combinations of food can be wrapped in banana, breadfruit, or ti leaves and tied, then baked in the coals of an outdoor barbecue. This is a popular way of cooking food in a leisurely manner at a luau. These large leaves are even used to wrap food purchases at the markets in Polynesia.

Breadfruit almost seems to be a misnomer because its starchy character really suits it to serve as a replacement for potatoes. This large fruit can be prepared in virtually the same way that a potato would be. It plays a prominent role in the Polynesian diet, whether boiled, baked, or pounded to make a dish resembling poe. Polynesia also is home to another source of starch, arrowroot, which is generally used as a thickener by islanders.

*K*ey Terms

Adobo—Filipino stew using meats marinated in vinegar seasoned with bagoong, fried with onions and garlic, and then stewed.
Bagoong—Filipino fermented, salted shrimp paste.

Coconut cream—Pureed and strained creamy liquid prepared from freshly grated white meat of mature pared coconut and some hot water.

Coconut milk—Coconut liquid similar to coconut cream, but with more liquid.

Coconut water—Liquid drained from fresh coconut by puncturing its eyes; used as beverage, but not as a cooking ingredient.

Cocido—Hearty Filipino stew containing a variety of meats, Spanish sausage, chickpeas, saba (sweet cooking bananas), tomato sauce, and lard.

Congee—Rice gruel often served at breakfast in Southeast Asia.

Hmongs—People native to the northern hill regions of Laos.

Kapi—Thai salty, dried shrimp paste.

Khmers—People native to Cambodia.

Longyi—Long, sarong-like cloth worn in Burma, tucked in at the waist or hiked up in the very hot weather.

Mons—People native to Burma.

Nam pla—Fermented fish sauce popular in Thailand.

Nuoc cham—Vietnamese condiment made with chili peppers, citrus juice, garlic, onions, and vinegar.

Nuoc mam—Fermented, salted fish sauce popular in Vietnam.

Patis—Fermented, salty fish sauce popular in the Philippines.

Poe (poi)—Starchy paste of boiled and pounded, peeled taro root popular in Polynesia.

Recipes

Shrimp Curry (Myanmar) (Serves 4–6)

3/4 lb shelled, deveined, raw shrimp
1/2 tsp turmeric
1 1/4 tsp paprika
1 tbsp shrimp sauce
1 tsp grated fresh ginger
2 garlic cloves, minced
3 medium onions, diced
1/4 c peanut oil
1 c tomato paste
1 c water

1. Marinate shrimp for 1 hour in turmeric, paprika, and shrimp sauce mixture.
2. Saute ginger, garlic, and onions in oil gently for 2 minutes.
3. Add shrimp and stir-fry briefly until shrimp is beginning to turn pink.
4. Add tomato paste diluted with water and heat while stirring for 1 minute.
5. Serve with hot rice.

Beef Curry (Thailand) (Serves 4)

3 c coconut milk
1 tbsp red curry paste
2 tsp turmeric
1 star anise
1/2 cinnamon stick
3 bay leaves
1 1/2 c cubed (1") potatoes

3 onions, coarsely chopped

1. Bring 1 cup coconut milk, curry paste, and turmeric to a boil; stir while reducing to about 1/4 cup.
2. Stir in remaining ingredients; cover and simmer for 45 minutes.
3. Serve with hot rice.

Fresh Coconut Milk* (Makes 1 cup)

1 c chopped white coconut meat (from fresh coconut)
1 c hot water

1. Poke holes in coconut eyes and drain the coconut water out.
2. Bake at 375°F for 15 minutes.
3. Use hammer to tap shell open.

4. Remove coconut meat; pare the brown covering, leaving only white coconut meat.
5. Blend coconut meat and water until coconut is very fine.
6. Squeeze through layers of cheesecloth to strain out the coconut, leaving the milk, which will keep for 2 days in the refrigerator.

* Canned coconut milk can be purchased to save time.

Chicken Soup with Mint (Cambodia) (Makes 4 cups)

1 lb boneless, cubed chicken breast and/or thighs
3 tbsp rice
1 garlic clove, minced
2 tbsp thinly sliced green onions
Water to cover
1 tsp salt
1/2 tsp ground pepper
1 1/4 tsp sugar
1/4 c lime juice
2 tbsp chopped mint leaves

Fish sauce

1. Put all ingredients except lime juice and mint in a large saucepan; cover with water.
2. Simmer, covered, for 30 minutes or until chicken is tender.
3. Add lime juice and heat briefly.
4. Add mint just before serving with a dash of fish sauce.

Pineapple Fried Rice (Thailand) (Serves 4)

2 small pineapples with tops
2 tbsp oil
1/2 lb pork, diced
2 green chilies, seeded and minced
1 onion, minced
3 c cooked rice
1/4 lb cooked, shelled shrimp
2 tbsp fish sauce
4 tsp soy sauce
6 tbsp roasted cashews
2 scallions, chopped
1 green chili, seeded and sliced
2 red chilies, seeded and sliced

3 tbsp coarsely chopped mint leaves

1. Split pineapples (tops attached) in half; use sharp knife to cut out the pulp, discarding core and chopping the pulp into pieces.
2. Heat oil in a wok and stir-fry chilies, onion, and pork until pork is well browned on all sides.
3. Add rice, shrimp, pineapple pieces, sauces, cashews, and scallions. Heat while stirring to thoroughly mix and bring to serving temperature.
4. Place filling in pineapple shells and garnish with chilies and mint.

Fish Chowder (Serves 4–6)

1/2 c pureed pimiento
1/2 c chopped onion
1 garlic clove, minced
2 tbsp peanut oil
1 lb fish fillet, cubed
1 tsp salt
1/2 tsp pepper

4 c coconut milk
1 1/2 c parboiled, cubed potatoes

1. Stir-fry pimiento, onion, and garlic in oil until onion softens (about 5 minutes).
2. Add fish and heat gently for 4 minutes.
3. Add salt, pepper, coconut milk, and potatoes.
4. Simmer 20 minutes before serving.

Shrimp-Pepper Curry (Malaysia) (Serves 4)

2 onions, chopped finely
2 hot chilies, seeded and finely chopped
1 green pepper, coarsely chopped
3 tbsp peanut oil
3 tomatoes, chopped
1/3 c slivered, blanched almonds
3 basil leaves, chopped
lemon grass, smashed (3 inches)
1/2 tsp thyme
1 tsp salt
1 zucchini, thinly sliced
1/2 lb fresh, cleaned shrimp

1 c coconut milk
2 tbsp flour

1. Saute onions and peppers in oil for 3 minutes.
2. Add all ingredients except flour and coconut milk, and simmer for 4 minutes.
3. Stir coconut milk gradually into flour until smooth, then stir this slurry into the other ingredients.
4. Stir continuously while heating to thicken sauce.
5. Serve over hot rice.

Crab Rolls (Vietnam) (Serves 6–8)

Filling

2 oz translucent mung bean threads (cellophane noodles)
5 dried Asian mushrooms (1" diameter)
1 lb ground pork (lean)
1 onion, finely chopped
3/4 lb cooked crab meat, minced
4 egg yolks, beaten
3/4 tsp salt
3/4 tsp pepper

Wrapping

1 lb egg roll wrappers
1 egg, beaten
Oil for deep-fat frying

1. Hydrate noodles in cold water and mushrooms in warm water for 30 minutes; drain and cut into 2" lengths.
2. Stir pork and onions while frying in a skillet so that pork is in small pieces and shows no trace of pink.
3. Add all other filling ingredients and mix thoroughly.
4. Shape about 2 tablespoons of the mixture into a rod 4" long and 1" in diameter. Repeat until mixture is all shaped.
5. Wrap each rod by placing diagonally (between opposite tips) on a wrapper and folding over the tips; brush egg along borders, then roll up the wrapper to firmly enclose the filling.
6. Deep-fat fry about four rolls at a time at 375°F until they are golden brown (about 4 minutes). Keep warm in 275°F oven and serve hot.

Ginger Beef with Coconut (Indonesia) (Serves 6)

2 c chopped onions
2 garlic cloves, minced
1 tbsp ground coriander
1 tsp freshly grated ginger root
1/4 tsp turmeric
1/4 tsp ground pepper
1 1/4 lb beef round steak in 1" cubes

4 c coconut milk

1. Combine all ingredients in a Dutch oven.
2. Heat to a boil while stirring slowly.
3. Cover and bake in 375°F oven until beef is fork tender (about 2 1/2 hours). Add water, if needed.
4. Serve with hot rice.

Fish Soup (Philippines) (Serves 6–8)

2 c canned tomatoes and juice
1 1/2 c chopped onion
1 qt water
1 1/2 tsp salt
1 lb firm white fish, cubed
1 c shredded cabbage
1 c peeled and cubed eggplant

1 c string beans (1 1/4″ pieces)
Juice of 1 lemon

1. Heat tomatoes, onion, water, salt, and fish to a boil and simmer for 10 minutes.
2. Add vegetables and simmer for 5 minutes more.
3. Stir in lemon juice.

Sweet Poe (Tahiti) (Serves 6–8)

1 large pineapple, pared and cored
2 mangoes, peeled and seeded
2 papayas (1 lb each), pared and seeded
3 bananas, peeled
6 tbsp arrowroot starch
1 c brown sugar
1 tsp vanilla extract
1 c coconut cream

1. Coarsely chop all of the fruits, then place in a large mixing bowl and sprinkle with arrowroot starch, brown sugar, and vanilla.
2. Gently mix together completely.
3. Transfer to buttered baking dish (14″ x 8″ x 2″) and bake in 375°F oven for about 1 hour (until top is golden). Cool before chilling in refrigerator. Serve with chilled coconut cream.

Mango and Glutinous Rice (Thailand) (Serves 4–6)

1 c sticky rice (glutinous sweet)
1/4 c sugar
1/2 c coconut milk
2 ripe mangoes (pared, seeded, sliced crosswise in 1/4″ slices)
4 mint sprigs or leaves for garnish

1. Prepare rice according to package directions. Drain.
2. Dissolve sugar in coconut milk.
3. Stir coconut milk into rice and heat slowly until almost dry. Chill.
4. Place serving of rice on four dessert plates and arrange slices of mango alongside the rice. Garnish with mint.

Summary

Southeast Asia includes the countries of Myanmar (Burma), Thailand, Cambodia, Laos, Vietnam, and Malaysia on the Asian continent, and also island nations: Singapore, Indonesia, the Philippines, and Polynesia. Mountains dominate the northern portions of this section of the continent, with monsoons being responsible for the heavy rainfall that is so important to growing rice. This cereal is the foundation of the diets throughout the region.

The generally warm and very moist weather enables farmers to grow a variety of tropical and subtropical fruits and vegetables. Among the more common are coconuts, mangoes, papayas, citrus, bananas, greens of many types, chilies and other peppers, and tomatoes. Fish from the sea and also from freshwater are good sources of protein. Augmenting the aquatic contributions are chickens, ducks, beef, and pork where religion does not prohibit certain flesh foods. Spices in abundance are grown in many parts of Southeast Asia.

The original inhabitants of this region were conquered by invaders from different directions throughout history, with Kublai Khan coming from the north in the 13th century, China from the east at various times, and Europeans and Arabs from the west before the 18th century. There also were numerous battles between the native groups, particularly between the Khmer, Thai, and Burmese. Thailand managed to remain independent of invaders from afar, but Burma and the peninsula of Indochina were ruled by foreign powers during the colonial era (notably by the French, British, and Dutch).

Religion plays a significant role in the countries throughout Southeast Asia. Buddhism is prominent, particularly in the nations on the continent. Hinduism is dominant on the Indonesian island of Bali and is practiced to a lesser extent in neighboring countries. Islam is the major religion in the Malay Peninsula and much of Indonesia as well as the southern island region of the Philippines. Catholicism dominates in most of the Philippines (heritage from the Spanish control) and is practiced by some minorities throughout the region. The art and dances of Southeast Asia frequently have religious inspiration. Intricate designs in handicrafts vary a bit from country to country, but clearly interconnect the various cultural groups. Bright colors and generous use of gold contribute to the dazzling impact of many of their buildings as well as their costumes, carvings, and jewelry.

The traditional eating style of Southeast Asia is to eat with the fingers, although people living near China in Vietnam use chopsticks, and many others today choose silverware. Rice provides the backbone of the diets for people here. Wheat also finds its way prominently into meals in the forms of noodles and breads. Chicken, duck, eggs, pork, fish, and soybean products (tofu and tempeh) are the sources of protein in diets, the specific choices being determined by religious dictates for some. Tropical fruits and vegetables are used generously; often, chilies and many indigenous spices and herbs are added to dishes to create unforgettable flavors (and heat). Sauces utilizing soy, coconut milk, or fish as principal ingredients form the basis for creating many of the recipes of the region.

Study Questions

1. Describe how the geography and climate influence the food patterns of people in Southeast Asia.
2. Where are the following countries and islands located: (a) Cambodia, (b) Myanmar, (c) Philippines, (d) Borneo, (e) Vietnam, (f) Thailand, and (g) Laos?
3. Trace the roles played by various European nations in Southeast Asia during the past 200 years.
4. Contrast the typical foods of Thailand with those of Polynesia.
5. Describe a dish that is typical of each of the following: (a) Thailand, (b) Myanmar, (c) Philippines, (d) Malaysia, (e) Laos, (f) Tahiti, and (g) Indonesia.

Bibliography

Barer-Stein, T. 1999. *You Eat What You Are*. 2nd ed. Firefly Books, Ltd. Ontario, Canada.
Basche, J. 1971. *Thailand: Land of the Free*. Taplinger Publishing. New York.
Cummings, J. 1998. *Laos*. 3rd ed. Lonely Planet. Oakland, CA.
Forman, W., R. Mrazek, and B. Forman. 1983. *Bali: Split Gate to Heaven*. Orbis. London.
Layton, L. 1990. *Singapore*. Marshall Cavendish. New York.
Mansfield, S. 1997. *Guide to Philippines*. Globe Pequot Press. Old Saybrook, CT.
Munan, H. 1990. *Malaysia*. Marshall Cavendish. New York.
Pearcy, G. E. 1980. *The World Food Scene*. Plycon Press. Redondo Beach, CA.
Steinberg, R. 1970. *Pacific and Southeast Asian Cooking*. Time-Life Books. New York.
Taylor, C., T. Wheeler, and D. Robinson. 1996. *Cambodia*. 2nd ed. Lonely Planet. Oakland, CA.
Yin, S. M. 1990. *Burma*. Marshall Cavendish. New York.

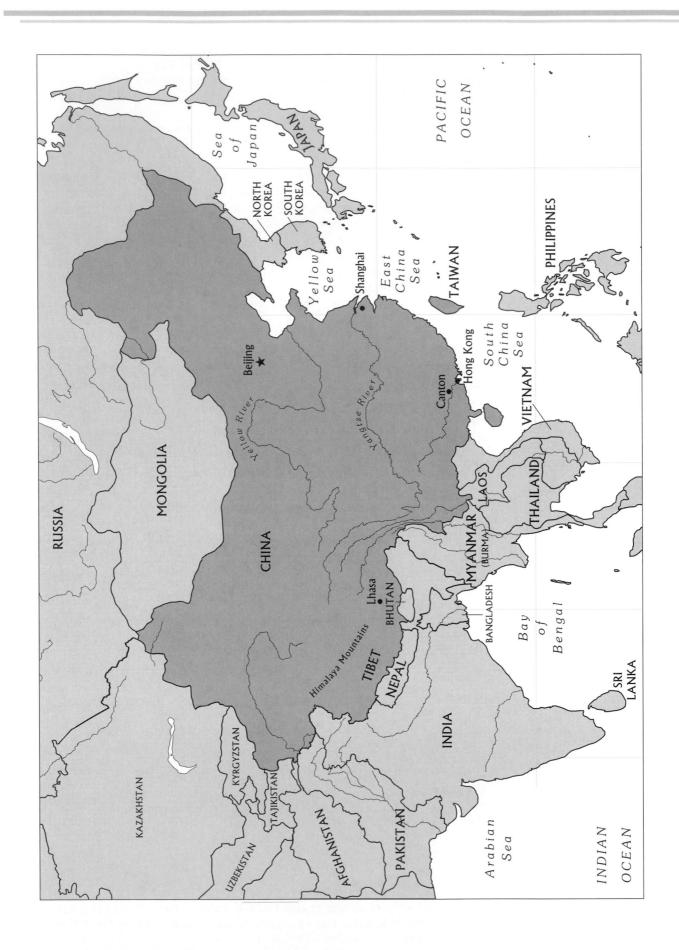

17

China

Geographic Overview

China, the most populous nation in the world, is a sprawling giant stretching across the equivalent of four time zones from the Yellow, East, and South China seas on its eastern shores to Afghanistan, Pakistan, and India on the west. Its long northern border abuts Russia, Mongolia, Kazakhstan, and Kyrgyzstan; southern neighbors include Vietnam, Laos, Myanmar, India, Bhutan, and Nepal. Although China's reach from east to west is even broader than the continental United States, all clocks are set to the time appropriate to Beijing, the capital. The result is that on a day when the sun rises at 6:00 A.M. in Beijing, it does not appear in Tibet until about 10:00 A.M. according to the clock.

Some of China's mountains form spectacular terrain, particularly in its Himalayan peaks along the southwestern borders, and include Mt. Everest at more than 29,000 feet (the world's highest mountain). From this region of numerous peaks towering above 25,000 feet and Tibet's plateau that is more than 12,000 feet above sea level, China tends to slope downward toward the east, causing the Yangtze and other rivers to flow generally eastward to the sea. However, there are several other mountain ranges that contribute to beautiful scenery in many parts of China. Another unique geographic feature of China is the Gobi Desert in the north.

The vastness of China and its mountains make it a land with diverse weather patterns—severe winters in the north and tropical conditions in the south. Rainfall tends to be heaviest in the summer in the south and diminishes as the storms move toward the northwest. In the winter and spring a dry wind sweeps down from Mongolia and Siberia, bringing an abundance of dry desert sand from the Gobi Desert, but almost no rain.

The combination of mountains, deserts, and high plateaus causes agriculture to be feasible on only a little more than 10 percent of the land. Added to this problem is the fact that the very large population needing to be fed is concentrated heavily along the east coast and is competing for space in areas well suited to agriculture. Yet another vexing problem is the climatic variations that tend to swing between floods and droughts. Extensive irrigation and the massive Yangtze dam project are directed toward attempting to control the problems created by erratic rainfall. China's challenge to produce enough food for its people remains ongoing.

Farm productivity varies with the climatic conditions, with a single crop being produced annually in the north and as many as three crops during the same period in the southern region. The principal cereal crop in the north is wheat, but rice is grown in abundance in the southern and eastern farming regions, where it comprises the mainstay of the diet. Other cereals grown include corn, millet, a sorghum variety called *kaoliang,* and barley.

Soybeans, a particularly important food crop grown in the northeastern regions, are used for oil and many different food products throughout China. Other sources of oil are sesame seeds and rapeseed. Peanuts, sugar (from cane and sugarbeets), tea, apples, pears, grapes, and such semitropical fruits as citrus, bananas, and pineapple are also produced commercially. Local farmers provide some vegetables too.

Pigs are the meat animal raised most commonly, and cattle are also raised for meat. Sheep are raised for meat and wool. Horses are popular in the region of Inner Mongolia, where tribesmen are noted for their riding skills. In the desert regions of China, camels are also raised for meat and other uses. Perhaps the most exotic animal involved in agriculture is the yak, which is used in Tibet to work fields as well as to provide food and clothing. Silkworms are important because their cocoons are the source of fiber to make the famous silks of China. Both saltwater and freshwater fish are yet another dimension of the protein supply.

History and Culture

The known history of Chinese civilization goes back more than 3,500 years, although evidence of earlier residents (Peking Man and others) dates back more than 600,000 years. More than 20 dynasties have ruled China since 1766 BCE. Qin Shihuang's dynasty, which began in 221 BCE, resulted in much progress in writing, education, business development, and transportation networks despite being marked by gross human rights abuses. The discovery of the terracotta warriors buried near Xian has directed attention to this ancient ruler. He also is credited with efforts to unite many protective walls in the north to construct the Great Wall that was vital to helping to block invasions from Mongolia.

The Han Dynasty followed Qin's death and lasted for over 400 years, during which development of foreign trade, notably the Silk Road, linked China and its exotic culture with Rome and other distant markets. Considerable turmoil followed the era of the Han rule. Eventually, the Tang Dynasty established control, and artistic and scholarly endeavors flourished. Several other dynasties reigned after the Tang period, including rulers from Mongolia. The Ming Dynasty was in power for almost 300 years, beginning in 1368. This rather warlike period involved wars against the Japanese and the Mongols. Far-reaching sea voyages as distant as eastern Africa were a hallmark of the Mings. Tourists are aware of this dynasty because of the Ming tombs outside of Beijing. Artistic achievements also remain from this era.

Beginning with the Portuguese arrival in 1516, Europe spread its influence in trade with China. The most unsavory part of that phase of Chinese history was the British involvement in developing the opium trade during the Qing Dynasty in an attempt to expand their commercial rewards, which led to the Opium War in 1840. Out of this conquest, the British negotiated a treaty that gave them control of Hong Kong until nearly the end of the 20th century. During the 19th century rule of the Qing Dynasty, China began to lose control of parts of its domain to other European powers and to Japan. France carved out the peninsula of French Indochina (Vietnam, Laos, and Cambodia), and Japan forced the Chinese to vacate Korea. Strong internal concerns about foreign influence in China culminated in the Boxer Rebellion in which foreigners and Chinese Christians were cornered in a fortified section of Peking in 1900 and fought off the Boxers for almost two months until a force of foreign troops liberated the besieged.

Revolutionary foment against the Qing Dynasty in the very early part of the 20th century resulted in the overthrow of the dynasty and establishment of the Republic of China with Sun Yatsen of the Kuomintang (Nationalist Party) serving as president until 1911. Quickly, Yuan Shikhai, the military head, forced Sun Yatsen's resignation and then named himself president for life when he was able to amend the constitution.

Following Yuan's death, diverse forces tangled until the People's Republic of China was established as a communist government in 1949. Chiang Kaishek played a significant role during this period, first leading military forces in an attempt to unify China, and subsequently pursuing an ongoing effort to eliminate the communists. In 1934 the communists, led by Mao Zedong and other future Chinese leaders, worked their way to the north of China in what is now called the Long March so that they could organize and mobilize peasant forces to drive out Chiang Kaishek and his Kuomintang associates. During World War II, Chiang directed his attacks on the communists and left the fighting of the Japanese primarily to the United States. By the end of World War II, the Chinese communists were so well armed and organized that they ultimately claimed mainland China, leaving Chiang Kaishek to flee with his associates—and also with the entire national gold supply—to Taiwan.

Chairman Mao Zedong stated the communist doctrines that became the "Little Red Book," which served as the basis for educating all Chinese. Mao's programs led to serious hardships for the citizens, especially when crops failed, and his leadership came into question. To regain solid control, in 1966 he began the Cultural Revolution, a very repressive program that ended with Mao's death 10 years later. Deng Xiaoping subsequently led the country into an era in which contact with foreign nations resumed. However, curbs on personal freedoms are still found in China. The tragic student demonstrations in Tiananmen Square in 1989 still linger in the minds of many (Figure 17.1).

The majority of Chinese are the Han, who originally were centered along the major rivers of central and eastern China. Among the minorities in China are the Zhuangs (in southwest China), the Huis (Muslims in northwest China),

Figure 17.1 The Forbidden City in Beijing lies just beyond Tianamen Square in Beijing.

Manchus and Koreans (northeast China), Mongolians, and Tibetans (in north and west respectively), as well as several other groups. This diversity contributes to the dimensions of culture throughout the outlying regions. The nomadic Mongolians live in *yurts* (sturdy round tents with domed roofs) and are noted for their skill in riding and raising horses. Prayer wheels are part of the daily lives of most Tibetans, and sturdy, thick-walled, small houses protect them from the fierce winters of their lofty plateau. The Han and other dwellers in the lower lands live in more confined spaces, often with extended families nearby, as the multitudinous population seeks housing.

Religion plays a minor role in the lives of many contemporary Chinese, although Tibetans and some Buddhists in other regions devote their lives to their faith, with monks once again being allowed to live in their monasteries with little interference from Beijing. Followers of Islam are concentrated in the northwestern part of China. Christianity was brought to China rather aggressively by Protestant and Catholic missionaries in the 19th century and still is the faith of a small fraction of the population despite the suppression of religion during the Cultural Revolution. Prior to the Cultural Revolution, the majority of people were followers of a mixture of Buddhism, with Taoism and Confucianism intermingled. Active practice of religion in people's daily lives is not encouraged by the government today, although it is tolerated.

Some mysticism surrounds various aspects of Chinese life. The traditional gods respected in China before the Communist era still are a part of life for many Chinese today, whether they are living in China or overseas. Familiar examples are the kitchen god, door gods, the god of wealth, god of happiness, and spirits of the bedroom, to name a few. Importance is placed on living in harmony with nature, a value that is exemplified by feng shui, the art of placing buildings, rooms within buildings, and exterior landscaping to optimize the balance of energies for good health and fortune. Traditional Chinese medicine also is related to the balance of yin, yang, and the five elements (water, fire, earth, metal, and wood) and is said to trace its origins to more than two millennia BCE. Extensive use of herbs, exotic sources of medicine, and reliance on needles of different metals in acupuncture are familiar aspects of medical treatment in China.

Art has long been a part of the Chinese culture. Even its form of writing places emphasis on calligraphy and beauty of brush or pen strokes. Paintings often incorporate careful brush strokes that define the distinctive style of Chinese painters. Even very intricate silk embroidery on silk reflects the importance of line to convey an artistic message (Figure 17.2). Porcelain has been such a hallmark of this country that dishes used throughout the world today are identified as "china," a clear recognition of the outstanding development of this art form in China by the time of Marco Polo. The art of cloisonné (enamel painted into a wire network and fired on metal vases or plates) is prominent among China's contributions to decorative arts. Intricate papercuts are another form of Chinese art.

Figure 17.2 Artistry combined with a needle and embroidery thread result in this young woman's highly skilled work

Opera is popular entertainment in China, with performances and productions quite different from western-style opera. The focus is a story, often with four performers; emphasis often is on vigorous dancing or action that may incorporate acrobatics. It is not unusual for music to be secondary in an opera, although some singing and musical instruments may be included. The musical instruments of Chinese origin that are particularly favored include the *erhu,* a two-stringed instrument made of wood and animal hide and played with a hair and bamboo bow. Children are taught to play this as well as the *pipa* (a lute), a zither called the *guzheng,* gongs *(daluo),* and western instruments such as the violin.

Physical fitness and achievement are important in China. The acrobats from China are seen not only in China but also in many other countries. Martial arts are practiced daily by many people in China. Tai chi is performed by many in public parks each morning and has become a form of exercise practiced by some in the United States.

In China, flowers play a leading role in the celebration of the Lunar New Year. Peach blossoms, narcissus, peonies, and pussy willow are sold in the flower market as symbols of good luck and prosperity for the New Year. Other plants that bring good luck are the miniature orange and the kumquat.

The Chinese New Year is a time of great celebration and occurs on the first day of the Chinese calendar, which is based on 12 lunar months. Each of the years in a 12-year cycle is named for an animal that came to Buddha's deathbed; the years are designated as the year of the rat, ox, tiger, rabbit, dragon, snake, horse, sheep, monkey, rooster, dog, and pig. Much importance is attached to the particular year in which a person is born. Celebration of the New Year can last for 2 weeks and end with the Festival of the Lanterns, but the festivities are concentrated in the first days, beginning with fireworks on New Year's Eve. Extensive housecleaning, new clothing, visits with family, and parades featuring the lion dance are all part of the holiday. Other traditional holidays celebrate various parts of the year, and political holidays honor important events, including the founding of the Communist Party of China, the birthday of the People's Liberation Army, and a national day honoring the government.

Food Patterns

Four rather distinctive styles of cooking, based largely on geography, characterize the cuisines found in China. The southern cuisine often is referred to as Cantonese food despite that the south's major city's name is now Guangzhou. Traditional stories regarding this popular style of cooking suggest that the chefs who fled from the kitchens of the Ming Dynasty in Peking when the dynasty came to an end traveled south and concentrated in Canton, where they incorporated local ingredients with their culinary skills and knowledge to bring Chinese food to new heights. Migrations of people from Canton resulted in the establishment of many restaurants around the world featuring some of the highlights of Cantonese culture.

The cuisine of eastern China relies heavily on foods from the sea. The large coastal city of Shanghai is identified with the eastern school of Chinese cooking. Light broths, egg rolls, and paper-wrapped foods are prominent in this cuisine.

The dish that seems to headline the northern or Peking cuisine is Peking duck, which retains that name today despite the city being renamed Beijing. Sweet and sour recipes, generous use of garlic, scallions, and wheat products, including noodles, are typical of northern cuisine. Mongolian fire pot is a contribution of this cuisine. Some emphasis is placed on elegant dishes appropriate to the status of Beijing as the political, artistic, and intellectual center of China.

Szechwan is the name usually given to the cuisine of western China. This designation conjures up images of burning sensations because of the abundant use of hot peppers. Many of the dishes are oily. Szechwan duck and hot and sour soup are favorites of this region.

Rice is a dominant part of most Chinese meals, even being used in the north of the country when it is affordable and available. A bowl of plain, boiled, long grain rice is served to each diner and is eaten as the *fan* (yin) part of the meal at the diner's pleasure. (The platters of food placed on the revolving center platform are the *ts'ai,* or yang, of the meal.) Rice may also be incorporated into various dishes. Sizzling rice soup is perhaps the most dramatic rice dish; *congee* (a thick rice porridge) is frequently served, particularly for breakfast.

The other cereal widely utilized is wheat, which finds its way southward from the northern fields in the form of wonton. The gluten in wheat enables wheat flour to be worked into dough, such as the wonton skins or wrappers that are used to encase many different types of fillings before being steamed, fried, or poached. Noodles are another wheat product used in China.

Dairy products are not a part of the Chinese diet, but extensive use of various soy products and some vegetables augmented by the practice of eating the soft bones of fish helps to meet calcium needs. The creative ways the Chinese have found for using soybeans include soy milk, soybean curd (tofu), black beans (preserved, fermented soybeans), fermented bean curd, sprouts, soy flour, and soy sauces (light, dark, and heavy). The excellent quantity and quality of soy protein adds important protein to the diet.

Pork is the meat most commonly used, but even this meat often is shredded or cut into small pieces as merely one ingredient in food mixtures. Religious dictates and also the cost of pork and other meats limit the amount of meat consumed. Many Chinese are vegetarians. The availability of soy foods is of particular importance for them, but tofu often is an ingredient in stir-fry dishes and other food mixtures. Poultry and eggs, lamb or mutton, and a little beef are other sources of protein. Among the less familiar sources of protein in Chinese diets are frog legs, camel, and shark fin.

Two important components of a typical meal are soup and a large fish cooked and presented whole to end the meal. Sometimes, more than one soup course is served. Typically, serving bowls of the meal items are placed on a lazy susan in the center of the table. Each person places some of the closest item onto his or her plate, and then the platform is rotated until all items have reached all of the people at the table. This procedure is used for the soup and fish dishes as well as for the other platters. Diners eat with chop sticks and a porcelain, flat-bottomed soup spoon. Since almost all of the food is cut into bite-sized or smaller pieces during preparation, chop sticks are effective tools for dining, once the technique has been mastered.

A key tool for preparing Chinese recipes is a sturdy cleaver. This device can be used to smash garlic cloves by pressing the broad, flat side of the blade down hard on the clove. Obviously, the sharp blade is well suited to the considerable amount of chopping that must be done to get the numerous ingredients ready for cooking. Even the flat end of the round handle can be used to grind peppercorns. A wok is a critical utensil because much stir-frying is done in this cuisine. A heavy frying pan is a bit less convenient to use, but it can serve as a substitute for a wok. A stack of bamboo steamer trays not only adds to the exotic feel of the kitchen, but is very effective in allowing steam to permeate the food in the various layers in the stack placed above boiling water. A rice cooker is a convenient contemporary utensil that simplifies preparation of Chinese food, which tends to be labor-intensive.

*K*ey Terms

Bird's nest soup—Cornstarch-thickened soup made with the mucilaginous lining of the nests of the Asiatic swiftlet, chicken broth, minced chicken, and egg white.

Bitter melon—Vegetable with a wrinkled green skin and an interior resembling a cucumber.

Black beans—Cooked and fermented soybeans preserved with ginger and salt.

Bok choy—Vegetable that grows as a bunch with thick, white stalks and a top of several large, coarse green leaves.

Boxer Rebellion—Violent uprising of a secret sect resulting in foreigners and missionaries being trapped in Peking for two months in 1900.

Cantonese (southern school)—Cuisine of the southern Chinese that features stir-frying, such dishes as egg rolls, dumplings (dim sum), and pork specialties, and generous use of vegetables, rice, and fruits.

Ch'a-shao-pao—Cantonese dish of steamed buns filled with roast pork.

Chi pao yu—Shanghai specialty; bits of seasoned raw fish wrapped in wax paper and fried in deep fat, then unwrapped and eaten.

Chinese parsley—Cilantro or coriander.

Chow mein—Parboiled noodles fried briefly with other ingredients; a Cantonese stir-fry with noodles.

Dim sum—Small, steamed dumplings filled with any of a variety of meat or vegetable fillings; favorites for snacks and lunches.

Eastern (Shanghai) school—Cuisine of the eastern seaboard of China, notably of Shanghai; light broths, seafood, egg rolls, and paper-wrapped foods are characteristic.

Five-spice powder—Popular Chinese spice made by mixing star anise, Szechwan pepper, cinnamon, cloves, and fennel.

Fan—Grain foods considered to be important as a balance with the ts'ai (other foods in the meal).

Fungi—Designation for mushrooms in some Chinese recipes; may include shitake, enoki, oyster, button, or other types of mushrooms, usually dried.

Ginger root—Gnarled root of ginger, which is usually peeled and grated; adds flavor as well as some heat to a recipe.

Hoisin sauce—Thick, brown, garlic-flavored bean sauce.

Kaoliang—Sorghum (grain) crop grown in northern China.

Kitchen god—Spirit of the hearth who determines wealth and longevity of people in the household; reports to Heaven annually regarding family's behavior.

Ku lao jou—Dish containing starch-coated fried cubes of pork, stir-fried green peppers, various vegetables, and pineapple cubes in a thickened sweet-sour tomato sauce.

Lotus root—Crunchy root of lotus (water lily) cut crosswise to use in stir-fries and soups, where its porous appearance due to many lengthwise cavities in the root adds visual interest.

Mongolian fire pot—Mongolian-designed unique chafing dish with a spot to burn charcoal, a chimney going up the center, and a surrounding round vessel where broth is kept hot enough for diners to cook their individual bites of meats and vegetables.

Northern (Peking) school—Cuisine of the northern region of China, which includes Peking duck and Mongolian fire pot as well as moo shu pork and other recipes that use wheat and wheat flour products.

Opium War—War in 1840 caused by British involvement in the opium trade in China; resulted in the long-term lease of Hong Kong to Britain.

Oyster sauce—Salty, dark Chinese sauce made with soy sauce and the flavor of oysters and other flavoring agents.

Peking duck—Traditional dish of northern China, which involves special roasting of a duck until the skin is very crisp; skin, a bit of duck meat, and green onion are wrapped in a thin pancake liberally splashed with hoisin sauce. Plum sauce is also served.

Plum sauce—Chutney made with plums, apricots, vinegar, chili, and sugar.

Seaweed—Various types of edible seaweeds and sea grass, as well as purple laver; usually used dried in soups.

Shark's fin—Usually transparent, yellowish, dried cartilage from the fin of a shark; this delicacy requires rehydration and is used in a soup.

Sizzling rice soup—Rice that has formed a crust on the bottom of a wok is deep-fat fried and then added to a hot broth, causing great sizzling sounds as it is stirred into the soup.

Snow peas—Flat, green peas in tender, crisp, edible pods.

Szechwan (western) school—Cuisine developed in western China, which is quite spicy and hot in character and uses considerable garlic, ginger, and oil.

Thousand-year eggs—Eggs (usually duck) preserved by packing them in a lime-clay mixture and storing for between 6 and 10 weeks, which transforms the white into a very dark, gelatinous material with a slightly fishy taste as the chemicals from the packing penetrate through the shells and throughout the egg.

Tofu (soybean curd)—Precipitate formed by adding calcium sulfate to a cooked soybean solution made from water and strained, ground soybeans; may be pressed to form firmer curd.

Ts'ai—Term designating the various other dishes that balance with the rice or fan (yin) in a meal; the yang part of the meal.

Water chestnut—Tuber that is sliced and used as a vegetable to add a crisp, distinctive texture; usually available canned.

Winter melon—Green, oblong melon similar in outward appearance to a watermelon, but with a white, pulpy interior and a seed-filled center.

Wok—Round-bottomed, two-handled metal pan used for stir-frying or as the container for boiling water for steaming food in bamboo steamer trays stacked on the wok.

Wonton—Small pouches of food wrapped in thin wheat dough (wonton wrappers) and cooked in a broth or deep-fat fried.

Yang—Positive principle including male sun, heaven, fire, brightness, good, wealth, and joy; complementary balance to yin.

Yin—Passive principle including female, moon, earth, water, darkness, evil, poverty, and sadness; complementary balance to yang.

Recipes

Bean Curd Szechwan (Serves 4–6)

1/3 lb uncooked shrimp, shelled and deveined
2 tsp cornstarch
4 tbsp oil
2 cartons bean curd, drained and cut into 1" cubes
1 tbsp sherry
1 tbsp soy sauce
1/2 c chicken broth
2 cloves garlic, minced
3 green onions, thinly sliced
2 tbsp cornstarch dispersed in 2 tbsp water

3/4 tsp chili powder

1. Cut shrimp into eighths and dredge thoroughly in cornstarch, then stir-fry in 2 tablespoons of oil until pink.
2. Heat 2 tablespoons of oil in wok, then stir-fry bean curd gently to avoid breaking curd.
3. Return shrimp to wok, add all other ingredients, and stir while heating to thicken the sauce.

Beef with Oyster Sauce (Serves 4–6)

2 dried mushrooms
1 lb flank steak
1 tbsp cornstarch
1 egg white
2 tbsp oil
2 tsp minced ginger root
1 clove garlic, minced
2 tbsp oyster sauce
1 tbsp soy sauce
2 tsp sherry
1/2 tsp sugar
6 water chestnuts, sliced
2 green onions, chopped

2 tbsp beef broth
1 tsp cornstarch in 2 tsp water

1. Pour boiling water over mushrooms; soak, then slice.
2. Cut beef in three lengthwise strips; cut strips crosswise in 1/8" slices.
3. Dredge beef pieces in cornstarch, then coat with egg white.
4. Heat oil in wok with ginger and garlic; stir-fry beef.
5. Add remaining ingredients and stir while heating until the sauce is thickened.

Char Siu Bao (Makes 12)

Bun Dough

1 pkg quick-acting dry yeast
1/4 c lukewarm water
1 tbsp sugar
3 c all purpose flour
1 c lukewarm milk

1. Dissolve yeast in 1/4 cup of lukewarm water; add sugar and let stand until it bubbles.
2. Place flour in mixing bowl; gradually stir in yeast mixture and then milk. Stir until well mixed, adding flour if dough is sticky.
3. Turn dough onto floured board and knead vigorously for 5 minutes, working in more flour if dough sticks.
4. Put dough in bowl, covered, and let stand until doubled (1 to 1 1/2 hours).
5. Divide dough into 12 pieces and flatten each to 1/4" thickness.

Filling

1/4 lb cooked pork, finely chopped
1 tbsp chopped green onions
1/2 clove garlic, minced
1 1/2 tbsp oyster sauce
1 1/2 tbsp sugar
1 tbsp soy sauce
1 1/2 tsp cornstarch
1/4 c water

1. In a saucepan, combine all ingredients and heat until thickened, stirring constantly. Cool slightly.
2. Fill each flattened dough with about 1 tablespoon filling; pleat sides and twist top of each bun.
3. Place each on a 3" x 3" square of wax paper and let rise until doubled.
4. Steam over rapidly boiling water for 10 minutes. Remove wax paper after steaming.

Chicken Walnut (Serves 4–6)

1 lb boneless, skinless chicken, cut into 1/2" cubes
1 tbsp cornstarch
1 egg white
1/3 c broken walnuts
1 green pepper, cut into 1/2" squares
1 sweet red pepper, cut into 1/2" squares
1 tbsp brown bean sauce
1 tsp sugar
1 tbsp chicken stock

1. Dredge chicken in cornstarch and dip in egg white; stir-fry in oil. Remove from wok.
2. Stir-fry walnuts and set aside.
3. Stir-fry peppers for 1 minute. Remove from wok.
4. Heat bean sauce, sugar, and stock for 1 minute while stirring.
5. Add chicken and peppers to wok and heat while stirring until hot.
6. Garnish with walnuts.

Chinese Peas with Water Chestnuts (Serves 4)

1 tsp minced ginger root
2 tbsp oil
1/2 lb Chinese snow peas (tips cut off)
1 can drained, sliced water chestnuts
1/4 tsp salt
1 tbsp cornstarch
1/4 c water

1. Saute ginger in oil in wok.
2. Add snow peas and stir-fry until bright green.
3. Add water chestnuts and salt.
4. Mix cornstarch with water and stir into vegetables.
5. Stir while heating until sauce thickens.

Chow Yung Cabbage (Serves 4)

1 bunch celery cabbage (Chinese cabbage)
2 tbsp oil
1 tsp grated ginger root
1 clove garlic, minced
1/4 tsp salt
1/4 c chicken broth
1 tsp sugar
1 tsp chili powder

1. Remove outer cabbage leaves; slice into diagonal slices 1/3″ thick. Set aside.
2. Heat oil, ginger, and garlic until wok is very hot.
3. Add cabbage and salt, and stir-fry for just under a minute.
4. Add broth and heat with a cover for 1 1/2 minutes.
5. Uncover; add sugar and chili powder. Heat while stirring just to mix.

Egg Drop Soup (Serves 4–6)

3 c chicken stock
1 tbsp cornstarch
2 tbsp water
1 tsp salt
1 egg, slightly beaten
1 green onion and top, chopped

1. Heat stock to boiling.
2. Stir in slurry of cornstarch in water; add salt and continue heating while stirring until slightly thickened and clear.
3. Stir very slowly while slowly adding egg. Turn off heat.
4. Garnish with chopped green onion, and serve.

Hot and Sour Soup (Serves 4–6)

5 dried Chinese mushrooms
1/2 lb fresh bean curd (tofu)
1/3 c canned bamboo shoots
3 c chicken stock
1/4 lb lean pork, slivered
1/2 tsp salt
1/4 tsp pepper
1 tbsp rice vinegar
1 tbsp soy sauce
4 tsp cornstarch
2 tbsp cold water
1 egg, slightly beaten
1 1/2 tsp sesame oil
2 green onions and tops, sliced

1. Soak mushrooms for 30 minutes in warm water. Drain. Cut in thin strips.
2. Shred drained bean curd and bamboo shoots. Set aside.
3. In a large saucepan, heat stock, mushrooms, pork, salt, pepper, bamboo shoots, vinegar, and soy sauce to a boil. Reduce heat, cover, and simmer for 4 minutes.
4. Add bean curd and cornstarch mixed with water and stir while heating until thickened.
5. Stir simmering soup while slowly adding egg and sesame oil.
6. Garnish with green onion, and serve.

Mongolian Lamb Fire Pot (Serves 6–8)

2 oz cellophane noodles
1/3 lb Chinese (celery) cabbage
1/4 lb fresh spinach
1/4 c soy sauce
1 tbsp sesame seed oil
1 tbsp sherry
1 1/2 tsp brown sugar in 1 1/2 tsp hot water
1 tbsp smooth peanut butter in 2 tbsp boiling water
1/8 tsp cayenne pepper
1/2 tbsp fermented red bean curd
5 c chicken stock
1 scallion, minced
1 garlic clove, minced
1 1/2 tsp grated ginger root
2 tbsp Chinese parsley (cilantro)
1 1/2 lb lean lamb in paper-thin slices 2″ x 3″ each

1. Soak noodles in 1 cup warm water for 30 minutes, then cut into noodles 6″ long.
2. Blanch 3″ pieces of cabbage for 3 minutes; drain and pat dry, then arrange beside noodles on a platter.
3. Wash spinach thoroughly and remove stems; pat dry and add to platter.
4. Combine soy sauce, oil, wine, brown sugar mix, diluted peanut butter, pepper, and red bean curd in a bowl; place about a tablespoon of the mixture into each person's soup bowl. Put remainder in serving bowl.
5. Heat the stock to boiling; transfer to the hot fire pot at the dining table. Arrange an individual plate of lamb and a soup bowl at each plate.
6. Add scallions, garlic, ginger, and parsley to the stock; diners then drop in lamb pieces, which they remove when desired.
7. Ladle stock into soup bowls.
8. Heat vegetables and noodles for 1 to 2 minutes, then ladle with the last of the broth into the bowls.

Moo Goo Ga Pen (Serves 4–6)

4 dried Chinese black mushrooms
1 tbsp oil
1/4 lb mushrooms, sliced
6-oz can water chestnuts, drained and sliced
1/4 c water
1 c celery, sliced in 1″ diagonal pieces
1/4 lb Chinese pea pods, ends trimmed
1 tsp salt
1 tsp sugar
1 lb boneless, skinless chicken breast in strips 2″ long
1/2 tsp grated ginger root
1 tsp soy sauce

1 tsp cornstarch in 2 tsp warm water

1. Soak Chinese mushrooms in water overnight; slice thinly.
2. Heat oil in wok; stir-fry both kinds of mushrooms and the water chestnuts.
3. Add water and steam, covered, for 2 minutes.
4. Add celery, pea pods, salt, and sugar; steam 2 minutes, then remove all food from wok.
5. Stir-fry chicken for 4 to 5 minutes.
6. Add vegetables, ginger, soy sauce, and cornstarch slurry; stir while heating until sauce thickens.

Peking Shrimp (Serves 4–6)

3/4 lb raw shrimp, shelled, deveined, and cut in half
1 tbsp cornstarch
2 tbsp oil
2 green onions, thinly sliced
1 c celery, thinly sliced
2 tsp grated ginger root
5 tbsp catsup
1 tsp chili powder
1 tbsp sugar

1/4 c chicken broth
1 tbsp sherry

1. Dredge shrimp in cornstarch and stir-fry until they are pink. Remove from wok.
2. Saute onion and celery for 1 minute.
3. Add shrimp and rest of ingredients to wok and heat while stirring until mixture is bubbling hot.

Shrimp Dim Sum (Makes 16)

Dough

1/4 c boiling water
1 1/4 c all purpose flour
1 1/2 tsp oil
4 1/2 tsp cold water

1. Stir boiling water into flour; add oil and cold water, and mix to form a ball.
2. Knead dough vigorously to create a smooth surface; cut into 16 and flatten each into a circle.

Filling

1 tsp cornstarch
1/4 tsp sesame oil
2 tsp soy sauce
1/2 tsp sherry
1/4 lb shrimp, shelled, cleaned, and finely chopped
2 1/2 tbsp bamboo shoots, finely chopped
1 tsp brown sugar
Optional garnishes: sliced red chili, soy sauce, green onion pompoms, shrimp crackers

1. Stir together cornstarch, oil, soy sauce, and sherry.
2. Stir in shrimp, bamboo shoots, and sugar.
3. Place spoonful of filling on a circle; lift edges of dough and pinch to form a pouch.
4. Arrange pouches on damp towel in steamer and steam for 10 minutes.
5. Serve with garnishes or shrimp crackers, or both, if desired.

Sweet and Sour Pork (Serves 4–6)

1 lb lean pork in 1" cubes
1/4 c cornstarch
1 egg, slightly beaten
Oil for deep-fat frying
1 garlic clove, minced
1 green pepper (1/2" squares)
1 carrot, thinly sliced
1 stalk celery, thinly sliced
1 c canned pineapple cubes, drained
1/2 c chicken stock
2 tbsp brown sugar
2 tbsp white sugar
1/4 c red wine vinegar
1 tsp soy sauce

1 tbsp tomato paste
1 tbsp cornstarch in 2 tbsp cold water

1. Dredge pork in cornstarch, then dip in egg and roll again in cornstarch.
2. Deep-fry pork in wok at 375°F, stirring to separate and brown all sides; remove to dish lined with paper towel and keep warm in 275°F oven.
3. Pour oil from wok, then stir-fry garlic, green pepper, carrot, celery, and pineapple for 4 minutes or until tender.
4. Stir in remaining ingredients and heat, stirring until thickened.
5. Stir in pork. Serve.

Chengdu Chicken (Serves 4–6)

3/4 lb boneless, skinless chicken cut into small cubes
2 tbsp cornstarch
1 egg white, slightly beaten
2 tbsp oil
1 green pepper in small cubes
2 red chilies, seeded and diced
2 green onions, chopped
1/2 tsp grated ginger root
1 tbsp hoisin sauce
1 tsp chili bean paste
1 tbsp rice wine
1/2 c salted, roasted cashews

1. Dredge chicken in cornstarch; dip in egg and roll again in cornstarch.
2. Stir-fry chicken in oil, turning constantly to brown on all sides (1 1/2 minutes). Remove to dish lined with paper towel and keep warm in 275°F oven.
3. Remove oil from wok and stir-fry green pepper, chilies, onions, and ginger for 1 minute.
4. Add chicken and remaining ingredients, except for cashews. Heat while stirring until hot.
5. Stir in cashews, heat very briefly, and serve.

Wonton Soup (Serves 4–6)

Filling

1/4 lb finely chopped, shelled shrimp
1/4 lb ground pork
1 tsp grated ginger root
1 tsp sherry
8 water chestnuts, finely chopped
1 mushroom, finely chopped
1 tbsp chopped parsley
1 tbsp soy sauce
2 green onions, finely chopped
1 egg
1/2 pkg wonton skins

1. Gently combine ingredients completely.
2. Place 1/2 teaspoon filling at center of a wonton skin and fold in half to make triangle; overlap lower two corners and seal together with drop of water (see note).
3. Add wontons to boiling water; when water returns to boil, lower heat and simmer for 5 minutes. Use colander to drain thoroughly.

Soup

4 c chicken broth
1 tbsp sherry
1 tbsp soy sauce
1/2 tsp sesame oil
1 bunch bok choy (1" pieces)

1. Heat broth, sherry, soy sauce, and sesame oil to a boil, then add wontons and heat to a simmer.
2. Add bok choy and heat briefly before serving.

Note: Wontons can be deep-fat fried at 375°F to golden brown and served with soy or sweet and sour sauce as an appetizer.

Summary

China is a very densely populated nation in Asia, which reaches across approximately one sixth of the world from east to west. Geographically, it includes the Himalayas and other mountain ranges, the Gobi and other deserts, high plateaus, river valleys, and a long seacoast that reaches into tropical regions. The combination of many people to feed, much land unsuited to farming, and widely varying rainfall from year to year sometimes has led to serious food shortages even though the land can produce a wide variety of crops in good years.

The history of China goes back more than 600,000 years, with records being available of events during the more than 20 dynasties that have ruled since 1766 BCE. Some of the more prominent dynasties have been the Qin Shihuang, Han, Tang, and Ming. European trade encounters by ship began with the Portuguese, who were followed by the French and British. The Opium War in 1840 and the Boxer Rebellion against foreigners in 1900 were the result of friction between these foreign influences and the native Chinese.

The formation of the Republic of China with Sun Yatsen as president occurred in 1911, marking overthrow of the dynastic form of rule. Considerable internal problems developed subsequently, culminating in the Long March of the Communists to northern China, followed by their ultimately forcing Chiang Kaishek's Kuomintang, or Nationalist Party, from the mainland to Taiwan and the establishment of separate rule there. Communist rule has been under the leadership of various people during the 20th century, including Mao Zedong and Den Xiaoping. The Cultural Revolution began in 1966 and lasted for 10 disastrous years, from which the people and economy are still struggling to recover.

The people in China are primarily Hans, but there are many other minority groups, such as the Tibetans and the Mongols. Many Tibetans are Buddhists, and so are some others throughout China. Muslims tend to be concentrated in the northwestern region. Christians (the result of a strong missionary movement from abroad earlier) are scattered in other regions, but definitely are the minority religion. Taoism, Confucian thought, and Buddhism are generally intermingled in eastern regions of China, but religions are still not prominent because of the actions during the Cultural Revolution designed to eliminate most religious worship. Nevertheless, there are many mystical traditions that add richness to the culture and even to the medicine of China.

Art takes various forms, including calligraphy, painting, embroidery, cloisonné, papercuts, and fine porcelains. Opera is an important tradition, which relies heavily on acting and dancing, with a bit of music. Music is valued and has developed along a form quite different from western music and is well suited to the instruments that are featured, including the *erhu* and the *guzheng*. Physical fitness efforts include tai chi and martial arts.

Food patterns in China include Cantonese (elegant dishes from southern China), Shanghai (eastern seafood and paper-wrapped foods), Peking (northern, featuring use of wheat noodles and Peking duck), and Szechwan (western dishes emphasizing hot spices and use of oil). Rice is the backbone of the Chinese diet. Pork is the most common meat, but beef, poultry, lamb, and some other meats are used, almost all being used sparingly in small pieces combined with various other ingredients. Soybeans in a wide array of forms are used extensively in Chinese cooking. Chopping the many ingredients consumes most of the time required to prepare Chinese foods. Stir-frying and frying are common methods of cooking and require little time once the food is ready to be cooked. A wok, cleaver, and steamer are essential kitchen items.

Study Questions

1. For each of three dynasties in China's history, (a) name the dynasty, (b) indicate the years each ruled, and (c) discuss the important contributions and achievements.
2. Why is wheat a more common cereal in the diet of people in northern China than in the southern region? Identify some dishes that include (a) wheat, and (b) rice.
3. Name at least four food products made from soy, and identify recipes in which each can be used.
4. What meats are often found in Chinese menus? Discuss ways in which they are included. What factors limit use of the various meats?
5. What religions are of some importance in China today? What factors have contributed to their role in Chinese lives?
6. Select at least two examples of cultural contributions China has given to the world, and describe representative works.

Bibliography

Barer-Stein, T. 1999. *You Eat What You Are.* 2nd ed. Firefly Books, Ltd. Ontario, Canada.

Buckley, M. 1994. *China.* 4th ed. Lonely Planet. Oakland, CA.

Ferroa, P. 1991. *China.* Marshall Cavendish. New York.

Fessler, L. 1963. *China.* Time, Inc. New York.

Fitzgerald, C. P. 1969. *The Horizon History of China.* American Heritage Publishing. New York.

Hahn, E. 1968. *Cooking of China.* Time-Life Books. New York.

Kramer, M. 1988. *Illustrated Guide to Foreign and Fancy Food.* 2nd ed. Plycon Press. Redondo Beach, CA.

Pearcy, G. E. 1980. *The World Food Scene.* Plycon Press. Redondo Beach, CA.

Petrov, V. P. 1976. *China: Emerging World Power.* 2nd ed. Van Nostrand. New York.

Tan, A. 1991. *The Kitchen God's Wife.* Ballantine Books. New York.

Tom, K. S. 1989. *Echoes from Old China.* Hawaii Chinese History Center. Honolulu.

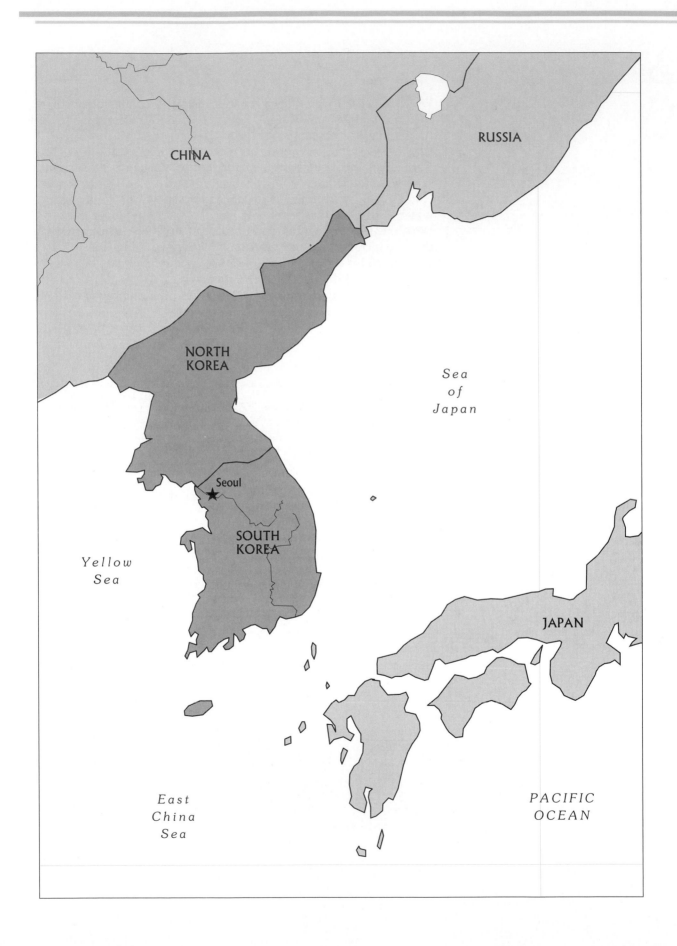

18 Korea

Geographic Overview

The Korean peninsula, which has been divided into the countries of North Korea and Republic of Korea south of the 38th parallel since 1953, consists of mountains on the east (Figure 18.1) dropping to coastal plains on the west. This peninsula, attached to the eastern edge of Asia, borders China on the north, with the Yellow Sea separating Korea's western shore from mainland China and the East Sea separating Korea from Japan's islands on the east. The whole peninsula is about 600 miles long and less than 150 miles wide.

The rugged terrain of much of Korea presents great challenges in food production to meet national needs. Much progress has been made agriculturally in South Korea since the Korean War ended in 1953. Although only a little more than 20 percent of the land is suitable for farming, the nation has constructed irrigation projects, mechanized much of the production, focused efforts on improving crop strains for better yields, and even built innumerable greenhouses to permit growth of crops that otherwise would not survive the harshness of the climate. With far fewer people actually farming, food production has nevertheless been significantly increased as a result of the many technological efforts that have been directed toward agriculture.

As is true in other Asian nations, rice is the major grain crop in Korea. Barley and corn (Figure 18.2) are other important grain crops. Soybeans play an essential role in the diet and are raised in great quantities. The climate of Korea is favorable for growing apples, peaches, persimmons, and grapes. Tangerines thrive in the very southern part of the country. Greenhouses are used extensively to raise vegetables.

Figure 18.1   The jagged mountains near the east coast of the northern part of South Korea are softened in the spring by countless blossoms on the cherry trees.

As the Korean economy improved following the Korean War, livestock production began to increase. Cattle (both for meat and dairy), pigs, goats, and rabbits are raised in numbers adequate to meet demand. Chickens are raised in huge numbers too. In a slightly different vein, silkworms are produced for their fine strands needed in making silk cloth; they also are considered a delicacy to eat (Figure 18.3).

History and Culture

Old Chosŏn is considered to be the earliest kingdom in Korea, holding the power for about 1,200 years beginning in the 24th century BCE. This was followed by splits that resulted in three tribal states in southern Korea and four in the north, which were considered a part of Han China.

The period of the Three Kingdoms was very significant in Korean history, lasting from 57 BCE to 668 CE. The Shilla Kingdom in the southeast was established in 57 BCE, the Koguryŏ Kingdom in the north in 37 BCE, and the Paekche Kingdom in the southwest in 18 BCE. Chinese influence was discarded; Buddhism was the religion of many. Shilla conquered Paekche and Koguryŏ in the 7th century, forming the Unified Shilla Kingdom with Kyŏngju as its capital. The golden age of Shilla rule lasted 250 years and resulted in many advancements in Korean culture and arts (Figure 18.4).

Figure 18.2   Corn is a staple crop in the Korean diet.

Figure 18.3 Silk worms (pan perched on the box) are just one of the delicacies offered for sale to visitors to a mountain shrine.

The Koryŏ Dynasty that ruled from 918 to 1392 established Buddhism (Figure 18.5) as the state religion. Korea derived its name from Koryŏ. The final dynasty in Korean history was the Chosŏn Dynasty, which ruled from 1392 until 1910 from Hanyang (now called Seoul). During this period, the Korean alphabet, called *han-gŭl,* was developed to greatly simplify reading based on phonics rather than on the thousands of Chinese characters. Confucian thought replaced Buddhism among the Chosŏn rulers. King Sejong the Great, who ruled from 1418 to 1450, sponsored many intellectual developments in music, science, medicine, and language. Tangible achievements under Sejong's rule included not only the development of han-gŭl, but also written notation of music, astronomical maps, a text on Chinese medicine, and developments in movable metal type.

Korea's location between China and Japan has caused it to be the target of numerous foreign military efforts over the centuries. Near the end of the 16th century, Japan's General Hideyoshi invaded, but Korea's General Yi foiled the Japanese by using turtle-shaped iron-clad ships to defeat the Japanese navy support. Eventually, the Japanese persevered and forced many Korean artisans and scholars to go to Japan, where they influenced developments, particularly in the arts.

Figure 18.4 The Bulguska (temple) built in the 8th Century by Shilla rulers is restored now and listed as an international cultural property of UNESCO.

Figure 18.5 The giant Buddha dominates a mountain park in northeastern South Korea.

Manchu invaders from the north also invaded Korea—twice in the 17th century. Subsequently, Korean rulers focused on an internal view of their peninsula, only to be interrupted toward the end of the 19th century by western nations demanding trade opportunities. Japan also began to attempt to develop trade and ultimately took over the Korean peninsula in 1910, after several years of violence, as part of its move to conquer China. Considerable resistance to Japanese control developed over the decades, but liberation of Korea did not occur until the end of World War II. Unfortunately, the decisions made after that war by the major winning powers (United States, Britain, Russia, and China) ultimately led to the Korean War in 1950 being fought over the division of the two Koreas along the 38th parallel. More than 50 years after the start of that war, the two parts of Korea are still divided; the south is a highly developed nation, and the north is quite isolated and continually short on food and other needs for its people. Because of this isolation, the remainder of this chapter describes the Republic of Korea, often called simply Korea or South Korea.

Korea has changed dramatically, emerging as a high-tech nation in a period of about 50 years, but many aspects of its heritage are cherished today. People usually have three names, with the surname usually being first (although the order is westernized by increasing numbers now). Among the surnames frequently seen in America are Lee, Kim, and Pak (often changed to Park), Cho, and Han. Family is of great importance. Familial ties encompass relationships with extended parts of the clan and special appreciation for the elderly and the experiences they contribute to the family. The family fosters expectations of great personal effort by each person to develop physically and intellectually and to make the best contribution to the group and its nation.

Sports and games are important to Koreans throughout life. The parks and various playing fields for soccer, baseball, volleyball, and basketball attest to this interest, which was illustrated by Seoul's hosting of the 1988 Summer Olympiad. Intellectually challenging board games are played by people of all ages, as can be seen in city parks when the weather is favorable. Kite flying is another favorite activity.

Although Koreans have quite eclectic tastes in music today, there is great appreciation for traditional music, which is characterized by three beats in a measure—clearly different from the two beats used in both Japanese and Chinese compositions. The *changgo*, a drum with the shape of an hourglass, plays a key role in providing powerful and intricate rhythms for the dances that are part of the cultural heritage from the courts of earlier days and from the countryside. Flutes, zithers, and double-reed instruments (e.g., the oboe) add the melodies. Korea has also contributed world-class performers in classical western music.

Although the art of making pottery in Korea can be traced back to China, advancements were made by the Koryŏ Dynasty, which produced wonderful pieces of celadon (softly tinted bluish-green), and by artisans during the Chosŏn period after 1392, who developed fine white porcelain. Paintings of the same period reflected the importance of Buddhism and Confucianism in people's lives. The fact that the Japanese conquerors took many artists and artisans back to Japan to add their influence to Japanese art is clear testimony to the achievements of Korean artists by the 16th century. Evidence of their work and of later artists can be found throughout Korea in temples, monasteries, public buildings, and museums.

Religion can be practiced freely throughout Korea, a freedom that provides several choices. Buddhism and Confucianism have had very long histories in this country and are clearly in favor today. Added to these now is Christianity, which was brought by missionaries about 200 years ago, the Catholics first and the Protestants in 1885. Buddhism has the largest number of followers, with Protestantism ranking an unchallenging second place and Catholicism far behind. Islam has become a small part of the scene since the Korean War. Small indigenous religions also exist.

The role of women has expanded in recent years, whereas for centuries earlier, women were accorded a bit of freedom if they were physicians, *haenyo* (divers), *kisaeng* (entertainers), or shamans. Now, many women work in a wide range of jobs and are well educated. Nevertheless, there still are a few women who dive for seafood off the shores of Cheju, the island off the southern tip of Korea. Most women in Korea wear western dress, although for special occasions they wear a *hanbok*, a two-piece dress consisting of a short jacket called a *chogori*, which is tied off-center with a bow, and a long, gathered skirt called a *chima*. Rarely, men may wear the traditional costume of bloomer trousers and a special coat (*turumagi*) over a vest.

Many Koreans celebrate the new year twice—at the beginning of the calendar year in January and again at the first part of the first lunar month of the lunar year, which varies and may fall in February. The Lunar New Year is a special time to honor a family's deceased ancestors. The Moon Festival in the middle of the first lunar month is important to farmers as a means of predicting the weather for the coming growing season. As is true in other Asian countries, Buddha's birthday is a cause for celebration on the eighth day of the fourth lunar month during the spring for all Buddhists. A lantern parade is a highlight of this day. Children's Day is celebrated on May 5 in honor of all children—not just boys, who sometimes are viewed with special favor, especially during their first year of life. Special festivities are held publicly, and children are often dressed in special costumes for the parades and demonstrations of various martial arts. July 15 and August 18 are national holidays marking the constitution and liberation in 1948. October 3 marks Tangun Day, the legendary founding of Old Chosŏn in 2333 BCE.

For generations, hardy women living on Cheju island, just south of the Korean peninsula, have spent several hours daily diving in the cold waters along the shore to harvest various fish and other types of seafood. Their careers as divers extend well into their later years. Wet suits now make this a slightly more comfortable job than in years past, but these remarkably strong women still have one of the most challenging jobs on Cheju.

Food Patterns

The first word that leaps to mind when thinking about the foods of Korea is *kimchi*. This very traditional mainstay traces back centuries, during which time the pickling of vegetable crops and storing in large crocks for use over the long winter and early growing season resulted in a variety of kimchi types. This means of preservation enabled Koreans to have vegetable in their diets despite the time of year. The huge crocks in which a family's kimchi supply was stored might be buried in the ground or stored outside in a cool spot that made it easy to remove kimchi as needed for meals. Production of the annual kimchi supply provided an opportunity for plenty of sociability while chopping the vast quantities of cabbage and other vegetables that were to be pickled. As much as 10 gallons of kimchi per person needed to be made prior to modern times, when canned and even some fresh produce became available to augment kimchi. Cabbage (Chinese or round), cucumbers, and *daikon* (long, white variety of radish) are the most frequent components of kimchi and are augmented with generous quantities of salt, onions, hot red pepper, ginseng, garlic, scallions, ginger, and other seasonings, such as salted or dried shrimp. The preserving action in kimchi is the result of the large amount of salt and the fermentation period, which develops acidity. Kimchi is served at all Korean meals, sometimes as one of the main dishes and sometimes as an accompaniment.

Rice is another cornerstone of Korean meals. Its form may vary, but most commonly, boiled, short grain rice is served in individual bowls. Rice flour made from sweet glutinous rice is used in making rice balls and rice cakes that sometimes are served as desserts. Rice porridge is a popular food, particularly at breakfast; sometimes it is mixed with red beans, bean sprouts, or other vegetables. Stir-fried dishes featuring rice are also popular. A traditional dish for New Year's is *tuk-kuk* (rice cake soup).

Soups are served frequently at any or all of the usual three meals a day. The variety of soups can be quite wide, ranging from being primarily broth with only a few seasonings (often hot pepper and garlic or onion) to others that include slivers of meats or fish as well as vegetables. Individual bowls are used for serving soups, and these soups may be sipped from the bowl, with a porcelain spoon being used when required for the vegetables or other ingredients.

Korea's geography readily explains the enthusiastic inclusion of fish in the diet, for the seas surrounding the peninsula provide generous bounty for the table. Crabs, shrimp, clams, oysters, bream, cod, and herring are just some of the seafood available in the shoreside markets in Pusan and other coastal cities. Beef, pork, chicken, and eggs are other sources of protein in Korean diets. Sometimes, recipes that are primarily meat dishes are prepared, typically as a barbecued meat *(bulgogi)*. More commonly, meats are slivered or shredded to flavor and augment vegetables and soups that extend the meat to serve more people. Dairy products are not generally part of the Korean diet.

Roasted chestnuts are a favorite snack on cold days (Figure 18.6), and these may also be used in preparing mixed dishes. Two other nuts—pine nuts and walnuts—are also incorporated in various dishes to add flavor, texture, and protein. Pine nuts are thought to help assure a long life.

Many Korean dishes are generously flavored with garlic, hot seasonings (ginger and red pepper, for example), and sesame seeds or oil. Soy sauce is another dominant flavoring. Sauces containing soy sauce mixed with such ingredients as scallions, vinegar, garlic, red pepper powder, sesame oil, and sugar are

Figure 18.6 Roasted chestnuts are a tempting snack on a cold morning in Seoul.

Figure 18.7 Meals in Korea traditionally are eaten sitting on the floor at a low table, with the shoes removed.

served as accompaniments to a meal. *Kochujang* is a red pepper and bean paste that often is found either as a condiment or as an ingredient in a meat or vegetable mixture.

Seaweed of various types can be found dried or fresh at markets along the seaside. *Laver* (edible lettuce-like seaweed) sometimes is brushed with sesame seed oil and toasted until crisp. Soy sauce may be used as a dip for seaweed. Some Korean soups feature seaweed as an ingredient.

Koreans eat three meals daily, often including a hearty breakfast and a light lunch. Snacking is a very common part of eating patterns. However, overweight is not a problem for most Koreans.

Korean meals traditionally are served on long, low tables, and diners sit shoeless on the floor (Figure 18.7). Each person is given chopsticks, a bowl of rice, and a bowl of soup. The other foods are placed in the middle of the table, and people serve themselves using chopsticks. Numerous dishes, including sauces and other condiments, typically are all served at the beginning of the meal and replenished as needed during the meal. Eating generally assumes priority over conversation while people are dining.

One particularly favorite meal features leaf lettuce brushed with a touch of sesame seed oil piled high on a platter (Figure 18.8). Holding a lettuce leaf, diners add various tidbits from the many dishes on the table and roll the lettuce leaf into a tight bundle to be eaten with enthusiasm (and perhaps some kochujang). This traditional meal is called *sang-chi-sam*. Another specialty is *samgye t'ang*. This is a chicken about the size of a Cornish hen, which is stuffed with rice, ginseng, and chestnuts, placed in a large individual bowl, topped with broth, and then baked until the meat is ready to fall from the bones. Such an individual feast is not likely to happen often, but it is a favorite. Korean hot pot *(shinsollo)* is similar to the Mongolian fire pot of China.

Figure 18.8 Lettuce leaves brushed with sesame seed oil are used to wrap several different vegetables and other fillings.

Noodles play a rather prominent role in the Korean diet. They may be made fresh in the home using wheat flour and egg to make a dough that subsequently is cut into noodles that are boiled in soups or used in other dishes. Wonton skins made with wheat flour are used to make dumplings. Buckwheat is also used to make noodles. Barley and corn (steamed ears) are other cereals in the Korean diet.

Teas of various types are popular beverages in Korea. Green tea is brewed from dried, unfermented tea leaves harvested from tea bushes in Korea or nearby countries. Ginseng may be brewed for its health benefits. Other herb teas featuring such flavors as ginger and cinnamon also are favored beverages that may be thought to have medicinal qualities. Fruit teas flavored with dried tangerine peel, pomegranate, citron, and other fruits are also popular.

Key Terms

Bulgogi—Grilled, marinated beef or other meat.

Chima—Long, gathered skirt that is part of traditional dress for Korean women.

Chogori—Short jacket tied off-center and worn with a chima to complete the traditional dress for Korean women.

Han-gŭl—Phonetic Korean alphabet developed under the leadership of King Sejong in the 15th century.

Kimchi—Fermented, pickled vegetables (particularly cabbage).

Kochujang—Red pepper and bean paste used as a condiment and also as an ingredient in Korean recipes.

Koryŏ—Dynasty that ruled Korea from 918 to 1392 and subsequently was the source for the name Korea.

Laver—Edible seaweed; popular in Korea.

Samgye t'ang—Whole small chicken stuffed with rice, ginseng, and chestnuts, covered in broth, and baked until meat almost falls from bones.

Sang-chi-sam—Lettuce-wrapped meal containing many tidbits from numerous dishes selected by the diner.

Sejong the Great—Dynamic 15th-century Korean leader who sponsored development of han-gŭl, written music, movable type, astronomy, and a medical book.

Shinsollo—Korean hot pot.

Takpaesuk—Whole small chicken stuffed with rice, covered in broth, and baked until meat almost falls from bones.

Tuk-kuk—Rice cake soup.

Recipes

Bulgogi (Korean Barbecued Beef) (Serves 2–4)

1 lb beef, sliced bacon-thin
1/4 c soy sauce
2 tbsp sugar
4 tbsp minced green onion
1 tbsp minced garlic
2 tbsp toasted sesame seeds
1 tbsp sesame oil

1/4 tsp red pepper

1. Marinate beef in marinade (made by mixing all other ingredients together) for at least 4 hours in refrigerator.
2. Grill over charcoal or broil beef strips for 1 minute on each side.

Chap Chai (Serves 4–6)

2 oz glass noodles (transparent bean threads)
1/4 lb beef, sliced cross grain (bacon-thin)
1 garlic clove, minced
3 tbsp soy sauce
1 egg
4 dried mushrooms (soaked 30 minutes, drained, sliced)
Cooking oil
1 onion, sliced vertically
2 carrots, julienne style
1 zucchini, julienne style
1 tbsp sugar
2 tsp sesame oil
1/4 tsp red pepper
2 green onions, thinly sliced

1. Add noodles to 1 quart of boiling water and boil 3 minutes, stirring once. Drain and cut into 6" lengths.
2. Marinate meat for 15 minutes in mixture of garlic and soy sauce.
3. Blend egg; cook in thin sheet in small skillet, then slice into 1/4" strips for garnish.
4. In sequence, saute each of the following until done, then remove (adding oil to skillet as needed): mushrooms, onions, carrots, zucchini, meat.
5. Combine noodles, vegetables, and meat with sugar, sesame oil, pepper, and any remaining marinade. Heat through, then serve garnished with egg and green onions.

Chao-Mein (Fried Noodles) (Serves 4–6)

2 oz Chinese noodles
Oil for frying
1/2 onion, sliced vertically
1/2 carrot, julienne style
1/4 lb shelled, chopped shrimp
2 dry mushrooms, soaked and sliced
2 oz bamboo shoots, rinsed and drained
1/4 lb fresh bean sprouts
1 stalk celery, sliced
1 tsp cornstarch
1 tsp sugar
1 tsp salt

1. Boil noodles in 1 quart of water until tender (7 to 10 minutes), stirring every minute. Rinse in cold water; drain well.
2. Fry noodles in 2 tablespoons hot oil for about 2 minutes; set aside.
3. Stir-fry onion and carrot for 2 minutes in 3 tablespoons oil.
4. Add shrimp, remaining vegetables, and 3 tablespoons of water; cover and steam for 5 minutes.
5. Whisk together cornstarch, sugar, and salt with 1 tablespoon of water.
6. Pour over vegetables and heat while stirring to thicken the sauce.
7. Serve over fried noodles.

Clam Casserole (Serves 4–6)

20 clams
1/4 lb beef, chopped
2 garlic cloves, minced
2 tbsp soy sauce
1 tsp red pepper powder
6 c boiling water
1/2 lb firm tofu, cubed
1/2 bunch watercress, cut in 2" lengths
4 scallions, cut in 2" lengths

1. Shuck and clean clams.
2. Mix beef thoroughly with garlic, soy sauce, and red pepper.
3. Add boiling water to beef in saucepan and simmer for 5 minutes.
4. Add clams and tofu, and simmer until clams are cooked.
5. Add watercress and scallions. Simmer for 1 minute, then serve.

Egg Soup (Serves 4–6)

1/4 lb beef, sliced thinly
1 garlic clove, minced
1 tsp sesame oil
2 tsp soy sauce
4 c boiling water
1 egg, slightly beaten
1 dried mushroom, soaked and sliced
1/2 tsp salt
1/4 tsp pepper

1 green onion, chopped

1. Mix beef, garlic, sesame oil, and soy sauce well.
2. Brown meat, then add water and simmer for 20 minutes.
3. In small skillet, cook egg in a sheet; slice in 1/4" strips for garnish.
4. Add mushrooms, seasonings, and green onion; garnish with egg.

Kimchi (Serves 4–8)

4 c Chinese cabbage, cut in 1" squares
1/4 c salt
6 green onions and tops, chopped
2 garlic cloves, minced
2 tsp ginger root, grated
1 tsp sugar
1 tbsp chili powder

1. Sprinkle cabbage with salt and let stand 1 hour.

2. Rinse cabbage in three changes of water.
3. Mix cabbage with remaining ingredients.
4. Transfer to large jar; put weight on cabbage to hold it below water (adding water as needed to cover cabbage).
5. Cover and let stand at room temperature for 2 days, then store in refrigerator for at least a week. (May be stored up to 1 month in refrigerator.)

Persimmon Punch (Serves 5–10)

2 oz ginger root, peeled and sliced
10 cinnamon sticks
10 c water
1/2 c sugar
5 dried persimmons
1 c water
1 tbsp pine nuts

1. Boil ginger and cinnamon sticks in water until liquid turns a pleasing red.
2. Remove ginger and cinnamon, add sugar, and cool.
3. Cut persimmons in half, removing core and seeds, then soak in water for 1 hour. Discard water.
4. Add persimmons to red liquid an hour before serving.
5. Garnish with pine nuts, and serve.

Shrimp Soup (Serves 4–6)

5 c water
4 tbsp soy sauce
1/2 tsp salt
15 medium shrimp, shelled
1/2 bunch watercress, cut into 2" lengths
2 scallions, cut into 2" lengths

1/4 tsp red pepper powder

1. Combine water, soy sauce, and salt; heat to boiling.
2. Add shrimp, watercress, scallions, and pepper; simmer for about 5 minutes until shrimp are done (turned pink).

Shinsollo (Serves 4–6)

6 c boiling water
1/2 daikon, cut into 1/2" crosswise slices
1/2 lb beef, thinly sliced
Salt and pepper to taste
1/3 cake of tofu
1 tbsp minced garlic
1/4 c flour
3 eggs, slightly beaten
3 tbsp oil
3 tbsp soy sauce
1 tbsp sugar
1 tbsp minced scallions
1 tsp sesame oil
1/2 tsp pepper
1 carrot, cut in 1/2" by 2" strips
5 pieces dried mushroom, cut in 1/2" by 2" strips
1/4 lb white fish fillet
10 medium shrimp, peeled

1. Pour boiling water over daikon and half of the beef; simmer until daikon and beef are tender, then remove them from the broth. Season broth with salt and pepper, and cool.
2. Combine cooked beef with bean curd, garlic, salt, and pepper, then form 20 meatballs. Dredge meatballs in flour, dip in egg, and fry to golden brown.
3. Shred remaining beef and mix with the soy sauce, sugar, scallions, sesame oil, and pepper.
4. Boil carrots; soak mushrooms.
5. Cut fish in thin slices 2" long; dredge in flour, dip in egg, and fry until golden brown.
6. Cook remaining egg in thin sheet and slice in strips 1/4" by 2".
7. In a hot pot, arrange a layer of daikon around the bottom, top with the shredded beef, then radially and artistically alternate rows of other ingredients, including shrimp, and finally add the beef broth.
8. Heat for at least 5 minutes so that everything is cooked.

Stir-Fried Rice (Serves 4–6)

1/4 lb beef, shredded
2 tsp minced garlic
4 tsp sesame oil
1/4 tsp red pepper powder
1 tbsp soy sauce
1 1/2 c shredded carrots
4 c cooked rice
3 tbsp green peas
2 tbsp chopped scallions

1. Mix beef with garlic, sesame oil, pepper, and soy sauce.
2. Saute carrots in oiled skillet, using medium heat, until tender.
3. Remove carrots, then saute beef mixture until beef is done.
4. Combine all ingredients in oiled skillet and stir-fry over medium heat for about 3 minutes or until hot and the raw vegetables are cooked a little.

Sweet Rice Chestnut Dessert (Serves 4–6)

3 1/2 c sweet rice
3/4 c brown sugar
2 tbsp sesame oil
4 1/2 tsp soy sauce
1 c chestnuts, boiled and peeled
1/2 c chopped dates
1/2 tsp ground cinnamon
4 tsp pine nuts

1. Wash and soak sweet rice for 10 to 12 hours; drain.
2. Steam rice in covered steamer until tender.
3. Mix rice with remaining ingredients, reserving the pine nuts for garnish.
4. Heat mixture, covered, in a double boiler over gently boiling water or in a rice cooker for 20 minutes.
5. Garnish with pine nuts, and serve.

Tashima Daikon Soup (Serves 4–6)

1/2 lb daikon, thin slices, 1/2" by 2" 2 oz beef, shredded 4 c water (total) 5 oz tashima (seaweed) 4 1/2 tsp soy sauce 1/2 tsp sesame oil 1 tsp minced garlic 2 tsp sliced scallions 1/8 tsp red pepper powder	1. Gently boil daikon and beef in 1 cup of water for 3 minutes. 2. Add tashima and 3 cups of water; simmer until vegetables are tender. 3. Remove tashima; cut into 1/2" by 2" strips. 4. Add cut tashima and remaining ingredients to soup; cook 3 minutes. Serve hot.

Toasted Tashima (Seaweed) (Serves 4–6)

5 sheets tashima
1 tbsp sesame oil
1/2 tsp salt

1. Brush one side of seaweed with sesame oil and sprinkle with salt.

2. Place seaweed in single layer on cookie sheet and toast in 450°F oven briefly on both sides until color turns slightly green.
3. Use kitchen shears to cut into rectangles of desired size.

Vegetables and Rice (Serves 4–6)

2 c rice 4 c water 1/4 lb chicken, chopped 1/4 lb mushrooms, chopped 3/4 c shredded carrots 1/2 c bean sprouts 3/4 c green beans, julienne style 4 tsp soy sauce 1/2 tsp salt 1/8 tsp pepper 1/4 c soy sauce	2 tsp sesame oil 1 1/2 tsp red pepper powder 1 tsp sugar

1. Combine rice, water, chicken, vegetables, 4 teaspoons soy sauce, salt, and pepper in rice cooker or large saucepan.
2. Turn on rice cooker, or boil gently in saucepan until rice is done.
3. Combine remaining ingredients to make sauce to serve with rice.

Summary

The Korean peninsula extends south from the eastern edge of Asia, bordered between China and Japan. Limited farmland is available because of the mountainous terrain, but the Republic of Korea (South Korea) has effectively worked to raise rice, barley, corn, fruits and vegetables suited to the climate, and livestock (cattle, pigs, goats, rabbits) and poultry. Fishing in the seas surrounding the land adds significantly to the food supply, as does harvesting of seaweed.

Following the kingdom of Old Chosŏn for many centuries, the region eventually evolved into the Three Kingdoms shortly before the time of Christ. The Shilla Kingdom conquered both the Koguryŏ and Paekche kingdoms and established the Unified Shilla Kingdom, with Kyŏngju as its capital, in the 7th century. This was followed by the Chosŏn Dynasty (1392 to 1910), which ruled from the city that subsequently has been named Seoul. King Sejong made many contributions, including the development of han-gŭl in the 15th century. Korea has been invaded by the Manchu from the north and by the Japanese from the east several times. Western nations also demanded trade with Korea in the 19th and 20th centuries. Ultimately, Korea was divided after World War II, leading to the Korean War and to the isolation of North Korea in sharp contrast to the very rapid development of the Republic of Korea in the south.

Korean culture emphasizes the family and its expectations of individual members to reach their physical and intellectual potential for the family and for Korea. Consistent with this expectation are many public parks with sports facilities and the availability of opportunities to develop abilities in music, dance, and art. Freedom of religion has resulted in the presence of Buddhism, Confucianism (or a blend of these two), Christianity (Protestant followers outnumber Catholic, but both are available), and Islam. A few other religious groups have a few followers too.

Various holidays are tied to the lunar months (Lunar New Year, Moon Festival, and Buddha's birthday, for example). Others are specific dates, starting with New Year's Day on January 1. May 5 is Children's Day. National holidays are July 15 (celebrating the constitution) and August 18 (commemorating liberation in 1948).

Typically, Koreans eat a large breakfast and two other meals daily, plus several snacks. Kimchi, rice, soups, fish, kochujang (red pepper and bean paste), garlic, onions, daikon, lettuce, carrots, beans, seaweed, and red pepper powder are key foods in the diet. Meals usually are served at low tables, with diners sitting on mats in their stocking feet. Chopsticks and porcelain soup spoons are used for eating. Soup and rice are served in separate bowls to each diner. Other dishes are placed in the center for all diners to share. Desserts are served occasionally and often feature rice. Tea of various types may be the beverage.

Study Questions

1. How does the geography of Korea shape its food supply?
2. Trace the influence of other nations on the history of Korea.
3. Describe the food patterns of Korea, being sure to include a description of kimchi.
4. Identify at least four ways in which rice is used in Korean foods.
5. Define the following: (a) chogori, (b) chima, (c) han-gŭl, (d) shinsollo, and (e) tuk-kuk.

Bibliography

Barer-Stein, T. 1999. *You Eat What You Are.* 2nd ed. Firefly Books, Ltd. Ontario, Canada.

Chu, W. Y. 1985. Traditional Korean Cuisine. *L. A. Korea Times.* Los Angeles.

DeLand, A. and R. Miller. 1994. *Far East 94/95.* Fielding Worldwide. Redondo Beach, CA.

DuBois, J. 1994. *Korea.* Marshall Cavendish. New York.

Kim, H. E. 1985. *Facts about Korea.* 18th ed. Hollym Corp. Seoul, Korea.

Kim, Y. J. 1995. *Kyongju, Old Capital of Shilla Dynasty Enlivened with 2000-Year History.* Y. S. Kim. Seoul, Korea.

Rutt, R. 1964. *Korean Works and Days.* Charles E. Tuttle. Rutland, VT.

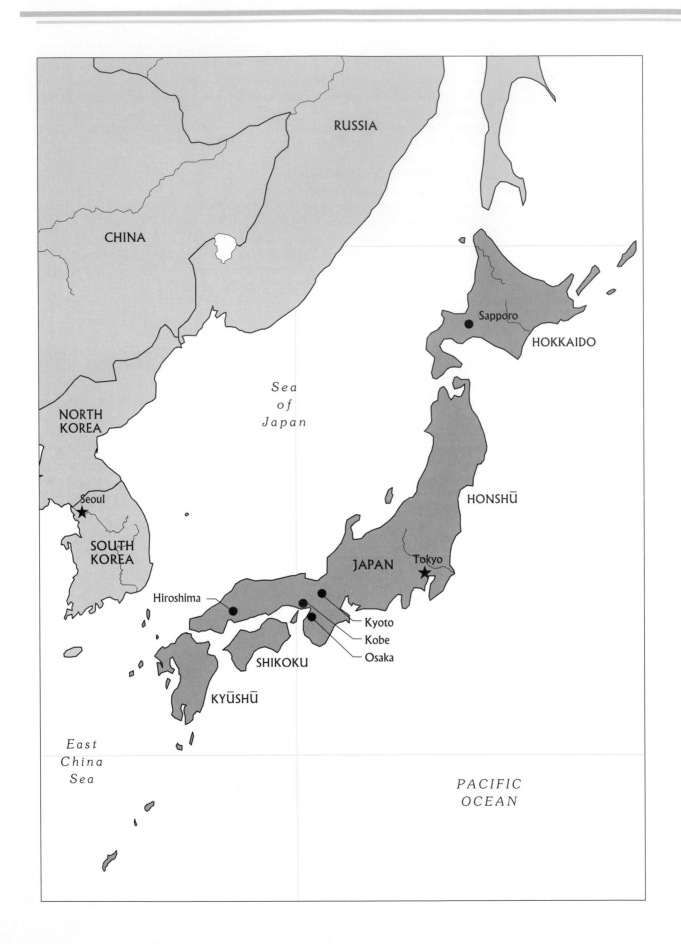

19 Japan

Geographic Overview

Japan, the island nation just east of the Asian continent, consists of four main islands stretching from latitudes equivalent to those of New England to Florida. The northernmost island is Hokkaido; Sapporo, its principal city, is familiar to many as the home of the 1972 Winter Olympics, a fact which attests to its cold and snowy winters and its mountainous terrain. A bit south and west of Hokkaido is the large main island of Honshu. Tokyo is located on its southern coast about where Honshu's shoreline turns westward. Shikoku is a comparatively small island roughly paralleling the western peninsula of Honshu and just a bit south of it. The fourth island, Kyushu, lies west and southward from the tip of Honshu and Shikoku. Kyushu has quite a mild, rather subtropical climate due to its southern location. In fact, Kyushu is close enough to the Korean Peninsula that this island apparently was the route by which early people from the mainland entered the region that is now Japan. The Chinese referred to what is now Japan by the name *Jihpen*, Land of the Rising Sun, which indicated its location to the east of China.

Geographically, Japan experiences considerable shifting and earth movements, the result of its volcanic origins and the movement of tectonic plates. Mt. Fuji on the island of Honshu has its lovely, symmetrical volcanic peak rising more than 12,000 feet. It is but one of seemingly endless mountains that comprise about 85 percent of the surface of Japan. Only limited areas of relatively flat land are available throughout the country, and a huge population competes with farmers for this space. This competition for land has forced development of terracing and other efforts to expand the land that can be used for people and crops.

The Japanese are masters at maximizing crop yields from the land that is dedicated to agriculture. Fields generally are small, but intensively farmed, and almost no land goes to waste. Rice can be grown to produce two crops annually, and vegetables also are planted and fertilized to achieve very high yields. Production of livestock is rather limited because of land limitations, but labor-intensive tending of cattle results in such high-quality meat as the world-famous *kobe* beef.

The limited availability of suitable land for farming has fostered development of the fishing industry and the harvesting of seaweeds for food. Fortunately, Japan's seas surrounding its islands provide important quantities of highly desirable foods that are featured prominently in Japanese cuisine. In fact, Japan's large fishing fleets pursue their catches in waters very far from their shores as well as close to home.

History and Culture

People made their way to the Japanese islands from China, Manchuria, and probably other parts of Southeast Asia before the end of the 3rd century CE. Unification of some of the groups began to occur in the 4th century, and Shinto began to emerge as a unifying religious tradition, which emphasized harmony and social unity. Then Buddhism was introduced from China in the 6th century and began to be interwoven with Shinto traditions (Figure 19.1). By the 8th century, the center of government was established at Nara on the major island of Honshu about 125 miles west of Tokyo. Near the end of the 8th century, Kyoto became the center of government.

The Heian period lasted from 794 to 1185. Although language and art showed strong Chinese influence, this period produced much literature and art that was distinctively Japanese. Governance also underwent changes, with the power gradually shifting from the emperor to very strong clans or families to military leaders (shoguns). The court of the emperor served a largely ceremonial role. The Fujiwara family gained control during the Heian period, only to be overshadowed by intensive power fights that resulted in Minamoto Yoritomo establishing his shogunate in Kamakura, while the emperor's court remained in Kyoto. By 1333 the shogunate was moved back to Kyoto.

Numerous civil conflicts continued until Tokugawa Ieyasu became shogun. He moved his government to what is now Tokyo in 1600, although the emperor was in Kyoto. It was during his reign that Portuguese Christian missionaries,

Figure 19.1 This Buddhist shrine in Nara, Japan, attracts many Buddhists and other visitors.

who had arrived in the middle of the 16th century, were driven out of Japan. In fact, the only Europeans allowed to stay were some traders from Holland. Essentially, Japan sealed itself off from the West until 1853. A strong class system was established by the Tokugawa shoguns: samurai (warriors), farmer, artisan, and merchant (in descending order of prestige). Subsequently, the fact that merchants were the ones who gathered economic strength resulted in a shift in their status to a higher level.

Opening of contact with the West occurred as a result of Commodore Perry's visits, first in 1853 and again in 1854, to establish a treaty that opened two Japanese ports for limited trade with the United States. Other nations soon followed with their own trade treaties. Japan's isolation ended. Then, the Meiji period unfolded with Emperor Meiji moving his government to Tokyo (called Edo at that time). Considerable development of the country took place internally, and Japan began to seek recognition in the world. China and Russia were the targets by 1912, when the Meiji era closed. Japan's expansion continued under Emperor Hirohito. Military actions by Japan were conducted in Manchuria in 1931 and in China in 1937. The attack on Pearl Harbor in 1941 certainly was an event that stands out in American history. Japan's defeat in 1945 left the nation in ruins. However, remarkable recovery and development from that time to the present have enabled Japan to emerge as a strong economic power in the world community (Figure 19.2).

Religion in Japan today is a somewhat nebulous aspect of the lives of people. Shinto, which is perhaps better described as a philosophical approach to life than as a discrete religion, plays a subtle role in Japanese traditions. Nature and harmony in life are values attributed to Shinto. Simple beauty provides harmony, as is evident in all aspects of Japanese art.

Buddhism is clearly evident in Japan, although not nearly as strongly as in other neighboring countries in Southeast Asia. In Japan, there is a melding of philosophy and religion by many worshipers. People feel free to embrace aspects of Shinto and Buddhism to suit their own spiritual needs. Christianity also plays a role in the lives of some Japanese; missionaries began to return to bring their message to Japan after the country was once again open to them during the Meiji rule.

The combination of Shinto and Buddhist worship resulted in construction of lovely temples and shrines throughout Japan. The sacred ground of a Shinto shrine is carefully defined by rope, white gravel, and *torii* (distinctive arch or gate to a Shinto shrine) so that people considered to need purification will not enter until ritually purified. Various architectural styles of Shinto shrines can be found in Japan. A particularly large and impressive one is the Heian Jingu shrine in Kyoto. The shrine at Nikko is another Shinto shrine often visited. Buddhist tem-

Figure 19.2 The streets of Tokyo, the present capital of Japan, are crowded near the entrance to this shrine within the city.

Figure 19.3 The large Buddhist shrine at Nikko consists of several buildings on the hillside.

ples (Figure 19.3) or shrines may also be built in various styles and sometimes are built rather close to a Shinto shrine. Their architecture may be somewhat more intricate than the Shinto shrines and may feature a pagoda-type roof (Figure 19.4).

The Japanese tea ceremony is an elaborate ritual that follows a lengthy, carefully choreographed program designed to emphasize beauty in all aspects of preparing, serving, and drinking tea artfully made using finely powdered tea leaves. Even the beauty of the cup is emphasized to enhance the interaction between the person preparing the beverage and the guest. Traditionally, the tea ceremony was performed by men, although this ability is carefully taught to young Japanese women today.

Another tradition that can be traced to Shinto practices is the public bath. Public baths evolved as a social, carefully prescribed tradition in Japan. Bathers are expected to wash themselves with soap and to rinse thoroughly before entering the public bath. Actually, the communal bath is a place for soaking, relaxing, and chatting with family or friends. In some parts of Japan, natural hot springs conveniently provide the setting for public baths.

Two types of traditional Japanese entertainment have a long history of performances that are highly stylized presentations of very old folk stories. *Noh* dramas are presented by actors wearing wooden masks. Action is very slow, and performances are long. A shorter, lighter version is called *kyōgen*. A particularly dramatic form of traditional Japanese entertainment is *kabuki*, which traditionally is danced by men wearing white face makeup, startling wigs, and very elaborate costumes. A performance might include sword fights, music, dancing, and even acrobatics.

A related tradition is puppeteering, which is called *bunraku*. Large, elaborate puppets are crafted with amazing costumes for the various roles in a play. The

Figure 19.4 Pagodas in Japan feature intricate detail on the various roof levels.

puppeteers breathe life into these puppets as they maneuver their characters, giving them voice and emotion to bring complex stories to the audience.

The Japanese love sports, but perhaps the most unique sport presented here is sumo wrestling. The stars of this sport are extremely heavy, often in excess of 350 pounds. They are an amazing sight as they enter the ring in their loin cloths and proceed to try to force a part of the opponent's body to touch the floor or to exit the ring. This is a sport that is steeped in centuries of tradition. A far more recent passion is the sport of baseball, which was imported to Japan by Americans following World War II.

On quite a different note of entertainment are the geishas. These women are well schooled in the fine art of flower arranging, in the tea ceremony, and in musical performance. Japanese men have enjoyed the tradition of geishas for many centuries as entertainment away from home.

Ceramics are a highly refined art in Japan. Their simple designs and excellent glazes are recognized throughout the world. One of their finest examples is the instantly recognizable Imari porcelains from Kyushu, a type that traces its roots to the importation of Korean craftsmen in 1616 following the Japanese invasion.

Japanese art reflects the pleasure conveyed by simplicity of line and subtlety or even absence of color. The calligraphy and brush art created by a combination of artistic strokes of varying widths of black on a simple white paper are representative of Japan. Scrolls painted with care and subtlety of color often depict nature at different seasons of the year. Wood blocks are used to create another distinctive Japanese art form, wood block prints. Although Japanese artists obviously had opportunities to become aware of the art of China and Korea, the style of art in Japan clearly is identifiable as its own. Origami, the art of paper folding, is yet another unique form of Japanese art.

Love of nature is reflected in the beauty created in Japanese gardens (Figure 19.5). Artful use of water, plants and trees of varying sizes and colors, and stones and gravel results in tranquil havens for quiet meditation and enjoyment. One of the features sometimes is an arched footbridge over a stream or pond. Artistically raked gravel provides harmony of line and peace in some gardens. Bonsai, the art of dwarfing a tree to create uniquely sculpted small trees, may be incorporated in designing a Japanese garden. A pot containing a small bonsai is likely to find its way into the home. If cut flowers are displayed, they will be arranged according to the rules of *ikebana* (flower arranging).

Japanese music is performed on traditional instruments and provides sounds very distinctive from western music. Stringed instruments with varying numbers of strings, a range of sizes, and different shapes are often featured in Japanese musical performances. The *samisen* has three strings and resembles a banjo in shape. The *koto* is the Japanese version of a zither, its 13 strings made of

Dance is an integral part of Japanese life, for both spectators and participants. Originally, dances were performed to help assure a good harvest or other need, such as successful fishing; other dances were to honor a god or a spirit. An example is the coal miner's dance (Tanko Bushi), which depicts the miners digging coal, pushing the filled carts, and carrying sacks of coal.

Figure 19.5 Peaceful gardens with flowers and artfully trimmed shrubbery and trees exemplify the Japanese love of nature.

silk, which provides a smooth sound when plucked. Another type of Japanese lute is the *biwa*, which has four strings and a short neck. The elegant style of music, called *gagaku*, dates from the Heian era and was centered at Nara. Big drums punctuate the music produced by playing flutes, stringed instruments, and other drums and reeds.

The Japanese love holidays and celebrate quite a few special ones, starting with New Year's Day on January 1. This may feature the wearing of kimonos and family celebrations. Boys are especially prized and honored on Children's Day, which is a national celebration held on May 5. The vernal and autumnal equinoxes are also major holidays, tracing their roots back to the early eras when most people were farmers and therefore very attuned to agricultural seasons.

Food Patterns

Japanese food patterns prominently feature two crops: rice and soybeans. Rice may be prepared in different ways, most commonly today being cooked in a rice cooker and served either in a separate bowl or with other ingredients. A prized form of rice is *mochi*, a rice cake made especially for the New Year celebration. Glutinous rice is first steamed until tender and then placed in extremely large wooden mortars where many people take turns pounding the rice with heavy wooden mallets to make a very sticky rice paste. This paste may be shaped into cakes that can be grilled or perhaps wrapped in seaweed and then dipped in soy sauce. Chunks of dry mochi can be deep-fat fried and eaten as a snack. Rice also makes its way to Japanese tables in the form of rice vinegar, *mirin* (sweet rice wine), and sake, the strong rice wine made by using *Aspergillus oryzae* for fermenting to an alcoholic content of 15 to 17 percent. Sake is served warm in special tiny cups.

Soybeans are found in many forms in the Japanese diet. Tofu has long played a significant role as a source of plant protein. Soy sauce, *miso* (fermented bean paste), and *okara* (powdered, dried pulp byproduct of tofu production) are often used in Japanese cooking.

Numerous kinds of fish and seaweeds are harvested from the seas around Japan. Not surprisingly, both of these foods are eaten in virtually all homes and restaurants. Sometimes, fish may be prepared with extreme care and served beautifully without any cooking—a dish called *sashimi*. Regardless of the type of fish being used for making sashimi, the key to success is great skill in cutting correctly with exactly the right sharp knife. Of course, only the freshest fish can be used, and service should be prompt to assure food safety.

Figure 19.6 Sushi is skillfully prepared using the freshest ingredients and artfully arranged for service.

Sushi preparation also is an art, one involving careful selection of lovely and delicate ingredients (various seafoods or vegetables, or both) to be arranged alongside vinegared rice (Figure 19.6). Sometimes, sushi is pressed into molds to form long fingers. A familiar style is made by arranging a layer of dried seaweed *(nori)* on a bamboo mat, then artfully arranging the ingredients on the seaweed before rolling carefully and tightly to enclose the filling as a long tube and ultimately slicing crosswise for lovely round slices with the seaweed serving as the outer covering. Vinegared ginger is usually served as an accompaniment for both sashimi and sushi. Another favorite condiment is *wasabi* (grated horseradish).

Tempura is quite a different but extremely popular way of preparing shrimp and vegetable slices. Surprisingly, this Japanese favorite food actually was brought to Japan by the Portuguese missionaries, and the tradition remained even though the missionaries were forced to leave. In fact, the name *tempura* is derived from the Latin *Quattuor Tempora*, the designation the Catholic fathers gave to the four times a year they were required to eat seafood rather than meat. The batter-dipped and fried shrimp were the way in which this special food was prepared, and the Japanese were quick to adopt the dish (and also to add thinly sliced vegetables to their tempura).

Soups are a part of Japanese cuisine, and *dashi* is central to preparing some soups. Dashi is a stock made with *katsuo-bushi* (dried fillet of bonito) and *konbu* (dried kelp). Fortunately, dashi is now available as an instant mix for use in making clear soups *(suimono)*, which may be garnished with a small curl of lemon rind, a bit of shrimp, or other artistic touch. Suimono can be varied by including a slice of tofu, perhaps a bamboo shoot sliver, and a bite of fish fillet. Miso soups range from sweet to quite salty in taste. For breakfast, this traditional soup (made using fermented soybean paste) is augmented with a bowl of rice, pickles, and green tea.

Noodles are another vital part of most Japanese diets. Those made with buckwheat flour from the north of Japan are called *soba*. Noodles made using wheat flour are named *udon* and are particularly popular in southern Japan. Soba noodles typically are a gray color and rather thin, while udon may be either flat or round and sometimes fairly wide and thick. The cooked noodles may be served with a dipping sauce or in a broth. In either case, they are politely sucked into the mouth, accompanied by an audible and appreciative slurping sound.

Vegetables frequently are pickled *(tsukemono)* and served as accompaniments at meals. Mushrooms of various types (shitake, for example) are used in their dried form in an array of recipes. Bamboo shoots and lotus root are important both for the texture they add and for their artistic appearance. Burdock *(gobo)*, Japanese eggplant, *kabocha* (Japanese pumpkin squash), daikon (giant white radish), cucumbers, and spinach are among the vegetable ingredients in

Figure 19.7 Fresh vegetables and thin cuts of meat are being grilled at the table in this Japanese restaurant.

Japanese meals (Figure 19.7). Vinegared salads (*sunomono*) are served at many meals.

Sukiyaki is a well-known one-dish meal from Japan despite the fact that it was developed in Japan in the mid-19th century when Westerners settling there brought their love of beef with them. Although Buddhism is a religion that values life, this dish featuring very thinly sliced beef and generous amounts of favorite Japanese vegetables cooked together quickly with soy sauce, dashi, and mirin for flavoring quickly became a favorite dish in Japan.

The presentation of food is an artistic statement as each dish is arranged for the table. A variety of small dishes suited for specific items is used to add the appropriate setting for the different menu items. Individual servings are small, and several dishes will be served at a meal, often accompanied with appropriate sauces to highlight the flavors. Chopsticks are used for dining, although broth of soup may be sipped from the diner's bowl. Meals are a time for experiencing the pleasure and beauty of food. Although dining at home is a regular practice, guests ordinarily are entertained at a restaurant. Families and individuals also dine out fairly often.

Key Terms

Bunraku—Puppet shows featuring large, complicated puppets very skillfully presented, often in traditional stories.

Dashi—Clear soup stock made with dried fillet of bonito and kelp.

Honshu—Largest of the islands of Japan; Tokyo is on Honshu.

Ikebana—Japanese art of arranging cut flowers.

Kabuki—Traditional, highly stylized drama with elaborate costumes and makeup, often featuring dancing and some music performed by men.

Mirin—Sweet rice wine.

Miso—Fermented soybean paste.

Mochi—Rice cake made by pounding cooked sweet glutinous rice; traditional for New Year's celebration.

Nori—Dried seaweed available in thin, greenish-black sheets; used for wrapping sushi and other foods or as a garnish.

Sake—Strong rice wine, usually served warm.

Sashimi—Very carefully cut and arranged slices of raw fish.

Shinto—Early religion of Japan that focused on nature and considered the Emperor to be a descendant of the sun goddess.

Shogun—Military rulers in Japan prior to 1867.

Soba—Noodles made from buckwheat flour from northern Japan.

Suimono—Clear Japanese soups.

Sukiyaki—Thinly sliced beef simmered with Japanese vegetables, soy sauce, mirin, and dashi in a pot at the table.

Sunomono—Vinegared salads.

Sushi—Vinegared rice and small bits of other ingredients pressed into a mold or rolled tightly into a long log encased in a layer of nori and sliced vertically.

Tempura—Batter-coated, deep-fried shrimp and thinly sliced vegetables.

Torii—Distinctive gateway to a Shinto shrine.

Tsukemono—Pickled vegetables.

Udon—Noodles made with wheat flour, typical of southern Japan.

Wasabi—Finely grated, delicate green horseradish; also available as a powder.

Recipes

Azuki and Mochi Gome (Red Beans and Rice) (Serves 4–6)

1 1/4 c azuki
1 qt water
2 c sweet rice (mochi gome)
2 tsp black sesame seeds (toasted)

1. Soak rinsed beans in cold water overnight. Heat to high simmer and simmer until tender (45 min-

utes). Drain beans, saving liquid for preparing the rice. Refrigerate beans.
2. Rinse rice in colander under running water until water runs clear. Soak rice at least 8 hours in bean liquid in refrigerator.
3. Drain rice (discarding liquid); add 1 cup cooked beans and steam for 45 minutes. Add salt if desired.
4. Serve with garnish of toasted black sesame seeds.

Deep-Fried Tofu (Serves 4–6)

12 oz tofu
Oil for deep-fat frying
1/2 daikon, grated
1/2 carrot, grated
2/3 c soy sauce
1/4 c mirin (or sherry)
1 tsp grated ginger root

1. Drain tofu; place between paper towels and top with pie plate holding heavy can (for weight). Remove liquid every few minutes during 30-minute draining period. Discard all but the curd. Cut curd into bite-sized cubes.
2. Heat oil to 400°F, then fry tofu for 4 minutes.
3. Garnish tofu with grated daikon and carrot. Serve with sauce of soy sauce, mirin, and ginger.

Dashi (Soup Stock) (Serves 8)

2 qt water
3 " square sheet of dried kelp (konbu)
3/4 c dried bonito

1. Heat water to boiling, then add konbu.
2. Add konbu and then remove it as soon as water returns to a boil.

3. Immediately add dried fish and turn off heat. Let stand 2 minutes.
4. Strain through cheesecloth in a strainer to clarify stock. Serve as a soup with simple garnishes or use in other recipes.

Oyako Domburi (Rice Topped with Chicken and Eggs) (Serves 4–6)

1 lb boneless, skinless chicken
1 1/2 c chicken stock
1/3 c soy sauce
2 tbsp sugar
1/4 c sake
3 dried mushrooms, soaked and sliced
1/4 c bamboo shoots
1/2 onion, sliced
1/2 c peas
6 eggs, beaten

2 sheets nori (seaweed)
Hot cooked rice

1. Simmer chicken in stock until tender; shred.
2. Add soy sauce, sugar, sake, and vegetables. Simmer 5 minutes.
3. Heat to boiling and stir in eggs.
4. Serve immediately over hot, cooked rice in individual domburi bowls; garnish with toasted strips of nori.

Sweet Potato Sweet (Okashi) (Serves 6–8)

2 sweet potatoes, pared and cut in 1″ thick slices
1 2/3 c sugar
2 c water
Pinch of salt
3 egg yolks

1. Boil sweet potatoes until tender. Remove from water to cool.

2. Heat sugar and water to boiling and boil for 3 minutes. Cool.
3. Mash potato before blending with salt, syrup, and yolks. Heat over very low heat, stirring constantly until thick and fluffy. Cool.
4. Form into balls 1 1/2″ in diameter.
5. Shape each ball into a chestnut-like appearance by placing in a cloth and twisting to force out extra liquid.

Autumn Sweet (Ohagi) (Serves 4–6)

1 c short grain rice
1 c glutinous rice
2 2/3 c chunky sweet red bean paste

1. Rinse rice until water is clear. Boil rice until tender in salted water.

2. Thoroughly mash rice after it has cooled for 10 minutes (use wooden spoon or Cuisinart).
3. Shape into spheres the size of golf balls. Coat some with a layer of red bean paste; make others with a center of red bean paste and an outer shell of rice.
4. Serve as dessert with green tea.

Chunky Sweet Red Bean Paste (Makes 3 cups)

1 c azuki (red beans)
3 c water
1 c sugar

1. Wash beans thoroughly, then cover with water and bring to a boil.
2. Drain beans and simmer in 3 cups of water until beans are tender and water is almost gone.
3. Stir in sugar and salt to make chunky paste.

Shrimp and Melon Soup (Serves 6)

5 c dashi
2 tsp sake
1 tsp soy sauce
1/2 tsp salt
1/4 honeydew melon, peeled and cut into 1" cubes
6 cooked medium shrimp

1. Simmer dashi, sake, soy sauce, and salt with the melon cubes until melon is tender (10 to 15 minutes).
2. Remove melon and place 3 cubes in each soup bowl; add 1 shrimp to each bowl, then gently pour the dashi into each bowl.

Sukiyaki (Serves 4–6)

1 lb sirloin, sliced very thin
1 can (8 1/2 oz) bamboo shoots
1 can (8 1/2 oz) yam threads (shirataki)
1 cake tofu, cut in bite-sized cubes
2 stalks celery, sliced diagonally
6 green onions, cut into 2" lengths
1 bunch watercress, cut into 2" lengths
1 gobo (burdock root), slivered
2 tsp oil
3 tbsp sugar
1 c sake
1/2 c soy sauce
2 c water (more as needed)
4 eggs

1. Arrange beef, bamboo shoots, yam threads, tofu, celery, onion, watercress, and gobo on platter for cooking at the table.
2. Preheat electric skillet, then add oil and cook the first 1/4 of the beef quickly to light brown. Move cooked beef to side of skillet and keep adding beef until it is all cooked and moved to one side.
3. Add sugar, sake, soy sauce, and water, and heat to simmer, then add one ingredient at a time, cook each, then move aside for the next ingredient.
4. Diners serve their own plates while seated around the skillet at the table and dip each bite of hot food in the egg provided at each place. Hot rice, perhaps a pickle, and green tea complete the meal.

Sushi (Vinegared Rice) (Serves 6–8)

2 c short grain rice
2 1/2 c water
2" square of dried kelp (konbu)
1/4 c rice vinegar
2 tsp salt
2 tbsp mirin
3 tbsp sugar
Suggested ingredients: Shrimp, crab, caviar, mushrooms, cucumber, spinach, dark tuna, various fish, nori, toasted sesame seeds, pickled ginger, soy sauce.

1. Wash rice thoroughly; combine with water and soak for 30 minutes.
2. Add konbu, cover, and heat to boil; reduce heat and simmer for 10 minutes until water is absorbed.
3. Turn heat to low for 5 minutes; remove from heat and let stand 5 more minutes. Discard konbu. Turn out to cool on large platter.
4. Meanwhile, heat rice vinegar, salt, mirin, and sugar to a boil and then cool it.
5. Thoroughly mix the vinegar sauce with the rice and cool to room temperature.
6. Sushi can be used by adding other tidbits of ingredients and squeezing into small balls, by making a roll of nori enclosing carefully arranged sushi and such items as bits of fish and vegetables before slicing into rounds, or by encasing in a thin omelet in which similar ingredients are used to make an attractive packet.

Tempura (Serves 4–6)

Raw shrimp, shelled, butterflied
1/2 lb green beans, cut in half
1/2 lb Japanese eggplant, peeled and cut into 1/2″ thick slices
1/4 lb snow peas
1/8 lb mushrooms, sliced
1 sweet potato, peeled and cut into 1/4″ thick slices
Lotus root, bamboo shoots (optional)
3/4 c dashi
1/4 c soy sauce
1/4 c mirin
Oil for deep-fat frying
1 egg
3/4 c ice-cold water
1/2 c flour
1/4 c cornstarch
1/2 tsp baking powder
1/4 daikon, grated

1. Assemble shrimp and vegetables for dipping in batter.
2. Boil dashi, soy sauce, and mirin for sauce; cool.
3. While oil heats to 375°F, make batter: Beat egg and water, and then stir in sifted dry ingredients (flour, cornstarch, and baking powder) just enough to moisten the flour.
4. Dip shrimp and vegetables individually in flour and then in batter to coat completely. Fry only a few pieces at a time to keep oil at 375°F. Fry for 1 minute, then turn to fry the other side for 1 minute to light golden color. Drain on paper towels.
5. Keep warm in oven until frying is finished.
6. Serve with dipping sauce (dashi, soy sauce, and mirin, from step 2) garnished with grated daikon.

Teriyaki (Serves 4)

1/2 c mirin
1/2 c soy sauce
1 tbsp sugar
1/2 c beef stock
2 tsp cornstarch
1 tbsp water
1 lb beef tenderloin, cut into 1/4″ thick slices
1 tbsp powdered mustard mixed with hot water to form paste

1. Unless using bottled teriyaki sauce, briefly heat mirin in saucepan and ignite to burn off alcohol

before adding soy sauce, sugar, and beef stock and bringing to a boil. Cool.
2. Make smooth slurry of cornstarch, water, and 1/4 cup of teriyaki sauce (from step 1). Heat to boiling while stirring to make glaze.
3. Preheat hibachi or broiler.
4. Dip each slice of beef in teriyaki sauce (from step 1) and broil 2 inches from heat for 1 minute on each side.
5. Serve on individual plates with a little glaze (from step 2) spooned on the strips and a little mustard paste.

Udon and Chicken (Serves 4)

10 oz udon (uncooked wide noodles)
6 c water with 1 tsp salt
1 qt dashi
2 tsp soy sauce
1 tsp sugar
1 1/2 tsp salt
1/3 lb boneless, skinless chicken breast, cut into thin strips
2 scallions, cut into 3″ strips

1. Boil noodles in salted water; turn off heat and let rest for 5 minutes. Place in colander and rinse in cold running water for 5 minutes.
2. Heat dashi to boiling, then add soy sauce, sugar, and salt, and return to boil.
3. Add noodles and heat to boiling, remove them to four soup bowls. Add chicken and scallions to soup and boil for 2 more minutes.
4. Ladle broth, chicken, and scallions over noodles.

Umani (Vegetables with Chicken) (Serves 2–4)

2 shitake mushrooms
1 gobo, pared and cut into 1" pieces
1/2 lb boneless, skinless chicken breast, cut into slivers
1 tbsp oil
2 carrots, pared and cut into matchsticks
1 can bamboo shoots, sliced
1 c dashi
1 1/2 tsp sugar
1 tsp soy sauce
1 tsp salt

1/2 c frozen peas

1. Soak mushrooms for 2 hours; discard water and stems, and slice caps in 1/2" strips.
2. Boil pieces of gobo for 5 minutes and drain.
3. Stir-fry chicken in oil for 3 minutes, then add vegetables (except peas), dashi, and sugar. Cover and simmer for 5 minutes.
4. Add mushrooms, soy sauce, and salt, and simmer for 10 minutes.
5. Add peas and simmer for 3 minutes.

Vinegared Shrimp and Cucumber (Serves 2–4)

1 c rice vinegar
1 c dashi
1/4 c soy sauce
1 1/2 tbsp sugar
2 cucumbers, peeled, seeded, cut into very thin slices
Salt
1 can small shrimp, drained

1. Heat vinegar, dashi, soy sauce, and sugar to simmering, and then cool.

2. On a cutting board, spread cucumber and sprinkle salt over all slices; knead 1 minute and put in a mixing bowl (without rinsing cucumber).
3. Pour about half of sauce over cucumbers and squeeze gently; drain and discard liquid.
4. Mix remaining sauce with the cucumbers.
5. Serve shrimp and cucumbers in small dishes to each person.

Yakitori (Serves 6)

Bamboo skewers
1/2 c sugar
1/2 c brown sugar
1 c soy sauce
1/4 tsp grated fresh ginger root
1 clove garlic, minced
1 tbsp mirin
2 whole boneless, skinless chicken breasts cut into 1 1/4" cubes
6 scallions, cut into 1 1/4" lengths

1. Soak bamboo skewers in water.
2. Combine sugars and soy sauce, and heat until sugar dissolves.
3. Add ginger root, garlic, and mirin. Stir and set aside.
4. Alternate chicken and scallion on skewers.
5. Dip skewers to coat chicken and scallions with sauce, then broil (hibachi or broiler) for about 3 minutes; dip in sauce again and broil second side for 3 more minutes.
6. Spoon a little sauce on skewers when served.

Summary

The nation of Japan has four major islands with rugged, volcanic terrain, limited tillable land, and restricted space for housing its population. Its proximity to Korea and China accounts for the migration of people into Japan and the resultant cultural influences that are evident despite the unique interpretations in Japanese art and music.

Shintoism was the first religion, but Buddhism arrived from China in the 6th century and became intertwined with the earlier religion. Culture flourished during the Heian period (794 to 1185). The capital was moved from Nara to Kyoto, where the Emperor reigned. However, a powerful shogun, Minamoto Yoritomo, moved his center to Kamakura. A later shogun, Tokugawa Ieyasu, made his capital in Edo (now Tokyo) although the Emperor retained his court in Kyoto.

Portuguese missionaries brought the message of Christianity to Japan in the 16th century, and traders from Europe followed. All but a few Dutch traders were forced to leave Japan near the beginning of the 17th century, and the internally focused Japan developed a strong class-system society with the samurai at the top and merchants at the bottom. Commodore Perry opened Japan to trading with America in the 1850s, and other nations quickly followed during the reign of Emperor Meiji, a period when merchants gained considerable status. Meiji moved his capital to Tokyo and began Japanese aggression toward China and Russia. Emperor Hirohito continued expansionist efforts in Manchuria and China before his early conquests in the Pacific region and the attack on Pearl Harbor that directly brought the United States into World War II. Since the end of the war, Japan has rebuilt as an industrial nation.

Religion can be seen in Japan in the form of Shinto and Buddhist shrines, some Christian worshipers, and other sects. Art and traditions have evolved along the Shinto traditions with emphasis on nature, beauty, simplicity, cleanliness, and adherence to ritual. The tea ceremony, noh and kabuki performance, bunraku, and sumo wrestling all reveal overtones of traditions. These qualities are evidenced in the musical performances on unique Japanese instruments and also in the dances performed by geishas. Wood block prints, artfully painted scrolls, graceful calligraphy, origami, and artistically crafted ceramics are prized aspects of Japanese art.

Beauty is also emphasized in the simple, elegant styling used in presenting foods in restaurants and homes. The cereal featured in the diet is rice in many different forms and types; sushi (vinegared rice), steamed rice alone or as part of a variety of dishes, mochi (pounded rice featured as a cake at New Year's), rice vinegar, mirin (sweet rice wine), and sake (strong rice wine) are familiar in Japanese diets. Soybeans also are seen in many different forms: soy sauce, miso (fermented soy bean paste), okara (powdered byproduct of tofu), and tofu. Fish, whether raw (sashimi), batter-dipped and fried (tempura), or dried (bonito in dashi), are very prominent because of their variety and availability from the seas surrounding the islands. Seaweeds are also popular. Clear soups (suimono) and miso soups are found as part of most meals. Noodles from buckwheat flour (soba) and from wheat flour (udon) are eaten frequently, often with broth and other ingredients as accompaniments. Pickled vegetables, such as gobo and daikon, are frequent small dishes in a meal. Sukiyaki and yakitori are dishes featuring beef or chicken. Typically, these meals are served in many small dishes with sauces or accents such as wasabi. Chopsticks are used for cooking, serving, and eating solid food items, which probably explains the Japanese practice of preparing meats and vegetables in small pieces.

Study Questions

1. Trace the interactions between Japan and other nations during the last 200 years.
2. Describe at least four traditions or art forms that are unique to Japan.
3. Define each of the following: (a) mochi, (b) mirin, (c) miso, (d) soy sauce, (e) tempura, and (f) dashi.
4. Explain why the sea is such a significant source of food for the Japanese, and identify some specific foods from the sea that are often eaten in Japan.
5. Identify and describe two types of Japanese noodles.

Bibliography

Adler, S., and S. Wolf. 2000. *Fodor's Japan.* 15th ed. Fodor's Travel Publications. New York.

Barer-Stein, T. 1999. *You Eat What You Are.* 2nd ed. Firefly Books, Ltd. Ontario, Canada.

Bosrock, M. M. 1997. *Put Your Best Foot Forward: Asia.* International Education Systems. St. Paul, MN.

Busch, N. F. 1972. *Horizon Concise History of Japan.* American Heritage Publishing. New York.

Golden, A. 1997. *Memoirs of a Geisha.* Vintage Books. New York.

Hinnells, J. R., ed. 1997. *A New Handbook of Living Religions.* Penguin. London.

Kinoshita, J., and N. Palevsky. 1990. *Gateway to Japan.* Kodansha International. Tokyo.

Kramer, M. 1988. *Illustrated Guide to Foreign and Fancy Food.* 2nd ed. Plycon Press. Redondo Beach, CA.

Pearcy, G. E. 1980. *The World Food Scene.* Plycon Press. Redondo Beach, CA.

Seidensticker, E. 1965. *Japan.* Time, Inc. New York.

Steinberg, R. 1969. *Cooking of Japan.* Time-Life Books. New York.

Tsuji, S. 1980. *Japanese Cooking: A Simple Art.* Kodansha International. Tokyo.

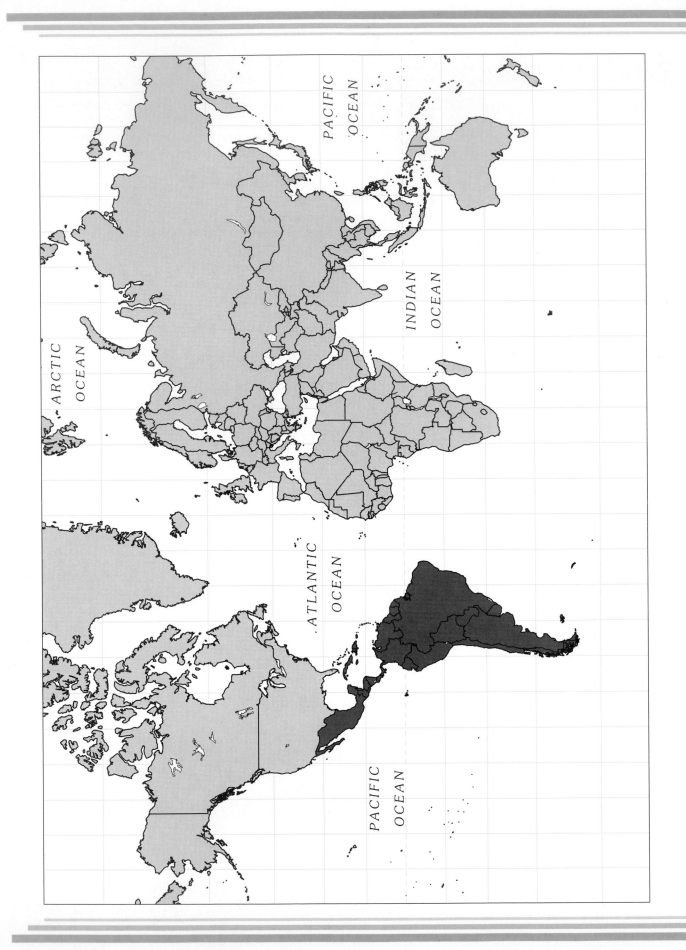

Part VI

Latin American Flavors

20 South America

Geographic Overview

South America is a continent with geographic features that include a very extended north–south range of mountains, the towering and rugged Andes. The rainforest of the Amazon River in the equatorial belt in the northeastern part of the continent is recognized as an invaluable resource for the world, one which must be protected in the fight against global warming. Surprisingly, the driest desert in the world lies less than 400 miles to the west.

The very heavy rainfall associated with rainforests makes agricultural development difficult in a large area of the Amazon basin. From an environmental perspective, allowing the forests to continue relatively undisturbed probably is by far the best use of the land. South America fortunately has much land that is well suited to raising livestock and crops. However, there are many arid regions in the interior of Argentina, Paraguay, and Bolivia where agriculture is barely possible.

Parts of Brazil and Argentina are well suited to agriculture of various types. The Argentine *gauchos* and their herds of cattle in the Pampas developed as a result of the European colonization of the region. The Incas and other Indians native to the continent were already growing potatoes, corn, and other crops on their high plateaus and in the valleys where they lived before the European conquests, and this land is still suited for farming today (Figure 20.1).

The northern part of South America actually lies north of the equator, and the equatorial heat plays a significant role in shaping the lifestyles and health of people throughout the region. Colombia lies adjacent to Panama and has coastline on both the Pacific and the Caribbean. Venezuela and its eastern neighbors of Guyana, Suriname, and French Guiana are arranged along the northeastern

Figure 20.1 Llamas are a source of wool as well as a beast of burden in the mountains of Peru.

shoulder of the continent facing the Atlantic. The highlands created by the northern end of the Andes in Colombia, Venezuela, and Ecuador provide a somewhat temperate relief from the tropical heat along the Caribbean and Pacific shores of these countries and also serve as the source of such important crops as potatoes, beans, sweet potatoes, manioc, cacao, peanuts, and pineapple. The benefits of living in higher elevations in the Andes were recognized by the Incans, who developed their many centers along the Andes on southward to Peru.

The countries of Peru and Chile hug the western side of the Andes, reaching to the Pacific. This results in two very long and narrow countries that together stretch approximately two-thirds the length of the 7,000-mile long Andes Mountains. The very southerly location of Cape Horn and the southern port at Punta Arenas are famous for their cold and blustery weather conditions, a sharp contrast to the tropical challenges on the northern end of the continent. Santiago and Valparaiso, Chile's major cities, are located about midway from north to south and are in the region that is well suited to farming. The fact that the seasons are reversed in South America from those in North America has resulted in active international trading in fresh produce, notably fruits and flowers, to augment American diets during the winter.

Chile's back-to-back neighbor is Argentina, which extends from the eastern side of the Andes peaks to the Atlantic Ocean until it forms a border with Bolivia on its northwest corner, Paraguay in the center, and Brazil and Uruguay for a distance along the northeastern edge. The Atlantic Ocean borders Argentina from Buenos Aires (Figure 20.2) all the way south to the tip of the continent. Only Bo-

Figure 20.2 The architecture of Buenos Aires clearly shows the effect of its European settlers.

Chickens sometimes are included on menus in West Africa.

A Masai man herds his cattle in the countryside outside Nairobi, Kenya.

Corn is grown by people in this village in Botswana.

A beautiful Muslim woman rests in a stall along a street in Djibouti, Djibouti in eastern Africa.

A safari jeep driver and his family sit outside their home in Botswana.

A cheetah patrols the Serengeti Plain with Mt. Kilimanjaro looming in the background.

This outdoor market near Nairobi, Kenya, teems with shoppers and farmers.

Women in a small Zimbabwe village weave baskets to sell when they are not farming.

Women and children eat within or near the huts where they live in villages in central Africa.

Paratha, used as a wrap for various fillings, highlights this vendor's wares in New Delhi, India.

Untouchables being fed at a Hindu temple in India.

Buddhist monks of the Yellow Hat Sect sound their horns in front of their temple in Darjeeling, India.

Darjeerling in the Himalayan foothills in northern India is the place where some of the world's finest teas are grown.

The peaceful gardens of Shalimar in Kashmir belie the intensity of border clashes between Pakistan and India in the disputed northern part of India.

Intricate windows in this palace in Jaipur, India, allowed women in the harem to look out on the street scene without being observed by others; in the distance the Amber Fort afforded protection to the people living in this part of Rajasthan (northwestern India).

Cremation pyres outside a Hindu temple in Katmandu, Nepal.

Boudanath, the largest Buddhist stupa in Nepal, casts watchful eyes in four directions in the Katmandu Valley.

Durbar Squares in Patan and Bhaktapur near Katmandu, Nepal preserve the cultural heritage of the Katmandu Valley.

Legumes of many types, essentials in the cuisine of Nepal and India, are marketed in open stalls, such as this one in Katmandu.

Tiger's Nest, a Buddhist monastery, was built clinging precariously to the steep mountainside and is accessible only by trail in Bhutan.

Large prayer wheels outside a small temple in Lhasa, Tibet, are turned when anyone passes by, while the tiny prayer flags high above flap in the wind constantly to send messages to heaven.

The Potala, seat of Tibetan Buddhism, looms impressively above Lhasa, Tibet despite the absence of the Dalai Lama who now lives in exile in India.

Tibetan monks perform their ritual chants for endless hours in Buddhist temples in which incense and yak butter candles add to the holy atmosphere. (Photo courtesy of Eileen Welsh)

The warm color of the walls adds a welcoming note to Norbulingka, the former summer home of the Dalai Lama in Lhasa, Tibet.

Shaggy yaks are used to plow fields on the Tibetan plateau. (Photo courtesy of Eileen Welsh)

The outdoor market in Yangon, Myanmar presents a tempting array of fresh produce amidst many friendly vendors.

Two young brothers at the Shwedagon Pagoda in Yangon seriously undertake their decision to be Buddhist monks (at least for a few days).

Two young Burmese boys chase after their goats in the midst of beautiful ruins of Buddhist temples near Pagan, Myanmar.

Two Burmese men pole along the shallow Irrawaddy River in Myanmar.

Trees bloom in the spring to brighten the remains of Sukhothai, the first capital of Thailand.

This wonderfully fearsome statue stands guard on the grounds of the Grand Palace in Bangkok, Thailand.

A festive dinner is hosted in the home of a prominent Bangkok physician.

Pagoda and temples with intricate designs on their walls are the site of worship for Buddhists in Luang Prabang, the old capital in northern Laos.

A worker makes rice wine at this still near Luang Prabang in northern Laos.

This young Laotian women is weaving in a textile workshop near Luang Prabang. © Owen Franklin / CORBIS

Surprisingly, the center tower of Angkor Wat is still splendid despite the ravages of the extremely wet climate for almost 1000 years and occupation by the militant Khmer Rouge for several years.

A Buddhist monk, one of many people who carry physical evidence of the atrocities of the Pol Pot years, serves as caretaker of his favorite Cambodian temple, Ta Prohm, which is being engulfed by the jungle near Angkor Wat.

Who could resist buying freshly barbecued kabobs from this smiling Cambodian vendor?

Children learn farm work at an early age in Cambodia; this boy is driving a pair of oxen in preparation for planting the next crop while rice matures on the family's land near Siem Reap, Cambodia.

Islam is the dominant religion in Malaysia and most of Indonesia. This modern mosque is in Kuala Lumpur, Malaysia.

Girls and women don fanciful costumes and masks in preparation for a dance performance in Siem Reap, Cambodia.

Colorful costumes and frightening masks are important to native dances performed on Bali in Indonesia.

Terraces such as these were built to grow rice on Bali centuries ago, and are still maintained and productive today.

Unlike the rest of Indonesia, which is Muslim, Bali has many Hindus, as can be noted in this festival parade.

Unique musical instruments, such as the gamelan are used to accompany dancers in Indonesia and other countries in Southeast Asia.

Rambutan (left of the apples) and passion fruit (lower right below the watermelon) are two tropical fruits used widely in menus in Southeast Asia.

Various edible green leaves are used to wrap small food packets in Cambodia.

Thai cookery springs to life in the mouth when various hot chilies are used generously.

livia and Paraguay lack a seacoast on the South American continent. Brazil comprises much of the very large area bulging eastward from the Andes to the Atlantic. Both Argentina and Brazil have land well suited to raising wheat and livestock. Argentina in particular is noted for its beef production, much of which is exported. Brazil grows sugarcane in considerable quantities and (along with Colombia) is an important source of the world's favored coffees, which are grown at intermediate elevations in the mountains. Cacao is another export crop from Brazil.

History and Culture

Machu Picchu, also dubbed the "lost city of the Incas," sits atop a mountain in Peru overlooking a tropical river flowing far below. Flanked by neighboring mountains, yet with a moderate climate, this city was the dramatic home of a large number of Incas when the Spaniards arrived in South America. After the Spanish conquest, this city faded into oblivion until it was discovered early in the 20th century and gradually opened as an important archeological site for tourists to visit.

Prior to the arrival of the early Spaniards, the dominant culture in South America was that of the Incas, which dated from about 1100 CE. Cuzco, located in a valley of the Andes at an elevation of 11,000 feet, was the center of the Inca civilization. They were a family-centered society in which animals (llamas and alpacas) were herded for their wool, thus providing clothing in addition to meat. Crops also were produced. Their religion was based on the Sun, and temples were built to the Sun and decorated with gold and silver as well as precious stones. The most important temple dedicated to the Sun was in Cuzco. Tragically, the decorations were destroyed by the conquering Spaniards, who melted down the gold and silver into bars to ship back to Spain. The Incas were noted for their roads and bridges that ran the length and width of their very large domain, providing effective links between even the outlying areas. The major sites included Ollantaytambo, Sacsahuaman, Pisac, and Machu Picchu, which would have served as forts to protect Cuzco from invaders.

Pizarro was the Spanish conquistador who led the expeditions southward from Panama beginning in 1524, after he had crossed Panama with Balboa. The conquest of the Incas was accomplished by a combination of bravery and fortitude in an arduous march to Atahualpo, chief of the Incas, and trickery that resulted in his capture. Spaniards began to occupy Peru, not only in the mountains at Cuzco, but also on the coast at Lima. Eventually, Pizarro was killed by some of his own men, but Spanish control of Peru continued for 300 years, marked by some of the horrors of the Inquisition and a Catholic legacy from the priests who continued to pursue their mission of saving souls in this foreign land.

Valdivia, a captain under Pizarro, was the Spaniard who led the efforts to expand into and take over Chile after Peru had been secured. Unfortunately for Spain, Chile proved to be more of an expense than an asset, for the costs to the Spanish crown greatly exceeded any profits from goods shipped from Chile. The region was not only geographically inhospitable, but it also was not rich in minerals. Interestingly, French ships traded in Chilean ports in the early 18th century and brought a distinctly French influence to Santiago and other Chilean towns despite the great distance from France.

Quesada was the Spanish conquistador who led his men into the rugged terrain of Colombia, finally reaching the highlands and making contact with the natives of this region. He fought two other groups of Spaniards while attempting to establish control of the region, but his overall results were minimal.

Farther to the south, Buenos Aires actually was founded twice on the banks of the Plate River somewhat inland from the Atlantic. The first settlers migrated farther into the continent in search of a more favorable location and successfully established Asunción in what is now Paraguay. Finally, a successful settlement was established in Buenos Aires in 1580. The Spanish intermingled freely with the native women wherever they went in South America, resulting in a constantly growing *mestizo* population. This hardy population accounted for much of the population growth during the 300 years of Spanish colonialism and was particu-

larly important in the early years. This accepted social pattern helped to reduce interracial tensions, an attitude that persists even now.

Cabral, a Portuguese captain, landed his ships in Brazil in 1500 and promptly claimed this big bulge of the continent for Portugal. Efforts to colonize were slow at first, but sugarcane was successfully introduced at Pernambuco in the north, and a few other settlements ranging to Sao Paulo in the south were able to grow; de Sousa was appointed governor-general of Brazil in 1549 by the King of Portugal, thus solidifying Portugal's domain amidst the Spanish claims. The Portuguese men also mingled with the natives of their region, which added significantly to the population of the settlements.

After 300 years of colonialism, South Americans evolved into revolutionaries. Simon Bolivar was the successful liberator of Venezuela and Colombia following several years of fighting and frustration. Considerable assistance from England and some help from the United States under President Monroe helped to eliminate Spanish shipping to South America and aided the revolutionaries. Unfortunately, the Spanish had carefully maintained a completely dominant governing role and had limited education for the colonial populations, which left South America ill-prepared for self-government.

In the other South American countries, others led similar efforts for liberation from European conquerors (Figure 20.3). Mariano Moreno was the architect of Argentina's May Revolution in Buenos Aires in 1810 and inspired the revolutionists in that country until his death. Actual liberation from Spain occurred in 1816. San Martin played a very prominent role in the liberation of Chile and then Peru while Bolivar was fighting in the northern part of the continent. Eventually, it was Bolivar who was in charge of the fight against the Spanish in Peru. At different times during the 19th century, the countries of South America finally threw off their bonds of colonialism. However, considerable internal political and military arguments persisted, leaving the vast majority of people living in a state of poverty and with very limited hope of a better life. The sharp economic division between the very wealthy upper class and the poor lower class remains even today.

Religion is largely Roman Catholic throughout South America (Figure 20.4), the result of the centuries of dominance by the various Catholic orders from the time of their arrival with the first conquistador. Although the Jesuits, Dominicans, and Franciscans established their missions independently in scattered parts of the continent, they all brought the message of the importance of believing in their God and worshiping in the churches they required their indigenous converts to build. The importance of a large place of worship with impressive gold and silver

Figure 20.3 Public buildings in Lima, Peru, feature architectural touches from Europe.

Figure 20.4   The statue of Christ the Redeemer on Corcovado, in Rio, is an amazing size—130 feet tall.

adornments was a clear priority, and the Catholic Church today still controls an amazing amount of wealth in South America despite the poverty level in which many of its believers still live. Although painting and other forms of art have developed rather minimally in South America, it is the Catholic Church that has served as the primary sponsor.

Music has been popular for centuries among the indigenous people of South America. The early instruments that they played included drums, rattles, and even crude trumpets made from shells, bone, or clay. Gourds were crafted for rhythmic sounds, and whistles were also carved. Such music still contributes to the culture today (Figure 20.5). In contrast to this type of native music, the music in the churches is basically European, reflecting the very strong influence of the Catholic missionaries.

Various folk dances occasionally can be seen. Perhaps the most familiar dance contributed by South America is the tango. This seductive dance has gained attention worldwide. Also, the exciting rhythms of South American music for dancing have made their way into contemporary music in other lands.

Not surprisingly, the culture of South America is varied, the result of (1) the influx of Europeans and their culture being superimposed on the original peoples of the regions, (2) the importing of slaves from Africa (notably in Brazil), and (3) the geographic barriers separating countries. Certainly, it is not surprising that the various parts of South America have much that is unique in each country and

Figure 20.5 Folk music is popular in Argentina and throughout South America

sometimes only limited commonalities. Perhaps the most significant common factors are the dominance of the Catholic Church and the predominantly mestizo population, the result of extensive intermingling between peninsular men (from Spain and Portugal) with native women.

Food Patterns

Food patterns in South America vary a bit by country, but they all embrace some foods developed by the indigenous population and others from the European and African immigrants. Such staples as manioc, corn, potatoes, tomatoes, chilies, bananas, pumpkin, squash, and beans were well established before the Spanish arrived. Game occasionally was added to the meals of the Indians. The pigs, cattle, sheep, and poultry brought by the Spanish thrived and became a significant part of the diet (meat, milk, and cheese) in the temperate parts of South America where they were introduced and raised. Plant crops brought by the Spaniards included garlic, onions, coffee, sugarcane, wheat, and rice.

In the northern countries of Colombia and Venezuela, corn is dried and used as flour to make a dough with some water and perhaps egg yolks. The dough may be flattened or shaped into balls, then baked or fried. Kernels of fresh corn sometimes are the key ingredient of fritters and pancakes. Banana leaves are used as the wrappers to encase a layer of corn flour dough with a filling of meat before steaming the packets, which are called *hallacas* (the South American version of a tamale).

Plantains are another popular tropical food. They are quite versatile and may be fried (sometimes twice, as is done when fried slices are pounded thin and refried to make crisp *tostones*), boiled, or grilled. *Yuca* (sweet cassava) is another starchy food that is used extensively in the lowland areas of the tropics. Coconut and its milk are also important foods.

In Bogotá (elevation about 8,500 feet), potatoes assume a significant role. Meats are also eaten more frequently if they can be afforded, but techniques such as stewing are essential to help tenderize them. Coffee is popular, particularly for breakfast, when it usually is served *con leche* (with warm milk). Breakfast typically is simply a bread and some coffee. The midday meal is more substantial and often followed by a siesta until the heat of the day has passed. South Americans follow the Spanish tradition of a late dinner (usually between 10:00 P.M. and midnight).

Brazil is particularly noted for its food, and much of the credit for its cuisine goes to the African slave women who cooked for the plantation owners in Bahia and the surrounding northeastern region. These women integrated their African food traditions with the local foods when they arrived in their new land. They used the roots of bitter cassava that the native Indians grated, squeezed, and cooked to yield manioc. They relied heavily on *dendé,* the oil from a West African palm tree with a yellow to reddish color, to fry their foods and add a distinctive hue and flavor to their dishes. Beans (usually black beans) and rice were other staples of their cuisine, often seasoned with an unusually hot chili pepper (*malagueta*) that is hotter than tabasco.

Stews containing meats, poultry, or seafood sometimes have coconut milk as a subtle flavoring. *Feijoada completa* is a favorite dish for a Saturday or other time when a long siesta is possible after the meal. This dish includes smoked and other meats, including sausage and bacon, the traditional beans, rice, hot sauces, manioc meal, and oranges. The beans effectively bind the fat from the sausage and bacon, which accounts for the urge to take a long siesta after feasting on feijoada.

Argentina's diet is focused on meat, which was the heritage from early gauchos. Grilled meats of various types are mixed to make *parrillada,* the Argentine favorite. Another favorite is *carbonada,* a stew of beef, rice, potatoes, corn, squash, sweet potatoes, and even apples. Empanadas, meat-stuffed fried or baked semi-circles of pastry, are popular. Italian immigrants added their touch to the food of Argentina with such universal dishes as spaghetti and lasagna. *Maté* is a beverage found in many South American countries, but Argentina claims it as its own. Part of the pleasure of the drink, which actually is a tea brewed from chopped yerba maté leaves, is the sociability of passing the gourd containing the maté so that each person can sip some through the straw. The straw in the elaborately decorated gourd is called a *bombilla* and is made of silver with an enlarged filter at its base to strain out the leaves.

Chilean sea bass is so treasured in the United States that it comes as no surprise that the Pacific waters off Chile are the source of many favorite foods of Chileans. This has been true since colonial times and perhaps before. *Sopa de pescado,* or fish soup, *curanto* (thick fish stew with meats and potato), *ceviche* (traditionally raw fish marinated for 1 to 4 hours in lime juice with onion until flesh becomes white and somewhat shrunken, but which is safe when heated and then chilled), and grilled or steamed fish are regular dishes at lunch or dinner.

Peruvians, Ecuadorians, and Bolivians in the higher valleys and plateaus of the Andes rely on potatoes as the staple in their diets. *Aji,* a very hot Andean chili, is used to spice potatoes and other dishes, particularly in Peru. A sauce seasoned with aji and containing water or milk and some cheese is very common in this region. Seafood is popular in Peru; in fact, ceviche may have originated there. Beef hearts in bite-sized pieces that are skewered and grilled are the traditional ingredient of *anticuchos,* although Peruvians often add other items, such as seafood. *Causa a la limeña* is an Indian-based dish of thick mashed potatoes, lemon juice, chopped onions, aji, and olive oil that may be served with hard-cooked eggs and shrimp. *Quinoa* is a grain that has been grown in the high valleys of the Andes since before the Spaniards arrived. Its seeds are a useful starch and protein source, although wheat is needed in addition if quinoa flour is to be used in making breads.

*K*ey *Terms*

Aji—Very hot Andean chili pepper; pronounced like the fish ahi: *ah-hee.*
Bolivar—Considered to be the liberator of South America from its European powers.

Bombilla—Fancy silver straw and filter used to sip maté from a gourd.

Cabral—Portuguese explorer who claimed Brazil for Portugal in 1500.

Café con leche—Coffee with warm milk, the style preferred in South America.

Carbonada—Argentinian beef stew with rice, corn, potatoes, squash, sweet potatoes, and apples.

Cuzco—Center of the Incan civilization in a very high (11,000 feet) Andean valley in Peru.

Ceviche—Raw fish marinated for 1 to 4 hours in lime juice and onion until flesh is opaque and the consistency of cooked fish; probably originated in Peru.

Dendé—Yellow to reddish oil from a West African palm, which was introduced into Brazilian cooking by women slaves.

Empanadas—Fried or baked semicircular pastries filled with meat and raisins; prominent in Argentina, but also in other South American countries.

Feijoada completa—Celebrated Brazilian dish of several meats (including sausages and bacon), beans, rice, hot sauces, manioc meal, and sliced oranges.

Hallacas—Colombian version of a tamale made by wrapping a layer of corn flour dough and a filling of meat or other ingredients in banana leaves and then steaming the packets.

Malagueta—Extremely hot South American pepper, also called aji.

Manioc—Granular flour prepared by peeling and then grating bitter cassava roots and squeezing out absolutely all of the juice, which is poisonous until subsequently boiled. The dry grated material is broken to a powder by pounding.

Maté—Beverage brewed in a gourd by pouring hot water over crushed leaves of yerba maté, producing a caffeine-containing beverage that is sipped through a bombilla; pronounced *ma-tay*.

Mestizo—Person of European mixed with Indian heritage.

Parrillada—Grilled mixture of meats, typical of Argentina.

Pizarro—Spanish conquistador who conquered the Incas and established Spanish dominance in Peru.

Quesada—Spanish conquisador credited with conquering Columbia.

Quinoa—Grain grown in the high Andes by Indians and eaten as a rich source of protein and starch in Peru and Chile; pronounced *keen-wah*.

Tostones—Twice-fried slices of plantain that are pounded thin before the second frying.

Valdivia—Captain under Pizarro who led the Spanish expansion to Chile from Peru.

Yuca—Sweet cassava; root used as a starch in the tropical regions.

ecipes

Arroz a la Peru (Serves 4–6)

1/2 lb veal, thinly sliced	1/2 c water
1/2 lb pork, thinly sliced	3/4 c rice
2 tbsp flour	1/2 clove garlic, minced
1/2 tsp salt	1/2 onion, chopped
1/2 tsp pepper	1/2 green pepper, chopped
2 tbsp oil	1/2 red pepper, chopped
1/4 c sherry	1 tbsp butter

1 hard-cooked egg, chopped
1 tbsp slivered almonds
1 tbsp raisins
1 1/2 tsp cornstarch in 2 tbsp water
1 tbsp chopped parsley

1. Dredge meats in mixture of flour, salt, and pepper, then brown in hot oil.
2. Add sherry and simmer for 5 minutes; add water and simmer until tender.
3. Meanwhile, boil rice according to package directions.
4. Saute garlic, onion, and peppers in butter in a skillet just until tender.
5. Combine sautéed mixture with the rice, egg, nuts, and raisins, and keep warm.
6. Add cornstarch paste to the meat pan and heat to boiling while stirring until thickened.
7. Serve rice mixture topped with the sauce and garnished with parsley.

Carbonada Argentina (Serves 6–8)

1 1/2 tsp crushed garlic
3/4 c chopped onion
1 tbsp oil
1 lb beef loin, cut into 1" cubes
1/2 c chopped green pepper
2 medium tomatoes, chopped
3/4 tsp salt
1/2 tsp cracked pepper
2 c beef broth
1/4 c sherry
4 dried peach halves, chopped
2 sweet potatoes, diced
2 potatoes, diced

1 c sweet corn kernels
1 medium pumpkin

1. Saute garlic and onion in oil for 2 minutes, then add beef, pepper, tomatoes, and seasoning.
2. Simmer, covered, for 20 minutes.
3. Add broth, sherry, peaches, sweet potatoes, potatoes, and corn; simmer for 45 minutes.
4. Meanwhile, cut a lid from the pumpkin and scrape out all seeds; butter and salt the interior.
5. Pour stew into pumpkin, top with lid, and bake in a shallow pan at 325°F for 30 minutes or until pumpkin is tender. Serve in pumpkin tureen.

Chicken Pie Venezuela (Serves 6–8)

1/2 c flour
2 c chicken broth
2 c canned tomatoes
3 c cubed, cooked chicken
3/4 c chopped onions
2 tsp diced pimiento
1/2 c sliced black olives
2 tbsp capers
2 c flour
1 tsp salt
2/3 c shortening
1/3 c water

1. Make slurry of flour and broth, stir in tomatoes, and heat to boiling, stirring constantly.
2. Add chicken, onions, pimiento, olives, and capers, and heat to boiling. Let stand without heat while making crust.
3. Cut shortening into flour and salt until particles are size of rice grains.
4. Toss flour with fork while adding water dropwise all around the bowl.
5. Press mixture with hands to form a ball firm enough to be divided in half and then rolled.
6. Roll both crusts into circles and fit one into a pie plate.
7. With slotted spoon, transfer filling into the bottom crust and pour in desired amount of sauce; add the top crust and pinch it closed all around the edge. Cut a 3" slit in center of top crust.
8. Bake for 10 minutes in 425°F oven and then reduce heat to 325°F and bake until top is golden and filling is bubbling.

Beef Empañadas (Serves 4–6)

1/2 tsp crushed garlic
1/4 c chopped onion
1/4 c red peppers, diced
1/4 c green peppers, diced
1 tbsp oil
1/2 lb sirloin, finely chopped
1/2 c beef bouillon
1/4 c raisins
1/2 tsp salt
1/2 tsp pepper
1/2 tsp chili powder
2 c flour
1 tsp salt
2/3 c shortening
1/3 c water

1. Saute garlic, onion, and peppers in oil, then sauté the meat; add bouillon, raisins, and seasonings, and simmer until meat is done, vegetables are soft, and the liquid is almost gone.
2. Cut shortening into flour and salt until particles are like rice grains.
3. Toss flour with fork while adding water dropwise all around the bowl.
4. Press mixture with hands to form 2 balls.
5. Roll each ball 1/8" thick; cut into circles 4" in diameter.
6. Place 1 tablespoonful of filling on the center of each circle. Moisten edge of circle with water, then fold over and press edges together to make a semi-circle with the filling sealed inside.
7. Bake in 400°F oven on baking sheet until browned (7 minutes), or fry in deep fat at 375°F.

Fruity Chopped Meat (Serves 4)

1 lb ground or chopped sirloin
1 tbsp olive oil
1/2 tsp salt
1/2 tsp black pepper
1 c minced onion
1 tsp crushed red chili peppers
1/2 tsp oregano
1/3 c orange juice
1 tsp orange zest

1/2 c raisins
1/2 c chili sauce

1. Saute meat in oil, salt, and pepper, stirring to break up the meat into small pieces.
2. Add remaining ingredients and simmer, covered, for 30 minutes, adding liquid if necessary to keep from sticking.

Peruvian Sopa (Serves 4–6)

6 c water
1/2 lb beef bones with much meat
1/2 c chopped onion
2 carrots, sliced thinly
1 1/2 c stewed tomatoes
2 tbsp chopped parsley
12 oz frozen lima beans
1 tsp salt
1/4 tsp pepper

1/3 c cornstarch stirred into 1/3 c milk

1. In water to cover, simmer beef, onion, carrot, tomatoes, and parsley for 2 hours.
2. Remove meat, debone, and return to pot.
3. Add lima beans, salt, and pepper, and simmer for 20 minutes.
4. Stir cornstarch slurry into soup and stir while heating for 10 minutes to thicken and blend.

Roasted Chicken with Chestnuts (Serves 4–6)

1 roasting chicken
1 c Chablis
3 tbsp lemon juice
1 tsp crushed garlic
2 tsp chopped chives
2 tsp minced parsley
1/4 tsp pepper
1/4 tsp nutmeg
1 c pureed chestnuts
4 slices bacon

1. Marinate chicken in marinade of wine, lemon juice, garlic, chives, and parsley in refrigerator for 1 day.
2. Remove chicken from marinade and stuff with well-blended mixture of seasonings and chestnuts. Place on rack in shallow pan and arrange bacon over it.
3. Roast until breast registers 170°F.

Ceviche (Serves 6)

1 1/2 lb bass or other firm, delicately flavored fish
3/4 c lime juice
3/4 c lemon juice
1 1/2 red onions, thinly sliced in rings
1 red chili pepper, minced
1/2 green pepper, chopped
1 red sweet pepper, chopped
1/4 tsp crushed garlic
1/2 c cooked corn kernels
1/2 green pepper, chopped

1. Arrange fish in single layer on a platter.
2. Prepare marinade of juices, onion, peppers, and garlic.
3. Pour marinade over fish, adding more juice if needed to cover all fillets.
4. Chill in refrigerator for at least 3 hours (fish will be opaque). Serve with garnish of cooked corn kernels and green pepper.

Sopaipillas a la Chile (Serves 4–6)

1 lb winter squash
1 stick cinnamon
1 c water
5 c flour
1 tsp salt
1 tbsp oil
Boiling water to moisten dough
Oil for deep-fat frying
1 1/2 c brown sugar
3/4 c water
1 tsp orange zest
1 stick cinnamon
1/4 tsp ground cloves

1. Boil squash in cinnamon water until tender. Drain and remove cinnamon; peel and mash the squash.
2. Stir in flour and salt, and then add oil with kneading action to work mixture into a dough, adding a little boiling water while kneading. Add just enough water to make dough that does not stick to board.
3. While kneading dough, heat oil in deep-fat fryer to 375°F.
4. Roll dough into 2" balls and fry three at a time for 3 minutes to golden brown. Drain on paper towels and keep warm in oven while frying rest of fritters and making syrup for dipping.
5. Boil remaining ingredients for about 4 minutes to make syrup. Dip fritters in hot syrup to serve.

Squash and Cheese (Serves 4)

1 lb winter squash, peeled, seeded, and sliced 1/2 tsp salt Water to cover 3/4 c cornmeal 1 tbsp sugar 1 tbsp butter 1/4 lb grated cheddar cheese	1. Boil squash in salted water until tender, then drain and mash. 2. Stir in cornmeal, sugar, and butter. 3. Stir while heating for 5 minutes over direct heat. 4. Place covered pan over simmering water and heat for 30 minutes. 5. Stir in cheese and continue heating just enough to melt cheese. Serve with a fish entrée.

Beef Pie (Serves 4–6)

3/4 lb round steak, chopped 1/2 c chopped onion 1 tbsp oil 3/4 c raisins 2 hard-cooked eggs, chopped 1/2 tsp salt 2/3 c grated cheddar cheese 1 1/2 c mashed potatoes 1/4 c buttered dried breadcrumbs	1. Brown meat and onions in oil. 2. Add raisins, eggs, salt, and half of the cheese; mix with beef, then transfer to casserole dish. 3. Top with mashed potatoes; garnish with remaining cheese and breadcrumbs. 4. Bake in 350°F oven until heated through and pleasingly browned (about 15 minutes).

Tomato Rice (Serves 4)

1/2 c chopped onion 1 1/2 tbsp oil 1 c long grain rice 2 c chicken bouillon 1 tomato, chopped 1/4 tsp salt	1. Saute onion in oil for 2 minutes; stir in the rice to coat it with oil. 2. Add other ingredients and simmer for 20 minutes until all liquid is absorbed.

Summary

The lands of South America embrace sharp geographic contrasts, from the towering Andes to the Amazon River with its vast rainforests and to extremely arid deserts. This range of conditions explains the types of foods that were native to South America (potatoes, tomatoes, cacao, sweet potatoes, and peanuts, for example). These unique crops were transported to Europe by early explorers, and other crops from Europe were introduced to South America, where they became important crops (wheat, cattle, and sugarcane).

Spain established a colonial empire in much of South America, beginning with Pizarro's conquest of the Incas and Peru. Valdivia was the Spanish captain who led the conquest of Chile. Quesada was credited with conquering Colombia, and the Spanish also settled and claimed Argentina. Cabral, the Portuguese captain, was responsible for Brazil becoming a Portuguese possession. Some other European presence, notably Dutch, German, Italian, and some French, also influenced the course of South America for 200 years. Bolivar spearheaded the 19th century liberation of the northern part of South America. San Martin and Moreno were important revolutionary figures to the south. Liberation was achieved in the 19th century, but stable governments have been difficult to establish.

The Catholic Church has played a very significant role in South America since the early days of the Spanish conquest. Priests came to establish missions and convert the Indians, a legacy that has continued to this day. Much of the population of South America is Catholic, and the arts have been fostered by the Church, as evidenced by the elaborate gold decorations and paintings in the churches.

Music in South America represents a blend of the Indian and European heritage and intermixing of these populations, plus the Negro heritage resulting from the slave trade during the colonial period, particularly in Brazil. Exciting rhythms and folk melodies are often performed with the help of drums, various rattles and percussive instruments, trumpets, and guitars. The tango is the most familiar of the dances that originated in South America.

Popular South American foods rely heavily on the use of corn, rice, potatoes, beans, pumpkins, squash, manioc, sweet potatoes, beef, pork, poultry, wheat, chilies, tomatoes, fish (in regions near the sea), and fruits ranging from tropical to apples and peaches of temperate climates. Much of the population has a rather limited diet because of lack of money, while some people are very rich and can afford to eat well. Breakfast usually is quite simple, the noon meal heavy, and the evening meal eaten very late (often 10:00 P.M. or later). Coffee is very popular as a beverage. Brazil's classic dish is feijoada completa, Argentina's is mixed grill, Chile's is seafood, and Peru may have created ceviche.

Study Questions

1. Identify where each of the following is located and describe the geographic factors influencing the foods available in each: (a) Colombia, (b) Chile, (c) Paraguay, (d) Bolivia, (e) Argentina, (f) Brazil, and (g) Venezuela.
2. Select one of the early conquerors or explorers of South America and find additional information about that person. How would you describe this individual and the influence he exerted on the region he conquered or explored?
3. What are four cereal grains that are grown in South America? Describe how each is prepared in South American kitchens.
4. Define (a) empanada, (b) manioc, (c) aji, (d) dendé, (e) maté, (f) mestizo, (g) quinoa, and (h) hallacas.
5. Name at least five fruits commonly used in South American meals.
6. Would the Incas have been eating pork prior to the Spanish conquest? Explain your answer.

Bibliography

Barer-Stein, T. 1999. *You Eat What You Are.* 2nd ed. Firefly Books, Ltd. Ontario, Canada.
Bernhardson, W. 1999. *Argentina, Uruguay, and Paraguay.* 3rd ed. Lonely Planet. Oakland, CA.
Bernhardson, W. 1997. *Chile and Easter Island.* 4th ed. Lonely Planet. Oakland, CA.
Crow, J. A. 1971. *The Epic of Latin America.* Rev. ed. Doubleday. Garden City, NY.
Leonard, J. N. 1968. *Latin American Cooking.* Time-Life Books. New York.
Pearcy, G. E. 1980. *The World Food Scene.* Plycon Press. Redondo Beach, CA.
Winn, P. 1999. *Americas.* Updated ed. University of California Press. Berkeley, CA.

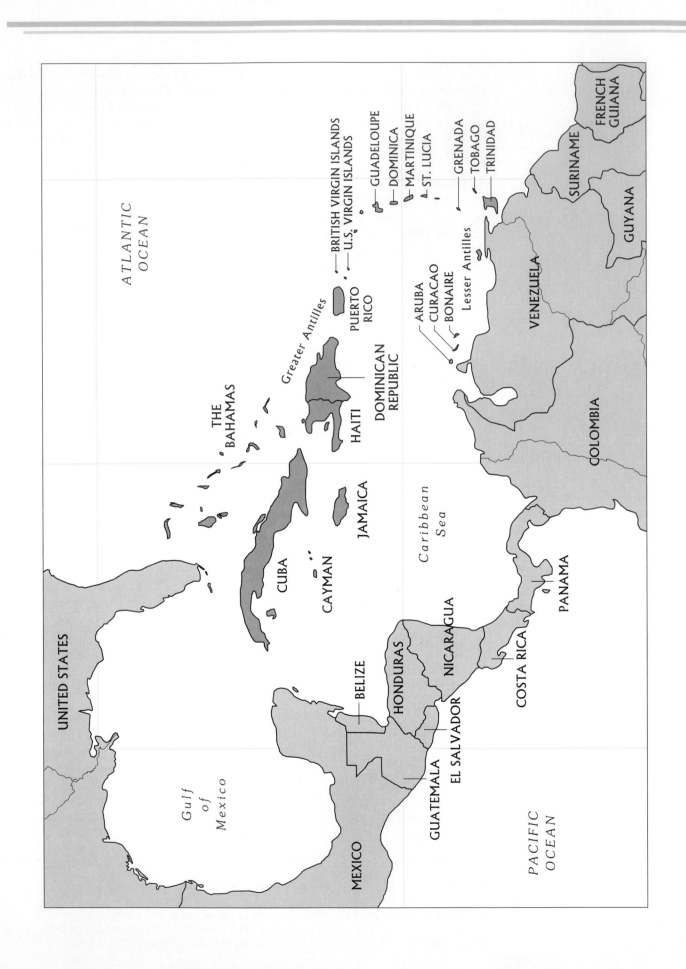

21 The Caribbean

Geographic Overview

The Caribbean Sea, with its lengthy crescent of islands arcing from just 90 miles south of the tip of Florida to within sight of the northern coast of South America, greeted Columbus in 1492 and excited him with its beauty and bounty. The island of Hispaniola (now divided into Haiti on its western end and the Dominican Republic) served as the staging grounds for him and other Europeans who followed. The total land mass of the many islands comprising this archipelago (collectively referred to as the West Indies) is only slightly larger than Oregon, but it is broken into around 7,000 islands. Cuba (the largest and closest to Florida), Jamaica just south of Cuba, Hispaniola, and Puerto Rico stretch eastward in a somewhat linear grouping called the Greater Antilles. The remainder of the islands in the crescent extend in an arc southward from a bit east of Puerto Rico on southwest to Grenada and Trinidad and Tobago.

The many islands and various governments can seem rather confusing. Just east of Puerto Rico are the Virgin Islands. Then, the island chain bends a bit toward the southeast in a grouping sometimes termed the Leeward Islands (including St. Kitts and Nevis). Continuing south and angling a bit westward, this chain of islands is called the Windward Islands (Figure 21.1). Finally, the islands near Grenada are called the Grenadines. Collectively, these and more comprise the lovely world of the Caribbean.

All of this region is situated in the tropical zone, enabling crops suited to warm and humid climes to flourish much of the time. However, the islands face the natural hazards of volcanic eruptions, earthquakes, and hurricanes, all of which can wreak periodic havoc in a seeming paradise. The rugged Atlantic

Figure 21.1 St. Lucia is a volcanic island in the Windward Islands of the Caribbean.

Ocean washes the eastern shores, and the Caribbean is the somewhat more tranquil sea to the west.

The crops that thrive in much of the region include sugarcane, bananas, coconuts, pineapples, citrus, and peppers. Rice, breadfruit, cacao, mangoes, coffee, and various spices also proved to adapt well to the islands when they were introduced by people from Europe and Asia. In short, plant foods of great variety generally were available to the early colonists and continue to be adequate for local use and even for export today.

History and Culture

Prior to the arrival of Columbus, the Caribbean was populated by different Indian groups. Originally, the Arawaks inhabited many of the islands and lived usually in peace. They were gentle and helpful when Columbus first arrived on Hispaniola, and this attitude tended to be the norm in the northern part of the Caribbean. Apparently, the Arawaks had been pushed gradually northward from the southern end of the Caribbean in earlier centuries as the Caribs pursued their warring ways northward from the South American mainland. The Caribs, who may have been cannibals a long time ago, were able to claim any of the Arawak islands that they coveted. It was the Caribs who presented the most warlike challenge to the various European expeditions seeking to establish their dominance over the Indians who were indigenous to the Caribbean. The combination of the superior weaponry of the Europeans and the new health risks they brought to the Indians resulted in almost complete destruction of the Indian population. Only a very few Indians can be found today. Some descendants of the Indians have mixed blood, the contribution of their conquerors half a millennium ago. These people are the mestizos.

The arrival of Columbus in 1492 altered life in the Caribbean forever. His report upon returning to Spain quickly led to return visits by Columbus and other European explorers. Christopher Columbus's brother Bartolemé established Santo Domingo in 1496 on Hispaniola. Santo Domingo served as the launching point for Cortés, who first went to Cuba and then on to Mexico. Ponce de León established a colony in Puerto Rico before proceeding to Florida via Cuba. Diego Valázquez de León is credited with establishing Santo Domingo in Cuba in 1514. Balboa and Pizarro journeyed to Panama and the Pacific Ocean from Santo Domingo, and Pizarro then proceeded southward for his conquest of the Incas and Peru.

The riches that were extracted from Spanish conquests in the New World and shipped back to Spain caught the attention of other European nations. France, the Netherlands, and England became involved in attempting to claim various Caribbean islands as they scrambled to obtain some of the potential wealth from the region. Some of the islands experienced numerous invasions as the competing powers attempted to gain permanent control. St. Lucia was variously in the hands of the British and the French at least a dozen times during the 16th and 17th centuries. The names of Soufriere (a town founded by the French) and Ft. Rodney (an English military fort; Figure 21.2) on St. Lucia subtly convey this tumultuous phase of its history. Many other islands in the Caribbean also exchanged hands more than once. A treaty was the means by which Haiti, the western third of Spain's Hispaniola, was given to France. Somewhat later, Haiti conquered and then ruled Santo Domingo (the eastern two-thirds of Hispaniola) until the Santo Domingans rebelled successfully, only to again be annexed by Spain. Neighboring islands share similar histories.

The rich shipments carried by Spanish galleons to Spain caught the attention of pirates as the ships traversed the Caribbean. Their attacks on shipping played a significant role in ending the Spanish dominance of the region. The competing European nations joined the fray as they attempted to gain control of the islands. Jamaica was the base for many pirate attacks. Among the most famous of the pirates were Henry Morgan and Blackbeard (actually named Edward Teach). Tales of their rich plunder have circulated in the intervening centuries. Today Spanish wealth still is being found on the ocean floor, where the remains of wrecks shelter gold, silver, and jewels, but salvagers have replaced pirates in the recovery of these treasures. The *Nuestra,* a Spanish ship that sank near Key West in 1622, contained so much booty that a portion of the relics located to date has been valued at as much as $500 million.

Settlements in the islands resulted in development of sugarcane plantations, a profitable but labor-intensive crop (Figure 21.3). Before long, the Indian labor supply proved inadequate, which led to importing slaves from Africa. In Jamaica and some of the other islands, slaves who escaped or who were freed by government decree or by owners were called Maroons. People of European ancestry who were born in the Caribbean and who often had some Negro blood were called Creoles (Figure 21.4), and this represents quite a large segment of the population in the Caribbean. After slavery was abolished in much of the region in the 19th century, workers were brought in from India and China to augment the labor force, which also added to the cultural milieu.

The United States was involved in Puerto Rico and Cuba as a participant in the Spanish-American War in 1898. The battleship *Maine* was destroyed in the harbor of Havana when it arrived to carry Americans from the revolution taking

Figure 21.2 A gun still points seaward from Ft. Rodney on St. Lucia, a reminder of the British forces that once ruled the island.

Figure 21.3 Sugarcane a very labor-intensive crop, spurred the market for slaves to tend the cane fields on the Caribbean islands in the 18th Century.

place in Cuba, which resulted in the United States declaring war. American forces invaded Puerto Rico that same summer, but the war was brief and ended with the Treaty of Paris being signed with Spain at the end of 1898. Various governmental arrangements between Puerto Rico and the United States have been tested, and Puerto Rico is now an American commonwealth. Cuba, however, became a communist state with Fidel Castro as its revolutionary leader and subsequently as president over four decades.

Many of the Caribbean islands have gained independence at various times in the 20th century. St. Kitts and Nevis were granted independence from the United Kingdom in 1983. Several other islands gained independence somewhat earlier: Jamaica in 1962, Barbados in 1966, the Bahamas in 1973, and Grenada in 1974, while St. Lucia in 1979 stayed in the British Commonwealth with independent status. The British influence clearly remains in these islands today. France granted independence to Haiti in 1804, but Haiti did not give independence to the Dominican Republic on its island until 1844. This island of Hispaniola shows distinct French influences. The small islands that comprise the Netherlands Antilles close to South America include Curacao, Bonaire, Saba, St. Eustatius, and St. Maarten, and all are still Dutch possession. The French still claim Martinique and Guadeloupe as their own too.

The major religions in the various islands reflect the colonial history unique to each (Figure 21.5). Cuba and Puerto Rico were under Spanish rule for that extended period, and Catholicism was firmly entrenched, albeit somewhat influenced by animism. Islands controlled by the French also had a strong Catholic

Figure 21.4 A Creole woman and her child at a street market on the island of Dominica.

Figure 21.5 The Catholic Church has a strong presence on many of the Caribbean islands, including Bequia in the Windward Islands.

The annual steel band competition that is held on one of the Caribbean islands generates stiff competition. Various steel bands compete on a makeshift stage, rolling their steel barrel drums onto the stage in a seemingly never-ending string of bands. The competition proceeds for several days until finally a winner is declared, giving the winning group and its island bragging rights until the next competition.

presence. The British brought the Anglican church (Figure 21.6) and also allowed other Protestant and Catholic churches. However, many of the residents throughout the islands also integrated religious practices brought from Africa by the early slaves. For example, some Jamaicans participate in spirit cults and witchcraft, both of which may incorporate aspects of animism. Rastafarianism, which traces its teachings to the Old Testament, has three different groups in Jamaica. Dreadlocks were worn by members; reggae music has its roots in Rastafarianism. Voodoo, with its animism, spells, and hexes, is a strong influence in Haiti and to a limited extent in the Dominican Republic.

Music and dance are very much a part of Caribbean culture and have had a distinct impact on the scene in the United States. Cuba's dances and the accompanying music include the rumba, congo, and mambo. Bomba and salsa music evolved in Puerto Rico, while reggae and calypso music and the limbo characterize Jamaican culture. The limping step of the merengue is a favorite in the Dominican Republic. These means of expression permeate various aspects of Caribbean life, ranging from generous use of music in religious services to much music and dancing in secular venues. Various types of drums, including bongos,

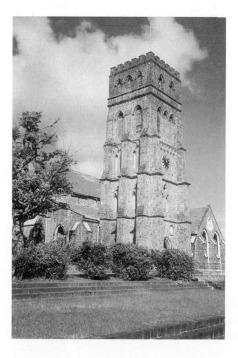

Figure 21.6 The British brought the Anglican Church to St. Kitts, where it still thrives today despite the island's independence from Britain.

usually play a prominent role, while maracas (gourds with seeds or beans inside to rattle in rhythm), *güiros* (notched gourds that create percussive rhythm when a stick is stroked across the notches), and claves (two hollow sticks hit together) add to the rhythmic excitement of Caribbean music. Guitars are often featured along with other instruments. Steel bands create exciting melodic and rhythmic music.

Literature has contributed to the culture of the Caribbean. Poetry has flourished on some of the islands, and novels and plays are also popular. Paintings by artists from the Caribbean often are very colorful and rather stylized with overtones of folk art. Folk art in such forms as masks, pottery, hammocks, leather work, and woodcarving also adds to the richness of the culture of the Caribbean.

Leisure activities often feature sports, with baseball being a particular favorite. Cockfighting by gamecocks equipped with sharp spurs is a very bloody but popular activity in the islands. Other sports include golf, basketball, cricket, and water activities. Storytelling is another favorite pastime.

Many of the holidays are religious celebrations, with Easter and Christmas being of particular importance. Independence Day celebrations occur at various times on different islands.

Food Patterns

The food patterns of people living in the Caribbean reflect the various preferences of earlier immigrants from Europe, Africa, India, and China as well as the indigenous crops of the region. The climate on most of the islands makes it possible to grow good crops, even some that were originally imported from great distances. Breadfruit, which is an important food in the diet today, was brought to the islands in the late 18th century from the South Pacific by the notorious Captain Bligh of *Mutiny on the Bounty* fame. *Akee,* a tropical tree fruit, arrived via slaves from Africa. Rice is now grown in the Caribbean, the result of the arrival of Chinese laborers. These crops and livestock are among the dietary additions resulting from immigration over the centuries. These provide interesting variety to the indigenous fruits and vegetables.

Coffee is a popular beverage in the region, particularly at breakfast when served with milk. Jamaica is a regional source of coffee beans. Sugarcane throughout the region is the basis of the production of rum, the favored alcoholic product and one that is of economic importance at markets around the world. Fruit juices are consumed generously to help fight the thirst resulting from the warm climate.

Menus vary a little throughout the islands, with family income and the dominant immigrant influences on a specific island shaping what is served at lunch and dinner. The ready availability and comparatively low cost of plantains, bananas, mangoes, oranges, yams, pumpkins, squash (Figure 21.7), beans of various types, cassava, taro, and okra make these popular, frequently served vegetables and fruits. Available meats include chicken, beef, pork, goat, and lamb, but cost limits the frequency and quantity that families may consume. Seafood (Figure 21.8), including imported dried, salted cod, originally brought for feeding slaves, is popular today.

Cassava bread is a legacy of the indigenous island dwellers from pre-Columbian times. The pepper-pot is another food tradition persisting from early times to today, especially in the southern islands of the Caribbean. Pepper-pot is a stew that is kept warm on the fire continuously for very extended periods, seemingly forever. New ingredients are added as needed and available so the flavors and textures are constantly evolving to provide a pleasing stew whenever a person is hungry. *Cassareep,* a bittersweet flavoring made from the juice of cassava root, gives its special touch to pepper-pot.

Figure 21.7 Various types of squash are key vegetables in the diet of the islanders of the Caribbean.

Callaloo is a thick, spicy green soup, often made with taro leaves, but with various ingredients added to complete it, depending upon the island where it is made. Callaloo is a green vegetable similar to spinach and is used in the soup in Barbados, along with okra, salt pork, coconut milk, and sometimes crabmeat. *Cocido* is a hearty stew featuring a variety of vegetables (potatoes, cabbage, green beans, and carrots), beef, and sausages, and flavored with *sofrito*. Sofrito is a hot, spicy sauce made of chilies, garlic, tomatoes, coriander, ham or bacon, and sometimes additional seasoning; this common sauce adds interest to many bland dishes. *Sancocho* is a Dominican stew featuring plantain, chicken, cassava, and such flavorings as vinegar, coriander, and pepper. Plantain is also the base for a Puerto Rican dish called *mofongo*, which is a mixture of mashed, boiled plantain, pork cracklings, and garlic; the mixture is fried in balls or baked like a pancake. *Sopito* is a coconut milk fish chowder made in the Netherlands Antilles.

Okra is a common vegetable that sometimes is added to give a different twist to a very basic starchy dish. For example, *coo-coo* is the dish made when okra is cooked with a simple cornmeal pudding called *funchi*. *Foo-foo* is a similar dish, introduced by African slaves, but okra is combined with mashed plantains.

Stamp and go is the intriguing name given to a Jamaican dish made with salted, dried cod in a heavy batter seasoned with onions, chilies, and annatto, and then fried. *Chicharrones* are another fried snack—pork cracklings. A somewhat different treat is *escabeche*, cooked fish marinated in vinegar and spices that results in a product related to the *ceviche* (made with raw fish) in South America.

Moros y Cristiano, considered to be Cuba's national dish, is made by cooking black beans and rice together with onions, green pepper, garlic, tomatoes, and various seasonings. Dominicans are fond of *pastelitos*, which are pastry turnovers

Figure 21.8 Fish fresh from the sea are important additions to the vegetables and fruits that can be grown on the islands in the Caribbean.

with a spiced, minced or ground meat filling. *Pasteles* are made in Puerto Rico by spreading a plantain leaf with mashed plantain or cornmeal paste, adding a filling of capers, meats, raisins, olives, and nuts, and tying the leaf into a packet, then steaming it like a tamale. *Keshy yena* is a unique favorite in Curacao and the Netherlands Antilles; an edam cheese with the top sliced off and the center hollowed out serves as the container for a filling of grated edam, meat mixtures, and seasonings, all of which is then baked in the oven.

Distinctive flavoring ingredients such as cloves and ginger are used (and many are grown locally) to heighten the appeal of some of the fundamentally bland foods of the Caribbean. Various chilies are used frequently. Allspice is from a pimento tree (not related to the pimiento of the Capsicum family). Mace (the reddish coating on ripe nutmeg) and nutmeg are grown in Grenada. Pepper is also raised in the Caribbean. Indian immigrants have brought curry and ghee to add to the richness of the flavors of the Caribbean. *Coui* sauce, a peppery mixture of hot peppers and cassava juice, is about as ubiquitous as cassareep, the other popular sauce based on cassava juice.

*K*ey Terms

Arawaks—Peaceful Indians who greeted Columbus when he arrived on Hispaniola.

Bacalao—Dried, salted cod.

Callaloo—Spicy, thick, green soup containing spinach or other green plus okra, salt pork, coconut, and crabmeat.

Carib—Fierce Indian tribe originating in South America and subsequently conquering the tribes in the Caribbean.

Cassareep—Bittersweet flavoring used in pepper-pot and made from the boiled juice of the cassava root.

Cassava bread—Native, rather flat bread made with powdered roots of cassava.

Cocido—Hearty Caribbean stew containing beef, sausage, vegetables, and sofrito.

Coo-coo—Cornmeal pudding with okra, which is served either hot or cold.

Coui Sauce—Popular Caribbean hot sauce made with cassava juice and hot peppers.

Creoles—People born in the Caribbean of European ancestry, often mixed with Negro blood.

Escabeche—Cooked fish marinated in vinegar and spices.

Foo-foo—Mashed plantains with okra.

Funchi—Cornmeal pudding prepared in the Caribbean.

Hispaniola—Caribbean island where Columbus landed and which eventually became the countries of Haiti and the Dominican Republic.

Keshy yena—Edam cheese stuffed with grated cheese, meat mixtures, and seasonings, then baked; from Netherlands Antilles.

Mace—Reddish coating on nutmeg, which is removed and dried for use as a spice.

Mestizos—Descendants of Indians and the conquering Spaniards.

Mofongo—Puerto Rican specialty made with mashed plantains, pork cracklings, and garlic, either fried in balls or baked as a pancake.

Moros y Cristianos—Cuban specialty containing black beans and rice cooked together with garlic, onions, green peppers, tomatoes, and seasonings.

Pasteles—Puerto Rican specialty made by spreading mashed plantain or cornmeal on a plantain leaf, adding a savory filling, wrapping, and steaming.

Pastelitos—Savory, small turnovers with meat filling made in the Dominican Republic.

Pepper-pot—Long-lived stew common throughout the Caribbean, flavored with cassareep, and containing meats and vegetables that are replenished from time to time as needed and available.

Rastafarianism—Jamaican religion traced to teachings in the Old Testament; members may have dreadlocks; reggae music originated in this group.

Sancocho—Stew popular in the Dominican Republic; contains plantain, chicken, cassava, vinegar, and pepper.

Sofrito—Hot, spicy sauce featuring chilies, tomatoes, garlic, ham or bacon, and coriander.

Sopito—Fish chowder made with coconut milk in the Netherlands Antilles.

Stamp and go—Jamaican dish featuring salted, dried cod suspended in a heavy batter containing chilies, onions, and annatto, and fried as a fritter.

Voodoo—Type of worship found in Haiti, based on spells, hexes, and animism; traced to African roots.

West Indies—Islands of the Caribbean, ranging from near Florida to the northeast coast of South America.

Recipes

Sofrito (Makes 3 cups)

1/8 lb salt pork, minced
1 tbsp minced garlic
1 1/2 c chopped onions
1 chili pepper, roasted, seeded, and minced
2 green peppers, chopped
1/4 lb ham, diced
3 tomatoes, seeded, peeled, and chopped
1 1/2 tsp minced coriander
3/4 tsp oregano
1/2 tsp salt

1/4 tsp pepper

1. Fry salt pork until crispy brown; save fat and discard pork.
2. Saute garlic, onions, and peppers until tender, stirring to avoid browning.
3. Add remaining ingredients and simmer, covered, for 30 minutes; stir occasionally.
4. Store in refrigerator.

Arroz con Pollo (Serves 4–6)

4 garlic cloves, minced
1 large red onion, chopped
2 tsp minced cilantro
1 tsp grated ginger root
1 1/2 tsp sofrito
3/4 tsp oregano
2 tsp black pepper
1/2 tsp salt
1/2 tsp saffron
1/2 tsp cumin
1/3 c lime juice
1/4 c red wine vinegar
1 1/2 lb boneless, skinless chicken pieces
1/4 c olive oil
1 1/2 c rice
3 c chicken broth
2 carrots, diced

1 bay leaf
1/2 c frozen peas
1/4 c minced stuffed green olives

1. Grind garlic, onion, cilantro, ginger, sofrito, oregano, pepper, salt, saffron, and cumin, then combine with lime juice and vinegar.
2. Marinate chicken in mixture for at least 4 hours in refrigerator.
3. Slowly fry chicken in olive oil for 25 minutes, slowly adding marinade.
4. Meanwhile, boil the rice in broth with carrots and bay leaf for 20 minutes. Stir in peas.
5. Transfer rice to baking dish, scatter olives on rice, and place chicken on top, pouring juices over it.
6. Cover and heat for 15 minutes at 350°F.

Black Bean Soup (Serves 4–6)

1 lb dried black beans
Water to cover beans 2"
1 tbsp salt
4 c chicken broth
1 c minced onions
1 1/2 tsp minced garlic
1/3 lb ham, diced
1/2 c tomato, seeded, peeled, and diced
2 tbsp malt vinegar
1/2 tsp cumin

Black pepper to taste

1. Rinse beans and place in saucepan; cover with salted water, heat to boiling, and simmer until tender (3 to 4 hours).
2. Remove from heat and puree 2 cups at a time in a blender, adding part of broth if needed.
3. Combine puree with the rest of the broth and other ingredients in pan, and simmer for 30 minutes, altering seasonings if needed.

Callaloo (Serves 4)

1 onion, minced
2 garlic cloves, minced
1 hot chili, whole
2 tbsp oil
1 lb spinach or taro leaves, washed and sliced in strips
2 c chicken broth
1 c coconut milk
1/2 lb okra, chopped
1 tsp salt
2 tbsp chopped cilantro
4 green onions, chopped

2 sprigs thyme, chopped
Dash of hot sauce
1/2 lb cleaned crab

1. Saute onion, garlic, and chili in oil until translucent.
2. Add greens and stir in other ingredients, except the crab, as the leaves wilt. Cover and simmer for 20 minutes, stirring occasionally.
3. Add crab and simmer for 5 minutes.
4. Remove chili before serving.

Coo-Coo (Serves 4)

1/2 lb okra, cut into rounds 1/4" thick (stems cut off)
2 c water
3/4 tsp salt
1 c cornmeal
1 tbsp butter

1. Boil okra in salted water and immediately reduce heat and simmer, covered, for about 10 minutes to tenderize okra.

2. Gradually stir in a thin stream of cornmeal and continue stirring constantly while heating until mixture becomes very thick.
3. Shape like a pancake on a serving plate; spread butter on the surface. Serve as a side dish with meat.

Keshy Yena (Serves 6–8)

1 ball edam cheese (2 lb), peeled
1 c minced onion
1/4 tsp cayenne pepper
1 tomato, minced
1/2 lb bay shrimp
1/2 tsp salt
1/4 tsp black pepper
1/4 c fine dry bread crumbs
6 stuffed olives, minced
1 tbsp minced sweet pickle
1 egg, beaten

1. Slice 1″ lid across top of cheese and scrape out interior of ball, leaving a shell 1/2″ thick. Grate cheese removed from the ball. Soak lid and shell completely covered in cold water for 1 hour. Drain.
2. Saute onion, then add pepper and tomato. Stir in shrimp, salt, and pepper when vegetables are tender.
3. In a bowl, mix the shrimp mixture with the grated cheese, bread crumbs, olives, pickles, and egg.
4. Put cheese bowl in a greased baking dish that is snug enough to hold the cheese as the bowl softens in the oven. Fill the cheese bowl with the filling and cover with cheese lid.
5. Bake in preheated oven at 350°F for about 25 minutes until top is lightly browned. Serve in the baking dish.

Moros y Cristianos (Serves 4–6)

1 c dried black beans
6 c water
1 1/2 tsp salt
3 strips bacon
1 garlic clove, minced
1 onion, minced
1/2 green pepper, diced
2 tomatoes, chopped
3/4 c rice
1 1/2 c water
Salt and pepper to taste

1. Rinse beans and cover with salted water in a saucepan; simmer for 3 to 4 hours until tender. Drain.
2. Fry bacon until crisp, and drain on paper towel. Crumble into bits.
3. Add garlic, onion, and green pepper to bacon drippings and saute for 3 minutes; add tomato and saute for 1 minute more.
4. Add bacon bits and sautéed mixture to beans, and mix well in saucepan.
5. Add rice and water, and stir while heating to a boil; cover and simmer until rice is done and liquid is gone. Season to taste.

Pastelitos (Serves 4–6)

Filling

1 lb ground chicken
2 oz ground ham
1/4 tsp oregano
1/4 tsp black pepper
1 garlic clove, minced
1 onion, minced
2 tsp vinegar
2 tbsp parsley
2 tbsp tomato paste
1/4 c water
1 tsp capers
8 ripe olives, chopped
2 tbsp oil

Pastry

2 c flour
3/4 tsp salt
2/3 c shortening
1/3 c water

1. Thoroughly mix filling ingredients together and saute slowly for 25 minutes, stirring occasionally.
2. Meanwhile, cut shortening into flour and salt to the size of rice grains.
3. Slowly sprinkle water on flour dropwise while tossing flour with a fork. Press into a ball. Divide in half and roll each half 1/8″ thick. Cut in 2″ squares.
4. Place teaspoon of filling on half of the squares, and cover each with the other squares. Seal edges.
5. Deep-fat fry at 375°F to golden brown.

Pasteles (Serves 6–8)

4 garlic cloves, minced
1/2 tsp cayenne pepper
1 onion, minced
1/4 c chopped chives
1 tsp thyme
1 lb ground beef
1 lb ground pork
4 tomatoes, diced
1 1/2 tsp salt
1 tsp Worcestershire sauce
1 c diced black olives
1/4 c capers
1/2 c raisins
4 c instant masa
4 c to 5 1/2 c warm water
2 lb banana leaves (or aluminum foil) cut into 12″ squares

1. Saute garlic, cayenne, onion, chives, and thyme for 5 minutes; add meats, tomato, and salt, and heat at medium for 30 minutes, then stir in Worcestershire sauce, olives, capers, and raisins. Simmer for 15 minutes.
2. Meanwhile, put masa in bowl and quickly stir enough water into masa to make a dough that is smooth and not sticky.
3. Rub leaves with oil, then put golf-ball-sized ball of dough between two leaves and roll dough very thin.
4. Put 2 tablespoons of filling in center of dough, fold dough to cover filling, wrap dough parcel in leaf, and tie with a string.
5. Place all parcels on a rack in a steamer and steam for about 40 minutes to cook the masa.

Stamp and Go (Serves 4–6)

1/2 lb dried, salted cod
1 c minced onion
1 1/2 tbsp oil
1 c flour
1/2 tsp salt
1 tsp baking powder
1 egg, well beaten
3/4 c milk
1 tbsp melted butter
2 tsp minced chilies
Oil for frying

1. After soaking cod for at least 12 hours (changing the water every 3 hours), rinse well in cold running water, then simmer it for 20 minutes in a pan of water deep enough to cover cod by an inch. Flake fish, removing bones and skin.
2. Saute onion in oil until translucent.
3. Stir flour, salt, and baking powder together thoroughly in a mixing bowl.
4. In another bowl, mix the egg, milk, and butter.
5. Pour liquid ingredients into flour mixture and stir briefly; add onion, cod, and chilies. Stir to make smooth batter.
6. Heat 1/2″ of oil in a skillet to 375°F. Drop a tablespoonful of batter into hot fat and fry for about 4 minutes, turning with slotted spoon to brown both sides. Add other fritters to fry at the same time, but do only a few at any time to keep the fat hot.
7. Drain on paper towels.

Piononos (Stuffed Plantains) (Serves 6)

1 lb lean ground beef
1/4 c cooked ham
1 garlic clove, minced
1/2 green pepper, chopped
1 long green chile, peeled, seeded, and chopped
1 onion, chopped
5 prunes, pitted
1 tsp oregano
1 tsp salt
1 tbsp malt vinegar
1 tbsp oil
1 tomato, seeded and chopped
1 tbsp raisins
2 tbsp chopped stuffed olives
1/2 c tomato sauce
3 ripe plantains
1/2 c lard
3 eggs, separated
1/4 tsp cream of tartar
Oil for deep-fat frying

1. Grind together meats, garlic, green pepper, chile, onion, and prunes; blend in oregano, salt, and vinegar.
2. Saute meat mixture in oil to brown, then add tomato, raisins, olives, and tomato sauce.
3. Stir and simmer for 25 minutes.
4. Peel plantains and cut each into four strips lengthwise. Fry for 5 minutes on each side in hot lard.
5. Roll plantain slice to make a ring 3″ in diameter and fasten overlapping ends together with a toothpick.
6. Stuff each circle with meat mixture.
7. Beat egg whites until foamy, then add cream of tartar; continue beating until stiff. Beat yolks and fold into whites.
8. Spoon egg mixture over all sides of each roll, then fry in deep fat at 375°F for 3 minutes, turning to brown both sides.

Summary

The Caribbean islands stretch southward in an arc from just off the tip of Florida to almost the northeastern coast of South America. Of the more than 7,000 islands in the region, the four largest are in the north: Cuba, Jamaica, Hispaniola (divided into the countries of Haiti and the Dominican Republic), and Puerto Rico, which is a commonwealth of the United States. Their tropical climate occasionally is punctuated by hurricanes, while earthquakes and volcanic eruptions sporadically cause serious damage. Nevertheless, the islands are suitable for raising a wide range of crops that flourish in a tropical setting.

Peaceful Arawaks and other Indian tribes lived throughout the islands until driven northward by hostile Caribs coming from South America. Then, the Spanish explorers, beginning with Columbus, arrived and began to exploit the region, shipping gold and other wealth through the Caribbean region back to Spain. The British, French, and Dutch followed as they struggled to gain control of various islands for their nations. Settlements followed, and sugarcane plantations quickly expanded beyond the labor supply the Indians provided. Slaves from Africa were brought in large numbers and bought by the planters of the Caribbean, forever altering the racial mix and the culture of the region. Pirates added to the violence and struggles for the islands in the 17th century. The abolition of slavery during the 19th century led to the immigration of workers from India and China, as well as from other countries, which further enriched the cultural mix. Independence has been acquired by many of the islands within the last century, but a few are still under foreign control.

The religion that predominates on each island usually reflects the beliefs of the country that has controlled it. Both Spain and France brought Catholicism to the islands, so there are many Catholics in the Caribbean, although the African slaves brought some of their traditions of animism with them and blended those with Catholic dogma. The Church of England and Protestant groups are dominant where England held sway. Haitians may practice voodoo, and some Jamaicans are Rastafarians. Religious holidays are celebrated in the various countries in colorful fashion. National holidays are also honored.

Music, dance, folk art, painting, and literature are very important and exciting aspects of Caribbean cultures. Rhythm is a key foundation to much of the music, and several types of drums and other percussive instruments originated in the region. Guitars add to the charm of their music and dances.

Food traditions show some overtones of the Europeans who conquered the islands, but the combination of the African slaves and their unique abilities to prepare tasty yet simple dishes using local foods really shaped the typical meals. Coffee and rum (made from the molasses derived from sugarcane) are the most popular beverages, although there are many excellent fruit juices that are also consumed widely. Yams, sweet potatoes, breadfruit, taro, cassava, plantain, corn, rice, okra, squash, pumpkin, beans of many types, meats, seafood, and tropical fruits are all available in the region. Some of the favorite regional dishes and popular sauces include sofrito, callaloo, coo-coo, foo-foo, funchi, pastelitos, pasteles, coui sauce, and cassareep.

Study Questions

1. Where are the following Caribbean islands located: (a) Hispaniola, (b) Curacao, (c) St. Kitts, (d) Grenada, (e) Cuba, (f) Puerto Rico, (g) Jamaica, and (h) Trinidad?
2. Why were pirates operating in the Caribbean, and what was the impact of their presence?
3. Why were African slaves brought to the Caribbean, and how did these immigrants influence the islands from their arrival on through today?
4. Match the island with the nation that granted its independence or that still controls it today.

    a. Haiti
    b. Curacao
    c. Cuba
    d. Jamaica
    e. Martinique
    f. Puerto Rico
    g. St Kitts and Nevis
    h. Bahamas
    i. Barbados

    1. United Kingdom
    2. France
    3. Netherlands
    4. Spain
    5. Spain, and then the United States

5. Define (a) Rastafarianism, (b) Creole, (c) bacalao, (d) cassareep, (e) sofrito, (f) pepper-pot, and (g) mestizo.
6. Identify at least three dances and three musical instruments that are a cultural part of the Caribbean islands.

Bibliography

Barer-Stein, T. 1999. *You Eat What You Are.* 2nd ed. Firefly Books, Ltd. Ontario, Canada.

Clark, S., and M. Zellers. 1972. *All the Best in the Caribbean.* Dodd, Mead, and Co. New York.

Ferguson, J. 1999. *Traveler's History of the Caribbean.* Interlink Books. Brooklyn, NY.

Foley, E. 1995. *Dominican Republic.* Marshall Cavendish. New York.

Gravette, A. G. 1990. *The French Antilles.* Hippocrene Books. New York.

Kramer, M. 1988. *Illustrated Guide to Foreign and Fancy Food.* 2nd ed. Plycon Press. Redondo Beach, CA.

Levy, P. 1995. *Puerto Rico.* Marshall Cavendish. New York.

McCullough, D. 1977. *Path Between the Seas.* Touchstone. New York.

Pearcy, G. E. 1980. *The World Food Scene.* Plycon Press. Redondo Beach, CA.

Porter, D., and D. Prince. 1998. *Frommer's 99 Caribbean.* Macmillan. New York.

Sheehan, S. 1994. *Jamaica.* Marshall Cavendish. New York.

Sheehan, S. 1995. *Cuba.* Marshall Cavendish. New York.

Tree, R. 1972. *A History of Barbados.* Random House. New York.

Viard, M. 1995. *Fruits and Vegetables of the World.* Longmeadow Press. Ann Arbor, MI.

Winn, P. 1992. *Americas.* University of California Press. Berkeley, CA.

Wolfe, L. 1970. *Cooking of the Caribbean.* Time-Life Books. New York.

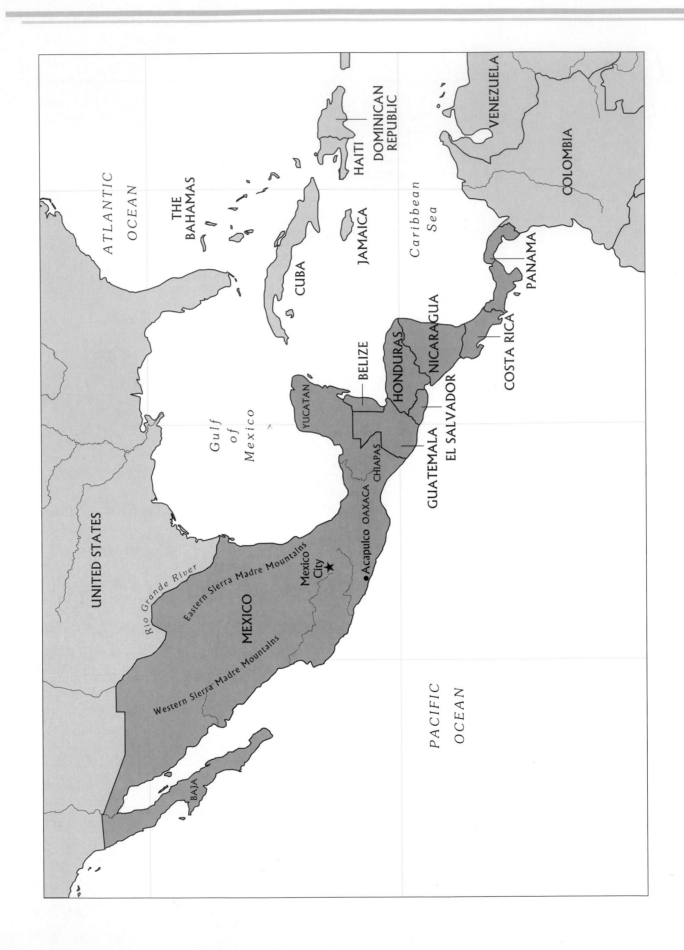

22 Central America and Mexico

Geographic Overview

The seven nations comprising Central America are relatively small countries (Figure 22.1), which together are equivalent in area to only about 25 percent of Mexico, their northern neighbor. From north to south, they begin with Belize, then Guatemala (just south of Belize), El Salvador (south and east of Guatemala), Honduras (north of El Salvador), Nicaragua (south of Honduras), Costa Rica (south of Nicaragua), and finally Panama (neighboring with Colombia in South America).

The landmass encompassed by these nations and Mexico stretches in a generally southeastern direction from the United States to Colombia in South America. However, there are two places that deviate from this picture. The Yucatan is a peninsula jutting northeast from southeastern Mexico toward Cuba, delineating between the Gulf of Mexico and the Caribbean. Even more surprising is that Panama basically is aligned in an east-west orientation, with the Panama Canal tracing a north-south channel between the Caribbean and the Pacific. The Caribbean beaches are the northern beaches, and the Pacific beaches are the southern beaches of Panama, facts which tend to generate geographic whiplash.

Belize is only a little larger than El Salvador, which is the smallest country in Central America. The entire eastern boundary of Belize is lapped by the waters of the Caribbean. Guatemala, Belize's western neighbor, is almost four times larger than Belize; it is bordered on the northwest by Mexico and on the southeast by Honduras and El Salvador. Guatemala and El Salvador have Pacific beaches. Honduras, the largest of the Central American countries, has a very long northern shoreline on the Caribbean. The total area of El Salvador, the smallest country, plus Nicaragua is equal to Costa Rica. Nicaragua, Costa Rica, and Panama each extend across from the Caribbean to the Pacific and have long shorelines in com-

Figure 22.1 Costa Rica, a comparatively small country in Central America, has coastline on both the Caribbean and the Pacific.

parison with the narrow width of their land, particularly in Costa Rica and Panama. Panama is a mere 30 miles wide at its narrowest point, and the Panama Canal traverses only about 50 miles as it provides the essential link ships need to go from the Caribbean to the Pacific. Panama is the third largest of the countries in Central America, and Costa Rica is about half the physical size of Panama.

The countries with Caribbean shores (Belize, Honduras, Nicaragua, Costa Rica, and Panama) are subject to hurricanes and traditionally have heavy rainfall in the coastal areas. Rainfall in the interior and along the Pacific is less, particularly from June to November. The low elevations in Central America are always hot and humid, not surprising in view of the tropical latitudes. The combination of heat and extensive swampy areas fosters health problems from insect vectors and microbiological sources; the name Mosquito Coast in Nicaragua and the notorious loss of life from malaria and other tropical illnesses during the construction of the Panama Canal are irrefutable evidence of such health hazards. The higher elevations in the inland regions reduce the difficulties a bit.

Geological factors add to potential problems in Central America, for two tectonic plates are the cause of very damaging earthquakes and volcanic eruptions (the Cocos Plate is slowly sliding under the Caribbean Plate). Among the active volcanoes are Poas in Costa Rica, Pacaya in Guatemala, and several others in these and other Central American nations (Figure 22.2). Although many subsis-

Figure 22.2 A volcano looms in back of Lake Atitlan in Guatemala.

Figure 22.3 The tip of Baja California ends in dramatic rocks in the sea at Cabo San Lucas, Mexico.

tence farmers till their small plots to raise beans, maize, fruits, and vegetables in Central America, the climate and soil allow successful agricultural enterprises. Among the export crops are pineapple, citrus, bananas, and coffee.

Mexico is the giant northern neighbor of Central America. From north to south, Mexico stretches more than 2,000 miles, and its shared border with the United States is almost 2,200 miles long. Mountains in the vicinity of Mexico City include Popocatepetl (a volcano 17,288 feet high). The Gulf of Mexico extends along the eastern edge of Mexico until the Caribbean commences on the eastern side of the Yucatan Peninsula. Baja, California (largely desert), reaches more than 800 miles southward from the northern border, forming a western peninsula separated by the Sea of Cortez and with the Pacific on its western edge (Figure 22.3). Between arid conditions (only 12 percent of the country gets enough rain for crops) and challenging terrain, Mexico has had limited agricultural productivity. Many of the farmers operate at a subsistence level, with corn, beans, and some rice or wheat being their common crops. The high elevation (7,500 feet) around Mexico City is suited for growing a variety of vegetables (such as tomatoes, potatoes, squash, and chilies) and wheat. Some livestock are raised in the north, and sugarcane is grown successfully in low areas along the Gulf of Mexico. Chocolate, vanilla, avocados, papayas, and guavas are available from the tropical lowlands.

History and Culture

Humans have lived in various parts of Central America and Mexico for more than 10,000 years, but archaeologists have found very limited evidence of the early people. Apparently, some crops were grown in Panama at least a millennium before the birth of Christ. With the exception of some interaction with the Incas to the south, little development occurred in the region of present-day Costa Rica and Panama until the arrival of the Spaniards. However, several Indian cultural groups arose in Mesoamerica, the region defined by archaeologists as reaching from the northern desert barrier of northern Mexico as far south as parts of El Salvador and Honduras. The Olmecs, who lived along the coast of the Gulf of Mexico, left huge basalt carvings depicting human heads as evidence of their level of achievement during their era from 1200 BCE to 400 BCE. Apparently, the abundant rainfall and good soil allowed them to not only raise the food they needed, but also to develop an organized society that constructed towns and conducted trade with other Indian societies throughout Mesoamerica. Shamanism and human sacrifices, as well as the slightly more friendly sport of playing ball, were parts of the Olmec culture that have been found in subsequent cultures of the region.

The Mayans developed their amazing culture in the tropical rainforests and jungles of Guatemala (Figure 22.4), Belize, and southern Mexico from about 600 BCE to 1200 CE. Their achievements included planned cities, construction of pyramids (Figure 22.5), a system of writing and recorded texts, and an accurate solar calendar that was superior to the calendar used in Europe at the time.

Concurrently with the Mayan developments along the coast, the *Zapotecs* were creating their center at Monte Alban near Oaxaca in the interior of Mexico. During its sphere of influence (500 BCE to 700 CE), there was considerable contact with the Toltecs living to the north of them at Teotihuacan, where the Pyramid of the Sun and the Pyramid of the Moon still stand only 30 miles from Mexico City. Although Teotihuacan dates from about 150 BCE to 750 CE (somewhat later than the founding of Monte Alban), its claim to being the home of the gods and evidence of physical dominance suggests that contact between the two groups may have been more brutal than friendly. The Mixtecs eventually established their dominance around Monte Alban and Oaxaca, while the Aztecs took over the region around Mexico City in the 1300s and ruled from Teochtitlan until the Spanish arrival and conquest in 1521.

Spanish influence in Panama and Costa Rica began to be felt in the early 16th century, with an attempt at establishing a settlement in Panama dating from 1510. The importance of this region was viewed by the Spanish to be primarily as a means of accessing wealth from elsewhere. Panama provided a route to bring out the valuables taken from the Incas in the Andes. Somewhat later, Spain used the overland route across the isthmus to transport goods offloaded from ships in the Pacific onto ships in the Caribbean waiting to load precious cargo to carry to Spain. In fact, this means of avoiding having to sail around Cape Horn was used (in spite of Henry Morgan and his pirates' attacks) until the British seized Portobela on the Caribbean side in 1739.

Although a successful Spanish settlement was created later in Costa Rica, the lack of local gold or silver caused the Spanish to basically ignore exploitation of the natives as they made their way northward to Nicaragua. The Spanish, traveling from their base in Panama, in 1519 established settlements in Nicaragua near the Pacific, including one on Lake Managua and one on Lago de Nicaragua. The latter had the trading advantage of a navigable river (Rio San Juan) to the Caribbean. Spanish forces from the north fought their counterparts from the

The Zapotecs developed a system of writing and a calendar. Further evidence of the level of development of this group is provided by the ruins of Monte Alban near Oaxaca in southern Mexico. Their skills in ceramics have been passed down over the ages and can be seen today in the region.

Figure 22.4   The Mayans built impressive pyramids and buildings in Tikal, Guatemala, which were overgrown by jungle, but are now being restored.

Figure 22.5 One of the two major pyramids in Tikal presents a climbing challenge to some tourists today.

south there. However, the English and also pirates of European heritage claimed the eastern Caribbean shoreline of Nicaragua.

Honduras was conquered by Cristobal de Olid under orders from Cortés, and Guatemala came under Spanish control when Alvarado, another soldier sent by Cortés to extend their conquests, seized much of both Guatemala and El Salvador with the help of Aztecs in 1524. Guatemala was ruled by Spain as a large region, which included the area from Guatemala south to Panama. Its capital was moved twice before being established in 1543 at what is now Antigua. The terrible earthquake of 1773 (Figure 22.6) caused so much damage that the final move was made to Guatemala City.

Figure 22.6 Antigua was the early capital of Guatemala, but the severe destruction caused by an earthquake in 1773 caused the seat of the government to be moved to Guatemala City.

Many stories swirl around the events that took place in Mexico when Cortés was capturing Montezuma and finally subjugating the Aztecs in the Mexico City area in 1521, but the loss of life and dignity the Indians suffered are changes that permanently altered the face of Mexico. Land was granted in very large parcels to Spanish soldiers, along with Indian servants to work the fields. The authority of the Catholic Church to convert the natives was granted to three mendicant orders: Franciscan, Dominican, and Augustinian. The Franciscans arrived in 1524 and busily began their work in converting the Indians to Christianity and then using them to build religious structures and housing for the friars. Some of the friars recorded history of times past, as told to them by the Indians, a legacy that has proven to be valuable to learning the background of the area. The Spanish occupation and the Catholic friars created a culture that encompassed some of the Indian heritage, but added a greatly altered lifestyle that is still very much in evidence today. The principal language is Spanish (although some Indian languages can be found), the Catholic Church dominates the religious scene, and a strong class division (with the majority being required to labor hard for very little financial benefits) remains. Few pure Spanish are found in Mexico today, but considerable intermarriage between the Spaniards, Indians, and Africans occurred throughout the Spanish occupation, and most people of mixed racial heritage had little opportunity to escape their servitude and poverty.

French influence came into Mexico indirectly when the French Bourbons maneuvered Philip V onto the Spanish throne. Governmental changes effected by the French in Mexico (actually called New Spain) resulted in considerably increased revenues from the colony and somewhat improved income for the Mexicans. Despite this, there was a growing desire among the population throughout Central America and Mexico to become independent from Spain. Napoleon deposed the Bourbons in the rule of Spain and its colonies. Thus, upheavals in Europe paved the way for upheavals in the Spanish possessions toward the west. Among the names prominent in the efforts to obtain freedom are Miguel Hidalgo, who is celebrated on September 16 in recognition of his impassioned plea to the people to rise up in 1810; Morelos, a mestizo priest whose leadership was another vital part of the effort to become independent; and Iturbide, Guadalupe Victoria (actually, Felix Fernandez), and Vicente Guerrero, who were united in their final efforts to gain independence, which was proclaimed in Mexico City on September 27, 1821.

Instability characterized the Mexican government following its achievement of independence. Iturbide became Emperor Agustin I for a period of about a year, but Santa Anna gained control and drew up a constitution in 1824; Guadalupe Victoria became the first president. Vicente Guerrero, with the help of Santa Anna, became president in 1828, and Santa Anna was made president in 1833 (actually, he held that position 11 different times as the position ricocheted to different aspirants).

Santa Anna is credited with the United States' acquisition of Texas, New Mexico, Arizona, and California from Mexico. This phase of Mexican history traces back to the Bourbon decision in the early 1700s to attract settlers to occupy Texas for land grants from Mexico in the hope of creating loyal settlers to keep out the United States. This merely drew Americans, including Stephen Austin, who led the settlers against Santa Anna's army, leading to the siege of the Alamo by Santa Anna and his later defeat by Sam Houston's forces. The treaty signed in 1836 created Texas as an independent republic with the Rio Grande (known as the Rio Bravo by Mexico) separating Texas from Mexico. Texas remained independent until 1845, when it became a state in the United States. Furthermore, its claim of a very large amount of land as far west as western New Mexico and northward into parts of Colorado and Utah threatened considerable loss of territory that Mexico had claimed to possess. When General Zachary Taylor's troops were attacked by the Mexican army in a disputed area, President Polk had Congress declare war, and the Mexican-American War began. American generals moved across the disputed areas successfully to California and southward into Mexico, where they were confronted by Santa Anna briefly at Buena Vista. Surprisingly, Santa Anna left the battle scene; General Scott landed at Veracruz and fought his way to Mexico City, with the final assault taking place at Chapultepec Castle on September 13, 1847. The disputed areas became part of the United States. The sale of the Gadsden Purchase in 1853 by Santa Anna completed definition of the border between Mexico and the United States.

Problems continued for Mexico, with deep divisions growing between factions. Finally, Benito Juarez was installed as the first Indian president in 1860. Combined forces of Spain, France, and England blockaded the port of Veracruz because of debts owed them from Mexico. While the United States was busy fighting its own Civil War, the French decided to invade Mexico, resulting in heavy fighting at Puebla and finally the capture of Mexico City. Maximillian, an Austrian archduke, and his wife Carlotta were sent to rule Mexico, which they did from 1864 to 1867, when Juarez forced them out and had Maximillian executed. Juarez served as president from 1867 until he died in 1872, a time which created considerable stability in the government. The dictatorship of Porfirio Diaz followed for 34 years. He did much to modernize Mexico, but discontent was growing, which erupted into Civil War in 1910, fueled by such fighters as Pancho Villa, Pascual Orozco, Jr., and Emiliano Zapata. Frightful fighting and hardships on the citizenry marked the decade of the Civil War. Olvaro Obregón became president in 1920, followed by President Calles. The period since then has had various crises, but democracy has been maintained, and economic development has been moving ahead.

The major religion throughout Central America and Mexico is Catholic (Figure 22.7), the result of the extensive conversion efforts initiated by the Spanish friars of the colonial era. The Church has a powerful economic base throughout the region and is the center of many festivals and celebrations. The strong emphasis on the importance of family and extended family found throughout these countries has been fostered over the centuries by the teachings of the Catholic friars. Machismo and male authority within the family and the role of women as mothers and caretakers of the home are a firmly established pattern. Morality among women is expected and carefully guarded. Despite the dominance of the Catholic Church, religious freedom is respected.

Figure 22.7 The cathedral at Chichicastenango, Guatemala is a place of great activity on market day in the village.

Christmas is a time for special celebrations and features the *posadas* in Mexico, which is marked every night from December 16 through Christmas Eve by a procession featuring Mary and Joseph knocking on doors and seeking lodging for the night until they are welcomed into a house and the party begins. A piñata, usually in the shape of an animal or a star and made of papier-mâché or clay and loaded with treats, is the feature attraction, and it is broken by someone swinging a broom handle while blindfolded; the swinging continues until the treats are broken out of the piñata. Epiphany, the day (January 6) when the three kings are thought to have arrived, is the traditional time for Mexicans to exchange gifts. Various other religious and national holidays are also celebrated. Cinco de Mayo (May 5) celebrates the 1862 defeat of the French at Puebla.

Similar celebrations are held in the countries of Central America. An interesting addition to the religious holidays in Guatemala at Easter is the making of *alfombras* (a carpet made outdoors using flower petals and sawdust to make lovely and colorful patterns). All Saints' (Todos Santos) and All Souls' days (November 1 and 2 respectively) also are celebrated throughout the region. Candlelight vigils are held, and breads and other foods shaped to resemble skeletons and skulls are prepared for the honored memory of departed family members. Pilgrimages to special religious shrines also are a part of the culture. People from all over Central America gather at Esquipulas in Guatemala on January 15 to light a candle before a statue of a black Christ, the site of a miraculous cure in 1737.

Food Patterns

The foods commonly eaten in Mexico and Central America are a flavorful blend of the native plants and fish eaten by the Indians mingled with pork, spices, and other European ingredients brought by the Spanish invaders. Although there are some differences in various regions of Mexico and its neighbors to the south, most people today eat a diet that strongly reflects the heritage of the Indian ancestors (Figure 22.8). Corn, the hardy cereal crop that formed the foundation of the diet prior to the arrival of the Spanish, still is the dominant staple, augmented by wheat and rice brought by the Spaniards. Beans of various types, chilies, and tomatoes were eaten by early Indians, while today they are likely to be flavored with lard, onions, and garlic, the contributions of their conquerors.

Corn is featured on the menu all day long throughout this entire region. Tortillas appear at all meals. Their preparation often is done in factories today, but they frequently are made at home too. Preparation of tortillas requires *masa ha-*

Figure 22.8 Corn tortillas are the base for this plate of nachos, which is served with garnishes of peppers, tomatoes, and onions plus a generous scoop of guacamole.

rina, the flour made in earlier days by grinding hull-less, lye-soaked corn (*nixta-mal*) with a hand-shaped stone (*mano*) on a flat stone quern (*metate*). After masa harina is worked into a dough with added water, balls of dough are patted or pressed into flat circles about one-eighth inch thick and usually 6 to 8 inches in diameter. These flat disks of dough are baked on a flat, cast-iron griddle *(comal)* and served immediately, or the baked tortillas may be reheated (often by frying) when used later.

Wheat is used to make flour tortillas (Figure 22.9), particularly in the northern part of Mexico. The gluten in the wheat flour makes the tortilla dough easier to manipulate than the dough made with corn. This characteristic is evident in the much larger disks commonly made when preparing flour tortillas. The malleable texture of flour tortillas is illustrated effectively in burritos, the Mexican dish featuring a hearty filling such as beans or meat (or both) and other ingredients wrapped in a large flour tortilla and often garnished with salsa (sauce of chopped tomatoes or other ingredients and seasoned with chilies and various spices).

Several recipes use corn tortillas as their base. Tacos are made with tortillas (either fried to make a crisp shell or soft) folded in half to hold the desired filling made with any combination of beans, slivered meats, chopped tomatoes and lettuce, salsa, grated cheese, and sour cream. Enchiladas are another dish made with corn tortillas, but these are rolled with a filling and covered with a sauce and grated cheese, then baked (Figure 22.10). *Quesadillas* are made by placing a rather thin layer of grated cheese or other filling over half of a tortilla and then folding the other half over to make a turnover that is heated in the oven or sometimes fried. A tostada is made by frying a tortilla (either corn or flour) in a bowl shape to make it crisp, then generously filling it with layers of refried beans, slivered meats, chopped tomatoes, onions, cilantro, grated cheese, guacamole, and salsa. *Flautas* are made by putting a small amount of filling very tightly into a corn tortilla and rolling it into a pencil shape, then frying it until crisp. Guacamole, a favorite salsa of pureed avocado flavored with chilies and other seasonings, is often an accompaniment to flautas as well as many other dishes. Other dishes featuring corn tortillas are *chalapas* (fried tortillas topped with ingredients similar to those used in a tostada), *chilaquiles* (shredded tortillas, fried before baking with chili sauce), and *gorditas* (thick, small tortillas fried with meats or vegetables, or both, and cheese).

Tamales with a variety of fillings are popular throughout this region. Their place in the menu may be as the main part of a meal, while sweet tamales are a dessert item. Basically, tamales are a cornmeal dough with a filling; the filled tamale is wrapped in cornhusks (or banana leaves, in tropical regions) and

Figure 22.9 Flour tortillas are baked using a dough with enough gluten so they can be folded or rolled, as is demonstrated in these quesadillas accompanied by salsa and guacamole for added flavor excitement.

Figure 22.10 Enchiladas at the upper left on this sampler plate, quesadillas at the extreme left, chiles rellenos in the middle, rice, guacamole with corn tortilla chips, and refried beans complete this plate.

steamed until the dough is done and the filling is cooked. The wrapping is then discarded, and the tamales are devoured with enthusiasm.

Many different types of chilies are grown in Mexico and Central America, and are used as flavoring or even as a main ingredient, as in *chiles rellenos*. Anaheim (or California) long green chilies are used in making chiles rellenos, and various other dishes utilize these or other chilies (Table 22.1). Considerable care is required when working with chilies to avoid burning hands, mouth, and eyes with the juices and fumes that come from them while removing the seeds and interior veins—the extremely hot parts of the chilies. Chilies for chiles rellenos are singed over a gas flame or in the oven to blacken and crisp the skin for easy removal; the cleaned chile is filled with grated cheese and dipped in a frothy egg batter, then deep-fried (usually in lard).

Beans are a staple item in diets throughout Mexico and Central America. Frequently, they are fried with lard and sometimes cheese, a dish called *frijoles refrito* (refried beans). Sometimes, beans are served after they have been simmered until soft, but without adding lard or other fat. The protein content of beans is augmented with rice, often served as Spanish rice seasoned with tomatoes and chilies. These two protein sources complement each other to provide the equiva-

Table 22.1 Selected Chilies of Mexico and Central America

Chili	Color	Size and Shape	Comments
Anaheim (California)	Green	6 to 9 inches long, 1 1/2 inches wide at stem	Peel and seed fresh chile to reduce bite; available canned
Ancho	Dark green, bright red when ripe	8 inches long, 1 1/2 inches wide at stem	Mild to moderately hot; milder as it ripens
Chile roja	Red	Varies with type	General term for any red chile
Chile verde	Green	Varies with type	General term for any green chile
Chipotle	Red	2 1/2 inches long, 1 inch wide at stem	Hot, mature jalapeño pepper that has been smoked; available canned
Jalapeño	Dark green	2 1/2 inches long, 1 inch wide at stem	Very hot; available fresh and canned, pickled or plain
Pasilla	Dark green (immature, dark brown (ripe); chocolate colored (dried)	8 to 11 inches long, 1 1/2 inches wide at stem	Ranges from mild to hot; available fresh or canned
Yellow	Yellow	Varies with type	Very hot, varies with type

lent of a complete protein. This is of particular importance for people who may not be able to afford meat on a daily basis.

Lard is the preferred and commonly used fat in this cuisine. Before the Spaniards brought pigs, the fat content of the diet was very low because of lack of sources. The cuisine now has evolved to one encompassing many fried foods and generous use of lard in recipes. Butter is available, but has not replaced lard in cooking.

Milk and dairy products are somewhat limited, although fresh cheeses are available. Canned and sweetened condensed milk are the preferred sources of milk, a pattern that developed because these products do not require refrigeration until opened, and refrigeration is of limited availability to many. Milk may be used in cooking, but is not generally used as a beverage in this region.

Some unique items in the Mexican and Central American diets are *nopales* (leaves of prickly pear cactus, usually pickled or fried), *tajaditas* (fried banana chips), *jicama* (root vegetable with a crisp texture, often sprinkled with chili powder and eaten raw), and fruit of the prickly pear cactus. Beverages include *atole* (a thick, cornmeal-based drink), hot chocolate (often flavored with cinnamon and beaten with a carved wooden beater), tequila (twice-distilled alcoholic beverage prepared from sap of the *agave* or century plant, often served with salt and lime), and *pulque* (mildly alcoholic beverage from agave sap). Coffee, usually served *con leche* (with milk), is very popular.

Meal patterns are influenced by economic factors and rural or urban locations of families. Breakfast *(desayuno)* may be as simple as café con leche and a bread, pastry, or tamale before people leave for work, while rural workers may do some chores before eating a more substantial breakfast that includes beans and tortillas as well. To help hungry workers survive until the typically late lunch *(almuerzo)*, usually a tortilla-based dish and a beverage is served shortly before noon. The main meal is *comida,* which is eaten in midafternoon and followed by a siesta. The menu for this meal is large, often beginning with soup and continuing with beans, rice, and tortillas or a hearty main dish, a dessert (flan is a favorite), and a beverage. A very late afternoon refreshment is the *merienda,* a time for enjoying a sweet pastry or roll, such as *buñuelos,* and a beverage (perhaps atole, hot chocolate, or coffee). Finally, supper *(cena)* may be served sometime between 8:00 P.M. and midnight in the city. This may be as simple as leftovers from comida. Snacking often also adds to the food intake of most people.

Key Terms

Agave—Century plant; source of the sap used to make tequila and pulque.

Almuerzo—Late-morning, light meal (usually tortilla-based dish and a beverage) often eaten in Mexico and Central America.

Atole—Gruel-like, thick beverage with a cornmeal base.

Aztecs—Indians in power in Mexico City region from the 14th century until Cortés conquered them in 1521.

Burritos—Wheat flour tortillas wrapped around bean or meat filling.

Cena—Supper meal (light menu) served in Mexico and Central America in the evening.

Cinco de Mayo—Celebration on May 5 honoring Mexican defeat of the French at Puebla in 1862.

Chalupas—Fried tortillas topped with refried beans, slivered meat, chopped tomatoes and onions, and grated cheese.

Chilaquiles—Shredded, fried tortillas baked with chili sauce.

Comal—Flat, cast iron griddle used to bake tortillas.

Comida—Heaviest meal of the day, eaten in midafternoon, in Mexico and Central America; includes soup, main dish, beans, rice, tortillas, dessert, and a beverage.

Desayuno—Breakfast (usually coffee and pastry) eaten early in the morning in Mexico and Central America.

Enchiladas—Corn tortillas rolled around a filling and covered with a sauce before baking.

Flan—Baked custard dessert.

Flautas—Tightly rolled corn tortillas containing a small amount of filling that are fried until crisp.

Frijoles refritos—Cooked beans with added lard that are stirred to a pureed texture.

Gorditas—Thick, small tortillas fried with meats or vegetables (or both) and cheese.

Guacamole—Pureed avocado flavored with chilies and other seasonings; served as an accompaniment or a garnish.

Jicama—Brown root vegetable with crisp white interior, often served in raw slices with chili powder sprinkled on them.

Masa harina—Ground corn that has been soaked in lye.

Mayans—Indians living in Guatemala, Belize, and southern Mexico from 600 BCE to 1200 BCE.

Merienda—Late-afternoon, light refreshment eaten in Mexico and Central America.

Metate—Stone quern used for grinding nixtamal to masa harina.

Nixtamal—Hull-less, lye-soaked corn.

Nopales—Leaves of prickly pear cactus.

Posados—Procession of Mary and Joseph's search for lodging reenacted from December 16 until Christmas as part of Christmas festivities.

Quesadilla—Flour tortilla folded over a layer of grated cheese and heated.

Salsa—Sauce containing finely chopped vegetables and seasonings used to add flavor excitement to many Mexican and Central American dishes.

Tacos—Crisply fried or soft tortillas folded in half over a filling of beans, meats, and other ingredients.

Tajaditas—Fried banana chips.

Tamales—Masa harina spread on cornhusks and wrapped around a filling of meat or other ingredients, then steamed until done.

Tortillas—Dough of masa harina (or flour) and water, which is pressed into thin disks and baked.

Tostada—Bowl-shaped fried tortilla filled with beans, meat, chopped vegetables, guacamole, grated cheese, and sour cream.

Zapotec—Indians who developed the city of Monte Alban near Oaxaca in Mexico around 500 BCE.

Recipes

Arroz con Pollo (Serves 4–6)

2 lb chicken pieces
2 tbsp oil
1 green pepper, chopped
1 large onion, coarsely chopped
2 garlic cloves, minced
6 stuffed olives, chopped
2 tomatoes, chopped
2 tomatillos, peeled and chopped
1 tsp capers
1/4 tsp oregano

1/2 tsp salt
Pepper
2 1/2 c water
1 c rice

1. Brown chicken in oil in deep skillet or Dutch oven.
2. Add vegetables, seasonings, and water; cover and simmer for 45 minutes.
3. Add rice and simmer, covered, until rice is done (about 20 minutes).

Atole de Leche (Serves 4–6)

3 c water
1/2 c masa harina
1 cinnamon stick
3 c milk
1 c sugar (or to taste)

1. In a pan, stir water into masa; add cinnamon and heat while stirring until thickened.
2. Add milk and sugar; stir slowly while heating to a simmer.
3. Remove cinnamon and serve hot in mugs or cups as a beverage.

Buñuelos (Serves 12–16)

2 eggs, well beaten
1/4 c milk
2 tbsp melted butter
2 c all purpose flour
1/2 tsp salt
1 1/2 tsp sugar
Oil for frying
2 tsp cinnamon
2 tbsp sugar

1. Combine eggs, milk, and butter in a mixing bowl.
2. Sift flour, salt, and sugar together, then add to liquid ingredients and stir well to make a dough.
3. Form dough into 1" balls.
4. On a floured board, press each ball into a very thin disk.
5. Deep-fat fry each disk in 375°F oil to a golden brown. Blot on paper towels.
6. Sprinkle with cinnamon and sugar mix.

Burritos (Serves 4–6)

1 1/2 lb beef stew meat
2 onions, chopped
3 oz canned diced green chiles
1 1/2 tsp salt
6 flour tortillas

1. Combine beef, onions, chiles, and salt in a casserole; cover and bake at 225°F for 8 hours.
2. Shred beef after it is cooled.
3. Place about 1/2 cup of meat filling on a tortilla, fold right and left sides in about 1" over the filling; roll loosely, starting at the bottom so that the filling is encased in the wrap.

Chicken Enchiladas (Serves 4–8)

2 1/2 lb chicken pieces
Water to cover
Salt and pepper to taste
1 1/2 onions, chopped
8 corn tortillas
1 can (10 oz) enchilada sauce
1 c grated cheddar cheese

1. Cover chicken with water and simmer, covered, until very tender. Remove and discard skin and bones; shred chicken meat. Salt and pepper to taste.
2. Saute onions and chicken in oil until golden. Remove from skillet.
3. Fry each tortilla separately to soften.
4. Place about 1/2 cup chicken mixture on each tortilla, pour some sauce over each filling, then sprinkle with cheese.
5. Fold both edges loosely over the filling and invert when arranging enchilada in an oblong baking dish.
6. Sprinkle remaining cheese and sauce over the pan of enchiladas, then bake for 15 minutes at 350°F.

Chiles Rellenos (Serves 6)

6 long green chiles (or canned whole green chiles)
6 cubes of Monterey Jack cheese (1" x 1" x 1/2")
6 eggs, separated
1/4 tsp cream of tartar
1 c salsa or enchilada sauce

1. Blister chile skins under broiler or over gas flame; cool and peel, then core and remove seeds; put a piece of cheese inside each chile.
2. Make six rings about 5" in diameter using folded aluminum foil and arrange on jelly roll pan.
3. Beat egg yolks until thick and lemon colored; beat whites until foamy, add cream of tartar, and continue beating until peaks form.
4. Fold the yolks into the whites, gently but completely.
5. Spoon a large spoonful of egg batter into each ring of foil, then arrange the stuffed chiles in the rings.
6. Spoon remaining egg batter over the chiles and bake at 350°F for 20 to 30 minutes until golden brown. Serve with salsa or enchilada sauce.

Salsa (Makes 2 cups)

3 tomatoes, peeled and diced
1 can (3 1/2 oz) chopped green chiles
1 large onion, finely chopped
1/4 c finely chopped cilantro
1 garlic clove, minced
1 tsp salt

Black pepper to taste
Juice of 1 lemon or 2 limes
1 tbsp salad oil

1. Combine all ingredients.
2. Store covered in refrigerator for up to 4 days.

Guacamole (Makes 1 1/2–2 cups)

2 ripe avocados
1 tbsp lemon juice
1/2 onion, minced
1 tomato, peeled, seeded, and finely chopped
3 tbsp canned diced green chile
1 tbsp minced cilantro
1 tsp salt
1/4 tsp white pepper

1. Peel avocados, discard seeds, and mash flesh with fork until smooth.
2. Stir in lemon juice thoroughly.
3. Add remaining ingredients. Stir to mix, then cover with plastic wrap and refrigerate for no longer than a day. Serve as a dip or garnish.

Gazpacho (Serves 2–4)

1 garlic clove, minced
3 tomatoes, seeded, peeled, and diced
1 cucumber, seeded and diced
1 green pepper, seeded and diced
2 stalks celery, minced
1 onion, minced
2 c V-8 juice

1/3 c lemon juice
Tabasco sauce and pepper to taste

1. Combine all ingredients, cover, and chill thoroughly in refrigerator.
2. Serve very cold in chilled bowls.

Nopalito Salad (Serves 4)

8 medium nopales (cactus leave)
4 green onions, minced
1 tbsp chopped cilantro
2 tomatoes, diced
3 1/2 oz canned diced green chiles
1 tbsp salad oil
2 tbsp vinegar
Salt and pepper to taste

1/4 c grated cheddar cheese

1. Clean, remove stickers, and slice nopales in 1/8" x 1" strips.
2. Boil nopale strips for 15 minutes until tender but crisp. Drain and cool.
3. Combine all ingredients except the cheese.
4. Garnish with grated cheese.

Jicama Salad (Serves 4–6)

2 c peeled, diced jicama
1 green pepper, seeded and diced
1 medium onion, thinly sliced
1 cucumber, seeded and diced
3 tbsp canned diced green chiles
1 tbsp salad oil
2 tbsp lemon juice

1/4 tsp oregano
Pinch of cumin
1/2 tsp salt
Pepper to taste

1. Combine all ingredients and mix lightly.

Tamales (Makes 6 dozen)

2 lb beef chuck roast
2 lb fresh pork shoulder
1 tbsp salt
4 garlic cloves, pressed
Water to cover meat
2 pkg dried cornhusks
1/2 lb dried pasilla chiles
1 lb lard
1/4 c ground cumin
2 garlic cloves, minced
1 tsp salt
3/4 c shortening (yellow)
1/2 c chili powder
5 lb fresh masa (or add stock to masa harina to hydrate)

1. Stew meat, salt, and garlic in simmering water until fork tender (about 3 hours). Save stock; sliver and finely chop the meat.
2. Remove silks and any dirt from cornhusks; cover completely with very hot water and soak for at least 2 hours (or overnight).
3. Remove seeds and stems of chiles and simmer in at least 2 cups of water until soft and skin starts to peel. Mash through a colander, discarding the skins and saving the pulp.
4. Melt 1/2 pound of lard; add cumin, garlic, salt, and chiles, and simmer for 3 minutes, then add meat. Add a little of the stock if necessary to create a spreading consistency. Simmer until needed.
5. Melt 1/2 pound of lard and 3/4 cup shortening, and heat stock separately.
6. Work the fat mixture and chili powder into the masa harina and then gradually add enough stock to work the dough to a spreadable mass.
7. Spread individual cornhusks thinly with the masa, covering the left two-thirds of the husk, leaving the right edge bare. Place a long strip of meat filling down the middle of the masa.
8. Fold the left side of cornhusk over to the right edge of the masa; fold the right edge over to the fold on the left side of the tamale. Tie both ends with a strip of husk, or fold up one end to close the tamale; place vertically (closed end at bottom) on a rack in a Dutch oven.
9. Add 2 to 3 cups stock and continue arranging tamales in a circular pattern until all tamales are filled and the pan is full.
10. Cover tamales with cornhusks, and then steam in covered Dutch oven heated at simmering for 2 1/2 hours until masa is firm in a center tamale.

Note: This recipe is a project to feed a crowd. Preparation usually is a family project and serves as part of the entertainment for a family gathering. Tamales can be frozen for reheating in the microwave oven at a future date.

Frijoles Refritos (Serves 4–6)

1 lb pinto beans
Water to cover
1/2 c to 1 c lard
Salt and pepper to taste
1/4 c diced Monterey Jack cheese (optional)

1. Wash and pick over beans to remove pebbles; cover with water in a saucepan, heat to boil, and turn off heat. Let stand for 1 hour. Bring to boil again and simmer until tender, adding water if needed.
2. Drain cooked beans and mash with potato masher.
3. Heat 1/2 cup lard in a skillet; stir in beans. Heat, stirring constantly, and add more lard if beans are dry. Add salt and pepper to taste.
4. Turn off heat; add cheese (if desired) and let it melt. Serve immediately.

Panama Yam Fritters (Serves 4–6)

1/2 lb ground pork
1 tomato, chopped
1 onion, chopped
1 tbsp oil
1/2 tsp oregano
1/2 tsp salt
1/4 tsp pepper
1/2 tsp cayenne
2 tsp chopped parsley
1 egg, hard cooked and chopped
2 lb cooked, mashed yams
1 egg, beaten

Oil for frying

1. Fry pork, tomato, and onion in oil until no pink remains in meat. Turn off heat and mix in seasonings, parsley, and chopped egg. Set aside.
2. Knead yams and beaten egg into a dough.
3. Pat 3 tablespoons of potato to a flat disk, place 1 teaspoon of meat in the center, and bring up dough edges to cover the filling in a football shape.
4. Fry balls at 375°F in deep fat for 4 to 5 minutes. Serve hot.

Molé de Olla (Serves 4)

4 boneless, skinless chicken breast halves
1/2 lb dried pasilla chiles
1/4 lb dried California chiles
Boiling water to cover
1/3 c slivered almonds
3 garlic cloves, minced
1/2 onion, chopped
1 corn tortilla in small pieces
2 tbsp oil
4 whole cloves
1 stick cinnamon
6 peppercorns
2 tomatoes, seeded and peeled
1 c chicken bouillon
1 square unsweetened chocolate

1. Roast chicken uncovered at 400°F for 25 minutes.
2. Soak chiles covered with boiling water until soft. Drain, remove stems and seeds, and scrape pulp from peel.
3. Fry almonds, garlic, onion, and tortilla pieces in oil to golden brown. Drain.
4. Blend almond mixture, chiles, cloves, cinnamon, peppercorns, and tomato in blender, adding enough chicken bouillon to blend to a slightly thick, smooth consistency.
5. Simmer for 20 minutes, then add chocolate and heat just long enough to melt the chocolate.
6. Add chicken to the molé sauce and simmer for 5 minutes, stirring constantly until chicken is heated through.

Sopaipillas (Makes 30)

2 c all purpose flour
1 tbsp baking powder
1 tsp salt
2 tbsp lard
3/4 c water
Oil for frying
Honey

1. Combine flour, baking powder, and salt, then cut into lard to the size of rice grains.
2. Stir the water all at once into the flour mixture to make dough.
3. On a lightly floured board, knead the entire ball of dough until smooth.
4. Lightly flour the board and rolling pin; roll dough to a 15" x 18" rectangle. Cut into 30 3" x 3" squares.
5. Fry a few at a time in hot oil (375°F), turning with a slotted spoon as they brown and rise so that both sides are golden brown.
6. Drain puffs on paper towels. Serve hot, with honey available to drip into the hollow after a corner has been bitten off.

Mexican Rice (Serves 4)

1 c long grain rice
2 tbsp oil
1/2 onion, chopped
1/2 garlic clove, minced
1/2 tsp salt
2 c chicken broth
4 oz canned tomato sauce

1. Soak rice in hot water for 15 minutes, rub with hands, drain, and rinse. Repeat with cold water until water is clear. Spread drained rice on clean towel to dry.
2. Briefly saute rice in oil in a skillet, then add onion, garlic, and salt, and saute until tender.
3. Add broth and tomato sauce; cover and simmer until liquid is absorbed and rice is tender and fluffy (30 to 40 minutes).

Capirotada (Bread Pudding) (Serves 8–10)

3 c water
2 sticks cinnamon
1 c raisins
11 pieces panocha (Mexican cone-shaped sugar pieces)
5 tbsp butter
1 loaf French bread, cut in 1" thick slices
3 oz slivered almonds
2 1/2 c grated cheddar cheese

1. Boil water, cinnamon, raisins, and panocha for 5 minutes. Remove cinnamon and let mixture cool.
2. Melt butter in skillet and fry six slices of bread on one side to a golden brown. Set aside.
3. Toast both sides of remaining bread slices in oven at 350°F.
4. Cover the bottom of a greased 9" x 13" x 2" baking pan with the toasted slices.
5. Spoon half the raisin mixture and scatter half the almonds and cheese over the toasted slices.
6. Make a top layer of the butter-fried slices and top with remaining ingredients.
7. Bake in 350°F oven for 30 minutes to melt cheese.

Summary

Mexico and its Central American neighbors (Belize, Guatemala, El Salvador, Honduras, Nicaragua, Costa Rica, and Panama) stretch between the United States in the north and Colombia in the south to connect the two continents of the Americas. The terrain ranges from mountains to coastal lands, deserts to tropical jungles. Olmecs, Mayans, Zapotecs, and Toltecs were among the early dominant Indians; the Aztecs were in control of the large area centering around Mexico City when Cortés arrived from Spain in 1521 and conquered them. Other European intervention included the French, Spanish, and English invasion of Mexico and the brief reign of Maximillian and Carlotta from 1864 to 1867.

The major religion of the region is Roman Catholic, and many of the holidays are religious celebrations. The culture emphasizes the importance of families, with women being the mothers and caretakers and men being the authority figures in families.

Corn, beans, wheat, and rice are key ingredients of the diet throughout the region. Tortillas made from corn or wheat flour are universally popular and eaten at most meals. Lard is the preferred fat. Pork, poultry, and beef are also eaten, the amount being influenced significantly by the income level of the family. Other ingredients include tomatoes, chilies, cilantro, nopales, avocados, jicama, cumin, onions, garlic, and chocolate. Beverages include hot chocolate, atole, pulque, and tequila (the latter two from the agave or century plant).

Study Questions

1. Where are each of the following located: (a) Panama, (b) Mexico, (c) Yucatan Peninsula, (d) Nicaragua, (e) El Salvador, (f) Guatemala, (g) Costa Rica, (h) Honduras, and (i) Baja California?
2. Locate the region where each of the following were located and indicate the approximate time when they were in power: (a) Zapotecs, (b) Aztecs, (c) Mixtecs, (d) Olmecs, and (e) Mayans.
3. Define (a) tortilla, (b) jicama, (c) nopales, (d) masa harina, (e) tamale, (f) enchilada, and (g) tostada.
4. Identify and describe at least three types of chilies.
5. Describe a typical schedule of meals in Central America and identify the types of food that might be included in the menus.

Bibliography

Barer-Stein, T. 1999. *You Eat What You Are.* 2nd ed. Firefly Books, Ltd. Ontario, Canada.

Buckley, K. 1991. *Panama: The Whole Story.* Simon and Schuster. New York.

Cameron, S., and B. Box. 1999. *Mexico and Central America Handbook.* 10th ed. Passport Books. Chicago.

Cipriani, C. 1998. *Fodor's Belize and Guatemala.* Fodor's Travel Publications. New York.

Foster, L. V. 1997. *Brief History of Mexico.* Facts on File. New York.

Leonard, J. N. 1968. *Latin American Cooking.* Time-Life Books. New York.

McGaffey, L. 1999. *Honduras.* Marshall Cavendish. New York.

Noble, J., W. Bernhardson, T. Brosnahan, S. Doggett, S. Forsyth, M. Honan, N. Keller, and J. Lyon. 1998. *Mexico.* 6th ed. Lonely Planet. Oakland, CA.

Pearcy, G. E. 1980. *The World Food Scene.* Plycon Press. Redondo Beach, CA.

Reilly, M. J. 1991. *Mexico.* Marshall Cavendish. New York.

Rockwood, C. M. 1999. *Costa Rica.* Fodor's Travel Publications. New York.

Sheehan, S. 1998. *Guatemala.* Marshall Cavendish. New York.

Winn, P. 1992. *Americas.* University of California Press. Berkeley, CA.

Zingarett, D., J. Duvis, C. Gavey, P. Hellander, C. Miller, and D. Schecker. 2001. *Central America on a Shoestring.* 4th ed. Lonely Planet. Victoria, Australia.

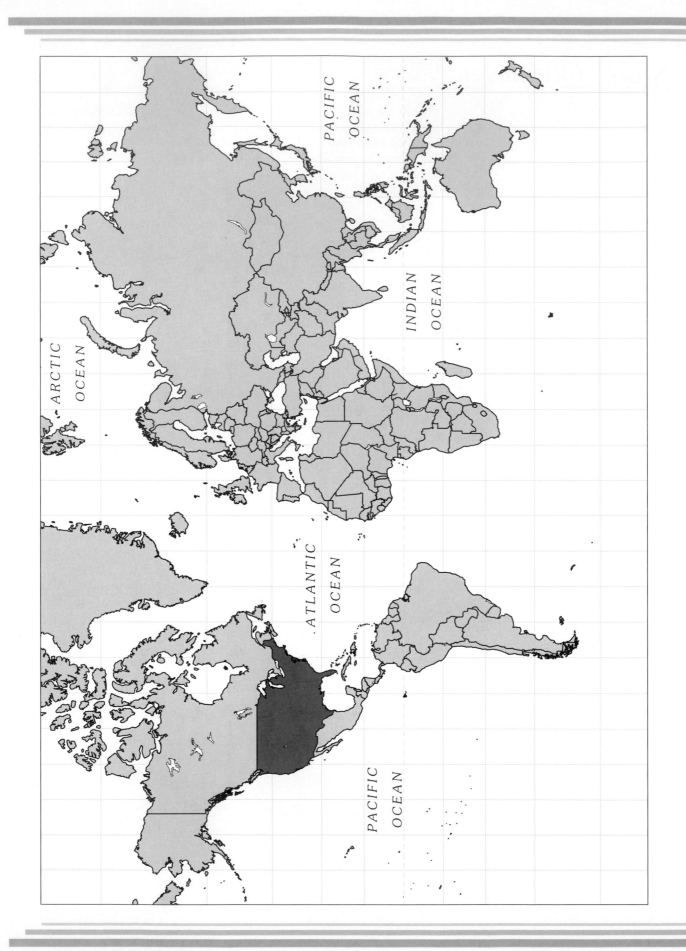

Part VII

America's Food Scene Today

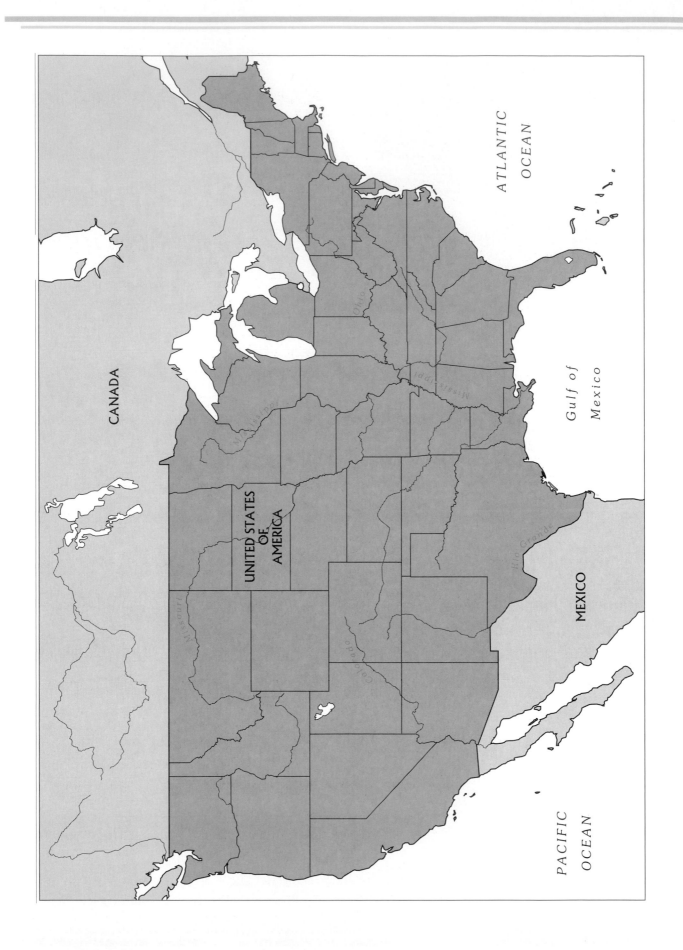

23 Who Is Eating What?

Evolving Demographics

The United States is a nation that has always admitted immigrants from other parts of the world to start new lives here. Dreams of better lives as a result of increased riches, freedom, and escape from political risks are just part of the many reasons that have brought people to seek America as their new home. Many immigrants in the 19th century were from Europe, with Great Britain, Ireland, and Germany contributing a little less than half a million people to the American influx between 1830 and 1860 (Rischin, 1989). These three countries plus Scandinavia were the source of about 10 million more new arrivals in the second wave of immigration that occurred between 1860 and 1890 (Figure 23.1). The third wave (between 1890 and 1930) brought a different mixture of Europeans: from Greece, Austria-Hungary, Italy, Poland, Russia, Portugal, and Spain. The numbers during this third European immigrant wave totaled another 22 million. These waves of emigration from Europe resulted in a population that was predominantly white people who had some commonalities as well as many differences. Their focus was on fitting in by learning English and working to support their families.

This European heritage presents only part of the picture, for workers from other parts of the world became part of the nation's population as this fledgling country developed agriculturally and industrially in the 18th and 19th centuries. African slaves were reluctant immigrants exploited by southern plantation owners to develop their lands and fortunes. This chapter in American history remains a legacy still being resolved as African Americans seek better lives for themselves and their families today. Asians also entered this country, as employers sought strong workers to aid in building railroads and other work required to develop

329

Figure 23.1 This church on Cape Cod, in Massachusetts, is representative of the religion familiar to Americans whose heritage was often rooted in Protestant parts of Europe.

the American West in the 19th century. The majority of these workers came from China (Figure 23.2), and many stayed in this country even after their original tasks were finished. Wars at various points around the world have been important in triggering immigration from Asia and other regions. Economic opportunity clearly is a strong factor motivating immigration to the United States, even in the face of legal limits on the numbers admitted annually. Illegal border crossings and smuggling via sea and air currently are taxing the U.S. Immigration and Naturalization Service's resources as an attempt is made to control immigration.

The trends in sources of immigrants over the years are presented in Table 23.1.

Figure 23.2 Buddhism was brought to the United States by early Chinese immigrants and then expanded as other immigrants from Asian countries have followed.

Table 23.1 Origins of U.S. Legal Immigrants from 1820 to 1976

Region of Origin	Approximate Percent of Total Immigrants					
	1820–60	1861–1900	1901–30	1931–60	1961–70	1971–76
Northern and western Europe	95	68	23	41	17	7
Canada	3	7	11	21	12	4
Southern and eastern Europe	–	22	58	17	15	13
Asia	–	2	3	5	13	32
Latin America	–	–	5	15	39	41
Other	2	1	–	1	3	3

Adapted from data from Population Reference Bureau.

Clearly, the demographics in the United States are changing significantly as a result of the decline in immigration from Europe and the dramatic increases from Asia and Latin America. These reflect legal immigration and ignore the significant numbers who enter illegally, particularly along the southwestern border that stretches from Texas to California.

Figures on immigration changes represent only a partial picture, because births and deaths in the resident population also contribute to demographic changes. The overall changes are occurring somewhat differently within the various states, and preliminary data from the census conducted in 1999 indicate some of these dynamics.

Preliminary information for California, one of the most dynamic states in terms of population (Figure 23.3), estimates that the state has 33.1 million residents, with less than half being categorized white (Table 23.2). No single ethnic group is dominant at the present time. In fact, whites represented less than half of the population in Los Angeles and two other counties in California as early as 1990.

Nationwide, the numbers of Asians and Latinos increased significantly, although African Americans remained the largest minority group. The figures are quite remarkable and clearly indicate that the United States is undergoing significant demographic changes that are creating an evolving pattern affecting almost all aspects of people's lives, including their diets and the foods available to them.

A comparison of the national and California percentages by ethnic groups reveals that these demographic changes are occurring differently in areas with large immigrant populations as contrasted with the nation as a whole. The striking increases in the Latino and Asian populations in California are partially the

Table 23.2 Demographic Changes in the United States and California

Group	United States		California			
	Preliminary 1999		1990		1999	
	Total (million)	Approximate Percent	Total	Percent	Total	Percent
White	224.6	73.9	17,089,221	57.1	16,526,103	49.9
Latino	31.3	10.3	1,775,669	26.0	10,459,616	31.6
Asian	10.8	3.6	2,766,862	9.2	3,763,072	11.4
Blacks	34.8	11.4	2,131,952	7.1	2,205,359	6.7
American Indian	2.3	0.8	186,407	0.6	190,971	0.6

Adapted from data presented in Los Angeles Times, August 30, 2000, A1, A16. Figures for 1999 are based on preliminary data from the U.S. Census Bureau.

Figure 23.3 Sikhs, many of whom are immigrants from India, celebrate their religion in central Los Angeles on a day of worship and a parade for Sikhs from as far away as San Francisco.

result of geography (a long border with Mexico and a logical entry point for arriving Asian immigrants). "Little Saigon" is the local designation for part of Westminster, Orange County, in southern California (Figure 23.4). This name is a proud indication that the area is the focal point for the largest Vietnamese American community in the United States (approximately 200,000 in southern California). Vietnamese political refugees arriving at the peak of migration in 1975, when Saigon fell, were distributed quite broadly around the nation. The cultural isolation this approach to resettlement created was too painful to many of the new immigrants. They moved a second time to cluster in cultural enclaves along the eastern seaboard from Boston to Washington, the Gulf Coast from Texas to Mississippi, the Pacific Northwest, San Jose and the Silicon Valley in California's Bay Area, and southern California's Orange and San Diego counties. The consequence of such population movements has been a growing appreciation of the culture, including the cuisine, of the Vietnamese, as they have brought demand for the unique food ingredients that help to define Vietnamese food and have

Figure 23.4 This large shopping mall in Westminster ("Little Saigon") attracts Vietnamese immigrants from all of southern California, it provides wonderful flavors of their original country.

Figure 23.5   This beautiful Hindu temple in southern California is a place of worship and comfort for many Hindus from India now living in the United States.

held their festivals and celebrations, not only for themselves, but for their new neighbors in their new land.

This broadening of cultural awareness and understanding of new food patterns is occurring in many parts of the country and for other immigrant ethnic groups as well as for the Vietnamese. The specific cultural and ethnic groups differ with the particular region or location within the country, but tremendous opportunities for becoming acquainted with new foods and other cultural components are widely available and continuing to increase as more immigrants arrive (Figure 23.5). Restaurants and ethnic markets are wonderful places to gain knowledge and to experience foods that may be quite new to you. The potential may be more varied in an urban setting. For instance, among the ethnic neighborhoods scattered around the Los Angeles area now are German, Chinese, Latino, Korean, African American, East Indian, Vietnamese, Japanese, and Thai. This list does not include the many other small spots where special ethnic markets and restaurants are clustered, and shoppers can also experience foods from the Middle East, Greece, Italy, and just about any other place you wish to name.

Special holiday celebrations (Figure 23.6) of ethnic groups also draw attention to the increasing cultural richness in America. Iranians now living in southern California (estimated to be about 600,000 in the region in 2000) mark their new year (coincident with the beginning of Spring, the vernal equinox) with a 13-day celebration that includes prayer, purification and rejuvenation of the spirit, gift-giving, and feasting, and which culminates in a huge gathering at a

Figure 23.6   Float in a holiday parade commemorates the vision of "Our Lady of Guadeloupe," an important celebration for Hispanic Catholics in East Los Angeles.

Figure 23.7 Jewish street corner display marking Hanukkah in Mission Viejo, California.

Immigrants from around the world have brought their religions with them, resulting in construction of places of worship quite different from the traditional churches and synagogues that dominated much of the United States until just the past few years. Religious structures in the United States now include Hindu shrines, Buddhist temples, and mosques, as well as Christian and Jewish places of worship. In 2000, Ramadan, Christmas, and Hanukkah happened to fall at roughly the same time. Public displays celebrating these three major religious events (Figures 23.7, 23.8, and 23.9) were featured together at a major intersection in Mission Viejo, California, clearly showing the rapid demographic shifts occurring in the United States today.

public park to mark the end of the celebration. Kwanzaa is an African American holiday (December 26 to January 1) celebrated in Los Angeles since 1966, an event that was spawned by Maulana Ron Karenga, who was at that time Chair of the Black Studies Department at California State University, Long Beach. This celebration of Black heritage has spread to various points in the United States and abroad to include parts of West Africa and is estimated to be enjoyed by 20 million people annually, despite the recent founding of this tradition. Cinco de Mayo, which is celebrated on May 5 in many locales with a significant presence of Mexican Americans, is yet another highly visible holiday celebration that emphasizes the importance of our nation's ever-broadening cultural heritage.

Religion is another increasingly diverse part of the nation's rich mixture of beliefs, traditions, and cultures. Eastern religions are in evidence in various communities around the United States today. Buddhist and Hindu temples now are available to worshippers, with Buddhist temples being considerably more numerous than Hindu. Jewish synagogues and temples are concentrated in New York, Los Angeles, Miami, Ft. Lauderdale, and Chicago (in descending number of worshipers). Surprisingly, the Jewish population in the United States exceeded that in Israel in 1997. There also are smaller groups that add to the religious scene—for example, the Ethiopian Christian Church. Eastern Orthodox churches often add their celebrations to the cultural mix too. Muslim presence in America can be seen anywhere from the mosque on a Navajo Indian reservation in New Mexico to those in cities, with worshipers originating from many parts of the globe (particularly from Southeast Asia) and various races (African American representing more than 40 percent).

Figure 23.8 Manger scene is displayed at Christmas time in Mission Viejo, California.

Figure 23.9 Giant photograph of a mosque on display in Mission Veijo, California, to celebrate the Muslim observance of Ramadan.

New Foods in the Marketplace

Depending on where you live, you may find some unfamiliar food items in your local markets and restaurants. These will be a clear indication of the evolving cultural blend in your neighborhood. A spirit of adventure will be helpful as you reach out for new food experiences. A basic ingredient guide may help you translate and enjoy your cultural food experiments. The listings in Tables 23.3 through 23.11 indicate the familiar food category into which different ethnic foods fit (breads and cereals, vegetables and fruits, meats and related protein foods, dairy, and fats and oils, and other—such as sweets and sauces).

Recent immigrants can find this new country a daunting place to find the familiar foods that formed their diets in their homeland. Labels are hard or

Table 23.3 Selected African Foods Categorized by Food Groups

Breads and Cereals	Produce		Meats and Proteins	Dairy	Fats and Oils	Other
	Vegetables	Fruits				
Corn	Amaranth leaves	Akee	Acacia seeds	Camel milk	Dendé oil	Cacao seeds
Fonio	Baobab pulp	Cape gooseberry	Agobono seeds		Palm oil	Coffee
Guinea Corn	Cassava	Cashew apple	Alligator			
Hungary rice	Chilies	Citrus	Antelope			
Kaffir corn	Fufu	Mango	Barracuda			
Millet	Gari	Melon	Bat			
Sorghum	Greens	Monkey bread pulp	Beef			
Tef	Iyan	Papaya	Bonito			
Wheat	Karkadeh flower pods and leaves	Roseapple	Bream			
	Manioc		Caterpillars			
	Peppers		Cod (dried, salted)			
	Plantain		Crickets			
	Potato		Crocodile			
	Sweet potato leaves		Dorado			
	Taro		Goat			
	Yam		Grasshoppers			
			Groundnuts			
			Grubs			
			Kaffir pea			
			Lamb			
			Legumes			
			Tilapia			

Table 23.4 Selected Asian Foods Categorized by Food Groups

Breads and Cereals	Produce		Meats and Proteins	Dairy	Fats and Oils	Other
	Vegetables	Fruits				
Acorn noodles	Amaranth leaves	Durian	Azuki beans	Donkey milk	Pork fat	Barley tea
Bao	Bamboo shoots	Fuzzy melon	Barracuda	Yak milk	Sesame oil	Bird's nest
Buckwheat	Bok choy	Japanese plum	Bat			Boxthorn tea
Congee	Bottle gourd	Kumquat	Beans			Five spice
Millet	Bracken fern	Loquat	Blowfish			powder
Mochi	Chinese cabbage	Lychee	Bonito			Ginseng tea
Rice	Chinese kale	Persimmon	Caterpillars			Rice vinegar
noodles,	Chinese mustard		Chicken			Rice wine
sticky	greens		Crab			Sake
sweet flour	Chinese spinach		Dog			Soy sauce
Soba	Cloud ears		Dried beans			
Sorghum	Daikon		Duck			
Udon	Eggplant		Eel			
Wheat	Garlic		Eggs (fermented,			
Wonton	Ginger root		preserved, quail,			
	Gobo		turtle)			
	Hairy cucumber		Fugu			
	Kelp		Miso			
	Kimchee (cabbage,		Mung beans, curd			
	cucumber, radish)		Pigeon			
	Laver		Pork			
	Lotus root		Roe			
	Mushrooms		Sea cucumber			
	Nori		Sea urchin			
	Peppers		Shark fin			
	Purslane		Shrimp			
	Seaweeds		Silkworm pupa			
	Snow peas		Snail Snake			
	Taro		Soy products			
	Wasabi		Tofu			
	Water chestnut		Yellowtail			
	Winter melon					

Table 23.5 Selected Indian (Asian) Foods Categorized by Food Groups

Breads and Cereals	Produce		Meats and Proteins	Dairy	Fats and Oils	Other
	Vegetables	Fruits				
Barley	Agathi leaves	Bananas	Almonds	Buttermilk	Ghee	Chutney
Chapati	Amaranth leaves	Cape gooseberries	Bengal gram dal	Milk	Peanut oil	Curry
Chickpea flour	Bottle gourd	Cashew apple	Black gram dal	Yogurt	Rapeseed oil	Garam masala
Corn flour	Breadfruit	Coconut	Bombay duck		Sesame seed oil	Saffron
Millet	Lily root	Durian	Bush beans			Sugarcane
Oats	Okra	Jackfruit	Cashew nuts			
Paratha	Onion	Loquats	Chana dal			
Puri	Plantain	Lychee	Chicken			
Rice	Purslane	Roseapple	Chickpeas			
Roti	Spinach		Conger eel			
Wheat	Tampala		Crocodile			
			Fish			
			Goat			
			Green gram dal			

(continued)

Table 23.5 Selected Indian (Asian) Foods Categorized by Food Groups (*cont.*)

Breads and Cereals	Produce		Meats and Proteins	Dairy	Fats and Oils	Other
	Vegetables	Fruits				
			Jujube			
			Kidney beans			
			Lentils			
			Mung beans, dal			
			Peanuts			
			Pigeon peas			
			Red gram dal			
			Squab			
			Turtle eggs			

Table 23.6 Selected Caribbean Islander Foods Categorized by Food Groups

Breads and Cereals	Produce		Meats and Proteins	Dairy	Fats and Oils	Other
	Vegetables	Fruits				
Barley	Amaranth leaves	Acerola	Bacaloa	Milk	Palm oil	Cocoa
Cornmeal	Beans	Akee	Barracuda	Yogurt	Pork fatback	Coffee
Rice	Breadfruit	Avocado	Beef			Rum
Rye	Calabaza (pumpkin)	Banana	Blood sausage			Sugarcane
Wheat	Callaloo	Barbados cherries	Chicharrones			molasses
	Carrot	Caimito	Chicken			
	Cassava	Cashew apple	Cod (dried, salted)			
	Celery root	Citrus	Dorado			
	Chayote squash	Coconut	Dried beans			
	Chichi	Cocoplum	Eggs (iguana, turtle)			
	Christophene	Mamey apple	Fish			
	Cocoyam	Mango	Goat			
	Corn	Naseberry	Iguana			
	Dasheen	Pineapple	Lamb			
	Eddo	Roseapple	Mackerel			
	Malanaga	Sapodilla	Marlin			
	Manioc	Soursop	Pigeon			
	Name	Star apple	Pigeon peas			
	Okra		Pork			
	Onion		Turtle, green			
	Palm hearts					
	Peppers					
	Plantain					
	Potatoes					
	Pumpkin leaves					
	Squash					
	Swamp potato					
	Tanier					
	Taro					
	Tomato					
	West Indian pumpkin					
	White sweet potato					
	Yam					
	Yautia					
	Yuca					

Table 23.7 Selected European Foods Categorized by Food Groups

Breads and Cereals	Produce		Meats and Proteins	Dairy	Fats and Oils	Other
	Vegetables	*Fruits*				
Barley	Beans	Apples	Bacalhau	Cheeses	Butter	Coffee
Buckwheat	Beets	Cherries	Baccala	Clotted cream	Olive oil	Beers
and kasha	Bracken fern	Grapes	Bacon	Cornish cream		Brandies
Millet	Cabbage	Plums	Beef	Crème fraiche		Liquers
Oats	Cardoon	Olives	Black pudding	Devonshire cream		Sauerkraut
Pasta	Carrots	Lingonberries	Blood sausage	Ice cream		Tea
Rice	Chickweed leaf	Pears	Bush beans	Milk		Vinegars
Rye	Cucumber		Caribou	Sour cream		Wines
Wheat	Dock		Caviar			
	Laver		Chickpeas			
	Leeks		Cod (dried, salted)			
	Mushroom		Conger eel			
	Onion		Eggs			
	Peas		Fish			
	Potato		Goat			
	Sweet peppers		Ham			
	Tomato		Horse			
	Truffles		Lamb			
			Mutton			
			Pork			
			Reindeer			
			Sausage			
			Squab			
			Veal			

Table 23.8 Selected Mexican and Central American Foods Categorized by Food Groups

Breads and Cereals	Produce		Meats and Proteins	Dairy	Fats and Oils	Other
	Vegetables	*Fruits*				
Amaranth grain	Amaranth leaves	Avocado	Bonito	Cheese	Lard	Atole
Cornmeal	Breadfruit	Banana	Chicharrones	Milk		Chocolate
Fideo	Calabacitas	Citrus	Chorizo			Coffee
Masa	(summer squash)	Guava	Cod (dried, salted)			Pulque
Pan dulcé	Cassava	Nance	Dorado			Sugarcane
Polvillo	Chiles	Naranjilla	Frijoles			Tequila
Quinoa	Chilies	Papaya	Garbanzo beans			Vanilla
Rice	Jicama	Pineapple	Goat			
Sopaipilla	Nopales	Sapodilla	Legumes			
Thin spaghetti	Palm hearts	Sapote	Marlin			
Tortillas	Plantain	Soursop				
	Purslane	Starapple				
	Squash	Strawberry pear				
	Squash blossoms	Tree melon				
	Taro					
	Tomatillos					
	Tomato					

Table 23.9 Selected Middle Eastern and North African Foods Categorized by Food Groups

Breads and Cereals	Produce		Meats and Proteins	Dairy	Fats and Oils	Other
	Vegetables	*Fruits*				
Bulgur	Amaranth leaves	Banana	Antelope	Camel milk	Olive oil	Coffee
Couscous	Cauliflower	Citrus	Bream	Donkey milk	Sesame oil	Grape leaves
Millet	Eggplant	Dates	Bush beans	Ewe milk		Mint tea
Pasta	Garlic	Figs	Camel	Feta cheese		Ouzo
Rice	Okra	Grapes	Caviar	Goat milk		Raki
Wheat	Onion	Loquat	Chicken	Yogurt		Retsina
	Parsley	Olive	Chickpeas			Tahini
	Potato	Papaya	Donkey			
	Spinach	Pomegranate	Lamb			
	Tomato		Legumes			
			Mutton			
			Nuts			

Table 23.10 Selected South American Foods Categorized by Food Groups

Breads and Cereals	Produce		Meats and Proteins	Dairy	Fats and Oils	Other
	Vegetables	*Fruits*				
Cornmeal	Amaranth leaves	Avocado	Bacon	Cheese	Dendé oil	Coffee
Quinoa	Apio	Banana	Barracuda	Milk	Palm oil	Sugarcane
Rice	Arracacha	Cashew apple	Beef			
Wheat	Breadfruit	Citrus	Bonito			
	Cassava	Coconut	Chicken			
	Chayote squash	Cocoplum	Cod (dried, salted)			
	Chocho	Jaboticaba	Dorado			
	Chuno	Mamey apple	Egg			
	Garlic	Melonpear	Fish			
	Manioc	Nance	Goat			
	Onion	Naranjilla	Guinea pig			
	Palm hearts	Papaya	Horse			
	Peppers	Pepino	Iguana			
	Plantain	Sapodilla	Lamb			
	Potato	Soursop	Legumes			
	Pumpkin	Starapple	Mutton			
	Taro	Tree melon	Pork			
	Tomato		Sausage			
	Yuca					

Table 23.11 Selected Southeast Asian and Pacific Islander Foods Categorized by Food Groups

Breads and Cereals	Produce		Meats and Proteins	Dairy	Fats and Oils	Other
	Vegetables	*Fruits*				
Mochiko (rice flour)	Amaranth leaves	Avocado	Aku	Carabao (water buffalo) milk	Palm oil	Bagoong (fermented fish)
Noodles	Bean sprouts	Banana	Bat	Milk	Sesame oil	Fish sauce
Rice	Breadfruit	Carambola	Bonito			Lemon grass
Wheat	Cassava	Cashew apple	Chicken			Sugarcane
Wonton	Chilies	Coconut	Dilir (fried fish)			
	Kelp	Durian	Dog			
	Laver	Fuzzy melon	Dolphin-fish			

(continued)

Table 23.11 Selected Southeast Asian and Pacific Islander Foods Categorized by Food Groups (*cont.*)

Breads and Cereals	Produce		Meats and Proteins	Dairy	Fats and Oils	Other
	Vegetables	Fruits				
	Manioc	Guava	Dried beans			
	Palm hearts	Jackfruit	Duck			
	Palmetto cabbage	Java plum	Egg			
	Plantain	Mango	Fish			
	Squash	Orange	Goat			
	Sweet potato	Papaya	Mahi-mahi			
	Taro	Pawpaw	Marlin			
	Tomato	Pineapple	Mung beans			
	Yam	Pomelo	Pork			
		Roseapple	Sea cucumber			
		Sapodilla	Seafood			
		Tamarind	Snake			
			Squab			
			Tempeh			
			Tofu			

impossible for them to read if they have not yet learned some basic English. The feeling of helplessness that shopping can create becomes easy to understand if you venture into an ethnic market and attempt to figure out what some of the foods are and how to prepare them. Fortunately, the large wave of immigrants in the last few years has created such demand for their basic food commodities in some communities that enterprising merchants are importing and stocking quite a wide assortment of the foods so important to immigrants (and also to others who seek knowledge and experience in the foods of other cultures).

Most cities have some ethnic markets appropriate to the cultural diversity of the specific locale. Lingering visits at such markets provide an invaluable look at the most important ingredients needed to prepare the dishes of that specific cuisine. Even more will be learned if you purchase some items and prepare them yourself. Each cuisine around the world has the potential to broaden your eating excitement. If you have a chance to visit a range of ethnic markets, your experiences with food can be broadened still more.

Ethnic restaurants offer yet another way of experiencing food from other cultures. The variety available in many American cities today is amazing. Try eating at an ethnic restaurant that features a cuisine you have never tried before. Read the entire menu and notice the items that are new to you. If you cannot read the menu, ask your server to explain each of the dishes so that you will know just what is available. The server's specific recommendations may help you figure out what you want to order so that you get a good introduction to the cuisine. Look around to see what diners from the culture of the restaurant are eating. Their choices can give excellent clues to finding favorites of that cuisine. You may want to make some notes about the foods you eat at your first meal and also jot down the names of dishes to order next time. Try other cultural restaurants too. Ask friends and acquaintances from other cultures where they like to eat and what they think are some of the best dishes to order.

World cuisines have developed over many centuries, in extremely varied settings. Foods sold in the United States are required to meet the standards established by the many laws governing food safety in this country. In some instances, long-standing traditions of preparation of certain foreign foods may come in sharp conflict with the law. A somewhat humorous illustration of such problems occurred in Los Angeles in the 1980s when the county's health department moved against a local producer of Peking duck because the steps in the production of this classical dish did not meet the temperature control standards for food handling in the city. Although no evidence was presented that Peking duck caused food-borne illnesses, action was initiated to halt its production. Finally, a truce was negotiated that included some modification of the original procedure. In 2000 some Vietnamese and Korean rice specialties, marketed as ready to eat delicatessen items, failed to meet required refrigerated storage conditions for selling them in California. Similar dishes sold in Vietnam and Korea are not refrigerated even during long, hot days. Clearly, such discrepancies cause hardships for new immigrants, but cooperative efforts are now being made to help draft acceptable, safe methods and standards that will assure safety without seriously altering palatability.

Shifting Food Patterns

No sudden transformation in food habits will occur the minute immigrants arrive in the United States, just as you probably are going to take a little time to accept some of the food specialties from their cuisines. However, changes in the habits and food choices do begin to occur over time with repeated contact and immersion in aspects of new food choices. Among the factors influencing changes in eating patterns among immigrant populations are the generation (whether a first generation new arrival, a second, or third generation), age of the individual, children in families, income level, occupation of workers, educational level (particularly of the food preparer), and living environment (rural or urban, isolated or in an ethnic community). These factors play roles of somewhat varying degrees of significance, depending on the individual and the unique cultural gap. For those with language differences, the transition has an added impediment. Children often pick up language skills rather quickly and can play a key role in helping parents learn about foods in the markets.

The first generation of immigrants (particularly if they are older when they arrive) is more resistant to giving up their original food patterns than is the second generation (Kallik, 1984). Second-generation food preparers are likely to retain part of their original food preferences, but often may make adjustments in the techniques used to prepare them as a means of saving valuable time. This generation may even give up most of its food traditions, leaving revival of their heritage to the eager third generation. The meal that is most likely to retain many of the cultural foods is dinner, for this is a time when the family is most likely to be together and to have a bit more time available. Breakfast and lunch patterns from the country of origin may give way fairly quickly to American patterns, particularly if these meals are eaten away from home.

The shift toward more American dietary patterns certainly is not necessarily a shift toward improved nutrition, for clearly Americans as a group are rapidly becoming an overweight population with eating habits that are not noted for being healthful. The desirable transition obviously is for new immigrants to pick up new habits that improve their nutritional status rather than cause new health problems.

Romero-Gwynn et al. (1993) found that second-generation Mexican American immigrants reported some healthful dietary changes, including decreased consumption of lard, cream, and chorizo (Mexican pork sausage). Offsetting these improvements, however, were decreased consumption of such healthful foods as atole, fruit juices, and pasta dishes with vegetables. The increased intakes of soda, mayonnaise, sour cream, white bread, and expensive ready-to-eat cereals are detrimental changes. Increased consumption of flour tortillas rather than corn tortillas, although seemingly not a change, actually is a shift for many immigrants from southern areas of Mexico where corn tortillas are the norm. Unfortunately, flour tortillas contain as much as 4 grams of fat in comparison with the usual 1/2 gram of fat in a corn tortilla. Substitution of lard with oil is a healthful change that many are making, although the amounts used may still be too great. Also, powdered, instant fruit drinks heavily sweetened with sugar are often an empty calorie replacement for the healthful fruit juices that were part of the diet in Mexico.

Satia et al. (2000) studied the dietary practices of 30 Chinese American women living in the Seattle area. They reported a shift to an American style breakfast, but retention of the Chinese style lunch by the majority and consumption of a Chinese dinner by all. Only some of the women still observed the importance of balancing yin and yang in food selections. Reasons cited for food selections included convenience of American foods, better quality of American beef, milk, and tofu (but poorer quality chicken and fish), and cost.

These examples illustrate possible shifts in dietary patterns that immigrants may make as they become assimilated into American society. Individuals obviously will make their own adjustments to their personal needs and living situations. Dishes from the various cultures may also undergo alterations as they become a part of the American scene. These changes may be due to the need to use somewhat different ingredients as substitutions when the original ones are not available. Restaurants and other food producers may alter some dishes a bit to attract Americans to their cultural dishes.

Interestingly, immigrants are not the only ones making changes in the food patterns of their heritage. Many Americans are learning more and more about foods from many points around the world. Even the fast food industry reflects this development, as evidenced by the growth of Mexican American items on their menus. Food courts and restaurants abound in Chinese foods, Greek dishes, Thai menus, and Vietnamese items, for example. Obviously, American tastes are changing and expanding too.

Key Terms

Cassava—Tropical plant that is harvested for the starch abundant in the roots.
Cinco de Mayo—Celebration on May 5 honoring Mexican defeat of the French in 1862 at Puebla; celebrations in the United States also recognize the Mexican Americans living in this country.
Daikon—Large, long Asian radish.
Durian—Large Asian fruit with bumpy skin and extremely strong smell.
Kwanzaa—African American holiday lasting a week at the end of the year to celebrate Black heritage.
Plantain—Very starchy banana, which is cooked before serving.
U.S. Immigration and Naturalization Service—Federal agency responsible for enforcing immigration and naturalization regulations and laws.

Summary

Early immigrants to the United States were primarily European, particularly British, Irish, and German at first, followed by Scandinavians and later a wave from Greece, Austria-Hungary, Italy, Poland, Russia, Portugal, and Spain. African slaves became an important part of the population in the southern states long before the Civil War and became free citizens after that war. Asians also came as workers in the western part of the country. Added to these earlier waves of immigrants are political refugees from Vietnam and other countries and many seeking improved economic opportunities from Mexico, Central and South America, the Caribbean, and Asian countries.

These immigrants have brought along their cultural heritage, which includes their cuisines, religions, and holidays. This diversity has created many ethnic markets and restaurants as well as new food items available in regular grocery stores. Many Americans embrace the increasing dining choices that result

The lovely smiles of Polynesians are as welcoming as the tempting fruits seen in this Tahitian market in Papeete.

Coconut palm trees and land crabs add to the available foods on Bora Bora in French Polynesia.

The starch-rich root of taro can be seen emerging from the ground looking somewhat like a bulb, with large green leaves on the plant.

The Ming tombs mark the remains of the powerful Ming Dynasty which ruled for about 300 years into the 17th Century.

The Great Wall of China was built to keep Mongol hordes from invading China, but it now is being besieged by tourists.

Chinese architectural designs stress harmony with nature, as can be seen in this poet's home in Chengdu.

Dried foods, including fish and mushrooms of various types, are sold alongside dried legumes and spices in this Beijing market.

This market boasts a wide selection of different rices for its customers.

Oranges are a special treat in Chengdu and may be served on a special platter placed on a lazy susan at dinner.

Buddhist monks in Shanghai chant their prayers and perform their rituals in this temple.

Bird cages on sale in the market in Xian, China, are evidence of the popularity of birds as pets in China.

Tai Chi and other forms of exercise are often done in groups in public parks in China.

To worship at this Buddhist temple on Cheju Island in South Korea requires a bit of a climb.

Haenyo (lady divers) still dive off the shores of Cheju Island south of the Korean Peninsula.

Large earthenware crocks used for storing kimchi throughout the remainder of the year.

Fish are sold on the wharf in Pusan very soon after they are delivered by fisherman.

Mollusks and crustaceans are part of the catch from the ocean that can be purchased at the large fish market in Pusan.

This lady models the full, gathered skirt (chima) and short jacket with its off-center bow (chogori), the graceful traditional and elegant dress of Korean women.

Diners eagerly eat their meal of smgye t'ang (rice-stuffed small hen baked in broth) and kimchi.

One of the four fierce temple guards that must be passed to enter this Buddhist temple in South Korea.

A young Buddhist monk in meditation at a Buddhist temple in the mountains of northeastern South Korea.

This giant Buddha is a prominent statue in Kamakura, Japan.

Gardens and blooming cherry trees brighten this home in Kyoto, the old capital of Japan.

The Golden Pavilion is one of the landmarks of Kyoto, Japan.

Heian Jingu is a Shinto shrine in Kyoto, the early capital of Japan.

This Shinto shrine is tucked into a small corner of a neighborhood in Kyoto, Japan.

Hot, baked sweet potatoes provide a welcome snack on a chilly day at the deer park near the temple in Nara, Japan.

Snow-covered Andes tower above the fields on the way from Cuzco to Machu Picchu in Peru.

Machu Picchu affords a commanding view of the river valley and all who approach this Incan village in the mountains of Peru.

The barbecue at this food stall in Montevideo, Uruguay, sizzles as various sausages, chickens, beef roasts, kebabs, and huge red peppers are grilled to perfection.

Peruvian women weaving cloth for the clothes they require for warmth in the high Andes.

The beaches of Rio de Janeiro (with Sugar Loaf in back) and their artfully inlaid sidewalks attract bathers from all over the world.

The view from Sugar Loaf Mountain shows off the city of Rio de Janeiro and its beautiful, sandy beaches.

High atop Corcovado Mountain, the statue of Christ the Redeemer stands as a protector above Rio de Janeiro.

The main cathedral in Cuzco, Peru, is a prime example of Catholic cathedrals built in South America.

Various meats being cooked on the barbecue at a ranch in Argentina.

This fisherman is busily mending his nets in preparation for more fishing off Union Island, his home in the Caribbean.

Taro, plantains, and lemons are among the choices for tonight's dinner on Dominica in the Caribbean.

Two old forts on the shore of San Juan, Puerto Rico were built in the days of the Spaniards to protect the island against invaders.

Various types of squash, eggplant, garlic, sweet potatoes, and cabbage are part of the natural bounty of food that can be grown in Costa Rica.

Avocados, beans, and many colorful hand-woven textiles are among the wares in the market at Chichicastenango, Guatemala.

Although the Panama Canal cleaves Panama, it actually serves as a unifying force as it facilitates shipping of food and other freight from ocean to ocean across the Isthmus of Panama.

Chichen Itza on the Yucatan Peninsula provides permanent reminders of the Mayan culture that once flourished there. (Photo courtesy of Paul Peterson)

Chiles rellenos, rice, beans, guacamole, and albondigas soup are the main course of this meal, which also includes tortilla chips and salsa.

China used by Maximillian and Carlotta during their brief tenure in Mexico reveal their remoteness from the culture of their Mexican subjects.

Hispanics celebrate their cultural heritage in a parade in East Los Angeles.

Sikhs in California celebrating their religious roots from India enjoy a communal vegetarian feast, religious service, and parade in downtown Los Angeles.

The comfort of their religion is provided to worshippers with an Indian heritage as they enter their own Hindu temple in Malibu Canyon just outside of Los Angeles.

from the growing diversity of cultures in this country. Immigrants also are adopting many of the foods and dietary practices of their new country. Sometimes these changes are nutritionally helpful, while others may be detrimental.

Study Questions

1. What ethnic and cultural groups live in your area? For each group, describe the food markets, unique food ingredients, and special menu items in their restaurants.
2. Visit an ethnic market and read the labels on five items for ingredient and nutrition information. Describe any problems you have in reading and understanding the labels.
3. What are the racial demographics of your school? Does the campus food service include food items that reflect this population? If so, identify the foods and, if possible, their frequency of service.
4. During the past week, have you eaten any foods that are considered to be part of any cuisine different from your heritage? If so, indicate each item and the typical frequency with which you eat it, and briefly describe what you like about it.
5. Which meal of the day is likely to be the first one that an immigrant will alter to the American style? Which meal is the last to be changed? Why do you think these changes occur in the order you indicated?
6. Why are some prepared cultural foods encountering problems in relation to American laws covering food in the marketplace?

Bibliography

Bouvier, L. F. 1977. International migration: Yesterday, today, and tomorrow. *Population Bull.* *34*(1), 6.

Bradley, B. 2000. *Journey from Here.* Artisan. Victoria, Australia.

Brown, L. K., and K. Mussell, eds. 1984. *Ethnic and Regional Foodways in the United States.* University of Tennessee Press. Knoxville, TN.

Four Winds Food Specialists. 1999. *Ethnic Foods Nutrient Composition Guide.* Author. Sunnyvale, CA.

Kalčik, S. 1984. Ethnic foodways in America and the performance of identity. In L. K. Brown and K. Mussel, eds., *Ethnic and Regional Foodways in the United States.* University of Tennessee Press. Knoxville, TN.

Lee, S. K., J. Sobal, and E. A. Frongillo. 1999. Acculturation and dietary practices among Korean Americans. *J. Am. Dietet. Assoc. 99*(9), 1084.

McIntosh, E. N. 1995. *American Food Habits in Historical Perspective.* Praeger. Westport, CT.

Norris, R. E., and L. L. Haring. 1980. *Political Geography.* Charles F. Merrill Publishing. Columbus, OH.

Pan, Y. L., Z. Dickson, S. Himburg, and F. Huffman. 1999. Asian students change their eating practices after living in the United States. *J. Am. Dietet. Assoc. 99*(1), 54.

Raj, S., P. Ganganna, and J. Bowering. 1999. Dietary habits of Asian Indians in relation to length of residence in the United States. *J. Am. Dietet. Assoc. 99*(9), 1106.

Rischin, M. 1989. Immigration. In *World Book Encyclopedia 10:* 82. World Book. Chicago.

Romero-Gwynn, E., T. S. Gwynn, L. Grivettr, R. McDonald, G. Stanford, B. Turner, E. West, and E. Williamson. 1993. Dietary acculturation among Latinos of Mexican descent. *Nutr. Today 28*(4), 6.

Satia, J. A., R. Patterson, V. M. Taylor, C. C. Cheney, S. Shiu-thornton, K. Chitnarong, and A. R. Kristal. 2000. Use of qualitative methods to study diet, acculturation, and health in Chinese-American women. *J. Am. Dietet. Assoc. 100*(8), 885.

Stoddard, R. H., B. W. Blouet, and D. Wishart. 1986. *Human Geography: People, Places, and Cultures.* Prentice-Hall. Englewood Cliffs, NJ.

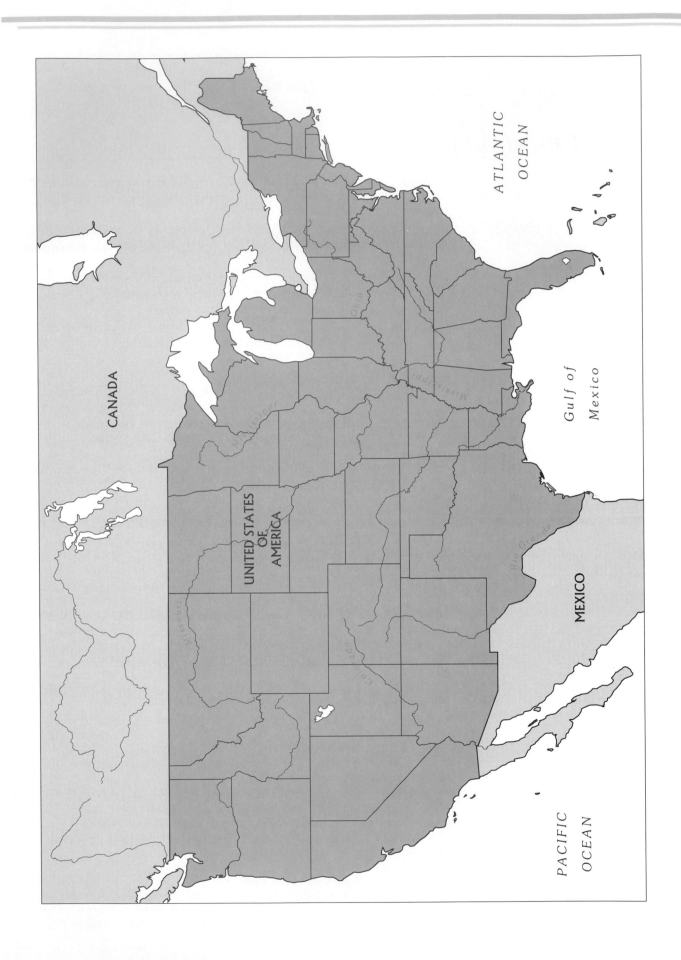

24 Diet Counseling in Our Cultural Milieu

The rapidly expanding cultural milieu in the United States is presenting significant challenges to dietitians and others who are involved in communicating messages of good nutrition. For true communication to take place between the client and the health professional, a mutual understanding needs to be developed. For this to happen, the dietitian needs to approach the counseling session with an understanding of the actual situation in which the client lives and a familiarity with the food patterns that probably form the basis for the foods that will be accepted and consumed. Familiarity is essential for people to accept suggestions about eating and diets. Obviously, there will be individual differences about the foods that immigrants from a particular country select as their favorites, but the general preferences within a country serve as a reasonable starting point for communication.

The chapters in this book provide considerable information that will help in understanding the culture and foods pertinent to working with individual clients. The various adaptations that have been made of the Food Guide Pyramid also will contribute additional insights regarding dietary recommendations and suggestions that may be appropriate. A discussion of these pyramids follows.

Equally as important is the way in which each counseling session is handled, for one country's view of good manners often is significantly different from another culture's customs and practices. Awareness of some of the possible pitfalls in communication is essential to effective counseling. This important topic is discussed in this chapter to provide a basic background in intercultural communication.

Adaptations of the Food Guide Pyramid

Despite the fact that controversy has swirled around the government's Food Guide Pyramid, this graphic and accompanying message will continue to be the focal point of nutrition messages in the United States. Its acceptance here has resulted in various proposals by professionals in other countries to adapt the concept to match the dietary preferences and available foods in their own countries or locales.

The Filipino Pyramid Food Guide (Figure 24.1) was presented in the Philippines in 1996 as a visual means of teaching good dietary practices to help avoid overweight and obesity while eating for good health. This guide consists of five groups:

- The foods in the first group, rice, root crops, corn, noodles, breads, and cereals, are pictured and named as the base of the pyramid, with the advice to "eat most."
- Two groups are included on the second level: vegetables are pictured on the left half, and fruits are on the right half, and captioned to "eat more."
- The third layer from the bottom is one group (fish, poultry, dry beans, nuts, eggs, lean meats, and low-fat dairy) and is captioned to "eat some."
- The apex of the pyramid is fats, oils, and sugar, with the admonition to "eat a little."

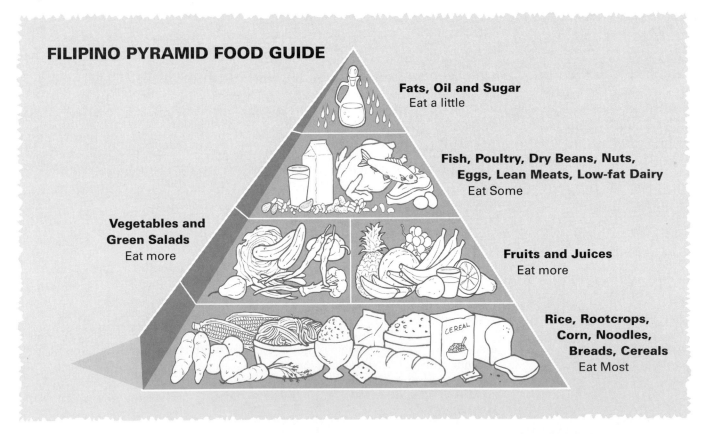

FILIPINO PYRAMID FOOD GUIDE

Fats, Oil and Sugar
Eat a little

Fish, Poultry, Dry Beans, Nuts, Eggs, Lean Meats, Low-fat Dairy
Eat Some

Vegetables and Green Salads
Eat more

Fruits and Juices
Eat more

Rice, Rootcrops, Corn, Noodles, Breads, Cereals
Eat Most

Figure 24.1 The Filipino Pyramid Food Guide. Developed by Sanirose S. Orbeta, M.S., R.D. and the Food and Nutrition Research Institute and endorsed by the Philippine Association for the Study of Overweight and Obesity. 1996.

An obvious departure from the pyramid developed by the United States is the elimination of the milk, yogurt, and cheese group, a move that was taken because it recognized the paucity of dairy foods in the typical Filipino's diet. The lack of emphasis on dairy may result in a somewhat low intake of calcium. The other key difference is the use of action words rather than specific recommendations on numbers of servings and serving sizes. However, proponents of this guide find this is a useful device for promoting interest in eating more of the lower two levels of the pyramid and less of the upper two levels.

A Piramide Alimentaria para Puerto Rico (Macpherson-Sanchez, 1998) was developed in Puerto Rico (Figure 24.2) using the U.S. pyramid as its launching point, but adapting it to the unique requirements engendered by the tropical setting. To highlight the importance of adequate water intake to Puerto Ricans, a stylized triangle that looks like the pyramid's shadow appears at the base and reminds people to drink six to eight glasses of water daily. The foundation block of the pyramid is identified as *cereals y viandas* (7 to 12 portions) and includes pictures of some foods in this group. Viandas are defined as bland plant foods high in starch, such as green bananas, yuca, breadfruit and its seeds, plantains, sweet potatoes, potatoes, white yams, yautia, and malanga. Cereals include rice, oats, wheat, barley, and corn (as kernels as well as the dried, granular meal). The second level is divided in half, with *hortalizas* (non-starchy vegetables) on the left and *frutas* on the right (2 to 4 servings for each group). The next level also is divided in half: *leche* (milk and dairy) on the left and *carnes y sustitutos* (including

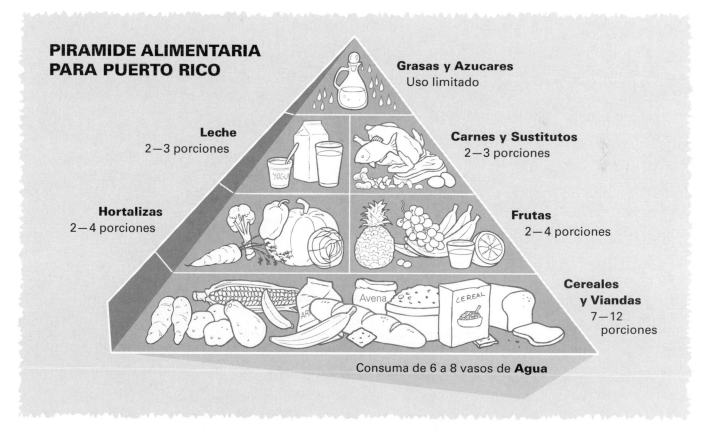

PIRAMIDE ALIMENTARIA PARA PUERTO RICO

Grasas y Azucares
Uso limitado

Leche
2—3 porciones

Carnes y Sustitutos
2—3 porciones

Hortalizas
2—4 porciones

Frutas
2—4 porciones

Cereales y Viandas
7—12 porciones

Consuma de 6 a 8 vasos de **Agua**

Figure 24.2 Piramide Alimentaria para Puerto Rico. Developed by the University of Puerto Rico with the U.S. Department of Agriculture. 2nd ed. 1995.

legumes, nuts, and eggs in addition to meat and poultry; 2 to 3 servings for each group) on the right. The peak is *grasas y azucares* (fats and sugars, to be in limited use). Minor variations in recommended servings are the result of shifting starchy plant foods such as potatoes into the bottom category rather than counting them as vegetables in this pyramid.

The Chinese version of a guide for daily eating is a five-tiered pagoda (Figure 24.3). At the base of the Chinese Food Guide Pagoda is cereals (300 to 500 grams) such as rice, wheat and baked breads from wheat, noodles, and corn. The second tier is vegetables (400 to 500 grams) and fruits (100 to 200 grams). The middle tier specifies three different types of protein-rich foods daily: meat and poultry (50 to 100 grams), fish and shrimp (50 grams), and eggs (25 to 50 grams). Directly above this tier is the fourth tier with two categories to be met: milk and milk products (100 grams) and beans and bean products (50 grams). No mention is made of sugars because they are not likely to be consumed in very large quantities in the typical Chinese diet. The pagoda reflects the limited intake of milk and dairy products that may need to be accommodated for those who are lactose intolerant; inclusion of tofu or other bean products in the fourth tier encourages calcium intake from this supplemental source. Use of the pagoda for the graphic provides a clear message that this guide is specifically for Asians.

The Mediterranean Diet Pyramid (Figure 24.4) presents the classic shape of a pyramid, but several modifications have created a pyramid that requires careful reading to encompass 11 categories and two additional suggestions that accompany this pyramid. The base of the Mediterranean Diet Pyramid is cereals (breads, pasta, rice, couscous, polenta, bulgur, other grains, and potatoes). As is

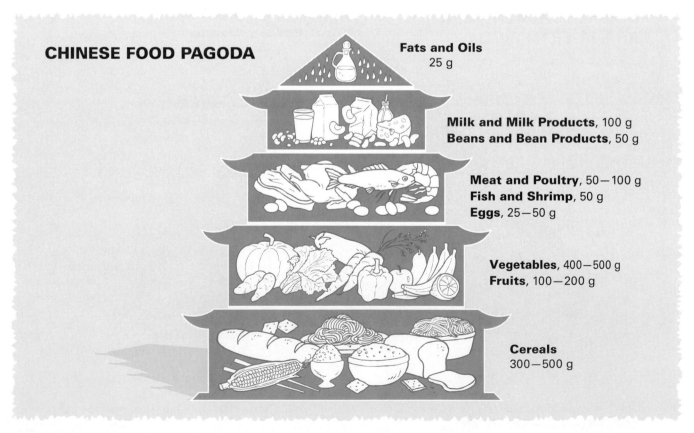

CHINESE FOOD PAGODA

Fats and Oils
25 g

Milk and Milk Products, 100 g
Beans and Bean Products, 50 g

Meat and Poultry, 50—100 g
Fish and Shrimp, 50 g
Eggs, 25—50 g

Vegetables, 400—500 g
Fruits, 100—200 g

Cereals
300—500 g

figure 24.3 Food Guide Pagoda for Chinese Residents. Developed by the Chinese Nutrition Society. 1999.

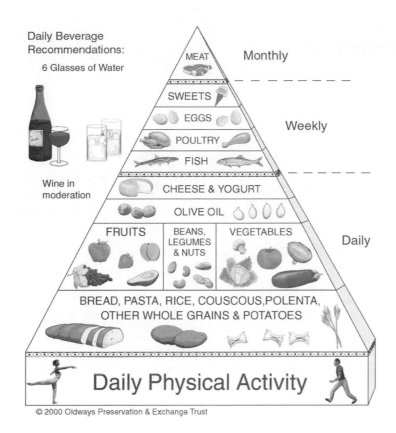

Figure 24.4 The Traditional Healthy Mediterranean Diet Pyramid. Co-developed by Oldways Preservation and Exchange Trust, the World Health Organization (WHO) European Office and the WHO/FAO Collaboration Center in Nutritional Epidemiology at Harvard School of Public Health. 1994.

basically true for the entire pyramid, the number of servings is not indicated, although foods from this foundation category are to be eaten daily. The next level, which is also to be eaten daily, places fruits on the left, covering about 40 percent of the space; beans and other legumes and nuts occupy about the middle 10 percent of this level; and vegetables comprise the right half. Olive oil in variable amounts, but daily, is the thin block above the fruits and vegetables. Cheese and yogurt, to be eaten daily, represent the next thin layer. Fairly thin layers then rise above the dotted line and the proviso is given that the following items (in ascending order on the pyramid) should be eaten a few times per week: fish, poultry, eggs (a very thin layer), and sweets. The tip of the pyramid is labeled red meat, with the recommendation that this should be eaten only a few times per month. To the left of the pyramid is the suggestion that one should have regular physical activity, and to the right is the suggestion of wine in moderation. This guide reflects the basic diet from the Mediterranean region, but is somewhat challenging to remember.

Dietary suggestions for people wishing to follow a "soul food" diet are depicted in yet another pyramid (Figure 24.5). Lactose-reduced milk, yogurt (low fat or fat free), and reduced fat cheeses are excellent choices for reducing discomfort for those with lactose intolerance and for keeping calories low if weight is a concern. To avoid high fat intake when selecting within the meat group, avoidance of such high-fat items as chitterlings (chitlins), fatback, pig feet, hog jowls, sausage, and pork neck bones is recommended. Emphasis on keeping snack foods and sweets to a minimum also is helpful.

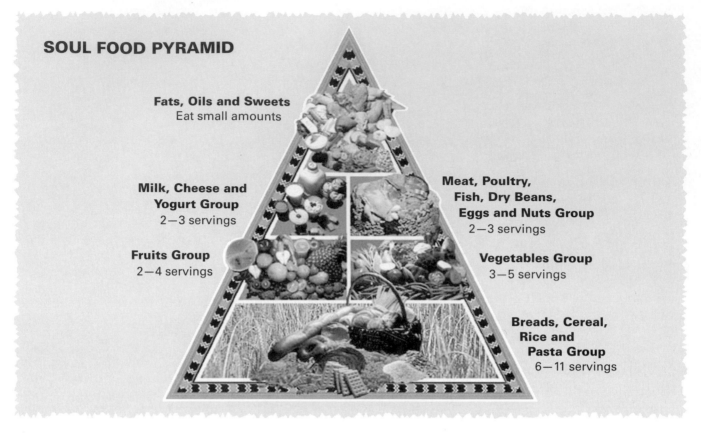

Figure 24.5   Soul Food Pyramid. Hebni Nutrition Consultants, Inc. 4630 South Kirkman Road #201, Orlando, FL 32819, website: *www.soulfoodpyramid.org.*

When counseling patients who are likely eating a diet that may be somewhat similar to one of these adaptions of the U.S. Food Guide Pyramid, you may find that the appropriate version is helpful in exploring food patterns and preferences. Then, you might shape your suggestions to take advantage of this visual. The picture will help to convey the message even when your words may be a little difficult for your client to understand.

*I*ntercultural Communication

Even when two people speak the same language, but come from different countries, there may be some confusion because of idioms, different definitions of the same word, or simply not understanding an accent. Add to this difficulty little or no knowledge of each other's language and communication drops to very limited or nonexistent. Unfortunately, the very different cultural backgrounds that the client and the health professional may have may magnify the problem because what is being said by the health professional may be understood quite differently from what was actually meant, even if an interpreter is helping with the session.

Another aspect of communication that needs to be considered is body language. Body language is subtle, yet it has a strong impact. The various movements you might make that are a normal part of your style of interacting with another person happen automatically unless you make a conscious effort to con-

An idea that you might find help-ful in refining your counseling skills is to arrange for a couple of friends to join you in videotaping a mock counseling session. One of the friends can be your client, and the other can videotape the ses-sion. You may be uncomfortable at first, but you probably will be able to relax enough to provide a good sample of your counseling techniques. You can review the tape privately if you prefer, or you can critique it with your friends to develop ideas that may be effective for you to use in actual counseling sessions. The chance to actually view yourself, as the client sees you, can be invaluable in improv-ing counseling skills.

trol a behavior that may be misinterpreted in the culture of your client. Consider the space you maintain between the two of you, whether there is any handshake or contact, and whether or not eye contact is acceptable or expected. Other possi-ble problems may occur because of hand motion, particularly the manner of pointing. Even your feet may be conveying messages contrary to your client's culture.

Recommendations you may make to your clients need to be made in the context of the beliefs and customs of the individual. Some foods simply are not allowed by religious beliefs. Others may be totally outside the typical diet of the culture. Special qualities may be attributed to some foods in a culture, thus mak-ing such foods of unique importance at special times, such as at childbirth.

The challenges of effective communication with your clients are apparent. For success in helping your clients, you will need to be familiar with the general cultural traditions of their backgrounds. Added to this knowledge is the need to establish the rapport with each client that will facilitate your understanding of the aspects of culture that are practiced by and important to him or her. Careful listening, including watching your client's body language, is a key to establishing good rapport and achieving effective counseling.

Although each client presents a somewhat different communication chal-lenge, consideration of the following points regarding cultural expectations will help you in establishing an appropriate context for your meeting.

- Language (English first or second, or none; other)
- Body language (personal space, greeting, eye contact, hands)
- Foods of the culture (kinds, beliefs, preparation, traditions)
- Religion (if food choices are influenced by it)
- Values regarding time

Obviously, the ability to speak in your client's language is extremely help-ful, but often may not be possible. If your client has limited knowledge of Eng-lish, you may need to speak slowly and in short sentences, using as simple a vocabulary as possible. Be sure to speak clearly, leaving a bit of space between words. Watch the eyes (unless culture does not permit) to determine whether you are being understood. It may be necessary to say the same thing in more than one way to get your message across. If you and your client have no language in com-mon, you will need to have an interpreter assist you in your meeting. Also, hav-ing appropriate visual materials and brochures written in the client's language may be helpful.

If at all possible, counsel in a conversational format in which you provide a small amount of information and draw your client into the conversation, perhaps with a simple question that will help you know whether you have been under-stood before moving to the next point. This type of dialogue may take time to es-tablish, but it is helpful in determining that your information is being understood correctly. Avoid asking questions that can be answered with a simple yes or no. Many people of other cultures wish to avoid embarrassing you or themselves by such an answer. For example, if you ask a client if he or she understands what has just been said, the answer will almost certainly be yes or a positive nod of the head, even if the client did not understand.

Questioning your client regarding any special foods enjoyed by the family, particularly those that may be served for holidays, can help strengthen the un-derstanding between you and aid you in creating dietary strategies that will be helpful to and used by the client. The insights you gain from such conver-sations may be of value in working with others from a similar background. Try to create an ever-expanding knowledge base about the cultures and the food patterns of your clients. Your work will not only be more interesting, but it also will become increasingly effective. Also, exploring whether there are some foods your clients avoid will help you to create realistic dietary suggestions that accomodate religious dictates or health beliefs regarding foods. Since health beliefs regarding such implied attributes as *hot* and *cold* (yin and yang) foods and their balancing in the diet vary even among people of the same country, individual client input is essential if you are to proceed appropriately in diet counseling.

Cultural attitudes toward time are highly variable, and these views tend to linger long after immigrants have settled in the United States. The typical American lifestyle that requires one eye to be on the clock at all times simply refuses to mesh with the more leisurely attitudes of countries where personal interactions take priority over punctuality. To establish rapport with some of your clients, you may have to take a few deep breaths to shift gears into a more relaxed and friendly style. Your warm, welcoming smile will not only relax your client, but will be surprisingly helpful in easing your frustration regarding the wasted time. Try it.

Many cultural differences can be found around the world, far more than can be included here. However, the following discussion will help pinpoint some of the distinctive ones that you may need to be aware of. Although many people in a particular culture may fit the descriptions, keep in mind that you are working with individuals, and they may have quite different beliefs and practices than those presented here. The key words to remember in your counseling are *listen, observe,* and *think* about your client as a unique individual, even though there are certain cultural patterns that are likely to be followed.

Customs and behaviors in the Far East vary a bit from country to country, but are generally somewhat restrained. In Japan there is particular appreciation of private space. A bow serves as the greeting, with the depth of the bow reflecting the importance and/or age of the person being greeted. If there is a handshake, Japanese usually prefer a weak grip. Men from South Korea may bow slightly and shake hands, sometimes with both hands, but women do not ordinarily shake hands. Touching is uncommon among Chinese. Business cards are very important when meeting people of Far Eastern background and are read carefully in appreciation of the title of the person on the card. Exchange of business cards is usually done in a formal manner that gives honor to the person giving the card, with the same appreciation being given to the donor of the other card. Body language also is important in the Far East; for example, avoid any prolonged eye contact, do not expose the sole of your shoe, keep the palm of your hand downward if pointing or beckoning, and avoid showing your mouth open (Japanese and Koreans often cover their mouths when smiling or laughing). Names may be confusing because the family name is often the first name in the sequence, with the given name following. Among key values are the importance of the family (superseding one's personal needs), respect for the elderly, paternalistic and rigid hierarchy in family organization, appreciation of formality and rules, indirect and circuitous dialogues, and dislike of confrontation and disagreements. Beliefs and superstitions (for example, hot and cold foods) are important. Personal questions may not be welcome. Beauty and style are particularly important to Japanese.

Customs in India and Southeast Asia vary a bit from those of the Far East, although there are certainly many similarities because of the numerous interactions over the centuries. Indonesians and Filipinos shake hands. Malaysians may extend their palms outward and touch fingers in greeting, while Thai, Balinese, Indian women, and some other Hindus greet people with their hands together in a prayer-like manner and sometimes with a slight bow, but Indian men shake hands.

Middle Easterners are often Muslims, and the customs of the region reflect this religious heritage. Women are important within their families and often quite protected from the rest of the world, which is evidenced in their wearing of the chador (or similar enveloping outer garment). The family and its honor are at the center of values, with males clearly recognized as the leaders of their families and male children being especially cherished. Men may embrace each other in greeting, may touch, and may stand quite close to others while talking. Punctuality is not a value in this part of the world, but warm hospitality is important. Expressing interest in the family's well-being precedes any business. Generosity often is so great that Middle Easterners may give you an item that you admired. Women and children may eat separately, after the men, but the foods served both sexes will usually follow Muslim laws: no alcohol; no pork, goat, dog, crabs, lobsters, or products containing them; fasting is required during Ramadan. Friday is a religious day, and no business is to be conducted. Judaism is prominent in Israel, which means that the religious day is Saturday and the food laws differ from those of Muslims: pork and shellfish are prohibited; Orthodox Jews require that their food be kosher (see Chapter 3) and that dairy and meat products be kept separate.

In the western hemisphere, Latinos also are a family-oriented, paternalistic society, which places the family (and extended family) as its dominant value. Women are expected to take care of the children and home, while men make the important decisions. When talking with others, sharing news of family takes priority over proceeding with the business at hand. Sociability is valued more than punctuality. Conversation and greetings often involve touching and standing close. However, South Americans often greet each other with a handshake rather than an embrace.

*K*ey Terms

Body language—Movements made without talking but that communicate attitude or feelings to another person.

Chinese Food Guide Pagoda—Educational tool developed in China to guide people in making healthy food selections.

Customs—Traditions that are common to a cultural group, such as shaking hands or bowing.

Filipino Pyramid Food Guide—Food guide developed in the Philippines to guide people in healthy food choices using the local foods.

Food Guide Pyramid—Educational tool used in the United States to guide people in making healthy food choices.

Mediterranean Diet Pyramid—Food pyramid designed to incorporate the foods common to the Mediterranean in a pattern that has 11 categories.

Soul Food Pyramid—Healthy food guide for persons who are lactose-intolerant and need to limit fat intake to control weight.

Viandas—Generic word used in the Piramide Alimentaria para Puerto Rico to include bland foods high in starch.

Summary

Health professionals today counsel many clients with cultural backgrounds quite different from their own heritage. Successful communication requires an understanding of the food patterns and cultural practices commonly followed in the client's culture. The Food Guide Pyramid has been adapted to some other parts of the world and can provide a basis for dietary counseling. The guides presently available include the Filipino Pyramid Food Guide, the Piramide Alimentaria par Puerto Rico, the Chinese Food Guide Pagoda, the Mediterranean Diet Pyramid, and the Soul Food Pyramid.

When counseling clients from other cultural backgrounds, many dimensions need to be considered in addition to the actual dietary information if your communication is to be effective. Among these dimensions are language, body language, food in relation to the culture, religion, and values (particularly about time). Some of the basic considerations for counseling Asians, Middle Easterners, and Latinos are mentioned in this chapter.

Study Questions

1. What food and cultural practices need to be considered before beginning to counsel a recent immigrant from the Middle East?
2. What food and cultural practices need to be considered before beginning to counsel a recent immigrant from China?
3. What food and cultural practices need to be considered before beginning to counsel a recent immigrant from Mexico?
4. Are there habits in your style of talking with another person that might need to be altered when you are working with clients from different backgrounds? If so, what are they, and how do you plan to make these changes?

Bibliography

Axtell, R. E. 1990. *Do's and Taboos of Hosting International Visitors.* John Wiley and Sons. New York.

Baldridge, L. 1985. *Complete Guide to Executive Manners.* Rawson Assoc. New York.

Basaran, P. 1999. Traditional foods of the Middle East. *Food Technol. 53*(6), 60.

Chinese Nutrition Society. 2000. Dietary guidelines and the Food Guide Pyramid. *J. Am. Dietet. Assoc. 99*(2), 886.

Curry, K. R. 2000. Multicultural competence in dietetics and nutrition. *J. Am. Dietet. Assoc. 100*(10), 1142.

Devine, E., and N. L. Braganti. 1995. *Traveler's Guide to Customs and Manners.* St. Martin's Press. New York.

Dresser, N. 1996. *Multicultural Manners.* John Wiley and Sons. New York.

Elkort, M. 1991. *The Secret Life of Food.* St. Martin's Press. New York.

Ge, K., and K. McNutt. 1999. Publication of the Chinese Guidelines and Pagoda: How it happened. *Nutr. Today 34*(3), 104.

Gordon, B. H. J., M. Kang, P. Cho, and K. P. Sucher. 2000. Dietary habits and health beliefs of Korean-Americans in the San Francisco Bay Area. *J. Am. Dietet. Assoc. 100*(10), 1198.

Harris, P. R., and R. T. Moran. 1987. *Managing Cultural Differences.* 3rd ed. Gulf Publishing. Houston, TX.

Harris-Davis, E., and B. Haughton. 2000. Model for multicultural nutrition counseling competencies. *J. Am. Dietet. Assoc. 100*(10), 1178.

Kleiner, S. M. 1999. Water: Essential but overlooked nutrient. *J. Am. Dietet. Assoc. 99*(2), 200.

Lukins, S. 1994. *All Around the World.* Workman Publishing. New York.

Macpherson, A. E. 1998. Food Guide Pyramid for Puerto Rico. *Nutr. Today 33*(5), 198.

Orbeta, S. 1998. Filipino Pyramid Food Guide: Perfect match for the Philippines. *Nutr. Today 33*(5), 210.

Packard, D., and M. McWilliams. 1993. Cultural foods heritage of Middle Eastern immigrants. *Nutr. Today 28*(3), 6.

Painter, J., J. Rah, and Y. Lee. 2002. Comparison of international food guide pictorial representations. *J. Am. Dietet. Assoc.* 102(4), 483.

Sonnenfeld, A. 1996. *Food: Culinary History from Antiquity to Present.* Columbia University Press. New York.

Tyler, V. L. 1987. *Intercultural Interacting.* Brigham Young University Press. Provo, UT.

Glossary

Adobo: Filipino stew using meats marinated in vinegar seasoned with bagoong before being fried with onions and garlic and then stewed (Ch. 16).

Aebleskiver: Small Danish doughnuts prepared in a special pan (Ch. 5).

Afrikaans: Language spoken by Afrikans (South African farmers of Dutch heritage); one of the official languages of South Africa (Ch. 14).

Agave: Century plant; source of the sap used to make tequila and pulque (Ch. 22).

Aji: Very hot Andean chili pepper; pronounced like the fish ahi: ah-hee (Ch. 20).

Aksum: Early, well-developed settlement in the highlands of Ethiopia of importance in the 4th and 5th centuries CE (Ch. 14).

Almuerzo: Late morning light meal (usually tortilla-based dish and a beverage) often eaten in Mexico and Central America (Ch. 22).

Alsace-Lorraine: Eastern region of France bordering Germany (Ch. 9).

Angkor Wat: Very large temple complex built by the Khmers in northwest Cambodia (Ch. 2).

Antipasto: "Before the pasta" (hors d'oeuvre); wide variety of tidbits or appetizers, often olives, breadsticks, pickled vegetables, or other simple items (Ch. 8).

Apfel strudel: Austrian pastry made with extremely thin dough spread with melted butter and an apple filling, then rolled into a log, sliced into 3-inch lengths, and baked (Ch. 6).

Appelflappen: Fried, batter-dipped slices of apple sprinkled with confectioner's sugar (Ch. 6).

Aquavit (Akvavit): Aged whiskey made in Scandinavia and considered by some to be the national Scandinavian drink (Ch. 5).

Arawaks: Peaceful Indians who greeted Columbus when he arrived on Hispaniola (Ch. 21).

Ardennes: Region north of Paris to the English Channel (Ch. 9).

Atole: Gruel-like, thick beverage with a cornmeal base (Ch. 22).

Avatar: Person who is so saintly that he is thought to be an incarnation of a deity (Ch. 3).

Aztec Empire: Empire extending to both coasts of central Mexico south to Guatemala that was controlled by Aztecs from 1345 to 1519 CE (Ch. 1).

Aztecs: Indians in power in Mexico City region from the 14th century until Cortés conquered them in 1521 (Ch. 22).

Bacalao: Dried, salted cod (Ch. 21).

Bagoong: Filipino fermented, salted shrimp paste (Ch. 16).

Baklava: Baked dessert made of multiple layers of phyllo brushed with butter and with honey or rosewater (or both) plus chopped nuts (Ch. 11).

Balsamic vinegar: Special herb-flavored vinegar, the best of which is made in the vicinity of Modena in northern Italy (Ch. 8).

Banraku: Puppet shows featuring large, complicated puppets very skillfully presented, often in traditional stories (Ch. 19).

Bantus: Very large group of Africans originally from west and central regions of Africa, but spreading eastward and south starting prior to colonial days (Ch. 14).

Bar mitzvah: Maturity celebration for Jewish boy (Ch. 3).

Bastila: Flaky-crusted pigeon pie flavored with ginger, cumin, cayenne, saffron, and cinnamon and dusted with confectioner's sugar; Moroccan specialty (Ch. 12).

Bat mitzvah: Maturity celebration for Jewish girl (Ch. 3).

Béarnaise sauce: Sauce similar to hollandaise, but with vinegar, shallots, and seasoning used in place of lemon juice (Ch. 9).

Béchamel sauce: Basic white sauce made with cream or milk and thickened with flour (Ch. 9).

Berbers: Natives of the mountains of North Africa noted for their fighting skills and horsemanship (Ch. 12).

Berlin Conference of 1884–85: Meeting at which European colonial powers divided the African continent without including Africans (Ch. 13).

Bet tai: Disc-shaped, yeast-leavened Arab wheat bread, usually about 14 inches in diameter (Ch. 12).

Betel nut: Nut from a climbing pepper that is chewed for its digestive qualities, and which has a deep red juice (Ch. 15).

Bird's nest soup: Cornstarch-thickened soup made with the mucilaginous lining of the nests of the Asiatic swiftlet, chicken broth, minced chicken, and egg white (Ch. 17).

Biscuit: Flat cracker or cookie (Ch. 4).

Bitter melon: Vegetable with a wrinkled green skin and an interior resembling a cucumber (Ch. 17).

Black beans: Cooked and fermented soybeans preserved with ginger and salt (Ch. 17).

Bliny: Small, thin Russian pancakes (Ch. 7).

Bodhisattva: Semidivine, mystical being incorporated in Mahayana form of Buddhism (Ch. 3).

Body language: Movements made without talking but that communicate attitude or feelings to another person (Ch. 24).

Boer: South African of Dutch descent (Ch. 14).

Boeuf bourguignon: French beef stew with vegetables and red wine (Ch. 9).

Bok choy: Vegetable that grows as a bunch with thick, white stalks and a top of several large, coarse green leaves (Ch. 17).

Bolivar: Considered to be the liberator of South America from its European powers (Ch. 20).

Bolshoi Ballet: World renowned Russian ballet ensemble (Ch. 2).

Bombilla: Fancy silver straw and filter used to sip maté from a gourd (Ch. 20).

Bordeaux: Western region of France that is home to some outstanding wines and cognac (Ch. 9).

Bordelaise sauce: Dark sauce made with meat juices, bone marrow, tarragon, shallots, and Bordeaux wine (Ch. 9).

Borrel: Dutch gin (Ch. 6).

Borsch: Russian soup featuring beets and cabbage (Ch. 7).

Bosporus: Narrow channel that separates Europe from Asia between the Sea of Marmara and the Black Sea (Ch. 11).

Bouillabaisse: Hearty fish stew from the Mediterranean coast of France (Ch. 9).

Boxer Rebellion: Violent uprising of a secret sect resulting in trapping of foreigners and missionaries in Peking for two months in 1900 (Ch. 17).

Braaivleis: Barbecues in the southern countries of Africa (Ch. 14).

Brahma: Creator god or universal spirit of Hinduism (Ch. 3).

Brahmans: Highest caste in Hinduism; priests and teachers (Ch. 3).

Brillat-Savarin: Author of The Physiology of Taste (Ch. 9).

Brittany: Peninsula jutting from the northwest corner of France (Ch. 9).

Bruschetta: Italian bread brushed with olive oil, garlic, and sometimes tomato, and then broiled (Ch. 8).

Bubble and squeak: Dish of leftover beef, potatoes, and vegetables that makes these noises while being fried together (Ch. 4).

Bulgogi: Grilled, marinated beef or other meat (Ch. 18).

Bulgur: Partially cooked and dried cracked wheat (Ch. 11).

Burghul: Granular cereal product made by boiling and drying cracked wheat (Ch. 12).

Burgundy: Region on the eastern side of France north of the Rhone Valley and southeast of Paris; also a wine produced in the region (Ch. 9).

Burnoose: Dark, cape-like, hooded garment worn by Arab men (Ch. 12).

Burritos: Wheat flour tortillas wrapped around bean or meat filling (Ch. 22).

Byzantium: Early name for the city now called Istanbul (Ch. 11).

Cabral: Portuguese explorer who claimed Brazil for Portugal in 1500 (Ch. 20).

Café au lait: Coffee with milk, the most common breakfast beverage (Ch. 9).

Café con leche: Coffee with warm milk, the style preferred in South America (Ch. 20).

Caffe latte: Coffee with a generous amount of milk added (Ch. 8).

Calabash: Dried hard shell of a gourd suitable for holding liquids or foods (Ch. 14).

Callaloo: Spicy, thick, green soup containing spinach or other green plus okra, salt pork, coconut, and crabmeat (Ch. 21).

Cannelloni: Ridged tubes of pasta that are designed to be filled with various stuffings for entrees or desserts (Ch. 8).

Cantonese (southern school): Cuisine of the southern Chinese which features stir-frying, such dishes as egg rolls, dumplings (dim sum), and pork specialties, and generous use of vegetables, rice, and fruits (Ch. 17).

Cape of Good Hope: Region at the southern tip of the African continent (Ch. 14).

Capellini: Angel hair (very thin, spaghetti-like pasta) (Ch. 8).

Cappuccino: Espresso topped with frothy white milk (Ch. 8).

Carbonada: Argentinian beef stew with rice, corn, potatoes, squash, sweet potatoes, and apples (Ch. 20).

Carcassonne: Walled city founded by Visigoths and serving as a fortress in southwest France during the Middle Ages (Ch. 9).

Carib: Fierce Indian tribe originating in South America and subsequently conquering the tribes in the Caribbean (Ch. 21).

Carthage: Important trading city on the Mediterranean shore of Tunisia (Ch. 1).

Casbah: Walled part of Arab city in North Africa (Ch. 12).

Cassareep: Bittersweet flavoring used in pepper-pot and made from the boiled juice of the cassava root (Ch. 21).

Cassava: Tropical plant that is harvested for the starch abundant in the roots (Ch. 23).

Cassava bread: Native, rather flat bread made with powdered roots of cassava (Ch. 21).

Cassoulet: Casserole dish from Toulouse made with white beans, onions, carrots, duck, and herbs (Ch. 9).

Cena: Supper meal (light menu) served in Mexico and Central America in the evening (Ch. 22).

Ceviche: Raw fish marinated for 1 to 4 hours in lime juice and onion until flesh is opaque and the consistency of cooked fish; probably originated in Peru (Ch. 20).

Ch'a-shao-pao: Cantonese dish of steamed buns filled with roast pork (Ch. 17).

Chalupas: Fried tortillas topped with refried beans, slivered meat, chopped tomatoes and onions, and grated cheese (Ch. 22).

Champagne: Region east of Paris where the sparkling wine is produced (Ch. 9).

Chapati: Pancake-like grilled whole wheat bread popular in India (Ch. 15).

Chi pao yu: Shanghai specialty; bits of seasoned raw fish wrapped in wax paper and fried in deep fat, then unwrapped and eaten (Ch. 17).

Chicharrones: Fried snack of pork cracklings (Ch. 21, 22).

Chilaquiles: Shredded fried tortillas baked with chili sauce (ch. 22).

Chima: Long, gathered skirt that is part of traditional dress for Korean women (Ch. 18).

Chinese Food Guide Pagoda: Educational tool developed in China to guide people in making healthy food selections (Ch. 24).

Chinese parsley: Cilantro or coriander (Ch. 17).

Chogori: Short jacket tied off-center and worn with chima to complete the traditional dress for Korean women (Ch. 18).

Chorten: Tibetan religious (Buddhist) monument, often with some gold or silver gilding (Ch. 3).

Chow mein: Parboiled noodles fried briefly with other ingredients; a Cantonese stir-fry with noodles (Ch. 17).

Churro: Spiral-shaped quick bread similar to a doughnut (Ch. 10).

Chutney: Chunky and flavorful sauce often served as an accompaniment to curry (Ch. 15).

Cinco de Mayo: Celebration on May 5 honoring Mexican defeat of the French in 1862 at Puebla; celebrations in the United States also recognize the Mexican Americans living in this country (Ch. 22, 23).

Circumambulation: Circling of a stupa or shrine by a Buddhist while meditating on the doctrines and offering food and flowers (Ch. 3).

Cloudberries: Orange-yellow, plump berries that are similar in shape to blackberries; primarily available briefly from the far north of Scandinavia in summer (Ch. 5).

Cocido: Hearty Caribbean stew containing beef, sausage, vegetables, and sofrito (Ch. 21); hearty Filipino stew containing a variety of meats, Spanish sausage, chickpeas, saba (sweet cooking bananas), tomato sauce, and lard (Ch. 16); Spanish meal consisting of three traditional courses (soup, cooked vegetables, and boiled meats), the specific ingredients being quite variable (Ch. 10).

Coconut cream: Pureed and strained creamy liquid prepared from freshly grated white meat of mature pared coconut and hot water (Ch. 16).

Coconut milk: Coconut liquid similar to coconut cream, but with more liquid (Ch. 16).

Coconut water: Liquid drained from fresh coconut by puncturing its eyes; used as beverage, but not as a cooking ingredient (Ch. 16).

Comal: Flat, cast iron griddle used to bake tortillas (Ch. 22).

Comida: Heaviest meal of the day, eaten in midafternoon, in Mexico and Central America; includes soup, main dish, beans, rice, tortillas, dessert, and a beverage (Ch. 22).

Congee: Rice gruel often served at breakfast in southeast Asia (Ch. 16); in China, flavoring, meat, or fish are sometimes added (Ch. 17).

Coo-coo: Cornmeal pudding with okra, which is served either hot or cold (Ch. 21).

Cortés: Spanish explorer in Central America, particularly Mexico, in the 16th century (Ch. 10).

Coui Sauce: Very popular Caribbean hot sauce made with cassava juice and hot peppers (Ch. 21).

Couscous: Cereal product made by drizzling water on wheat flour and rolling into small pellets, which are then steamed until fluffy (Ch. 12).

Crayfish: Freshwater crustacean; apparently introduced to Scandinavia via ships from Britain (Ch. 5).

Creoles: People born in the Caribbean of European ancestry, often mixed with African blood (Ch. 21).

Crêpe: Thin French pancake (Ch. 9).

Crumpet: Similar to an English muffin, but somewhat thinner and more springy (Ch. 4).

Culture: Customary beliefs, social forms, and material traits of a racial, religious, or social group (Ch. 2).

Curry: Hearty and well-seasoned stew-like dish featuring meat or legumes and served with several accompaniments (Ch. 15).

Customs: Traditions that are common to a cultural group, such as shaking hands or bowing (Ch. 24).

Cuzco: Center of the Incan civilization in a very high (11,000 feet) Andean valley in Peru (Ch. 20).

Cyrillic alphabet: Alphabet developed by Cyril and Methodius, Byzantine monks who lived in the 9th century; used in Russia and many Slavic regions (Ch. 7).

Daikon: Large, long Asian radish (Ch. 23).

Dal: Puree of lentils or other legumes, usually rather blandly seasoned (Ch. 15).

Dashi: Clear soup stock made with dried fillet of bonito and kelp (Ch. 19).

Dendé: Yellow to reddish oil from a West African palm, which was introduced into Brazilian cooking by women slaves (Ch. 20).

Desayuno: Breakfast (usually coffee and pastry) eaten early in the morning in Mexico and Central America (Ch. 22).

Devi: Hindu goddess, the wife of Shiva (Ch. 3).

Diaspora: Settling of Jews outside of Palestine (Ch. 3).

Diaz, Bartolomeu: Portuguese navigator who sailed around the Cape of Good Hope (southern tip of Africa) in 1488 (Ch. 10).

Dim sum: Small, steamed dumplings filled with any of a variety of meat or vegetable fillings; favorites for snacks and lunches (Ch. 17).

Dolmas: Stuffed grape leaves usually containing rice and often other ingredients; may be served hot or cold (Ch. 11).

Dravidians: Early people of southern India (Ch. 15).

Dulceata: Romanian dish of simmered fruits in very heavy syrup (Ch. 7).

Durian: Large Asian fruit with bumpy skin and extremely strong smell (Ch. 23).

Dutch East India Company: Trading company that established Cape Town as a post to restock its ships plying between the East Indies and Holland (Ch. 14).

Eastern (Shanghai) school: Cuisine of the eastern seaboard of China, notably of Shanghai; light broths, seafood, egg rolls, and paper-wrapped foods are characteristic (Ch. 17).

Einkhorn: Wheat species native to the Balkans, Anatolia, and adjacent areas of western Asia (Ch. 1).

Eintopf: Hearty German stew of meat, vegetables, and a cereal or dumplings (Ch. 6).

El Cid: Spanish military hero who fought many battles for both the Moors and the Catholics, and freed Valencia from the Moors in 1094 (Ch. 10).

Emmer: Early form of wheat native to Palestine and Syria; main form of wheat in prehistory and later grown in parts of Europe into the Christian period (Ch. 1).

Empañadas: Fried or baked semicircular pastries filled with meat and raisins; prominent in Argentina, but also in other South American countries (Ch. 20).

Empire of Ghana: Dominant power in West Africa from 5th to 11th century (Ch. 13).

Empire of Mali: Empire dominating trade from Senegal to Egypt from the 13th to the 15th century (Ch. 13).

Empire of Songhai: Dominant empire in West Africa (including Timbuktu) after splitting from Mali in the 14th century into the 16th century (Ch. 13).

Enchiladas: Corn tortillas rolled around a filling and covered with a sauce before baking (Ch. 22).

Escabeche: Cooked fish marinated in vinegar and spices (Ch. 21).

Escoffier: Chef considered to be the definitive writer about French cuisine (1846–1935) (Ch. 9).

Espresso: Very strong Italian coffee made by brewing dark-roast, finely ground coffee with steam (Ch. 8).

Ethnicity: Affiliation with a race, people, or social group (Ch. 2).

Etruscan: Group that settled in Tuscany and moved south, ultimately taking over Rome and contributing their alphabet, speech, and ability to wage war (Ch. 8).

Falafel: Dish made by forming a paste of soaked chickpeas and seasonings, shaping into balls or other shapes, and frying in deep fat (Ch. 11).

Fan: Grain foods considered to be important as a balance with the ts'ai (other foods in the meal) (Ch. 17).

Färikäl: Thick lamb stew with cabbage; popular stew in Norway (Ch. 5).

Feijoada completa: Celebrated Brazilian dish of several meats (including sausages and bacon), beans, rice, hot sauces, manioc meal, and sliced oranges (Ch. 20).

Feta: Soft cheese made from ewe's milk (Ch. 11).

Filipino Pyramid Food Guide: Food guide developed in the Philippines to guide people in healthy food choices using the local foods (Ch. 24).

Finnan haddie: Smoked haddock poached in milk on a bed of onions (Ch. 4).

Fiskebeller: Norwegian fishballs (Ch. 5).

Five Pillars: Basic requirements of Muslim religion (Ch. 3).

Five-spice powder: Popular Chinese spice made by mixing star anise, Szechwan pepper, cinnamon, cloves, and fennel (Ch. 17).

Flan: Baked custard dessert, usually served with caramel in it in both Spain and Portugal (Ch. 10, 22).

Flautas: Tightly rolled corn tortillas, containing a small amount of filling, which are fried until crisp (Ch. 22).

Flying buttress: External architectural feature to support the relatively thin, windowed walls of Gothic cathedrals (Ch. 9).

Fondue: Swiss dish prepared by melting cheese with wine in a chafing dish and using long-handled forks to dip cubes of bread into the cheese mixture (Ch. 6).

Fontina: Cheese well suited for making fondue; originally from Valle d'Aosta in northern Italy near Great St. Bernard Pass (Ch. 8).

Food Guide Pyramid: Educational tool used in the United States to guide people in making healthy food choices (Ch. 24).

Foo-foo: Mashed plantains with okra (Ch. 21).

Fool: Sweetened fruit puree blended with custard or cream; served cold (Ch. 4).

Forbidden City: Walled area in Beijing built by Chinese emperors as the seat of government and power (Ch. 2).

Foul: Mixture of cooked chickpeas and black or broad beans that have been soaked together for at least 2 days before being cooked; served with topping of garlic, olive oil, lemon, tomato, and cilantro (Ch. 11).

Franco: Spanish dictator for about 40 years in the 20th century (Ch. 10).

Frijoles refritos: Cooked beans with added lard that are stirred to a pureed texture (Ch. 22).

Frikadeller: Danish meatballs (Ch. 5).

Fruit soup: Dessert soup popular in Scandinavia; often made with various dried fruits that are readily available through long winters (Ch. 5).

Fufu: Starchy paste produced by pounding and boiling manioc or other rich source of starch and then dipping each bite in a spicy sauce (Ch. 13); starchy paste or dough made of cassava and popular in Kenya (Ch. 14).

Funchi: Cornmeal pudding prepared in the Caribbean (Ch. 21).

Fungi: Designation for mushrooms in some Chinese recipes; may include shitake, enoki, oyster, button, or other types, usually dried (Ch. 17).

Fusilli: Wavy, spaghetti-like pasta (Ch. 8).

Garam masala: Basic mixture of spices usually prepared in quantity and used as desired to season many different dishes in India (Ch. 15).

Gari foto: Stew of hard-cooked eggs, onions, and tomatoes (Ch. 13).

Gelati: Italian ice cream (Ch. 8).

Ghandi, Mahatma: Famous pacifist in India who led a 200-mile march to the sea in 1930 to protest the salt tax (Ch. 2).

Ghee: Clarified butter that has been cooked down a little to add flavor; expensive, but preferred fat for cooking in India (Ch. 15); clarified butter; considered a sacred food by Hindus because it is from the cow, a sacred animal (Ch. 3).

Ghiveciu: Romanian casserole consisting of browned chunks of pork or veal, browned vegetables, tomato paste, red wine, and green grapes (Ch. 7).

Gibanica: Yugoslavian layered cheese pie (Ch. 7).

Ginger root: Gnarled root of ginger, which usually is grated after being peeled; adds flavor as well as some heat to a recipe (Ch. 17).

Gnocchi: Yugoslavian small dumplings of wheat or cornmeal, or both (Ch. 7).

Gorditas: Thick, small tortillas fried with meats or vegetables (or both) and cheese (Ch. 22).

Goree: Island just off the coast of Dakar, Senegal, from which vast numbers of slaves were shipped to the Americas and Caribbean islands (Ch. 13).

Gorgonzola: Blue-veined cheese that originated in Gorgonzola near Milan in northern Italy and is now produced in the Po Valley (Ch. 8).

Gothic: Style of cathedral featuring pointed arches, high and thin walls containing stained glass, and strengthened by flying buttresses on the exterior (Ch. 9).

Gravet: Smoked salmon, a Norwegian delicacy (Ch. 5).

Great Rift Valley: Vast depression in the earth extending from Jordan south and west to Mozambique (Ch. 14).

Great Zimbabwe: Settlement in Zimbabwe featuring the Great Enclosure built of stone in the 14th century (Ch. 14).

Guacamole: Pureed avocado flavored with chilies and other seasonings; served as an accompaniment or a garnish (Ch. 22).

Gulyas: Hungarian stew made with chunks of braised meat, seasoned with onion and paprika, and varying amounts of liquid (Ch. 7).

Haggis: Scottish traditional pudding of oatmeal, variety meats, suet, onions, and seasonings boiled in a sheep's stomach; often served at dinners honoring Robert Burns, Scotland's famous poet (Ch. 4).

Hajj: Pilgrimage to Mecca; one of the Five Pillars (Ch. 3).

Hallacas: Colombian version of a tamale made be wrapping a layer of corn flour dough and a filling of meat or other ingredients in banana leaves and then steaming the packets (Ch. 20).

Han-gŭl: Phonetic Korean alphabet developed under the leadership of King Sejong in the 15th century (Ch. 18).

Harira: Hearty soup containing legumes, meat, and vegetables, and seasoned with spices and lemon; important for suppers during Ramadan (Ch. 12).

Hispaniola: Caribbean island where Columbus landed and which eventually became the countries of Haiti and the Dominican Republic (Ch. 21).

Hmongs: People native to the northern hill regions of Laos (Ch. 16).

Hoisin sauce: Thick, brown, garlic-flavored bean sauce (Ch. 17).

Hollandaise sauce: Sauce made of an emulsion of butter, egg yolks, lemon juice, and seasoning (Ch. 9).

Honshu: Largest of the islands of Japan; Tokyo is on Honshu (Ch. 19).

Hot cross buns: Easter yeast buns containing cinnamon, allspice, and raisins, and topped with a cross of candied orange peel or a strip of dough to represent the cross of Christ (Ch. 4).

Hummus: Dip made with pureed, cooked chickpeas, tahini, lemon juice, garlic, and olive oil (Ch. 11).

Hutspot: Hearty stew-like dish made in the Netherlands by simmering a large cut of meat with vegetables and then mashing the cooked vegetables before serving them with the sliced meat (Ch. 6).

Id al-Fitr: Three-day celebration marking the end of the Ramadan; the Feast of the Breaking of the Fast (Ch. 3).

Idlis: Rice cakes (Ch. 15).

Ikebana: Japanese art of arranging cut flowers (Ch. 19).

Ile de France: Region within a 50-mile circle of Paris (Ch. 9).

Illyrian: Group of people settling the Balkans prior to the Romans (Ch. 7).

Imam: Person who leads Muslims in their daily prayers (Ch. 3).

Incan Empire: Region of Andes in Peru controlled by Incas from about 1300 CE until Pizarro conquered it after his arrival in 1533 CE (Ch. 1).

Inquisition: Period when Spain required non-Catholics to convert or leave the country; torture sometimes was part of the imprisonment process in Spain, Peru, and Portugal (Ch. 10).

Irish stew: Stew of lamb cubes, potatoes, and onions simmered for a very long time to tenderize the stew meat; frequently served with red cabbage in Ireland (Ch. 4).

Jenné-Jeno: Very early town (before 500 CE) in Mali (Ch. 13).

Jicama: Brown root vegetable with crisp white interior, often served in raw slices with chili powder sprinkled on them (Ch. 22).

Jollof rice: Dish comprised of layers of meat, tomatoes and other vegetables, and steamed rice (Ch. 13).

Jugged: Slow, moist-heat cooking of meat in a covered clay pot (Ch. 4).

Ka'ba: Black stone cube with a meteorite in its wall; shrine in the center of Mecca of importance to Muslims (Ch. 3).

Kabob (kebab): Meat and sometimes other items grilled on a skewer (Ch. 11).

Kabuki: Traditional, highly stylized drama with elaborate costumes and makeup, often featuring dancing and some music performed by men (Ch. 19).

Kama: Hindu god of love (Ch. 3).

Kami: Supernatural beings (departed ancestors) in Shintoism in Japan (Ch. 3).

Kaoliang: Sorghum (grain) crop grown in northern China (Ch. 17).

Kapi: Thai salty, dried shrimp paste (Ch. 16).

Kasha: Buckwheat groats (or sometimes other cereals) boiled in liquid until light and fluffy; dish popular in Russia and its environs (Ch. 7).

Kashruth: Jewish dietary laws (Ch. 3).

Keshy yena: Edam cheese stuffed with grated cheese, meat mixtures, and seasonings, then baked; from Netherlands Antilles (Ch. 21).

Khatib: Person who reads the Friday sermon (Ch. 3).

Khmers: People native to Cambodia (Ch. 16).

Kibbeh: Deep-fat fried, egg-shaped shell of finely minced lamb and cracked wheat paste encasing a filling of another meat (Ch. 11).

Kielbasa: Polish sausage made of ground beef and pork well seasoned with garlic (Ch. 7).

Kimchi: Fermented, pickled vegetables (particularly cabbage) (Ch. 18).

Kippers: Herring prepared in the traditional Scottish way of splitting them and then salting, drying, and smoking to preserve them (Ch. 4).

Kitchen god: Spirit of the hearth who determines wealth and longevity of people in the household; reports to Heaven annually regarding family's behavior (Ch. 17).

Knedliky: Flat, circular potato or bread dumplings popular in the Czech Republic and Slovakia (Ch. 7).

Kochujang: Red pepper and bean paste used as a condiment and also as an ingredient in Korean recipes (Ch. 18).

Koldt bord: Literally, cold table; bread, butter, and cold dishes that are the beginning part of a smørgasbørd (Ch. 5).

Koran: Volume of writings (114 suras) given to the Prophet Muhammad by Allah (God) through the Angel Gabriel (Ch. 3).

Koryŏ: Dynasty that ruled Korea from 918 to 1392 and subsequently was the source for the name Korea (Ch. 18).

Kringle: Nut-filled coffee cake from Denmark (Ch. 5).

Krishna: Hindu god celebrated as the eighth incarnation of Vishnu (Ch. 3).

Kshatriyas: Second caste in Hinduism; warriors and rulers (Ch. 3).

Ku lao jou: Dish containing starch-coated fried cubes of pork, stir-fried green peppers, various vegetables, and pineapple cubes in a thickened sweet-sour tomato sauce (Ch. 17).

Kulich: Yeast-leavened Russian traditional Easter bread containing candied and dried fruits, nuts, and liqueur (Ch. 7).

Kutho: Kind or generous act that brings merit to help strive toward Nirvana (Ch. 3).

Kwanzaa: African American holiday lasting a week at the end of the year to celebrate Black heritage (Ch. 23).

Languedoc-Roussillon: Region in southern France that includes the marshy delta of the Rhone River (Ch. 9).

Lapskaus: Chunky and thick meat and potato stew (Ch. 5).

Lasagne: Broad, ribbon-like pasta used in casserole dishes (Ch. 8).

Lascaux: Area in southern France where cave paintings from prehistoric people have been found (Ch. 9).

Laver: Edible seaweed; popular in Korea (Ch. 18).

Lavosh: Armenian cracker bread; basically a very thin version of pita (Ch. 11).

Lebkuchen: German gingerbread cookies baked in a picture mold (Ch. 6).

Lebneh: Soft cheese made by draining whey from yogurt (Ch. 11).

Lefse: Norwegian flatbread (Ch. 5).

Lemon curd: Egg yolk-thickened sweet filling flavored with lemon juice and rind; often used as filling for tarts and pies (Ch. 4).

Levant: Lands at the eastern end of the Mediterranean Sea (Ch. 11).

Lingonberries: Mountain cranberry-like fruit particularly popular in Sweden (Ch. 5).

Longyi: Long, sarong-like cloth worn in Burma, tucked in at the waist or hiked up in the very hot weather (Ch. 16).

Lotus root: Crunchy root of lotus (water lily) cut crosswise to use in stir-fries and soups, where its porous appearance due to many lengthwise cavities in the root add visual interest (Ch. 17).

Lumache: Large, conch shell-shaped pasta suitable for stuffing (Ch. 8).

Lutefisk: Cod soaked in lye until very soft (about 3 days) before being rinsed in running water for 2 days and subsequently poached or boiled (Ch. 5).

Mace: Reddish coating on nutmeg, which is removed and dried for use as a spice (Ch. 21).

Magellan: Portuguese navigator who led the first circumnavigation of the world from 1519 to 1522; he died in the Philippines during the trip (Ch. 10).

Maghreb: Countries in the northwestern part of Africa: Morocco, Algeria, and Tunisia (Ch. 12).

Magyars: Ancestors of today's Hungarians (Ch. 7).

Mahayana: Buddhist sect prominent in Tibet, Mongolia, and the Himalayas (Ch. 3).

Malagueta: Extremely hot South American pepper, also called aji (Ch. 20).

Mamaliga: Romanian cornmeal mush similar to Italian polenta (Ch. 7).

Manicotti: Long, plain tube of pasta appropriate for stuffing (Ch. 8).

Manioc (cassava): Tropical plant from the lowlands of South America used as a source of root starch (Ch. 1); granular flour prepared by peeling and then grating bitter cassava roots and squeezing out absolutely all of the juice, which is poisonous until subsequently boiled. The dry grated material is broken to a powder by pounding (Ch. 20).

Mantra: Hindu incantation (Ch. 3).

Manu: Source of Hindu laws on living, and ancestor of Hindus, progenitor of human race and source of Vedas (Ch. 3).

Masa harina: Ground corn that has been soaked in lye (Ch. 22).

Mascarpone: Unripened Italian dessert cheese made from fresh cream; may be flavored with honey, liqueurs, or candied fruit (Ch. 8).

Maté: Beverage brewed in a gourd by pouring hot water over crushed leaves of yerba maté, producing a caffeine-containing beverage that is sipped through a bombilla; pronounced ma-tay (Ch. 20).

Mayan Empire: Region including the Yucatan Peninsula and Guatemala controlled by Mayans from 3000 BCE to about 1200 CE (Ch. 1).

Mayans: Indians living in Guatemala, Belize, and southern Mexico from 600 BCE to 1200 CE (Ch. 22).

Mealie meal: South African name for cornmeal (mealie means corn) (Ch. 14).

Medici: Powerful Florentine banking family; Cosimo, Lorenzo, and Catherine (who carried the excellence of Florentine cuisine to France when she married future King Henri II) are credited with influencing the artistic and culinary renaissance in the 15th and 16th centuries, particularly (Ch. 8).

Medina: Old native quarter of a North African city (Ch. 12).

Mediterranean Diet Pyramid: Food pyramid designed to incorporate the foods common to the Mediterranean in a pattern that has 11 categories (Ch. 24).

Menorah: Candelabra used in Jewish worship (usually with six arms plus elevated center holder) (Ch. 3).

Merienda: Late afternoon light refreshment eaten in Mexico and Central America (Ch. 22).

Meseta: High central plain in Spain (Ch. 10).

Mestizos: Descendants of Indians and the conquering Spaniards (Ch. 20, 21).

Metate: Stone quern used for grinding nixtamal to masa harina (Ch. 22).

Mihrab: Niche in an interior wall of a mosque to indicate the direction of Mecca for worshipers during Salat (Ch. 3).

Minaret: Slender tower with a balcony for the muezzin to call Muslims to prayer (Ch. 3).

Minbar: Staircase topped with a pulpit in a mosque (Ch. 3).

Minoan civilization: Well developed, artistic culture centered on Crete in the second millennium BCE until the volcanic eruption of Thera in 1625 BCE (Ch. 1).

Mirin: Sweet rice wine (Ch. 19).

Miso: Fermented soybean paste (Ch. 19).

Mochi: Rice cake made by pounding cooked sweet glutinous rice; traditional for New Year's celebration (Ch. 19).

Mofongo: Puerto Rican specialty made with mashed plantains, pork cracklings, and garlic either fried in balls or baked as a pancake (Ch. 21).

Mongolian fire pot: Mongolian-designed unique chafing dish with a spot to burn charcoal and a chimney going up the center, and a surrounding round vessel where broth is kept hot enough for diners to cook their individual bites of meats and vegetables (Ch. 17).

Mons: People native to Burma (Ch. 16).

Moors: Inhabitants of northwestern Africa (mixture of Arabs and Berbers) who invaded Spain in the 8th century (Ch. 10, 12).

Moros y Cristianos: Cuban specialty containing black beans and rice cooked together with garlic, onions, green peppers, tomatoes, and seasonings (Ch. 21).

Mosque: Place of worship for Muslims (Ch. 3).

Moussaka: Eggplant casserole usually containing lamb, onions, tomato sauce, and eggplant slices (Ch. 11).

Mozzarella: Cheese used on pizzas, originally made from buffalo milk, but now often made from cow's milk (Ch. 8).

Muesli: Breakfast cereal of toasted oats, nuts, and dried apples, developed by a Swiss doctor (Ch. 6).

Muezzin: Person who calls Muslims to prayer five times a day (Ch. 3).

Muhammad: Arabian prophet who founded Islam in 622 CE (Ch. 3).

Mulligatawny: Curry-flavored rich soup made with a chicken or lamb base; reflecting British period in India (Ch. 4).

Mycenea: Site of Agamemnon's palace and the governmental center of the Greek Peloponnesus and the eastern Mediterranean from the late 1500s BCE to about 1100 BCE (Ch. 1).

Naan: Oval-shaped whole wheat bread baked by sticking it to the wall of a tandoor (Ch. 15).

Nam pla: Fermented fish sauce popular in Thailand (Ch. 16).

Niger River: One of the longest rivers of the world, it runs across much of West Africa, running northward before turning east and south; has an interior delta and one at the coast (Ch. 13).

Nixtamal: Hull-less, lye-soaked corn (Ch. 22).

Nopales: Leaves of prickly pear cactus (Ch. 22).

Nori: Dried seaweed available in thin, greenish-black sheets; used for wrapping sushi and other foods or as a garnish (Ch. 19).

Normandy: Northern region of France just east of Brittany and lying along the coast of the English Channel (Ch. 9).

Northern (Peking) school: Cuisine of the northern region of China, which includes Peking duck and Mongolian fire pot as well as moo shu pork and other recipes that use wheat and wheat flour products (Ch. 17).

Nuoc cham: Vietnamese condiment made with chili peppers, citrus juice, garlic, onions, and vinegar (Ch. 16).

Nuoc mam: Fermented, salted fish sauce popular in Vietnam (Ch. 16).

Olmecs: Dominant cultural group in Central America from 1200 to 150 BCE; settled predominantly on the coast of the Gulf of Mexico along the Bay of Campeche west of the Yucatan Peninsula (Ch. 1).

Om: Sound chanted repeatedly for long periods to generate religious energy in Hinduism (Ch. 3).

Opium War: War in 1840 caused by British involvement in the opium trade in China; resulted in the long-term lease of Hong Kong to Britain (Ch. 17).

Osso buco: Braised veal shanks simmered with herbs and wine until very tender (Ch. 8).

Oyster sauce: Salty, dark Chinese sauce made with soy sauce and the flavor of oysters and other flavoring agents (Ch. 17).

Paella: Traditional dish of rice flavored with saffron and topped with cooked vegetables and meats (Ch. 10).

Pagoda: Several-storied shrine for Buddhists (Ch. 3).

Pannetone: Coarse, sweet yeast bread containing raisins and candied fruit (Ch. 8).

Paratha: Whole wheat bread circles about 7 inches in diameter and made with some ghee in the dough and in the frying on the griddle (Ch. 15).

Parmesan: Hard cheese often aged for more than 2 years; frequently grated over Italian dishes (Ch. 8).

Parrillada: Grilled mixture of meats, typical of Argentina (Ch. 20).

Parthenon: Classical Greek structure dominating the Acropolis in Athens (Ch. 2).

Paskha: Pyramid-shaped Russian Easter cake (Ch. 7).

Pasteles: Puerto Rican specialty made by spreading mashed plantain or cornmeal on a plantain leaf, adding a savory filling, wrapping, and steaming (Ch. 21).

Pastelitos: Savory, small turnovers with meat filling, made in the Dominican Republic (Ch. 21).

Patis: Fermented, salty fish sauce popular in the Philippines (Ch. 16).

Peking duck: Traditional dish of northern China, which involves special roasting of a duck until the skin is very crisp; skin, a bit of duck meat, and green onion are wrapped in a thin pancake liberally splashed with hoisin sauce. Plum sauce is also served (Ch. 17).

Peloponnesus: Peninsula extending off the southwestern region of Greece (Ch. 11).

Penne: Tubular pasta cut diagonally into pieces about an inch long (Ch. 8).

Pepper-pot: Long-lived stew common throughout the Caribbean, flavored with cassareep and containing meats and vegetables that are replenished from time to time as needed and available (Ch. 21).

Perigord: Area north of the Pyrenees where truffles are found (Ch. 9).

Pesto: Flavorful thick sauce made by pulverizing fresh basil and adding such ingredients as piñon nuts, parmesan cheese, garlic, and olive oil (Ch. 8).

Phyllo: Extremely thin dough that is formed into large sheets and serves as the main ingredient for desserts and some main dishes (Ch. 11).

Pierogi: Polish dish consisting of small pockets of dough containing a filling (vegetable or sweet) (Ch. 7).

Pirozhki: Small Russian pastries filled with meat (Ch. 7).

Pita: Pocket bread that is common throughout the Middle East (Ch. 11).

Pizaro: Spanish explorer who conquered Peru in the 16th century (Ch. 10, 20).

Plantain: Very starchy banana, which is cooked before serving (Ch. 23).

Plum sauce: Chutney made with plums, apricots, vinegar, chili, and sugar (Ch. 17).

Poe (poi): Starchy paste of boiled and pounded, peeled taro root, popular in Polynesia (Ch. 16).

Pombe: Kenyan beer (Ch. 14).

Posados: Procession of Mary and Joseph's search for lodging reenacted from December 16 until Christmas as part of Christmas festivities (Ch. 22).

Potala: Seat of Tibetan Buddhism and the former home of the Dalai Lama (Ch. 15).

Prester John: Mythical Christian leader of a domain deep in Africa (Ch. 14).

Prince Henry the Navigator: Portuguese leader who sponsored voyages of exploration aboard caravels to very distant places (Ch. 10).

Prosciutto: Thinly sliced, well-cured Parma ham (Ch. 8).

Provence: Region in southern France adjacent to the French Riviera (Ch. 9).

Pumpernickel: German dark, coarse bread made with unsifted rye flour (Ch. 6).

Punic Wars: Three wars fought between Carthage and Rome between 264 and 146 BCE (Ch. 1).

Puri: Deep-fat fried rounds of whole wheat bread that are puffed in the middle during frying (Ch. 15).

Quesada: Spanish conquistador credited with conquering Columbia (Ch. 20).

Quesadilla: Flour tortilla folded over a layer of grated cheese and heated (Ch. 22).

Quinoa: Grain grown in the high Andes by Indians and eaten as a rich source of protein and starch in Peru and Chile; pronounced keen-wah (Ch. 20).

Raclette: Swiss favorite consisting of melted cheese served with a sliced, boiled potato, sweet gherkin, and pickled pearl onions (Ch. 6).

Ramadan: Thirty-day fast in the ninth lunar month of the Muslim year (Ch. 3).

Rastafarianism: Jamaican religion traced to teaching in the Old Testament; members may have dreadlocks; reggae music originated in this group (Ch. 21).

Ratatouille: Highly flavorful medley of vegetables and herbs from Provence (Ch. 9).

Ravioli: Rectangular pasta pouches stuffed with ground meat or cheese (Ch. 8).

Rijsttafel: Rice table originating in Indonesia, but brought to the Netherlands by the Dutch East Indies Company; consists of highly spiced dishes and many other somewhat bland dishes, which are prepared at the table (usually in restaurants) (Ch. 6).

Risotto: Rice cooked for an hour or more, with saffron or other seasonings added (Ch. 8).

Roma: Nomadic group originating from India, but particularly numerous in Romania and spreading into most parts of Europe (Ch. 7).

Romano: Sharp, aged sheep's milk cheese; very hard cheese, ideal for grating (Ch. 8).

Rømmegrøt: Norwegian porridge of milk and sour cream thickened with flour and flavored with cinnamon and coarse sugar granules (Ch. 5).

Rösti: Swiss dish of parboiled, grated potatoes sautéed in sizzling butter to make a pancake-like disk that is browned well on both sides (Ch. 6).

Roti: Indian word for bread (Ch. 15).

Sachertorte: Austrian dessert; layered chocolate cake spread with apricot jam and topped with a chocolate glaze (Ch. 6).

Sadza: Zimbabwean name for a stiff corn porridge (Ch. 14).

Saffron: Orange to yellow spice; the stigma of purple crocus (Ch. 10).

Safsari: Robes worn by women in North Africa to cover their bodies and veil their faces (Ch. 12).

Sahel: Broad band of land across West Africa between the Sahara and the lush vegetation along the southern coast (Ch. 13).

Sake: Strong rice wine, usually served warm (Ch. 19).

Salat: Muslim daily prayer according to the Five Pillars (Ch. 3).

Sally Lunn: Light yeast bread baked in a tubular pan, sliced in half, then topped with whipped cream or melted butter; originated in Bath, England (Ch. 4).

Salsa: Sauce containing finely chopped vegetables and seasonings used to add flavor excitement to many Mexican and Central American dishes (Ch. 22).

Sambar: Spicy puree of lentils, which often is served with idlis (Ch. 15).

Samgye t'yang: Whole small chicken stuffed with rice, ginseng, and chestnuts, covered in broth, and baked until meat almost falls from bones (Ch. 18).

Sami: Nomadic reindeer herders (Lapplanders) living in the arctic reaches of Scandinavia; shorter stature and darker coloring than the Scandinavians from the lower parts of this region (Ch. 5).

Samosa: Fried pastry enclosing a filling (Ch. 15).

Samovar: Elaborate Russian device equipped with a chimney, a teapot for the essence of the tea, and a large area where the water is boiled for dispensing from the spigot (Ch. 7).

Sancocho: Stew popular in the Dominican Republic; contains plantain, chicken, cassava, vinegar, and pepper (Ch. 21).

Sang-chi-sam: Lettuce-wrapped meal containing many tidbits from numerous dishes selected by the diner (Ch. 18).

Sangria: Red wine with fruit juices (Ch. 10).

Sashimi: Very carefully cut and arranged slices of raw fish (Ch. 19).

Sauerbraten: German dish; roast marinated in vinegar and wine and simmered with seasoning until very tender, served with a gingersnap-containing gravy and red cabbage cooked with tart apples (Ch. 6).

Saum: Ritual of fasting; one of the Five Pillars (Ch. 3).

Schnitzel: German term for cutlets of veal or other meat cut thinly prior to cooking (Ch. 6).

Scones: Quick bread made from a dough that is rolled and cut into circles, then baked in a very hot oven; popular for teatime (Ch. 4).

Seaweed: Various types of edible seaweeds and sea grass, as well as purple laver; usually used dried in soups (Ch. 17).

Sejong the Great: Dynamic 15th-century Korean leader who sponsored development of han-gùl, written music, movable type, astronomy, and a medical book (Ch. 18).

Shahada: Creed that is one of the Five Pillars: "There is no god but God; Muhammad is the Messenger of God" (Ch. 3).

Shark's fin: Usually transparent, yellowish, dried cartilage from the fin of a shark; this delicacy requires rehydration and is used in a soup (Ch. 17).

Shashlyk: Russian version of shish kebabs (Ch. 7).

Shawarma: Thinly sliced chicken layered tightly with fat and formed into a solid that is grilled vertically on a rotisserie and sliced off in very thin slices (Ch. 11).

Shchi: Cabbage-containing soup made in Russia (Ch. 7).

Shepherd's pie: Deep-dish meat pie made with cooked meat and onions, and topped with a crust of mashed potatoes before baking (Ch. 4).

Shiite: Branch of Islam practiced by those who follow Ali, the prophet's son-in-law (Ch. 12).

Shinsollo: Korean hot pot (Ch. 18).

Shinto: Early religion of Japan that focused on nature and considered the Emperor to be a descendant of the sun goddess (Ch. 19).

Shiva (Siva): Destructive Hindu god (Ch. 3).

Shofar: Hollowed out ram's horn blown in the synagogue during Rosh Hashanah to call man to be aware of his shortcomings and to emphasize that God is the divine king (Ch. 3).

Shogun: Military rulers in Japan prior to 1867 (Ch. 19).

Shortbread: Very rich, flat, round cookie (biscuit, if using British vocabulary); often served with tea (Ch. 4).

Sibelius: Composer from Finland who lived from 1865 to 1957; his most famous orchestral work is "Finlandia" (Ch. 2)

Sinhalese: Descendants of Aryans living in Sri Lanka (Ch. 15).

Sinterklaas: Name for Saint Nicholas in the Netherlands (Ch. 6).

Sizzling rice soup: Rice that has formed a crust on the bottom of a wok before being deep-fat fried is added to a hot broth, causing great sizzling sounds from the rice as it is stirred into the soup (Ch. 17).

Slatko: Serbian dish made of fruit simmered with blossoms in a sweet sugar syrup (Ch. 7).

Slivova: Bulgarian plum brandy (Ch. 7).

Slivovitz: Plum brandy liqueur drunk by Czechs and Slovaks (Ch. 7).

Smørgasbørd: Very elaborate Scandinavian buffet with ample arrays of cold foods and hot dishes, as well as dessert choices (Ch. 5).

Smørrebrød: Scandinavian open-faced sandwiches, usually with a base of rye bread and butter and artfully arranged toppings (Ch. 5).

Snow peas: Flat, green peas in tender, crisp, edible pods (Ch. 17).

Soba: Noodles made from buckwheat flour from northern Japan (Ch. 19).

Sofrito: Hot, spicy sauce featuring chilies, tomatoes, garlic, ham or bacon, and coriander (Ch. 21).

Sopa de ajo: Garlic soup popular in Spain (Ch. 10).

Sopito: Fish chowder made with coconut milk in the Netherlands Antilles (Ch. 21).

Sosaties: Barbecued pieces of meat on a stick (Ch. 14).

Soufflé: Baked foam of egg whites combined with a yolk and chocolate (or cheese or other flavoring ingredient) sauce (Ch. 9).

Souk: Arab marketplace featuring specific types of shops, such as spice shops and gold shops(Ch. 12).

Soul Food Pyramid: Healthy food guide for persons who are lactose-intolerant and need to limit fat intake to control weight (Ch. 24).

Spanakopite: Main dish consisting of many layers of phyllo, spinach, and various other ingredients according to taste (Ch. 11).

Springerle: Anise-flavored, German picture cookie popular at Christmas (Ch. 6).

Spritsar: Swedish ring-shaped cookie often made at Christmastime (Ch. 5).

St. Peter's Basilica: Very large cathedral in the Vatican city (Ch. 8).

Stamp and go: Jamaican dish featuring salted, dried cod suspended in a heavy batter containing chilies, onions, and annatto, and fried as a fritter (Ch. 21).

Steak-and-kidney pie: Hearty, savory pie containing pieces of beef steak and kidneys in the filling (Ch. 4).

Stupa: Hemispherical mound with a central decoration, which serves as a shrine for Buddhists (Ch. 15).

Sudras: Fourth caste in Hinduism; menial workers (Ch. 3).

Suimono: Clear Japanese soups (Ch. 19).

Sukiyaki: Thinly sliced beef simmered with Japanese vegetables, soy sauce, mirin, and dashi in a pot at the table (Ch. 19).

Sunni: Branch of Islam practiced by those who follow the descendants of the fifth caliph (Ch. 12).

Sunomono: Vinegared salads (Ch. 19).

Sushi: Vinegared rice and small bits of other ingredients pressed into a mold or rolled tightly into a long log encased in a layer of nori and sliced vertically (Ch. 19).

Szechwan (western) school: Cuisine developed in western China, which is quite spicy and hot in character and uses considerable garlic, ginger, and oil (Ch. 17).

Tabouli: Salad containing soaked bulgur, minced parsley and mint, diced tomatoes, olive oil, and lemon juice (Ch. 11).

Tacos: Crisply fried or soft tortillas folded in half over a filling of beans, meats, and other ingredients (Ch. 22).

Tagine: Stew prepared in a round pottery bowl topped with a conical lid (bowl and conical lid also called tagine), a unique product of Morocco (Ch. 12).

Tahini: Paste of finely ground sesame seeds, sesame oil, and lemon juice (Ch. 11).

Taj Mahal: Mausoleum built by Shah Jahan in Agra, India, to honor the memory of his favorite wife, Mumtaz (Ch. 2, 15).

Tajaditas: Fried banana chips (Ch. 22).

Tak paesuk: Whole small chicken stuffed with rice, covered in broth, and baked until meat almost falls from bones (Ch. 18).

Talmud: Authoritative body of Jewish tradition (Ch. 3).

Tamales: Masa harina spread on cornhusks and wrapped around a filling of meat or other ingredients, then steamed until done (Ch. 22).

Tamils: Descendants of early invaders of Sri Lanka (Ch. 15).

Tandoor: Thick-walled, deep, jar-shaped clay oven used for roasting meats and baking naan (Ch. 15).

Tapas: Small plates of tidbits of food designed for nibbling while having a drink in the late afternoon or early evening (Ch. 10).

Taro: Tropical plant from Southeast Asia noted for its edible, starch-rich root (Ch. 1).

Tatars: Mongol invaders who originally gathered military might under Genghis Khan and who conquered Russia under his grandson's leadership (Ch. 7).

Tempura: Batter-coated, deep-fried shrimp and thinly sliced vegetables (Ch. 19).

Theravada: Southern form of Buddhism based on a monastic approach; in Thailand, Myanmar (Burma), Sri Lanka, Cambodia, and Laos (Ch. 3).

Thousand-year eggs: Eggs (usually duck) preserved by packing them in a lime-clay mixture and storing for between 6 and 10 weeks, which transforms the white into a very dark, gelatinous material with a slightly fishy taste as the chemicals from the packing penetrate through the shell and throughout the egg (Ch. 17).

Toad-in-the hole: Sausages cooked in a quick bread batter (Ch. 4).

Tofu (soybean curd): Precipitate formed by adding calcium sulfate to a cooked soybean solution made from water and strained ground soybeans; may be pressed to form firmer curd (Ch. 17).

Torah: First five books of the Old Testament, the foundation for Judaism (Ch. 3).

Torii: Distinctive gateway to a Shinto shrine (Ch. 19).

Tortiglioni: Spiral-shaped pasta (Ch. 8).

Tortillas: Dough of masa harina (or flour) and water, which is pressed into thin disks and baked (Ch. 22).

Tostada: Bowl-shaped fried tortilla filled with beans, meat, chopped vegetables, guacamole, grated cheese, and sour cream (Ch. 22).

Tostones: Twice-fried slices of plantain that are pounded to be thin before the second frying (Ch. 20).

Transylvania: Region in western Romania bounded by the Carpathian Mountains (Ch. 7).

Treacle: Very thick molasses (Ch. 4).

Trekboers: Boers who made the Great Trek to settle the interior of South Africa (Ch. 14).

Trifle: Elaborate dessert made in a pretty glass bowl, which has been lined with lady fingers or slices of pound cake and then filled with layers of stirred custard, whipped cream, slivered almonds, raspberries, and generously laced with sherry (Ch. 4).

Truffles: Dark, subterranean fruiting bodies of a fungi; especially rare and flavorful ingredient prized in French recipes (Ch. 9).

Ts'ai: Term designating the various other dishes in a meal that balance the meal with the rice or fan (yin) in the meal; the yang part of the meal (Ch. 17).

Tsetse fly: Vector for sleeping sickness, a very serious disease in parts of West Africa (Ch. 13).

Tsukemono: Pickled vegetables (Ch. 19).

Tuk-kuk: Rice cake soup (Ch. 18).

U.S. Immigration and Naturalization Service: Federal agency responsible for enforcing immigration and naturalization regulations and laws (Ch. 23).

Udon: Noodles made with wheat flour, typical of southern Japan (Ch. 19).

Ugali: Kenyan name for stiff cornmeal porridge (Ch. 14).

Untouchables: All Hindus not born into a higher caste (Ch. 3).

Vaisyas: Third caste in Hinduism; farmers and business-people (Ch. 3).

Valdivia: Captain under Pizarro who led the Spanish expansion to Chile from Peru (Ch. 20).

Vasco da Gama: Portuguese navigator who opened trade routes to India in 1498 and 1502 (Ch. 10).

Vedas: Four volumes of the collective wisdom on how Hindus must live (Ch. 3).

Velouté sauce: Basic flour-thickened sauce made with a fish or chicken stock (Ch. 9).

Viandas: Generic word used in the Piramide Alimentaria para Puerto Rico to include bland foods high in starch (Ch. 24).

Vishnu: Preserver god of Hinduism (Ch. 3).

Voodoo: Type of worship found in Haiti, based on spells, hexes, and animism traced to African roots (Ch. 21).

Voortrekkers: Boers who used oxen and covered wagons to make the Great Trek between 1835 and 1839; also called trekboers (Ch. 14).

Wasabi: Finely grated, delicate green horseradish; also available as a powder (Ch. 19).

Water chestnuts: A tuber that is sliced and used as a vegetable to add a crisp, distinctive texture; usually available canned (Ch. 17).

West Indies: Islands of the Caribbean, ranging from near Florida to the northeast coast of South America (Ch. 21).

Winter melon: Green, oblong melon similar in outward appearance to a watermelon, but with a white, pulpy interior and a seed-filled center (Ch. 17).

Wok: Round-bottomed, two-handled metal pan used for stir-frying or as the container for boiling water to create steam for steaming food in bamboo steamer trays stacked on the wok (Ch. 17).

Wonton: Small pouches of food wrapped in thin wheat dough (wonton wrappers) and cooked in a broth or deep-fat fried (Ch. 17).

Worcestershire sauce: Pungent sauce made of soy sauce, vinegar, and garlic and used quite universally at British tables; originated in Worcestershire, England (Ch. 4).

Yang: Positive principle including male sun, heaven, fire, brightness, good, wealth, and joy; complementary balance to yin (Ch. 17).

Yarmulke: Skullcap worn by Jewish men (Ch. 3).

Yassa: Dish made with lemon-marinated chicken or meat (Ch. 13).

Yin: Passive principle including female, moon, earth, water, darkness, evil, poverty, and sadness; complementary balance to yang (Ch. 17).

Yorkshire pudding: Puffy pudding baked on meat drippings in a very hot oven; batter is thin egg–milk–flour mixture similar to popover batter (Ch. 4).

Yuca: Sweet cassava; root used as a starch in the tropical regions (Ch. 20).

Zapotec: Indians who developed the city of Monte Alban near Oaxaca in Mexico around 500 BCE (Ch. 22).

Zeljanica: Yugoslavian cheese and spinach pie (Ch. 7).

Zukat: Purifying tax; one of the Five Pillars (Ch. 3).

Recipe Index

Subject Index